Responsible Investment

To my wife Melinda, my parents John and Carmel, and my siblings Jean, John, Irene, Maeve, Olive and Mary.

RS

To my wife Lisa and my children Holly and Noah.

CM

Responsible Investment

EDITED BY RORY SULLIVAN
AND CRAIG MACKENZIE

Greenleaf
PUBLISHING

This book has been compiled from the contributions of the named authors. The views expressed herein do not necessarily reflect the views of their respective companies. While all reasonable care has been taken in the preparation of this book, Greenleaf Publishing and the authors do not accept responsibility for any errors it may contain or for any loss sustained by any person placing reliance on its contents.

© 2006 Greenleaf Publishing Ltd

Published by Greenleaf Publishing Limited
Aizlewood's Mill
Nursery Street
Sheffield S3 8GG
UK
www.greenleaf-publishing.com

The paper used for this book is a natural, recyclable product made from wood grown in sustainable forests; the manufacturing processes conform to the environmental regulations of the country of origin.
Printed in Great Britain by William Clowes Ltd, Beccles, Suffolk.
Cover by LaliAbril.com.

British Library Cataloguing in Publication Data:
  Responsible investment
    1. Investments - Moral and ethical aspects
    I. Sullivan, Rory   II. Mackenzie, Craig
    332.6'042

  ISBN-10: 1-874719-03-9
  ISBN-13: 978-1-874719-03-8

Contents

Foreword

Stephen Timms MP

Minister for Pensions Reform, UK

In a modern economy, economic success goes hand in hand with social and environmental goals. A strong economy and a strong society are two sides of the same coin. This is the essence of sustainable development. Long-term economic success cannot be based on despoiling the environment or exploiting individuals or their communities. Economic success will not endure if parts of society are excluded from its benefits. Investment in people is an economic necessity rather than a social cost to be endured.

Over the past decade, this has increasingly been the view of many leading companies. They recognise that the effective management of social and environmental risks is fundamental to their success. They no longer see corporate social responsibility as peripheral, but as mainstream to the business, with a compelling business rationale. It is imperative that investors understand how these issues are being managed and can determine the value that they can add.

Investors provide efficient access to capital, the lifeblood for our economy. Their role in sustainable development is vital—in delivering products and services, in supporting innovation and in creating jobs and wealth. However, when incentives become misaligned, there is potential for markets and companies to harm society and the environment. A focus on short-term profits rather than longer-term growth and development is a frequent source of these problems.

Many investors—including pension funds—operate with a very long-term time horizon. They therefore have an interest in encouraging companies to deliver stronger self-regulation, more effective governance, improved incentive structures and more rational business practices. Through giving due weight to environmental and social factors in investment decision-making, investors can effectively signal to companies the economic importance of these issues. These actions are not peripheral to the process of allocating capital. They are integral to the investment process. Institutional investors—asset managers, insurance and pension funds—represent the savings of millions of individuals, and their role should properly be seen as creating wealth for individuals over the longer term.

Does government have a role to play? The answer, of course, is yes. Today's corporate social responsibility movement is contributing decisive innovations to tackling the social and environmental challenges that confront us, and government wants to encourage a larger contribution still. But government's role is not simply to pass laws and regulations. Rather, we should be fostering the economic, political and social environment within which companies can realise their potential to serve the public interest and deliver sustainable development.

In my first period as Pensions Minister, in 1999, I introduced a small change to the 1995 Pensions Act requiring pension funds to state in their Investment Principles the extent, if at all, that they take account of social, ethical and environmental issues in the selection, retention and realisation of investments. The measure was intended as a light-touch policy intervention, to focus attention on the social and environmental consequences of investment. From the contributions to this book—from asset managers and pension funds, as well as from companies, the trade union movement and civil-society organisations—it is clear that, since then, there has been a period of innovation in the investment management industry. Many of the authors acknowledge the important influence of this relatively modest measure. It is even more pleasing to see the real benefits, primarily through shareholder activism, in areas such as climate change and access to medicines, and more broadly through the new focus on integrating environmental and social factors into investment decisions.

This book demonstrates great progress, but it also highlights that there is much more still to be done. Many institutional investors have yet to implement shareholder activism effectively or to integrate fully social and environmental issues into investment decision-making. Some of the contributors to this book make practical suggestions about the kinds of actions that could be considered by government—not just further regulation, but market-based measures and greater use of voluntary information disclosure. One message that comes across loud and clear is that mainstreaming responsible investment requires much more widespread support from the pension funds and long-term asset owners whose interests are at stake.

This book also highlights the barriers to investors' ability to encourage higher standards of corporate performance on social and environmental issues. These barriers are greatest in areas where markets are failing, or when, for other reasons, it goes against companies' economic interests to take action. It is precisely in these areas that government may have the most useful role to play, creating the policy environment within which companies and investors will be encouraged to address challenges such as climate change, resource depletion, irresponsible sales and marketing practices, and bribery and corruption.

The book suggests that many of the barriers to corporate social responsibility relate to the time horizons of investors. Where investors have long-term investment horizons, they will often have an interest in seeing market failures corrected. We need to consider together how we—government, investors, companies, civil society—can foster the kind of long-term investment culture necessary to meet the needs of future generations of pensioners while supporting responsible and productive business practice today.

I commend the editors of this book—Rory Sullivan and Craig Mackenzie—and the many contributors. They present here valuable examples of leadership, of real changes in business practice, of innovation and of progress towards sustainable development.

This book gives welcome grounds for optimism that, under the right conditions, social and environmental issues can be integrated into core investment activities, that real economic value can be derived from doing so—and that institutional investors can be important contributors to achieving sustainable development.

Part I
Introduction and background

1
Introduction

Rory Sullivan and Craig Mackenzie
Insight Investment, UK

One of the most striking features of debates around sustainable development has been the manner in which attention has moved from solely focusing on the roles and responsibilities of government towards consideration of the roles and responsibilities of companies. This reflects the dramatic political and economic changes resulting from the fall of the Berlin Wall, the end of the Cold War, the pressures of economic 'globalisation' and the drive to attract foreign investment.

Since the early 1990s, companies have extended their supply chains ever more widely and deeply into the developing countries of Asia, Africa and South America, and have invested in countries that were previously 'off limits' for political or ideological reasons. While this has brought many economic benefits (both to the companies and to the countries in which they have invested), the benefits have not been unambiguously positive. Concern has been expressed about the adverse social and environmental impacts (e.g. global warming, biodiversity loss, resource depletion) of globalisation and the perceived power and influence of corporations *vis-à-vis* national governments. There has also been a heated debate about the proper role, responsibility and level of accountability of corporations in a 'globalised' economy, heightened by examples and allegations of corporate wrongdoing and inappropriate influence on government, both in the developed and the developing countries (see, for example, Balanya *et al.* 2000; Dobbin 1998; Korten 1995; Monbiot 2000; Woolfson and Beck 2005).

The fact that corporate activities have such a powerful and controversial impact on modern societies is important to investors for two reasons. The first is that these factors may affect investment returns. For example, shareholder returns in energy-intensive sectors may be reduced by the introduction of a tax on greenhouse gas emissions. Secondly, investors may have some moral responsibility for the harmful activities of companies and may, therefore, face pressure to correct these activities. For example, it has been suggested that one of the reasons why companies behave unethically is because of the pressure from investors to put short-term profits ahead of corporate responsibility. It has also been suggested (Monks and Sykes 2002) that another reason for unethical corporate behaviour is that investors fail to hold company boards properly to account for their corporate governance. The question of moral responsibility is of particular importance given that most investment today is conducted by a relatively small number of institutional investors[1] who manage the pensions and saving funds of millions of ordinary people. Therefore, the manner in which these institutional investors (pension funds and fund managers) invest and discharge their responsibilities as the providers of capital and the owners of companies has important consequences for society as a whole.

There is a growing belief that investors, in particular large institutional investors, have a responsibility to work proactively to address the environmental and social impacts of their investments. There have been demands from government as well as stakeholders, such as trade unions, that institutional investors act to ensure the probity of the companies in which they invest (Gribben and Faruk 2004). The rationale for these demands is that active shareholder participation can play a major role in encouraging high-quality corporate governance that will deliver long-term shareholder returns, while also offering the potential to deliver broader societal benefits. Over the past ten years, UK shareholders have used their power quite successfully to: create longer-term incentive structures for directors; increase board independence and executive accountability; create better risk management infrastructure (making it harder for incompetent or self-seeking managers to take unjustifiable risks with the business); and improve the quality of company policy, management systems and disclosures on issues such as climate change, bribery and corruption, supply chain labour standards, human rights and access to medicines.[2] These activities have contributed to important outcomes such as dramatically reduced prices of AIDS medicines, the withdrawal of companies from unhelpful industry lobby groups and improvements in labour conditions in retail supply chains.

---

1 At the end of 2003, 48.7% of all ordinary shares listed on the UK stock exchange (£666 billion of a total of £1,368 billion) were owned by insurance companies, pension funds and other institutional investors. Investors from the rest of the world held 32.3% of the ordinary shares with individuals holding a further 14.9% (National Statistics 2004). While the specific numbers vary, other countries have seen a similar concentration of assets in the hands of institutional investors (see, generally, Mallin 2004: 66-68; Monks 2001).

2 For a general overview of shareholder activism in Canada, Australia and the US, see Sparkes 2002: 311-65.

There has also been a growing recognition of the materiality[3] of social, ethical and environmental issues to investment decision-making. Examples of where these issues have impacted directly on company financial performance have included litigation (e.g. tobacco, asbestosis, product liability), regulation, taxation and other market instruments, and company failure as a consequence of probity failings (e.g. Enron). As a consequence, several fund managers have announced research programmes to better integrate these issues into their investment activities. Investment analysts have responded by increasing the amount of research they do in this area, and have produced reports on issues such as HIV/AIDS in the southern African mining industry, the effects of the EU's emissions trading scheme on European electricity utility companies, the implications of obesity for food producers and retailers, and the effects of climate change on the insurance sector.

About this book

What is responsible investment?

There is a lack of agreement on how responsible investment could be defined. According to Mansley (2000: 3), an initial definition could be something like:

> Investment where social, ethical or environmental (SEE) factors are taken into account in the selection, retention and realisation of investment, and the responsible use of the rights (such as voting rights) that are attached to such investments.

However, this is an extremely broad definition and leaves open a number of questions about the scope of these concepts and the manner in which these factors should be taken into account.

This book is being written at a time when the definition and practice of 'responsible investment' is under scrutiny. For a number of years, it has been assumed that the only ethical approaches available to investors were either to shun certain stocks (e.g. 'vice' stocks such as tobacco, gambling, alcohol and pornography) or to invest in certain positive activities (e.g. environmental technology or healthcare). While such approaches have the advantage of appealing to relatively simple conceptions of right and wrong,

---

3   The term 'materiality' is often used to describe the financial significance of specific issues. Information is defined as 'material' if its omission, mis-statement or non-disclosure has the potential to adversely affect decisions about the allocation of scarce resources made by the users of the financial report or the discharge of accountability by the management or governing body of the entity (AASB 1995). There is no real consensus on the level at which an issue becomes 'material', although a general rule of thumb is that companies should disclose events that lead to impacts of greater than 10% on a key financial performance indicator (such as profit, turnover or revenues), whereas impacts of less than 5% are generally not considered material (for useful reviews, see Faux 2002, · 2004). However, for environmental events, the level at which 'environmentalists' consider that companies should consider disclosing information is lower (e.g. Faux 2004). That is, many issues that are considered significant by environmental non-governmental organisations (NGOs) or other stakeholders (such as trade unions) are unlikely to be financially material.

they have struggled to become more than a relatively small part of the total investment market (for a further discussion on this, see Chapter 3). The reasons for this are various but include the relatively small proportion of the population that feels sufficiently strongly about such issues to make a positive choice on how its money is invested, and the perception that such investments carry a higher risk than conventional investments. From the perspective of encouraging companies to improve their performance on social, ethical and environmental issues, a blanket refusal to invest in a specific company also means that such investors (given that they represent a relatively small minority of shareholders) have limited ability to encourage higher standards of corporate responsibility (Sparkes and Cowton 2004: 48).

These limitations have created interest in alternative approaches to addressing social, ethical and environmental issues in investment. Two major strategies or responses have emerged. The first, as discussed above, is to enhance mainstream investment processes to explicitly analyse company performance on these issues, and then to incorporate the results into investment decision-making. The second is for investors to use the formal rights and informal influence granted to them as shareholders to encourage companies to pay appropriate attention to the management of social, ethical and environmental issues. Recent years have seen a dramatic increase in the number of investors using one or both of these strategies (see, generally, Eurosif 2003; Mansley 2000; Sparkes 2002), although across Europe as a whole, these investors remain in the minority.[4] The UK has been at the forefront of these changes with some £84 billion of pension fund assets now managed through engagement or shareholder activism mandates (Eurosif 2003: 23).

Who are the key actors?

The focus of this book is on what is referred to as the institutional market, which is a general term for investments managed or controlled by insurance companies, pension funds and investment managers, and investment managers in pension funds, mutual funds and other pooled investment vehicles. Institutional investors invest on behalf of large numbers of individuals who have their pensions and savings invested in these funds. Most pension funds operate under trust law. This imposes a 'fiduciary' obligation on the trustees and fund managers involved to serve the interests of those whose money is invested in these funds—these interests are usually interpreted in exclusively financial terms.

Pension funds may manage their money themselves or may appoint one or more fund managers to do so. In practice, the vast majority of pension funds use external investment managers (or fund managers). Fund managers are specialist organisations that manage the funds of investment intermediaries, particularly pension funds. While investment terms or objectives are agreed with clients, fund managers have the pri-

---

4 A recent survey estimated that some €336 billion of assets are now managed according to come sort of socially responsible investment strategy, with approximately half of this being shareholder activism (Eurosif 2003: 10). However, with the exception of the UK and the Netherlands, socially responsible investment remains a comparatively modest part of the total investment market and, across Europe as a whole, the share of assets managed in a socially responsible manner remains very small at around 2% (Eurosif 2003: 14).

mary responsibility for day-to-day investment decisions (Monks and Sykes 2002: 12).[5] In general, fund-manager performance is judged over relatively short periods (usually three years in the UK but with more regular, typically quarterly, reviews of performance). Consequently, there may be a significant mismatch between the periods over which fund managers are judged and the longer periods over which investment returns are required by beneficiaries.

Pension funds are advised in the selection and appointment of fund managers, and on a range of other issues relevant to their investments, by firms of investment consultants. The views that these consultants hold about particular managers or about particular investment strategies—including views on the investment relevance of social, ethical and environmental issues—are very important in determining which managers succeed in winning mandates.

What are the key questions?

To date, there has been little systematic analysis of the implications of these approaches (i.e. shareholder activism and enhanced analysis of social, ethical and environmental issues) for mainstream investment activities. In this book, through providing an account of emerging practice in addressing social, ethical and environmental issues in investment activities, we consider the following questions:

- Do responsible investment strategies actually contribute to improvements in the social, ethical and environmental (SEE) performance of companies?

- To what extent is it in investors' interests to encourage higher standards of corporate responsibility?

- Do responsible investment strategies enhance financial performance for investors?

The vast majority of the contributions to this book are from practitioners (fund managers, corporate governance or corporate responsibility specialists, investment analysts, investment consultants) or stakeholders (trade unions, non-governmental organisations [NGOs]), rather than academic commentators. This was a deliberate choice on our part. The practice of responsible investment has developed rapidly, and there has been little systematic analysis of how practitioners (as opposed to onlookers) actually implement responsible investment, or of how practitioners and stakeholders perceive the role of shareholder activism or enhanced analysis in mainstream investment processes. By inviting practitioners to contribute, we also expected to be able to address the final question above: namely, what are the strengths and weaknesses of current

---

5   Investment management styles can be divided into 'active' and 'passive'. Active funds are invested on the basis of financial analysis, conducted by fund managers and investment analysts. Some asset managers rely on their own in-house ('buy-side') analysts. Others rely more on research provided by 'sell-side' analysts who are employed by the stockbrokers used by fund managers to buy and sell shares. In contrast, passive management involves closely tracking a specific index (or basket of shares), such as the FTSE 100 (which reflects the collective price performance of the UK's 100 largest companies).

practice, and what are the barriers to making responsible investment a standard part of mainstream investment processes?

What is the scope of this book?

Given the particularly rapid development of new approaches to responsible investment in the UK in recent years, this book focuses primarily on the UK (although there are also articles from practitioners in the US and Switzerland). However, the lessons learned and conclusions drawn are also generally applicable to other countries, reflecting the increasing influence of the Anglo-American model of share ownership, and the relevance of social, ethical and environmental issues to all companies.

We concentrate our attention on investments in equities and bonds, specifically the relevance of social, ethical and environmental issues to the issuers of, and investors in, shares or debt and the manner in which institutional investors act to influence investee companies to address these issues. Clearly, these issues are also relevant to other investment classes, such as property or direct project investments. However, the manner in which investors analyse these risks and the avenues of influence available to investors are very different to those for equities and bonds, and so are outside the scope of this book.

It is important to note that this book does not focus specifically on the primary purpose of the capital markets: namely, the provision and efficient allocation of capital. This is by far the biggest social contribution of investors and is an essential ingredient of sustainable development. However, as noted above, the outcomes from investment in companies are not unambiguously positive. The focus of this book is on how the negative consequences of institutional investment can be minimised and the positive consequences enhanced.

Definitions

In the context of a book about investment in company securities (shares and bonds), the terms 'social', 'ethical' and 'environmental' are taken as relating to those aspects of corporate practice that are associated with corporate responsibility and sustainable development.[6] Institutional investors are likely to be particularly interested in those issues that have the potential to materially affect investment performance.

Under the category of ethical issues, we refer to issues such as responsible marketing (or the ethics of marketing), and bribery and corruption. Social issues include supply chain management (or the consequences of supply chain management practices, such as impacts on workers' health), human rights, workplace health and safety, and community relations. Finally, examples of the environmental issues that may be considered by investors include climate change, chemical emissions, resource consumption and impacts on biodiversity. In practice, these issues overlap significantly. For example,

---

6 For a more comprehensive overview of the issues that are likely to be of concern to institutional investors, see Sparkes 2002: 117-275 and Mansley 2000: 37-62.

damage to a river ecosystem as a consequence of pollution discharges may also have social or economic consequences by undermining the ability of local populations to obtain fish from the river.

We refer to corporate responsibility[7] (which is also commonly referred to as corporate social responsibility or CSR) as the set of ethical expectations that people have about companies' behaviour. These expectations relate to characteristics such as corporate integrity, honesty, fairness, taking due care of people's health and safety, respect for rights, avoiding environmental harm, accountability and impacts on wider society. We refer to corporate responsibility management as the policies, practices and programmes adopted by companies to address these issues.

Each company varies in the manner in which it manages corporate responsibility, depending on factors such as its size and activities, the particular issues associated with its business activities, stakeholder demands and the company's attitudes and values. Companies may manage these issues as an integral whole or may divide them into areas such as business ethics, environmental concerns, human rights, governance, community and stakeholder relations, and philanthropy. Irrespective of the specific labels that are applied, we wish to emphasise one fundamental point: it is our view that corporate responsibility should be a fundamental part of every company's values, strategies, and governance and management systems.

Structure

This book is divided into five sections. The first, comprising Chapters 1–3, examines the idea of responsible investment from an economics perspective (Chapter 2) and through a historical overview of the development of responsible investment (Chapter 3). Chapter 2 is of particular importance as the economic dimensions of responsible investment remain relatively under-developed, and one of the opportunities presented by this book is to draw together theory and practice in a more coherent manner. This economics perspective allows us to better understand the potential of, and barriers to, the development of practice, and it assists in analysing the case studies and other material provided by the contributors to this book.

The second (Chapters 4–12) and third (Chapters 13–18) sections of the book consider how social, ethical and environmental issues are taken into account in investment decision-making and shareholder activism respectively. Each section comprises a series of case studies where practitioners present their approach and experience in order to critically evaluate the financial, social, ethical and environmental outcomes from their work.

The fourth section (Chapters 19–31) subjects both the practice and theory to challenge and analysis. Critical perspectives on responsible investment have been obtained from different stakeholders: companies, NGOs, trade unions and academics. The authors reflect on their experiences with responsible investment and examine some of

---

7   For useful introductions to corporate responsibility and related concepts, see Elkington 1997 and Andriof and McIntosh 2001.

the broader questions, such as the role of investors in promoting sustainable development, the scope and legitimacy of activism and the barriers to responsible investment.

Finally, in the fifth section (Chapters 32–33), we draw together the different strands and themes of the book. Chapter 32 uses the case-study and analytical material presented to test and refine the hypotheses set out in Chapter 2. The chapter also considers the three key questions above (relating to the effectiveness and benefits of responsible investment and investors' interest in encouraging higher standards of corporate responsibility). In Chapter 33, we present some broader reflections around the contribution of responsible investment to sustainable development and the future direction for responsible investment.

References

AASB (Australian Accounting Standards Board) (1995) *Accounting Standard: Materiality. AASB 1031* (Melbourne: AASB).

Andriof, J., and M. McIntosh (2001) *Perspectives on Corporate Citizenship* (Sheffield, UK: Greenleaf Publishing).

Balanya, B., A. Doherty, O. Hoedeman, A. Ma'anit and E. Wesselius (1999) *Europe Inc.* (London: Pluto Press).

Dobbin, M. (1998) *The Myth of the Good Corporate Citizen* (Toronto: Stoddart).

Elkington, J. (1997) *Cannibals with Forks: The Triple Bottom Line of 21st Century Business* (Oxford, UK: Capstone).

Eurosif (European Sustainable Investment and Responsible Investment Forum) (2003) *Socially Responsible Investment among European Institutional Investors* (Brussels: Eurosif).

Faux, J. (2002) 'A Stakeholder Perspective of Material Disclosure Thresholds for Environmental Events', *Asian Review of Accounting* 10.2: 3-16.

—— (2004) 'The Effects of Materiality Thresholds on Decision-Making', paper presented at the *Bangkok International Conference of Applied Business Research*, Kasetsart University, Bangkok, Thailand, December 2004.

Gribben, C., and A. Faruk (2004) *Will UK pension funds become more responsible? A Survey of Trustees* (London: Just Pensions).

Korten, D. (1995) *When Corporations Rule the World* (London: Earthscan Publications).

Mansley, M. (2000) *Socially Responsible Investment: A Guide for Pension Funds and Institutional Investors* (Sudbury, UK: Monitor Press).

Mallin, C. (2004) *Corporate Governance* (Oxford, UK: Oxford University Press).

Monbiot, G. (2000) *Captive State: The Corporate Takeover of Britain* (London: Macmillan).

Monks, R. (2001) *The New Global Investors* (Oxford, UK: Capstone).

—— and A. Sykes (2002) *Capitalism without owners will fail: A Policymaker's Guide to Reform* (New York: Center for the Study of Financial Innovation).

National Statistics (2004) *Share Ownership: A Report on Ownership of Shares as at 31st December 2003* (London: National Statistics; www.statistics.gov.uk/downloads/theme_economy/ShareOwnership2003.pdf, accessed 17 November 2005).

Sparkes, R. (2002) *Socially Responsible Investment: A Global Revolution* (Chichester, UK: John Wiley).

—— and C. Cowton (2004) 'The Maturing of Socially Responsible Investment: A Review of the Developing Link with Corporate Social Responsibility', *Journal of Business Ethics* 52: 45-57.

Woolfson, C., and M. Beck (eds.) (2005) *Corporate Social Responsibility Failures in the Oil Industry* (New York: Baywood).

2

The scope for investor action on corporate social and environmental impacts*

Craig Mackenzie

Insight Investment, UK

The purpose of this chapter is to explore the extent of, and limits to, the role investors might play in addressing the harmful social and environmental impacts of the companies in which they invest. Such a focus may give the appearance that I think the glass is half empty; that companies in particular, and capitalism in general, are a source of problems that investors and others must solve. This is not, however, the case. Rather, I believe very strongly that the glass is half full. Companies competing in free markets have a hugely valuable role to play in creating many of the products and services, jobs, tax revenues and investment returns on which modern economies depend. They also have a vital and positive role to play in providing the investment, research and technology necessary to solve our most pressing social and environmental problems—from renewable energy technologies to medicines to treat diseases such as AIDS. Capitalism has many strengths, and investors play a crucial and positive role in providing and efficiently allocating capital.

Despite these important and positive contributions, few would dispute the fact that companies cause or contribute (whether wholly or partially, directly or indirectly) to many significant social and environmental problems, including climate change, loss of biodiversity, social exclusion, bribery and corruption, breaches of human rights, and

---

* I would like to thank Rory Sullivan for his extensive input to this chapter; and thanks also to Rob Lake, Sandy Black and William Claxton-Smith who provided comments on an earlier draft.

the production of dangerous goods and services. These negative outcomes raise two important questions:

- What, if anything, can the investors in these companies do to help address these problems?

- Do investors have an interest in taking action?

These questions are particularly relevant to large institutional investors. A few dozen large institutional investors own or control more than half the shares in the largest companies in the UK. A single large insurance company or asset manager, for example, will typically control more than 1% of the shares of an individual company. Collectively, these investors' decisions determine the price of company shares and the way votes are cast at annual general meetings.

Historically, large institutional investors have, as a rule, not taken specific steps to address social and environmental issues. In recent years, however, there has been an increased willingness among some of the biggest institutional investors to reconsider their role. In the UK (which is the main focus of the analysis in this chapter) this has been, in part, due to regulatory pressure, including a change in the 1995 Pensions Act requiring occupational pension funds to state the extent, if at all, they take account of social, ethical and environmental issues in investment; and the publication of the Myners report (Myners 2001) on shareholder activism by pension funds.

While there is now a willingness to ask what investors can do to address the harmful impacts of companies, few institutional investors (with the exception of those mentioned in this book) have sought to engage substantively in the debate about the role and responsibilities of investors on social and environmental issues. One reason may be because many think that, in fact, investors have little role to play; one goal of this chapter is to consider the merits of the arguments against such a *laissez-faire* outlook.

This chapter aims to understand what opportunities investors have to take actions that are likely to be effective in modifying corporate behaviour on social and environmental issues. Are there really specific actions that could lead to significant improvements in corporate performance on issues such as climate change, product safety, and bribery and corruption? If not, investors will have little or nothing to contribute. Even if investors *can* make a contribution, is it in their interests to do so? The question of interests is particularly important in the case of institutional investors. The activities of these investors are constrained by the fiduciary obligations defined by trust law. These obligations are usually interpreted as giving overriding priority to the financial interests of the beneficiaries of institutional investment funds. If an action that an investor might take to address a corporate responsibility problem is expected to be significantly detrimental to the financial interests of its beneficiaries, it will be legally difficult for trustees to endorse it. As we shall see, this raises important questions about the time horizons and breadth of the interests of beneficiaries.

In order to consider whether investors are likely to be both able and willing to take action, we need to answer a more basic question: what are the causes of harmful social and environmental impacts by companies? It is only by understanding these causes that we can answer questions about the role investors might play in modifying them, and whether it is in their interests to do so.

The first section of this chapter considers this question of causation, drawing on economic theories of market failure, agency problems and bounded rationality. The second section then considers the practical actions investors might take to modify or oppose these causes, with the third section looking at the question of whether investors have an interest in taking these actions. Finally I discuss what this analysis might lead us to expect investors to do in practice.

Causes of harmful corporate impacts

From an investor perspective, the causes of harmful corporate impacts can be divided into two categories:

- Negative social impacts that result when companies seek to maximise shareholder returns in circumstances of market failure

- Negative social impacts that arise when companies fail to maximise shareholder returns: for example, because of agency problems and bounded rationality

As we shall see when discussing investor interests later on, this distinction is very important.

Market failure

One of the most remarkable things about markets is how, under favourable conditions, they are able to align the interests of participants, both companies and shareholders, through market transactions and so make everyone better off. However, markets reliably deliver this outcome only when certain conditions—such as strong competition between companies, free flows of information and an absence of 'externalities'[1]—are met. When these conditions are not met, markets can fail to align the interests of companies and their investors with those of society; as a result, companies can face strong incentives to act in ways that can be socially harmful.

Not all forms of market failure are particularly harmful—some externalities are simply a minor inconvenience. So exploiting market failure in itself is not necessarily a cause of public concern. However, in many cases, exploiting market failure can have major negative consequences. Market failure could be the source of most of the serious and widespread harmful corporate impacts on society and the environment.

In the economics literature, there are four main categories of market failure: externalities; public goods; the inefficiency of monopoly power; and imperfect information.[2]

---

1   Externalities are where the benefits or costs of an exchange spill over onto other parties. Negative externalities occur when the actions of one party impose costs (as opposed to benefits for positive externalities) on another party. An example of a negative externality is environmental pollution, where the costs of, say, emitting carbon dioxide into the atmosphere are not borne by the companies or individuals responsible but by those impacted by climate change.

2   For a useful overview, see Cooter and Ulen 2000: 40-43.

The presence of externalities may result in market failure, as the price of a product or service may not reflect its social value (i.e. may not fully account for all the consequences of its production). Much of the thinking on externalities (and the public policy solutions that may be adopted to address them) is based on Pigou's *The Economics of Welfare* (Pigou 1920). According to Pigou, in the presence of such externalities, the market cannot provide the right price signals to companies and other economic agents and, as a consequence, the market fails to maximise social welfare.

The second category of market failure relates to 'public goods'. In environmental policy, the key public goods issue is the depletion of open access (or common property) resources by overuse.[3] Examples include clean air, rainforests and ocean fisheries. Other examples of public goods include national defence, policing or the provision of lighting in public places. It is in everybody's interests that these public goods are provided but it is practically impossible to charge individuals for their use (and individuals have no incentive to pay what the goods are really worth to them).

The other two categories of market failure relate to imperfect competition: namely, the inefficiency of monopoly power, and imperfect information. From an economic perspective, monopolies tend to lead companies to set prices too high and/or to produce goods of insufficient quantity or quality, to the disadvantage of consumers and others. Severe informational asymmetries can disrupt markets so much that a socially optimal solution cannot be achieved by voluntary exchange. If, for example, consumers cannot accurately assess the quality or costs of products or services, companies will face an incentive to rip them off. This in turn will undermine customer trust and participation in the market. Arguably, mis-selling of financial services products in the UK is an example of this problem (FSA 2004).

In situations where markets fail to align the interests of companies with those of society, governments can intervene with sanctions, through regulation, the imposition of taxes or other measures (e.g. facilitating tort litigation). The consequence is that there are few areas of modern business activity that are not controlled by a complex array of regulatory requirements, including, for example, regulations relating to employment, discrimination, health and safety, environmental protection, consumer protection, competition, contracting, advertising and accounting.

While much of the economics literature focuses on government responses to market failures, far less attention has been paid to ethical norms and the social sanctions that can result from their breach. In many situations, exploiting market failure involves breaching widely accepted ethical norms such as those relating to honesty, promise-keeping, due care, fairness, respect for rights and accountability. These norms are often supported by powerful social and psychological sanctions (Mackenzie 2005). For example, externalising the costs of disposing of toxic waste by dumping it in a local river breaches the duty of care a company has to its local communities. The sanctions that could be faced by the company are not only those associated with regulatory action or litigation but could include damage to relationships with local communities, adverse press coverage, loss of standing or credibility with industry peers and damage to relationships with environmental regulators.

3   This is often referred to as the 'tragedy of the commons' after Hardin's famous article (Hardin 1968).

Taken together, such government and social sanctions result in substantial costs as well as benefits from exploiting market failure. In market failure situations companies therefore face a dilemma. On the one hand, they may have an immediate financial interest in exploiting the market failure to their advantage. On the other, they are likely to face sanctions from government and society if they do. Where government and social sanctions are sufficiently large, 'rational' companies should have little difficulty in exercising self-restraint, and should choose not to exploit market failure because doing so is not in their long-term interest. Unfortunately, for various reasons, the picture is rarely this clear. Sometimes the problem is that the penalties are too small to deter companies from exploiting market failure, either because of a lack of effective enforcement or the inability of regulators to impose sufficient fines. In other cases, the problem is that the costs associated with exploiting market failure are primarily to intangible assets such as reputation and brand. Intangible costs are hard to value properly. Companies may therefore fail to place sufficient weight on the true costs of exploiting market failure. A third problem is that many of the penalties associated with market failure affect companies but not those who manage them. The problem here is that managers may choose to exploit market failure and ignore the costs for the company (this is a specific agency problem which we discuss further below). As a result of these problems, government and social penalties do not always deter companies from exploiting market failure. An uncomfortable feature of these situations is that companies or their managers have an interest in exploiting market failure, even when doing so is against the law.

Agency problems

The interests of company directors and employees may well not be the same as those of the shareholders. Indeed, in some cases they may be diametrically opposed. This problem has become known as the 'principal–agent problem' (Jensen and Meckling 1976). In the case of institutional investment, the principals are the shareholders and the agents are the executive management.[4] In theory this problem might be solved by careful monitoring of the executives to ensure they do not put their own interests ahead of those of the company. Efforts to ensure that companies have strong governance systems, with strong independent directors on the board and effective systems of internal control, are intended to do precisely this. However, there are limits to the effectiveness of such monitoring, so agency problems are likely to persist.

Agency problems are clearly an important issue for investors. As the shareholders of Enron and WorldCom have discovered, if executives put their interests ahead of those of the shareholders, tens of billions of pounds of shareholder value can be destroyed. Given that this book is focused on the harmful social and environmental impacts of companies, the issue we now consider is whether agency problems also *cause* social and environmental problems. There are a number of responses to this.

---

4   In fact, there are three sets of principal–agent issues that are considered in this book. The first are those relating to the shareholders and their agents (the executive management of companies). The second relate to situations where pension funds (the principals) delegate investment management responsibilities to investment managers (the agents). The third are those relating to companies and their employees (i.e. internal to the organisation).

One obvious answer is that shareholders are clearly part of society and most company shareholdings are, ultimately, controlled by the pension, insurance and mutual funds that contain society's savings. So, when executives rip off shareholders, they rip off the investing public. A second answer is that there are consequential impacts of governance failures. When companies fail (whether as a result of poor governance or from other causes), employees lose their jobs and local economies can be adversely affected. In the specific context of this book, there is a third answer to which we want to draw attention: namely, that agency problems can exacerbate market failure by undermining government and social sanctions. The reason why we emphasise this third point is that one major source of negative social and environmental impacts caused by companies arises when individual directors, managers or employees pursue their own interests and disregard those of the company as a whole. Many examples of fraud, corruption, health and safety failures, environmental accidents and customer rip-offs arise not because markets fail to align the interests of companies with their stakeholders but rather because company executives pursue their own interests at the expense of everyone else, including their company's shareholders.

According to the principles of agency theory, company executives will tend to act in ways that give rise to harmful social and environmental impacts when they have an interest in doing so (e.g. when doing so enables them to meet a sales target that will trigger a bonus, or when a reputation for aggressively cutting costs is rewarded with a promotion). As discussed above, this problem is particularly important in situations where the government and social penalties for exploiting market failure are targeted at companies rather than at those who manage them. When this is the case, agency problems mean that companies' executives may seek to exploit market failure for their own benefit, even though this may subsequently lead to substantial penalties for the company. Ripping off customers and slashing health and safety costs may lead to substantial regulatory penalties for the company in the long term, but, in the meantime, doing so may be the short cut for executive managers to achieve their financial performance-related bonuses.

Why would companies create such damaging incentives? One reason could be that the process of incentivisation is controlled by the executive managers themselves who have an interest in designing a remuneration framework that is more favourable to them despite adverse consequences for the shareholders. Another is ignorance. It is sometimes hard to foresee the unintended consequences of particular remuneration arrangements. A third problem is that it is often difficult for companies to give due weight to the costs of exploiting market failure. Specifically, while companies can gain tangible, immediate benefits from exploiting market failure, the government and social penalties of doing so are often uncertain, intangible and accrue only over the long term. For example, litigation against a company for externalising the costs of disposing of its toxic waste (e.g. by dumping it in a river) may occur years or even decades after the company profited from the externality. Furthermore, while the benefits of exploiting market failure are visible in the bottom line, the costs of government or social sanctions to correct market failure are often largely intangible: taking advantage of market failure may undermine customer loyalty and trust in the brand, it might weaken employee motivation and advocacy, or it might damage the company's reputation.

Because it is often relatively difficult for companies to monitor these costs and to base executives' incentives on them, self-seeking executives may seek to exploit market failures, even in the presence of substantial penalties, to the detriment both of society and the long-term interests of shareholders. For these reasons, agency problems are not only a problem in their own right but they also make the job of correcting market failures much more difficult.

Bounded rationality

It is said that there are two theories of history—the conspiracy theory and the cock-up theory. Agency problems belong in the former category. The cock-up theory explains another main reason why companies may have harmful impacts on society. Companies are not all-knowing or perfectly rational—they exhibit what economists refer to as 'bounded rationality' (Simon 1983).[5] In more familiar terms, they can be ignorant and incompetent. They make mistakes.

When companies employ ignorant or incompetent executives, when they use flawed technologies or badly designed processes, accidents happen. Companies often take unjustified risks and fail to exploit valuable opportunities. When an individual makes a mistake, the consequences are normally quite localised. However, the scale and power of companies mean that, when they make mistakes, the consequences can affect thousands of people. While many problems that we are primarily concerned about in this book arise because the interests of companies or their agents are not well aligned with those of society, we need to remember that there are also many that arise due to bounded rationality.

What can investors do?

This section offers a short outline of the main actions investors can take when their interests are affected by market failure, agency problems or bounded rationality. There are two broad areas of activity—those associated with shareholder activism and those associated with enhancements to investment analysis and decision-making.

Shareholder activism

One way that investors can play a role in encouraging companies to improve their social and environmental impacts is through shareholder activism. As shareholders, large

---

5   Bounded rationality captures the insight that companies tend to make suboptimal choices among competing options, where the courses of action chosen tend to be those that avoid uncertainty and are satisfactory (or are good enough in the circumstances). In addition, actors tend to use a range of heuristics (rules of thumb) to assist in their decision-making processes. Such approaches are not necessarily 'irrational'. For example, the costs of acquiring information may be prohibitive compared to the benefits of obtaining it, or ignorance may be a rational approach where transaction costs are high and the uncertainties that are of concern relate to the long-term survival of the business (i.e. short-term concerns may dominate decision-making processes) (see Korobkin and Ulen 2000: 1,075-76, 1,085).

institutional investors have a range of formal and informal rights and powers relating to companies. Formally, the shareholders have the right to vote to approve: the appointment of board directors, the board's remuneration policy, the appointment of auditors and, frequently, the annual report and accounts. They can also sell the company's shares if they don't like what the company is doing, potentially depressing its share price and raising its cost of capital. In addition, investors have informal powers such as the ability to meet and influence the board, the ability to generate media or press coverage, and to encourage other investors to exert their formal powers. These formal and informal powers mean that shareholders have significant ability—particularly if they act collectively—to influence the behaviour of companies. The idea that shareholders should use this power is endorsed and encouraged by the Combined Code on Corporate Governance (FRC 2003) and the Myners Principles (Myners 2001).

To what extent can these powers be used to address harmful corporate impacts on society and the environment? Turning first to agency problems, it is generally recognised that many agency problems can be tackled through effective systems of corporate governance. Among other things, effective governance requires boards to:[6]

- Be comprised of a majority of strong, independent non-executives

- Define clear policies authorising and constraining executive action

- Approve company strategy

- Ensure there are effective controls to monitor executive and staff performance, including compliance with policy

- Set suitably long-term and balanced incentives, bearing in mind the potential for agency problems

Most importantly perhaps, effective governance requires shareholders to ensure that the right people are appointed to the board in the first place.

If these requirements are met, and the company's system of governance is effective, the scope for agency problems, and for the harmful social and environmental impacts associated with them, should be reduced. However, corporate governance is not a 'one-off' activity. In order for shareholders to ensure that boards continue to function effectively, it is necessary that institutional shareholders monitor the quality of corporate governance on an ongoing basis and use the powers that they have to support good practice. Many governance failures arise in part because of the lack of effective shareholder scrutiny.

If activism is a useful tool to tackle agency problems, can it also be used to address market failure? One possibility is that investors may have an important role to play in supporting and encouraging the efforts of boards to deliver effective self-regulation. As discussed in the previous section, agency problems make the job of regulating market failure much more difficult. Where regulatory penalties are directed at companies and not executive management, agency problems may mean that managers continue to exploit market failure even when it is not in the interests of their company. In such

---

6   The most authoritative source of guidance on corporate governance in the UK is the Combined Code (FRC 2003). There is also a growing literature on this topic (see, for example, Cadbury 2002; Carver and Oliver 2002; Monks and Minnow 2003).

cases, action by regulators will be effective only if it is complemented by effective corporate self-regulation. The more investors succeed in encouraging strong governance to address agency problems, the more government and social penalties will be given due weight in the activities of executive managers and so by the company collectively.[7]

Self-regulation by boards, with the active support of shareholders, may have a broader role to play than simply addressing agency problems. As the Combined Code puts it (FRC 2003: section AI):

> The board should set the company's values and standards and ensure that its obligations to its shareholders and others are understood and met.

Arguably, boards should ensure that the company seeks to comply with its legal obligations, irrespective of the costs and benefits of doing so. If the law requires a company not to externalise its costs on the environment, then boards should ensure that the company meets this legal obligation, irrespective of the consequences for shareholders. Furthermore, the law is not the only source of obligations. As *The Economist* (2005) recently put it:

> managers ought to behave ethically as they pursue the proper business goal of maximising owner value—and that puts real constraints on their actions. In most cases, acting within these constraints advances the aim of the business, just as individuals find that enlightened self-interest and ethical conduct usually sit well together. But, for firms as for people, this will not always be true. Sometimes the aims of the business and rational self-interest will clash with ethics, and when they do, those aims and interests must give way.

Effective self-regulation is essential if companies are to meet their obligations in the face of market failure. In practice, this requires boards to:

- Withhold their approval of corporate strategies based on exploiting market failures that lead to harm

- Institute policies that prohibit executives from taking actions that exploit market failure

- Design incentives systems that penalise executives who breach such policies

- Ensure that the system of internal control monitors compliance

So, as I have argued elsewhere (Mackenzie and Hodgson 2005), boards can institute steps that ought to be more or less effective in leading companies to exercise self-restraint in the face of opportunities to exploit market failure. From a public-interest perspective, investors should provide the necessary support and encouragement to boards to enable them to do this. Whether they will, in fact, have an interest in doing so is discussed below.

---

7   Of course, where the penalties for exploiting market failure are weak or non-existent, exploiting market failure may be the profit-maximising strategy. Here, the elimination of agency problems would not have a positive effect.

Enhanced analysis

The second way that investors may be able to play a role in addressing the harmful social and environmental impacts of companies is through better financial analysis and investment decision-making.

Before discussing this issue, there are two points to make. The first is that there are reasons for thinking that investment decision-making affects corporate behaviour. The basic idea is that, collectively, the financial analysis and investment decision-making of stock market participants sets the share price for companies. Share prices, in turn, affect company behaviour, both directly by affecting the cost of capital and indirectly by motivating boards and executive behaviour. This is particularly true given that:

- The performance targets used by many companies to set executive bonuses are based, at least in part, on share price performance

- A large proportion of executive incentives are paid in shares or share options

- The company may be at risk of takeover if the share price falls too far

The second point is that, if investment analysis fails to place sufficient weight on the value of good corporate social and environmental performance or on the costs of poor performance, then the capital markets may create incentives for companies to cause (or fail to prevent) harmful corporate impacts on society and the environment.

Turning to the question of market failure, the uncomfortable fact is that, in the short term at least, economic theory predicts that corporate financial performance may improve when companies successfully exploit market failure (i.e. exploiting market failure is often the profit-maximising strategy). This means that in situations of market failure (that have not been corrected by effective government and social penalties), bad social and environmental performance can be good for profits. In such circumstances, investment analysts would be expected to attach a higher financial value to companies that exploit market failure than those that choose not to do so. This problem is not merely theoretical. In practice investors favour companies that are able to make super-normal profits because of market failure. For example, equity analysts often look for 'pricing power' (i.e. the ability to set prices well above the marginal costs of production). One source of pricing power is uncompetitive markets with high barriers to entry. Investment analysts typically reward companies with pricing power with higher share prices.

Because companies can benefit from exploiting market failure (in the absence of effective government and social penalties), the capital markets can send strong signals encouraging companies to exploit market failures. This is not always terribly detrimental to the public interest. For example, if the market for premium ice cream is uncompetitive and consumers end up paying a higher price, the harm done is relatively minor. However, if the market is for a basic necessity (e.g. water) and poor people are, as a result, priced out of the market, the public-interest consequences of the market failure are more acute. In such cases investors may end up playing an unhelpful role in the process. For example, a well-meaning executive might decide that it is simply unacceptable for the company to aggressively exploit a harmful market failure. He might then announce to the shareholders his intention to ensure that the company exercises self-restraint, accepting that this will reduce earnings significantly, but that this is the price of responsible behaviour. Unfortunately, the economics suggests that such an act is likely to be rewarded with a lower share price and a higher cost of capital (and possibly even calls for the board to sack the high-minded executive). If this is right, investors can sometimes create incentives for companies to exploit market failure and penalise companies that fail to do so.

The picture is, however, more complicated than this. As we noted in the previous section, governments and wider society typically attempt to impose penalties on companies that exploit market failure. When such penalties are sufficiently substantial (i.e. of appropriate magnitude, certainty and effect), companies may not overall have anything to gain from exploiting market failure. If investors give these penalties due weight, they will incentivise companies to exercise self-restraint. Unfortunately, there may be reasons for thinking that investors may not be very efficient at valuing the costs of exploiting market failure. The reason is that these costs typically accrue over the long term (e.g. a lawsuit in five years' time), and are often intangible (e.g. affecting brand equity and staff morale) and uncertain (e.g. will the government regulate effectively or not?). In contrast, the benefits of exploiting market failure are frequently immediate and tangible (e.g. lower costs, higher revenues). This problem is compounded by the fact that investors may be significantly better at taking account of the immediate and tangible benefits of exploiting market failure than in considering the long-term and intangible costs of doing so. To the extent that this is the case, investors may drive up share prices of companies that exploit market failure even when long-term shareholder value is being destroyed. Where this happens, investors are not merely a major source of pressure for companies to exploit market failure when doing so is the profit-maximising strategy, but may also create pressures to exploit market failure in the presence of otherwise effective social deterrents, even when doing so destroys long-term shareholder value. In such cases, the capital markets are effectively working against government efforts to address market failures. There is significant debate about just how serious this problem is (see, for example, Cuthbertson *et al.* 1997), as at least some of the long-term costs associated with government and social penalties are currently taken into account (e.g. risks of future litigation against tobacco companies). Furthermore, some investors are rather better than others at looking at long-term issues, and so escape criticism on this point.

What can investors do about this problem when it arises? The more that financial analysts assess the costs of government and social penalties associated with market failure, the stronger the signals will be for company executives to take these cost into account. In other words, where it is possible for investors to correct weaknesses in their analysis, they will be able to increase the incentives company executives face to reduce their harmful social and environmental impacts. This could be an important contribution, and go some way to mitigating the burden of responsibility investors have for encouraging the exploitation of market failure. However, while enhanced analysis could therefore be a very worthwhile activity, we should be clear about its limitations. Enhanced analysis may, in some cases, reveal that companies may be giving *too much* weight to the penalties of exploiting market failure. In such cases, better analysis may actually send socially undesirable signals to companies. A more important limitation, however, is that enhanced analysis does not, of itself, resolve problems of market failure; it only resolves problems associated with the capital markets' possible inefficiency in pricing-in the penalties associated with exploiting market failure. It is hard to see how mainstream investors could take action to correct market failure itself through their investment decisions (though, as we saw above, they are able to do so through shareholder activism). The problem is that the purpose of investment analysis is to value companies in purely financial terms. The ability of the capital markets to set an accurate share price and to allocate capital efficiently depends on the collective effectiveness of analysts in doing this. The basic problem of market failure is that the associated social or environmental costs are 'external' to the value of the company. As such, investment analysts interested solely in placing an accurate valuation on a company will have no reason to take these external costs into account (except, as we have discussed, in situations where society imposes significant penalties on companies that exploit market failure). If this argument is right, then enhanced analysis per se cannot be relied on to create incentives for companies to refrain from exploiting market failure.

The interests of investors

It has been argued that shareholder activism and enhanced analysis offer significant, if limited, potential to enable investors to address the harmful social and environmental impacts of companies. The next question is: to what extent can investors be expected to adopt these strategies? One way of looking at this question is to explore whether investors have an *interest* in doing so.

Before exploring this issue it is important to be clear that interests are an indicator of potential behaviour, not a determinant. There is a strong body of evidence (see, for example, Fehr and Fischbacher 2004) that self-interest is not the only driver of behaviour. Investors may well place their duties to clients or to wider society over their own financial interests. However, interests do drive individual and collective behaviour to some degree and so provide some indication of investor behaviour. It is also worth being clear that we accept that the interests in question are multiple and entangled. The interests that need to be considered include those of individual fund managers, the commercial interests of the asset management companies they work for, and the interests of the pension funds that hire them. The consequence is that the propositions on investor interests (outlined below) are best seen as providing a provisional framework for analysis rather than a definitive specification of interests.

Do investors have an interest in taking the actions described in the previous section to address the problems caused by companies? The answer to this question depends on the cause of the problem concerned. If the harmful corporate impact arises as a result of a company's failure to maximise shareholder returns because of agency problems or bounded rationality, then investors would seem to have an interest in companies taking action to address these issues. If, on the other hand, the harmful corporate impact arises as a result of the company's efforts to maximise shareholder value in situations of market failure, then it would seem that investors have no financial interest in seeing the problem corrected, even if this is to the detriment of society and the environment. If companies can maximise shareholder value by exploiting market failure, and if investors are interested solely in shareholder value maximisation, then it logically follows that investors have an interest in companies exploiting market failure. Given that market failure is the source of some of the most serious social and environmental problems, this conclusion, if accurate, would limit the extent to which society might look to investors to uphold the public interest.

This conclusion contains an important, if unpalatable, grain of truth. It is likely to be much more straightforward for investors to take action to reduce the harmful social and environmental impacts associated with agency problems and bounded rationality than it is for them to address market failure. However, ultimately, this picture is too simple. For a start, as discussed in the first section of this chapter, there are substantial government and social penalties associated with exploiting market failure. In the presence of sufficiently substantial penalties (or, at least, the threat of such penalties), investors may well not have an interest in companies exploiting market failure.

Understanding the reasons why investors might, or might not, have an interest in encouraging companies to exploit market failures requires consideration of the varied perspectives of different kinds of institutional investors. In our view, there are three key dimensions on which the perspectives, and hence the interests, of investors vary: time, economic breadth and relative/absolute returns. These dimensions affect the extent to which investors are likely to have an interest in companies exploiting market failure.

Some investors have a very short-term focus, seeking to make their money on the basis of short-term movements in the markets. Other investors have much longer-term time horizons. Pension funds, for example, have liabilities stretching decades ahead. Their aim should be to ensure they have the funds to meet those liabilities. Investment time horizons are important in the context of market failure. As we discussed above, there is often a time lag between the benefits of exploiting market failure and the costs associated with government and social penalties. If you are interested only in short-term profit or returns maximisation, you don't need to care all that much about the long-term downside of these penalties, particularly if they are uncertain and intangible. If, on the other hand, you are a long-term investor, you have stronger reasons to care about the long-term costs associated with short-term behaviours, and will have a stronger interest in companies exercising self-restraint in the presence of market failure (at least those market failures that attract or may attract significant government and social penalties).

Another very important perspective is the *breadth* of investments. Some investors have their capital invested in hundreds of companies right across the economy, whereas others have holdings in only a few dozen companies. When it comes to market failure, if you are a shareholder in only one company, you will care only about the benefits and costs that accrue to that company and you will not care about the costs its behaviour imposes on other companies. If, on the other hand, you invest in companies across the economy, you will care about the costs and benefits for other companies too. This is an important issue, and one that is discussed further in Chapter 19. The exploitation of a market failure by one company will frequently be detrimental to others. To take a very simplified example, a coal-fired power station emitting greenhouse gases will contribute to climate change so leading to increased flood risks which may require water utilities to upgrade their piping and sewerage systems to be able to cope with extra volumes of water. Thus, the water utilities will be required to pick up some of the financial costs arising from the environmental damage caused by the coal-fired power station (and other greenhouse gas emitters).

The third important dimension is the manner in which investors assess their investment performance. Most investors measure their performance relative to a benchmark based either on the performance of their peer group or on the returns of a stock market index. Relatively few evaluate their investment performance in absolute terms. What does this mean in practice? Let us imagine that, in one year, the stock market falls by 10% but your fund only falls by 8%. If you care about absolute returns, the year's performance is rather disappointing. You have lost 8% of your capital. If, on the other hand, you care only about relative performance, you will be feeling rather pleased with yourself. You have lost less money than the benchmark index. In particular, as is commonly the case, if you are an individual fund manager and your annual bonus is based on beating the stock market by, say, 1%, you will be delighted by a fall of 8% relative to a 10% fall by the benchmark index—you have beaten your performance target and the resulting bonus will probably make you several tens of thousands of pounds richer as a result!

This issue of absolute and relative returns has implications for investors' interests in tackling agency problems. If you care about absolute performance you have, over the long term at least, an interest in companies addressing agency problems and bounded rationality. Generally speaking, you will want to support initiatives that encourage good governance because this should lead to higher absolute investment returns across the market. If, on the other hand, you care about relative performance you may not be very interested in encouraging better governance. You can add relative performance with badly governed companies just as much as you can with well-governed ones. Your only consideration is whether the market is over- or underestimating the scale of the governance problem. If the market is underestimating a problem, you may be able to beat it by reducing your holding in the company concerned. If it is overestimating the problem, you can beat it by increasing your holding. In either case, it doesn't matter how severe the company's agency problems are. Furthermore, if you did try to do something about the problem through shareholder activism, the financial benefits of any success you have in improving governance will be shared by all the company's other investors. This will cancel out most, or even all, of the relative gain in performance that would have resulted from your hard work; so why bother?

Implications for investor interests on corporate social and environmental impacts

Applying the investor characterisation above leads us to number of hypotheses:

- Investors with a short-term focus will have an interest in companies exploiting market failure, even in the presence of government and social penalties that impose costs over the long term. Long-term investors, however, will not have an interest in companies exploiting market failure when there are sufficient government and social sanctions

- Narrowly focused investors will not be affected when the companies they invest in exploit market failure in a way that imposes substantial costs on other companies. Broadly focused investors, on the other hand, will not have an interest in companies exploiting market failure when doing so is to the detriment of the other companies in their portfolio

- Investors that are both long-term and broadly based will not have an interest in companies exploiting market failure when doing so is to the detriment of companies as a whole over the long term: for example, because it may result in heavy-handed regulatory interventions. They will prefer self-regulation in such cases

- Investors concerned about relative returns will be interested only in addressing market failure and agency problems to the extent that doing so will enable them to beat their performance benchmark. Their interest in taking action to improve things may therefore be limited

If this analysis is roughly correct, quite a lot hangs on whether investors' interests are short-term, relative and narrow or long-term and broadly based. It is to this question that we now turn.

Where do investors' interests really lie?

The good news is that most of the main institutional asset owners would appear to have, at least in theory, an interest in long-term, absolute, broadly based investment returns. A typical pension fund will invest in hundreds of companies across the whole economy, with a view to meeting its obligations to pay the pensions of workers who will retire in 30 years' time. This perspective means that such a fund will have an interest in addressing agency problems and bounded rationality. The fund will also have an interest in discouraging companies from exploiting market failure when doing so imposes greater long-term costs on the companies concerned or on other companies in the economy, whether directly through the imposition of government regulation or indirectly through other more intangible social penalties. As a result, it may be the case that it will not be in the interests of the fund to exploit any major sources of market failure.[8]

Unfortunately, this conclusion may be too good to be true. While institutional asset owners may, in theory, have these long-term, economy-wide interests, when it comes to managing pension fund assets in practice it seems that the investment perspective is more focused on short-term, narrow and relative performance. A substantial proportion of the assets of most pension funds are parcelled out to asset management companies with a mandate to beat a peer-group benchmark index over a three-year period. A large pension fund may divide its assets into a number of separate mandates, each managed by a separate manager and each fairly narrowly invested in portfolios of, perhaps, 50 stocks. This means that, even though the fund as a whole may be invested right across the economy, each individual portfolio will have much narrower exposure. Investment decisions are typically made on the basis of analysis of the value of individual companies. Investment performance is assessed relative to a benchmark such as the UK FTSE All Share Index on a quarterly or annual basis. If managers fail to deliver sufficient relative performance over these shorter time scales, they may well be sacked.

As a result, even though pension funds typically have long-term, broadly based, absolute interests in corporate performance, the way that pension fund assets are man-

---

8   The long-term, economically broad, absolute-performance orientation of pension funds is, to varying degrees, shared by life assurance funds and by many of the individuals that invest their long-term savings in mutual funds.

aged seems to place emphasis on the short-term, relative returns of narrowly focused portfolios. If this is correct, then the real interests of pension funds may not be fully reflected in their investment practice. Even short-term investors will have reasons to consider the discounted stream of cash flows beyond the time horizon of their three-year mandates. However, short, narrowly focused mandates, subject to quarterly and annual performance testing, are unlikely to justify the time and effort necessary for asset managers to conduct the extensive analysis of long-term, economy-wide factors that may affect the interests of pension funds in the long run.

This leaves us with the uncomfortable, albeit tentative, conclusion that, in spite of their real interests and needs, institutional investors may not have an interest in addressing market failure. They may not give due weight to the long-term, economy-wide costs of market failure in investment valuations, and they may not use their influence as shareholders to encourage companies to exercise self-restraint in the presence of market failure. Indeed, if, as suggested above, pension fund assets are invested as if they are only interested in short-term performance *relative* to the benchmark, such investors may not even be very interested in tackling agency problems and bounded rationality.

Conclusion

The previous sections have outlined a model for thinking about the role investors, particularly institutional investors, might play in addressing the harmful social and environmental impacts of the companies in which they invest. Given the scale and complexity of the issues addressed by this model, considerable caution should be exercised about the conclusions drawn from it. They are hypotheses rather than hard claims proven beyond doubt. Indeed, I hope that the subsequent chapters in this book will allow readers to assess their validity. It is also worth reiterating that, while this chapter has identified some important problems that arise when companies and markets work badly, we believe that companies and markets often work very well. By providing and efficiently allocating capital to companies, investors play a hugely positive role in creating value.

Shareholder activism

Shareholder activism to improve the quality of corporate governance and self-regulation may be effective as a mechanism to address agency problems and bounded rationality. Such activism can be useful in addressing market failure by helping to correct the agency problems that sometimes undermine effective regulatory action and by enabling a company to exercise better self-restraint in the presence of market failure.

Nevertheless, the power of activism to address market failure should not be overstated—the strength of the incentives created by market failure may make it very difficult for companies to self-regulate, even with the active support of their shareholders, and particularly if dominant competitors choose not to show the same self-control. In such situations, investors may have little choice but to lend their support to efforts to develop more effective government and social interventions to correct market failure (Mackenzie and Hodgson 2005). Shareholder activism, then, is likely to serve as a supplement to, rather than a replacement of, government and social efforts to correct market failure.

Enhanced analysis

Investors may be able to support efforts by companies to address agency problems and bounded rationality by giving due weight to these issues in their investment analysis. If capital markets are inefficient for this reason, then the better investors become at accurately valuing these factors, the stronger the incentives created by the capital markets for companies to address these problems.

On the other hand, there is not all that much that investors can do through enhanced investment analysis to address market failure. The problem is that exploiting market failure can be a profit-maximising strategy and, when it is, investment analysis will tend to reward companies that exploit market failures with a higher share price. Unfortunately, within conventional investment analysis frameworks, it is hard to see how investment analysts can address this problem while still preserving their role in the efficient allocation of capital.

This problem has a further implication—there may be situations where investors develop programmes of shareholder activism to urge companies to exercise self-restraint in the presence of market failure while simultaneously, through their investment decision-making, acting in ways that disincentivise such self-restraint. That is, in the face of market failure, investors may undermine the effectiveness of shareholder activism in support of self-regulation by sending contradictory signals through their investment decisions.

There may be some cases where the capital markets are inefficient at valuing the uncertain and intangible long-term costs associated with government and social efforts to address market failure. Where this is so, enhanced investment analysis that gives due weight to these costs will strengthen the effect of efforts to correct market failure, and reduce harmful social and environmental impacts as a result. Here activism and investment decision-making can work in parallel to encourage corporate self-restraint in the face of market failure.

Investors' interests

A key factor in determining whether investors will take the actions described above is the extent of their interest in doing so. Long-term, broadly based investors with an interest in the absolute performance of their investments will have an interest in taking action to address agency problems, bounded rationality and, in many cases, market failure through both enhanced analysis and shareholder activism. However, their interest in addressing market failure will be more qualified than in addressing agency problems or bounded rationality, as it depends on the extent to which the long-term and economy-wide costs of exploiting market failure exceed the benefits.

The ability of long-term broadly based investors to address market failure through enhanced analysis will be limited, for the reasons described above. Even though these investors may not have an interest in companies exploiting market failure, the fact is that financial analysis tends to take place at the stock-specific level rather than the economy-wide level. From the perspective of standard investment approaches it is hard to see how stock-specific financial analysis can be 'enhanced' to take account of economy-wide costs of a company's activities when these costs will have no impact on the company's economic value. In the absence of alternative models of investment analysis, it is possible that such long-term investors may have little choice but to seek to discourage companies from exploiting market failure through activism and public policy advocacy, while simultaneously taking investment decisions that punish companies that exercise such restraint. It is hard to see how such inconsistency can be avoided. However, the interests of long-term, broadly based investors are probably better served by inconsistent action to address market failure through activism and public policy advocacy than by consistent inaction.

While long-term, broadly based investors will have an interest in addressing many of the causes of harmful corporate impacts on society, the same is less true for investors with a focus on short-term relative performance. Such investors may well have little interest in addressing market failure at all. Furthermore, they are also unlikely to have much interest in supporting shareholder activism to address agency problems or bounded rationality, partly because the benefits of such activism will accrue only over the long term and partly because all shareholders will benefit from any gains, eliminating most of any *relative* performance benefits.

On the other hand, short-term, narrowly focused investors with an interest in the relative performance of their investments may have *some* interest in enhanced analysis to take account of agency problems and bounded rationality, giving due weight to the penalties associated with exploiting market failure. However, they will only be interested in such analysis to the extent that such factors are likely to affect individual share prices over the short term.

Most institutional asset owners, such as pension funds have long-term, broadly based, absolute performance interests. However, the way their assets are invested appears to indicate that they behave as though they have short-term, narrow, relative performance interests. To the extent that this is true, the model would predict that, in the absence of new interventions from pension funds, investment consultants or regulators, asset managers will find it difficult to justify extensive programmes of enhanced analysis or shareholder activism on environmental or social issues, even when such activity may be in the interests of pension funds. If this is correct, the key question for the future is: to what extent can institutional investors act to ensure that their long-term, broadly based interests are fully expressed by those who manage their money?

In conclusion, our model suggests that investors can take action through shareholder activism and enhanced analysis to address agency problems and bounded rationality and, to a lesser extent, market failure. Investors can also address agency problems and bounded rationality through enhanced analysis. Market failure cannot be addressed in this way, although better analysis of the costs of government and social penalties may be useful. However, the model predicts that current investment practice is not likely to lead to the kind of widespread uptake of enhanced analysis that would drive share prices, or the widespread shareholder activism necessary to deliver majority support for greater self-regulation by companies in the face of market failure. In order for this to happen, pension funds and other asset owners would need to find ways to ensure that their long-term, broadly based interests in absolute investment returns are more fully reflected in the practices of their asset managers.

References

Cadbury, A. (2002) *Corporate Governance and Chairmanship* (Oxford, UK: Oxford University Press).

Carver, J., and C. Oliver (2002) *Boards that Create Value* (New York: Jossey Bass Wiley).

Cuthbertson, K., S. Hayes and D. Nitzsche (1997) 'The Behaviour of UK Stock Prices and Returns: Is the Market Efficient?', *Economic Journal* 107.443: 986-1,008.

Cooter, R., and T. Ulen (2000) *Law and Economics* (New York: Addison-Wesley).

Economist (2005) 'Survey on Corporate Social Responsibility', *The Economist* 20 January 2005.

Fehr, E., and E. Fischbacher (2004) 'The Nature of Human Altruism', *Nature* 425: 785-91.

FRC (Financial Reporting Council) (2003) *Combined Code on Corporate Governance* (London: FRC, www.asb.org.uk/documents/pagemanager/frc/combinedcodefinal.pdf).

FSA (Financial Services Authority) (2004) *Treating Customers Fairly, Progress and Next Steps* (London: FSA, www.fsa.gov.uk/pubs/other/tcf_27072004.pdf).

Hardin, G. (1968) 'The Tragedy of the Commons', *Science* 162.

Jensen, M., and W. Meckling (1976) 'Theory of the Firm: Managerial Behavior, Agency Costs, and Ownership Structure', *Journal of Financial Economics* 3.4: 305-60.

Korobkin, R., and T. Ulen (2000) 'Law and Behavioural Science: Removing the Rationality Assumption from Law and Economics', *California Law Review* 88: 1,051-144.

Mackenzie, C. (2005) 'Moral Sanctions', *Journal of Corporate Citizenship* 15.4: 49-61.

—— and S. Hodgson (2005) *Rewarding Virtue: Effective Board Action on Corporate Responsibility* (London: Business in the Community).

Monks, B., and N. Minnow (2003) *Corporate Governance* (Oxford, UK: Blackwell).

Myners, P. (2001) *Institutional Investment in the United Kingdom: A Review* (London: HM Treasury, www.hm-treasury.gov.uk/media/2F9/02/31.pdf).

Pigou. A.C. (1920) *The Economics of Welfare* (London: Macmillan).

Simon, H. (1983) *Reason in Human Affairs* (Stanford, CA: Stanford University Press).

3
A historical perspective on the growth of socially responsible investment

Russell Sparkes*

Chief Investment Officer, Central Finance Board of the Methodist Church, UK

Socially responsible investment (SRI) is a field that has developed over several decades. While this book focuses on the currently prevalent approaches to SRI in the UK institutional market—namely activism/engagement, and enhanced analysis and integrated investment analysis—it is important to recognise that these approaches have emerged from some 40 years' experience with SRI. The aim of this chapter is to describe the evolution of SRI over this time, and to reflect both on the current state of practice and the future challenges for SRI. It presents the history of SRI in the UK in three main stages—the early work of church investors, the launch of ethical investment unit trusts in the mid 1980s and the 'mainstreaming' of SRI following the implementation of the SRI pensions legislation in 2000.

The historical record illustrates two other points that tend to be overlooked in discussions about SRI. The first is the fundamental importance of the legal background, as legal concerns inhibited the growth of the institutional SRI market in the UK until they were addressed by the SRI pensions regulations that came into force in 2000. The second is that public anxiety about geopolitical issues has been an important factor behind the expansion of SRI, particularly for institutional investors such as public-sector pension funds.

---

* This chapter is written in a personal capacity, and the views expressed here should not be taken as reflecting those of the Central Finance Board of the Methodist Church.

Some comments on definitions and terminology

This chapter is not intended to examine whether there is any difference between 'ethical' or 'socially responsible' investment—these terms are treated as essentially equivalent.[1] The key point from a chronological perspective at least is that 'ethical investment' was the standard terminology in use until the end of the 1990s, since which time SRI has come into general use. For the purposes of this discussion, SRI is defined as 'an investment philosophy that combines ethical or environmental goals with financial ones' (Sparkes 1994a: 4).

The UK church investors, who were the original pioneers of UK SRI, have normally used what would now be referred to as 'a mixture of exclusion and engagement'. However, when 'commercial' SRI funds first became available to the general public, they were marketed in fairly straightforward terms of avoiding investment in areas such as alcohol and tobacco. This approach to SRI has been variously described as 'exclusion', an 'avoidance approach' or (mostly in the US) 'ethical screening'.[2]

In the late 1990s, a major switch occurred when certain large insurance companies started discussing SRI issues with companies in which they had investments; this is normally described as 'engagement'. The late 1990s and early years of the 21st century also saw greater interest in shareholders using their formal rights as shareholders to force companies to take action on specific corporate governance and corporate responsibility issues.[3]

Driving forces for SRI

It is probably fair to state that, in the public's mind at least, SRI is generally identified with ethical/SRI unit trusts, i.e. funds based on ethical 'screening' or exclusion. Since their inception 20 years ago there has been a rapid growth in such funds, and most media comment has focused on these unit trusts. However, a focus on ethical unit trusts misses the huge amount of work undertaken in this area initially by church investors

1   For a discussion of this topic, see Sparkes 2001.
2   The simple exclusion criteria of many original ethical unit trusts led to them being severely criticised by philosopher Roger Scruton (in Anderson 1996) who argued: 'This Report suggests that their own investments might variously be accurately labelled "investments reflecting investors' opinions", "investments reflecting fashionable causes", "scrupulous investments", "ethically simplistic investments" . . . the overall objection to ethical investment codes is their aggressive simplicity . . . a simplicity which ill fits them for their ethical work . . . there is no reason why the various investment institutions should not continue to serve [their customers] and their preferences. The only objection this Report makes is that they should not describe what they are doing as "ethical" investment.'
3   While such a development has the potential to achieve social and environmental goals, it is important to recognise that not all shareholder activism is for social purposes. Indeed, such actions first took off on a wide scale as 'greenmail' in the US in the 1980s. Greenmail was a technique that involved aggressive investors buying a strategic stake in companies and forcing them to liquidate assets, often involving the abandonment of social issues and cutbacks in employment, in order to buy off the shareholder activists.

and, more recently, by pension funds and other institutional investors. Such a restricted focus could lead to the erroneous conclusion that SRI is no more than a successful example of 'ethical consumerism' whereas, in fact, SRI is probably more accurately described as a response to major geopolitical issues such as the Vietnam War, apartheid South Africa, a widespread sense of growing environmental crisis, major corporate governance failures and related concerns about executive pay, fears about the consequences of globalisation and, most recently, pharmaceutical issues in part related to HIV/AIDS.

Ethical investment and the law

> Tawney himself said that to explore the economy without exploring the legal institutions within which it exists is like a geographer discussing the river systems without mentioning the mountains, but it has been more popular among economists to stress the 'invisible hand' of the market than the 'visible hand' of the law (Jones 1989).

It is surprising how little attention is paid to legal matters in most discussions of SRI. This probably occurs because most writers on the subject take the legislative framework as a 'given'. While this is a reasonable approach when writing about developments in one country at one moment in time, it is potentially misleading when attempting to extend the lessons learned in one country to another whose legal systems may greatly alter what is permissible or prohibited. Furthermore, legal frameworks within countries are not constant but are liable to change significantly over time. This is certainly true of the trust law which governs SRI in the UK.

The period 1984–91 saw the two definitive court cases in English law on SRI and fiduciary duty—the Megarry and Nicholls cases.[4] The first of these cases, *Cowan v. Scargill* (commonly referred to as the Megarry case), was the famous legal battle brought by Arthur Scargill in 1984 to force the trustees of the mineworkers' pension fund to avoid investment overseas or in alternative sources of energy that were a rival to coal. The case hinged on the question of whether pension funds could or should take account of ethical or social factors in deciding investment policy. Judge Sir Robert Megarry's judgement was very clear: a pension fund was a trust like any other, and hence the trustees were subject to an overriding duty to act in the best interests of the beneficiaries of the trust. Megarry defined the 'best interest' of a pension fund as being the greatest financial return on its investments subject to a degree of prudence, on the grounds that the sole purpose of a pension scheme was financial (i.e. to fund pension benefits). He therefore ruled that the union trustees could not enforce their policy.

The second case related to the campaign against apartheid South Africa. In 1991, the Bishop of Oxford and two other clergymen went to the High Court under Vice-Chancellor Nicholls. While the stated goal of the case was to require the Church Commissioners to include ethical considerations in their investment policy, the true objective

---

4   These and other cases are described in detail in Sparkes 1994a: ch. 11.

was to require the Commissioners to disinvest from British companies with any kind of presence in South Africa. The effect would have been to increase the proportion of the stock market excluded from the Church Commissioners' investment universe from 13% to 37%. The Bishop of Oxford lost his case, with the judge ruling that the basic principles of fiduciary duty had not changed. However, Lord Nicholls did make some minor concessions which distinguished the legal position of charities from that of pension funds, noting that UK law did recognise that unethical investment could deter potential donors, alienate supporters and employees, and damage a charity's reputation. He stressed, however, that he thought that such exemptions from the fiduciary duty to maximise returns would be fairly rare in practice.

Although the focus of this book is primarily on UK SRI, it is pertinent to note that the US approach is very different, with shareholder activism being centred around the utilisation of the rights of share ownership to assert ethical goals. Much of the difference in approach can be traced to the differences in legal systems, with US investors benefiting from specific rights to file shareholder resolutions granted to them by the Securities and Exchange Commission (SEC); specifically, the process for filing a shareholder resolution is much easier and the ownership thresholds to be met are much more liberal than in the UK. In addition, US pension schemes are required to treat voting rights as they would any other asset, i.e. they should be used in the best interests of beneficiaries, independent advice should be taken on their use and records should be kept of voting activity to demonstrate that such assets are being utilised.

The pioneering role of church investors

The earliest ethical investors were the churches on both sides of the Atlantic. Ethical investment grew naturally out of the churches' desire to integrate the management of their financial assets with their beliefs; in so doing they working within a venerable tradition. At about the same time as Adam Smith was setting out his vision of the 'invisible hand' of the market, John Wesley argued for a link between ethics and ethical investment in a sermon, *The Use of Money*, published in 1760. Wesley was a social reformer who was one of the first public figures of his day to speak out against the slave trade. Wesley stressed the importance of the right use of money and saw the role of the investor 'not as a proprietor, but as a steward'. He went on to say that we should gain all we can but (Wesley 1760):

> Not at the expense of life nor at the expense of our health, nor without hurting our mind. Therefore we may not engage or continue in any sinful trade . . . not hurting our neighbour in his substance (i.e. wealth), nor by hurting our neighbour in his body.

Hence, Wesley ruled out obtaining property through gambling or pawnbroking or excessive interest rates, while he also condemned profits made through the supply of products that damage health, such as strong liquor. For his time Wesley's thinking was surprisingly sophisticated. For example, he condemned spirits, but not wine, arguing that:

> We may not gain by hurting our neighbour in his body. Therefore we may not sell anything which tends to impair health. Such is, eminently, all that liquid fire, commonly called drams, or spirituous liquors . . . We may not gain by hurting our neighbour, by ministering, either directly or indirectly, to intemperance . . . it concerns all those who have anything to do with taverns.

It is interesting that, in his 1999 speech setting out the proposed new SRI regulations, the UK Pensions Minister Stephen Timms MP used Wesley's *Use of Money* sermon as the basis of his speech, noting its emphasis on stewardship:[5]

> In Wesley's words, penned some 250 years ago, we are told we are 'placed here [on Earth] not as proprietors, but as stewards . . . we are entrusted for a season with goods of various kinds; but the sole property of them does not rest with us'. Central to his message is the idea of stewardship: that everything we gain or are given is only conditionally ours. We are not the absolute owners of our wealth; rather we are custodians or stewards. This is a way of thinking that has become more familiar to us in recent years: we recognise that our children and grandchildren will have to deal with the environmental problems we leave them, and we have already begun to address the damage we have done. So perhaps Wesley's words have a resonance for us that they did not have for the people of his own time.

The historical record shows that the earliest 'ethical investors' were the Christian churches, not just in the UK, but also globally. While this chapter focuses on the UK, church investors also played a pioneering role in the development of SRI in the US, in Canada, on the continent of Europe and in Australia.[6] Church investors also invented many of the SRI techniques that have subsequently become standard practice, such as the use of exclusion criteria, dialogue or engagement with companies, and shareholder activism.

It is also worth noting that it was the desire of some Christian individuals to make broadly based ethical investment funds available to the general public, which led to the creation of modern SRI unit trusts in the first place. The world's first socially responsible mutual fund was launched as long ago as 1928 in the US, when temperance groups followed the legal prohibition of the sale or manufacture of alcohol in the US with the creation of the Pioneer Fund, which excluded investment in alcohol or tobacco. However, this fund was never marketed to the general public and remains fairly small to this day. A similar process occurred in Sweden in 1965 when the Swedish temperance society inaugurated the Ansvar unit trust for its members. This was the first ethical unit trust launched in Europe, although again its sales were effectively restricted to the affinity group. The first ethical fund targeted at a mass audience was the Pax World Fund, a mutual fund (i.e. a unit trust) which owed its conception to two New Hampshire Methodist ministers. It has been extremely successful, with its initial funds of $100,000 in 1971 growing to over $1 billion by 2001. Pax, which means 'peace', was set

5   Speech to PIRC Corporate Social Responsibility Conference, London, 21 April 1999.
6   For information on US history and practice regarding SRI, the works produced by Domini and Kinder (1984), Domini *et al.* (1992) and Domini *et al.* (1993) are invaluable. See Bassler *et al.* 2001, Ellmen 1998 and Knowles 1997 for histories of SRI in Germany, Canada and Australia respectively. For a more up-to-date review of SRI in Europe, North America and the Pacific, see Sparkes 2002: chs. 12, 13, 14.

up to create an investment vehicle that would enable investors to avoid investing in companies believed to be profiting from the Vietnam War. The Pax fund also excluded traditional 'sin stocks' such as tobacco and gambling.

In the UK, ethical investment dates back to 1948 with the creation of the modern-day Church Commissioners 'to manage the investments entrusted to us to maximise our financial support for the ministry of the Church of England, particularly in areas of need and opportunity'. The Church Commissioners and other Church of England bodies such as the Central Board of Finance (CBF) and the Pensions Board operate under a common ethical investment policy which was based initially on negative exclusion: specifically, investments in armaments, gambling, tobacco, breweries or newspapers.

Vietnam and South Africa

US shareholder rights were little used until the late 1960s when public opinion was ignited by concern about the Vietnam War. The first SRI proxy resolutions filed by church groups and student bodies related to Vietnam (e.g. the resolution submitted to Dow Chemical's annual general meeting in 1969 questioning that company's production of the defoliant Agent Orange).[7] In 1971 the US Episcopal Church filed a shareholder resolution on South Africa at General Motors' annual general meeting.[8]

The issue of apartheid in South Africa proved a key driving force for the development of SRI, particularly in the US. In the early 1970s US church investment funds, university foundations, and state and local pension funds pressurised American companies to desegregate their operations in South Africa. In the early 1980s, states such as Connecticut and Wisconsin required all US companies in which their pension funds were invested to follow the Sullivan Principles of non-segregation of all races in eating, comfort, locker room and work; and of equal and fair employment practices for all employees. Anti-South African activism hardened following that country's declaration of a state of emergency in 1985. Anti-apartheid activists campaigned for state, local government, university and labour pension funds to pressurise US companies operating there to withdraw. This campaign received the backing of some of the largest pension funds in the US, e.g. those of New York State and California.

There were similar campaigns in the UK, particularly against Barclays Bank, which controlled the largest bank in South Africa, and the giant Anglo–Dutch oil company Royal Dutch/Shell, believed to be a significant supplier of oil to the apartheid regime. A 'shadow board' was set up that helped to co-ordinate a boycott of Barclays Bank, one of the biggest consumer boycotts ever held in Britain. Activists persuaded a variety of charity and pension funds to withdraw their money from Barclays. In August 1985 Bar-

---

7   Incidentally, concern over corporate involvement in Vietnam led to the establishment of the Council for Economic Priorities (CEP) in 1969, the world's first SRI research service.

8   These actions resulted in the formation of the Interfaith Center on Corporate Responsibility (ICCR) in 1973. ICCR is an interfaith grouping of 275 Protestant, Catholic and Jewish institutions whose members have investment portfolios worth well over $100 billion. ICCR has been the leader in US shareholder activism since its foundation and, despite the growth in US shareholder activism over the last 30 years, ICCR was still the single largest filer of social proxy resolutions in 2003.

clays submitted to pressure when it announced that it would not be taking up its rights in a share issue by Barclays National in South Africa, reducing Barclays South Africa to an associated company in which Barclays owned merely 40%.

Demands within the churches for more information on corporate involvement in South Africa led to the establishment of the Ethical Investment Research Service (EIRIS) in 1983. The main initial supporters were the Society of Friends (Quakers), Quaker charitable trusts and the Methodist Church. Since that time, EIRIS Ltd has become the dominant provider of SRI research in the UK, with its services used by the majority of UK SRI unit trusts.

In the UK, the controversy around South Africa led to investors engaging with companies on the issue. The issue also resulted in the creation of the first ethical investment advisory committee, when acrimonious debate within the Methodist Church led to a decision to formally establish an Ethics of Investment Committee in 1983. The Committee had two key functions: to provide ethical investment advice to the church's investment arm, the Central Finance Board of the Methodist Church (CFB); and, most importantly, to produce an annual 'ethics report' publicising its activities. The latter was a good model of transparency and disclosure that could, and perhaps should, have been more widely followed by the SRI industry later. The CFB also pioneered 'engagement' with companies, holding discussions with Shell and Barclays regarding their activities in South Africa.

The launch of ethical investment unit trusts in the UK

The 'pioneering' stage of UK SRI came to an end in May 1984 when, for the first time, a retail ethical investment fund—the Friends Provident Stewardship Fund—was made available to the general public. This development resulted in SRI itself receiving much greater media attention and public recognition. There was a strong church influence behind the fund, as Charles Jacob MBE, the former investment manager of the CFB of the Methodist Church, was a prime inspiration.

In the late 1970s there was considerable debate within Friends Provident (FP), a medium-sized insurance company originally established on Quaker principles, as to what extent its funds should continue to be invested in accordance with Quaker ethical values. By the early 1980s, FP's management concluded that, while the company could no longer avoid investments in areas such as alcohol and tobacco, it would create a small fund, the FP Stewardship Fund, for those who wished to avoid such investments. There were considerable delays in getting legal approval from the Department of Trade and Industry, but this finally occurred early in 1984. Stewardship's original aims and objectives included both positive and negative criteria, although media attention focused on the negatives, contributing to the perception of retail SRI as being based on the avoidance of 'sin stocks' such as alcohol, tobacco and armaments. There are two other things about FP Stewardship that need to be highlighted. First, FP originally did little ethical research itself, outsourcing most of the work to EIRIS, which used its database to generate an 'approved list' based on the criteria devised by Stewardship's Ethics Committee. Second, FP adopted a 'twin track' approach to SRI, with its ethical research unit and its fund management team having little contact (i.e. the research team had no involvement in fund management, and the fund managers had little or no involvement in the ethics). This model was adopted by FP for legal reasons to do with fiduciary duty, and this approach has been generally copied by other SRI funds. The conventional legal wisdom of the 1980s believed that, following the Scargill case, SRI research should be only advisory in nature and totally separate from fund managers. Fund management companies were worried that, if SRI analysts advised on stock selection and portfolio construction, they would be left open to legal challenge if the subsequent investment performance was poor.

If the churches were one influence on the launch of FP Stewardship, another influence was increasing public suspicion of corporate activity and demand for consumer activism in the UK. The most visible sign of this trend was the work of Social Audit,[9] founded in 1973, and inspired by Ralph Nader's work in the US.

When FP launched the Stewardship Fund, the received wisdom was that it would remain a tiny niche product, essentially serving those with Quaker ideals who were unhappy with FP's move towards a more mainstream investing style. Outsiders forecast that it was unlikely ever to exceed £5 million in size. Such pessimism was to prove totally unjustified; within a year of launch the unit trust had investment assets of over £30 million. FP subsequently added various pension and unit-linked products under the overall Stewardship brand. The total assets in Stewardship surged from £188 million in 1990 to £1,638 million by the end of the decade.

Other financial services companies noticed the rapid growth of the Stewardship Funds. FP itself issued a range of other ethical investment funds, such as FP Stewardship Income and FP North American Stewardship. The next few years saw a variety of new entrants decide to launch ethical funds. These included the Buckmaster (now Credit Suisse) Fellowship Trust, Abbey Ethical, NM Conscience, Allchurches Amity Trust and Scottish Equitable Ethical. Figure 3.1, first published in *Professional Investor* magazine in March 1994, shows the growth of ethical investment over the period 1984–93.[10] Another indicator of the growing maturity of SRI occurred in 1988 with the foundation of the Social Investment Forum (SIF) in the US to promote and explain SRI to a wider audience.[11]

Green investing

The next major global issue to propel SRI forward was a growing public sense of environmental crisis, following a series of high-profile environmental incidents including the Three Mile Island incident in the US in 1979, the catastrophic explosion at Cher-

---

9   Headed by Charles Medawar, Social Audit audited, generally without the co-operation of the management, a number of large companies looking at social, employment, consumer, environmental and financial impacts.

10   Indeed, this was probably the first time that a magazine targeted at investment professionals thought SRI worthy of notice.

11   The UK Social Investment Forum was established in 1991.

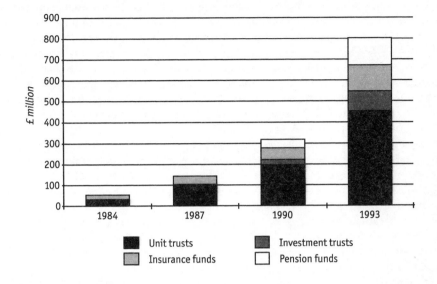

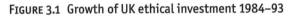

FIGURE 3.1 Growth of UK ethical investment 1984–93

Source: Sparkes 1994b

nobyl in 1986, growing evidence in the 1970s of the damage being caused by 'acid rain' to Europe's forests, the toxic gas leak at a chemical plant in Bhopal in 1984 which killed 3,500 people and injured 50,000 more, and the 1986 leak from a Swiss chemical factory which caused heavy pollution in the Rhine. Public concern was expressed most visibly in 1990 when the Green Party won 15% of the UK vote in the European elections, an event that sent shock waves through the British political establishment.

In 1988, the nature of UK SRI changed significantly when environmental assessment became an integral part of SRI analysis, a significant change to the earlier SRI approach of avoiding 'sin stocks' such as alcohol and tobacco. This occurred through the creation of the Merlin research unit, an organisation later taken over by the Jupiter fund management group. A genuine trailblazer, Merlin was the pioneer of green investment in the City of London on the back of the vision and energy of two people in particular— Tessa Tennant, who had spent six years at the Green Alliance before working at Franklin Research, a leading US SRI firm, and Mark Campanale who had worked in Africa following a master's degree in agricultural economics.

Merlin's approach was radical in two ways: first, in the way it made the environment an essential component of SRI and, second, in the way it shifted SRI analysis away from negative exclusion towards a more positive 'best-in-class' approach. Merlin was also the first to identify sustainable development as a means of creating new investment opportunities (e.g. it was an early investor in the Norwegian recycling packaging company Tomra). Merlin was the first commercial SRI provider to take up the engagement methodology pioneered by the churches regarding companies operating in South

Africa. The development by Merlin of such an integrated approach was a key part of the evolution of mainstream SRI thinking.[12]

In 1989, Merlin launched Merlin International Green—the first-ever SRI investment trust. There was such a high level of public interest in green issues at the time that a number of other fund management houses rushed to follow their example and roll out environmental funds. The year also saw the launch of the Henderson Green PEP, the Homeowners Green Chip Trust, the Eagle Star Environmental Trust and the TSB (now Scottish Widows) Environmental Investor Trust. The following year saw the inception of the CIS (Co-operative Insurance) Environ Trust and the Clerical Medical (now Insight) Evergreen Trust while, in 1991, the insurance company National Provident (NPI) entered the SRI market with the launch of the NPI Global Care Trust which had a strongly green flavour.

Indeed, the late 1980s saw increasing awareness in financial markets that the environment was becoming big business. One of the UK's leading stock brokers, James Capel, produced a 'green index' of 30 companies involved in environmental services, with a 70-page annual review of the sector, *The Green Book*. However, high enthusiasm in 1989 marked the peak of environmental investing; the Capel Green Index, having risen from an initial level of 100 in January 1989 to 147 in August 1989, then fell back to a low of 87 in November 1990 before slowly rising again. As can be seen from Table 3.1, over the five years from its inception at the end of 1988, the index steadily under-performed the main UK equity benchmark (the FTSE All Share Index).

	1988–90	1990–92	1993	5 years to end 1993
Capel Green Index	−6.1%	+39.6%	+16.1%	+52.1%
FT All Share	+20.4%	+41.5%	+27.7%	+117.7%

TABLE 3.1 Performance of the Capel Green Index

In the late 1990s, technology mania swept the global financial markets. In an unfortunate echo of what had happened ten years earlier, renewable energy stocks and the forecast 'hydrogen economy' were seen as offering almost limitless investment opportunities. In the late 1990s, many SRI funds increased their exposure to relatively risky shares that had the tendency to go up much more than the market as a whole when equities were rising, as they were in the late 1990s. However, they could also be expected to drop sharply when, or if, the market turned down. This strategy, which led to some SRI funds producing strong relative investment returns during the late 1990s

12   In May 1994, Tennant and Campanale left Merlin to join National Provident (NPI) setting up the NPI Global Care (SRI) team. Since this is now the Henderson SRI team, Tennant and Campanale may be credited with founding two of the UK's current leading SRI fund managers.

bull market, resulted in weak performance when the bubble burst in the spring of 2000.[13]

The period 1990–99 saw steady growth in retail SRI funds, with Henderson/NPI emerging as a strong contender to ISIS (Friends Provident). In 1999, the Australian insurance group AMP took over NPI, and the NPI SRI team was transferred over to Henderson Global Investors, the asset management arm of AMP. Mark Campanale became closely associated with NPI/Henderson's drive to make SRI be seen as a positive rather than a negative investment approach. This was achieved through emphasis on a 'best-in-class' approach, seeking investment in 'industries of the future'. In the late 1990s, the Henderson SRI investment funds began to win sizeable institutional mandates. In 2000 alone, the Henderson SRI team doubled its total SRI assets to over £1 billion. This was achieved primarily on the back of mandates for local authority pension funds. This was an important development for the UK SRI market as, for the first time, fund management companies saw that SRI offered the chance to win not just retail funds but potentially much larger institutional mandates for pension fund and charity clients.

It was mentioned earlier how initially the FP Stewardship SRI fund, the retail market leader, based most of its research on negative ethical screens. By the middle of the 1990s this approach was updated by the recruitment of Craig Mackenzie (previously a researcher on SRI at Bath University) to establish a significant internal SRI research capability. In October 1998, FP announced the creation of a six-person 'engagement unit'. Around this time, FP branded its fund management and research activities under the 'ISIS' label, with the business having its own stock market quotation.[14] Although ISIS retained its traditional approach of keeping SRI research and fund management strictly separate, it hoped that in-depth analysis of social and environmental problems could be used by pension funds to 'engage' with companies over such concerns. This engagement product was actively promoted under the name of 'responsible engagement overlay' or REO™. In June 1999, the company won a £20 million mandate for REO™ from Aberdeen City Council, followed by Lothian Council in June 2000 for a £350 million REO™ agreement. Other REO™ customers included the AEW trade union pension fund and the giant Dutch pension fund PGGM; some of these REO™ mandates were 'unbundled', i.e. were on a stand-alone basis.

The late 1990s also saw increased use of formal shareholder rights and the growing convergence between SRI and corporate governance. Turning first to the use of formal shareholder rights, in May 1997 a NGO coalition filed a shareholder resolution at the annual general meeting of the Shell Transport and Trading Company. Shell had been widely criticised over its planned disposal of the Brent Spar oilfield platform in the North Sea along with allegations of links to human rights abuses in Nigeria. The resolution requested Shell's management to: behave in a more socially and environmentally

---

13   One the most visible signs of green investment mania emerging from the 1990s 'tech boom' was the Merrill Lynch New Energy Fund, launched in October 2000. While this was not explicitly an SRI fund, the fund's focus on renewable energy probably attracted many individual SRI investors. Merrill Lynch's stated objective was to raise £35 million, but such was the public's enthusiasm that £200 million was subscribed, a large pool of capital for a small investment universe. Unfortunately for investors in the Merrill Lynch New Energy Fund, the expected growth did not materialise, with the fund's share price declining in 2001–2002.

14   In 2004, ISIS merged with the long-established investment trust company Foreign & Colonial, with the new investment management business being renamed F&C.

responsible way; draw up a detailed policy on the environment and human rights; appoint a specific board member with responsibility for its implementation; and have an independently audited report on the implementation of its policy. The proposal surprised everybody by receiving the support of over 11% of the votes cast, and Shell management subsequently addressed the concerns raised by the resolution. With regard to the relationship between corporate governance and SRI, corporate governance had traditionally been seen as of limited interest to most SRI funds. This began to change in the mid-1990s with growing public concern about large executive pay rises in companies whose profitability looked under pressure, and where redundancy programmes were being implemented. One of the most high-profile examples was British Gas, where demonstrators objecting to rising executive pay in that company campaigned outside its 1995 annual general meeting. Eleven pension funds tabled a shareholder resolution calling on the company to change its methods of determining executive pay, with the resolution receiving over 18% of the vote, an astonishing percentage for a resolution opposed by the company.

2000 SRI pensions legislation

The next major development in the growth of UK SRI occurred on 3 July 2000, the day new SRI pensions regulations came into effect. The new measures obliged all UK private sector pension funds to consider SRI and voting rights as part of their overall investment policy, and to disclose:

- The extent (if at all) to which social, environmental or ethical considerations are taken into account by trustees in the selection, retention and realisation of investments

- The policy (if any) of directing the exercise of the rights (including voting rights) attaching to investments[15]

In 1997, the then Minister for Trade and Industry Margaret Beckett had publicly expressed the government's view of the importance of shareholder voting:

> I look forward to more institutions actively using their voting assets, and to pension fund trustees, and other clients, routinely asking managers how they have voted. Better still, institutions should explain their voting policies and volunteer the information on how they have voted (quoted in Sparkes 2002).

The introduction of the 2000 SRI pensions regulations led to optimism in some quarters that SRI would rapidly move from fringe to mainstream. While the full mainstreaming of SRI has yet to happen, the pensions regulations certainly led to major changes in the size and composition of the UK SRI market. In December 1997, two years

---

15   At the time, many observers were surprised to see that shareholder voting (which was seen as relating primarily to corporate governance) was coupled together with SRI. This reflected the increasing impatience of the government with the apparent indifference of institutional investors to use their voting rights as shareholders to stop apparent abuses such as excessive executive pay.

before the SRI legislation was laid before Parliament, the value of total SRI assets in the UK was some £22.7 billion, dominated by church and other charity investors who had over 50% of the SRI assets under management at that time (£12.5 billion). By the end of 2001, the overall total of socially responsible investment funds in the UK had risen almost tenfold to £224.5 billion. Churches and charities were overtaken by pension funds and insurance companies as the major players, owing to the 'engagement' activities of large insurance companies and asset managers such as Friends Provident and Henderson.[16]

A number of factors contributed to this change. Some very large pension schemes, mainly those linked to the public sector such as Hermes (Post Office) and the Universities Superannuation Scheme (USS),[17] adopted SRI policies. From the mid-1990s, under the leadership of Alastair Ross-Goobey, Hermes, the manager of over £35 billion investment funds mostly for BT but also with some external clients, became known for its corporate governance activism. In 2001 Hermes adopted the following statement of investment policy for its BT client:

> The letters of appointment of every investment manager of the Scheme instruct the appointee, in its investment policy, to consider the following when selecting the shares in which they invest the Scheme's assets: A company run in the long-term interests of its shareholders will need to manage effectively relationships with its employees, suppliers and customers, to behave ethically and to have regard for the environment and society as a whole . . . Similarly, the letters of appointment request that the manager uses its best endeavours to exercise the ownership rights associated with shares.

One important sign of the growing influence of SRI in the financial markets has been the development of coalitions of SRI funds working together on subjects such as transparency and disclosure, and pharmaceutical ethics. Probably the most significant of these is the Institutional Investors Group on Climate Change (IIGCC), a forum for collaborative effort by institutional investors on issues related to climate change. IIGCC seeks to:

- Promote better understanding of the implications of climate change among members and other institutional investors

- Encourage companies and markets in which IIGCC members invest to address any material risks and opportunities to their businesses associated with climate change and a shift to a lower-carbon economy

- Occupy the overlap between 'interested investor' (aware of the implications of climate change) and 'responsible investor' (acting to manage the risks climate change poses to investments). IIGCC does not seek to become a 'campaigning investor' (advocating immediate or otherwise radical changes in energy and economic activity)

The second major development behind the rapid transformation of SRI was the move by a number of large insurance companies to apply SRI criteria across all their equity

16   This development is discussed in depth in Chapter 13 of Sparkes 2002. See also Mansley 2000.
17   See, further, Chapter 14 by Peter Casson and David Russell.

funds. Friends Provident (ISIS) was the first to do so in the summer of 2000, moving beyond the Stewardship unit trusts to apply engagement to all of its equity funds with investment assets worth £15 billion. Friends Provident's example was quickly followed by three other major UK insurance companies: Co-operative Insurance Services (CIS); Henderson/NPI and CGNU. By the end of 2001, these four insurance companies had added £103 billion of UK equity assets to the SRI UK investment universe.

Another sign of growing interest in UK SRI occurred in August 2000 when seven key members of the Henderson SRI team, including SRI fund manager Clare Brook and head of SRI research Anne-Maree O'Connor, were head-hunted to join Morley (see Chapter 6). Morley was the investment management side of CGNU (now Aviva), one of the UK's largest insurance companies. This was the first time that socially responsible invest-ment expertise was thought valuable enough to be worth 'head-hunting'. The pattern was repeated a year later when Craig Mackenzie and colleagues from Friends Provident left to join Clerical Medical (now Insight), the fund management arm of HBOS.

When the 2000 pensions regulations were announced there was considerable opti-mism that SRI would be adopted as a core product by the investment mainstream. This has not really occurred. Although many conventional UK fund management houses have appointed some SRI expertise, this is often limited in scope. UK SRI is therefore still dominated by a relatively small number of financial services companies, such as Hen-derson; Insight and Friends Provident (ISIS/F&C). These 'leaders' share the following characteristics:

- Significant retail and institutional funds SRI funds under management

- Substantial SRI research and fund management teams[18]

- High-profile team leaders such at Karina Litvak at F&C, Rob Lake and Nick Robins at Henderson, and Craig Mackenzie at Insight, who are all successful at generating media coverage for their engagement and activism activities

- Strong internal operating procedures and 'ethics audit trails'

Reflections on the current state of play[19]

The good

- SRI has entered the mainstream in the UK, although it is still not *the* main-stream approach

---

18   In 2004, the author made a comparative study of the engagement activity produced by the UK fund providers, and was particularly impressed by the quality of the work from F&C and Insight.

19   In May 2003, the author was invited to give my thoughts on the future of UK SRI to the board of the UK Social Investment Forum at a management 'awayday'. Some of the points I made in my pre-sentation, *The Good, The Bad and The Future*, are presented here.

- Large charities (with income over £1 million) are required to consider social, environmental and ethical factors when setting their investment policy, and small charities should do so as a matter of best practice

- There has been rapid growth in interest in SRI in Europe, including the foundation of the European Social Investment Forum (Eurosif) in 2001

The bad

- There is growing scepticism among some independent financial advisers (IFAs) and NGOs about SRI. These concerns are linked to increasing scepticism about the value of corporate social responsibility (CSR) (see, for example, Christian Aid 2004)

- Investors appear reluctant to use their formal rights to encourage change in companies

- The use of 'engagement' has blurred the image of SRI. For example, as noted by Eric Borremans, head of sustainable development at BNP Paribas:

  > Engagement-only runs the risk of becoming a public relations exercise and is too detached from fundamental analysis. If you really want to create change in a company you need a significant shareholding and do a lot of lobbying with the management. A typical engagement overlay may not provide the means for driving that change. We don't send letters and requests or come in with an agenda for change—and we don't try and tell them what they should do.

- Demand for SRI in the institutional market has not developed as rapidly as hoped after the 2000 SRI pensions regulations came into force

The future

- While the amendment to the UK Pensions Act was a major change, countries such as Australia have since overtaken the UK. Since March 2002, Australian pension and insurance funds have had to disclose their fund's compliance with the SRI regulations, with the Australian Securities and Investment Commission (ASIC) having the power to inspect SRI claims. If similar powers were adopted and enforced in the UK, it would enable investors to distinguish between SRI funds that are really trying hard to provide a good SRI service for their investors and those funds adopting a compliance approach at minimal expense

- New boutiques are likely to emerge, offering more tailored services and products for their clients

- SRI investment managers need to provide detailed SRI audit trails, demonstrating their claims regarding the outcomes that have been achieved from engagement and activism

In conclusion, there is a growing convergence between SRI and corporate governance: this is a welcome and important development. However, we are still some way from seeing a proper alignment of SRI and social activism (see, further, Sparkes and Cowton 2004; Lydenberg 2005): that is, a financial system that is both responsible and responsive to changing societal values and expectations. For SRI to act as a positive mechanism for change, so ensuring that companies work in the public interest, requires the provision of accurate, objective and rigorously produced non-financial information on corporate activity, as well as fundamental changes in the way institutional investors utilise their shareholding rights as owners to implement change and guide corporate executives in a positive direction. These are the next challenges for responsible investment.

References

Anderson, D. (ed.) (1996) *What has 'ethical investment' to do with ethics?* (London: Social Affairs Unit).

Bassler, K., M. Kuhlo and P. Stoll (2001) *Ethisches Investment: Strategien für Kirchliche Geldanlagen* (Stuttgart: Gesangbuchverlag).

Christian Aid (2004) *Behind the Mask: The Real Face of CSR* (London: Christian Aid).

Domini, A., and P. Kinder (1984) *Ethical Investing* (Reading, MA: Addison-Wesley).

——, —— and S. Lydenberg (1992) *The Social Investment Almanac* (New York: Henry Holt).

——, —— and —— (1993) *Investing For Good: Making Money while Being Socially Responsible* (New York: Harper Business).

Ellmen, E. (1998) *The Canadian 1998 Ethical Money Guide* (Toronto: Lorimer).

Jones, N. (1989) *God and the Moneylenders* (Oxford, UK: Blackwell).

Knowles, R. (1997) *Ethical Investment* (Sydney, Australia: Choice Books).

Lydenberg, S. (2005) *Corporations and the Public Interest: Guiding the Invisible Hand* (San Francisco: Berrett-Koehler).

Mansley, M. (2000) *Socially Responsible Investment: A Guide for Pension Funds and Institutional Investors* (Sudbury, UK: Monitor Press).

Sparkes, R. (1994a) *The Ethical Investor* (London: HarperCollins).

—— (1994b) 'The Rewards of Virtue', *Professional Investor*, March 1994: 20-22.

—— (2001) 'Ethical Investment: Whose Ethics, Which Investment?', *Business Ethics: A European Review* 10.3: 194-205.

—— (2002) *Socially Responsible Investment: A Global Revolution* (Chichester, UK: John Wiley).

—— and C. Cowton (2004) 'The Maturing of Socially Responsible Investment: A Review of the Developing Link with Corporate Social Responsibility', *Journal of Business Ethics* 52.1: 45-57.

Wesley, J. (1760) 'The Right Use of Money', in *47 Sermons* (Peterborough, UK: Epworth Press, 1974).

Part II
Enhanced investment analysis and decision-making

4

Does a focus on social, ethical and environmental issues enhance investment performance?

Rory Sullivan, Craig Mackenzie and Steve Waygood
Insight Investment, UK

The starting point for considering whether the enhanced analysis of social, ethical and environmental (SEE) issues improves investment performance is the belief that these issues affect company earnings. SEE issues are a major part of the business environment and can affect earnings through a number of mechanisms, including:

- Government intervention (e.g. command-and-control regulation, economic instruments such as the EU's emissions trading scheme for greenhouse gas emissions)

- Litigation seeking redress for harmful corporate impacts (e.g. asbestos litigation)

- Damage to stakeholder relationships and to brand and reputation (e.g. the controversies around the use of sweatshop labour in the clothing and footwear industries)

- Direct impacts (e.g. the effects of increased rainfall and other changes in weather patterns as a result of climate change)

- Changing patterns of consumer behaviour (e.g. demand for healthier foods)

Companies that develop effective strategic responses to these issues have the potential to outperform those that do not.

To the extent that SEE issues are major drivers of earnings, investment analysts have an interest in understanding them, and in understanding the quality of companies' responses. If reliable information on how these issues affect company performance is available, then investors that give this information due weight in their investment decisions should outperform those that fail to do so. Expressing this argument another way, ignoring material information about corporate earnings is rarely a sensible investment strategy. While this argument should be relatively uncontroversial, it does not necessarily follow that more focused or enhanced analysis of SEE issues will deliver even better performance. The reason is that the capital markets may already be efficient at taking account of this kind of information and, as a consequence, it is possible that all the analysis that can productively be done on these topics is already being done. If this is the case, focusing even more resources on SEE issues will not enhance investment performance. Our experience in discussing this topic with analysts, whether on the sell side or the buy side, is that very often analysts and investment managers do have access to information about major SEE issues, and give due weight to this information in investment decision-making. For example, we have found that analysts are generally very well aware of the financial implications of issues such as impending environmental regulations, tobacco litigation and major potential sources of reputation damage. This awareness is simply because analysts follow companies closely and have a good understanding of material earnings drivers. However, current analysis may well be imperfect. For example, the costs of government regulation might be uncertain, intangible and long-term. It is possible that the capital markets are relatively inefficient at placing a financial value on actions that have these types of characteristics. If this is the case, investors that have access to better information or who can analyse these issues more effectively may deliver better investment returns than the market as a whole.

What do the available data tell us?

One way of testing the hypothesis that better investment returns can be generated in this way would be to look at the performance of fund managers who claim to do enhanced analysis to see whether their funds have, in fact, outperformed. Unfortunately, there is a lack of good research on this topic. There are, however, quite a few studies on the question of whether corporate performance on SEE issues affects share prices. For example, there is a significant body of evidence that social, ethical and environmental issues can be material to financial or share price performance,[1] and there have been a number of empirical studies on the relationship between environmental

---

1 Examples include the share price impacts of: the disclosure of poor environmental performance data (Hamilton 1995); major environmental accidents such as Union Carbide's 1984 chemical leak in Bhopal, India (Blacconiere and Patten 1994); companies that are the subject of public announcements concerning fraud, price fixing, bribery or patent infringement (Gunthorpe 1997); and corporate reputation crises such as those faced by Shell in the mid-1990s (Knight and Pretty 2001).

performance and financial performance.[2,3] These studies are not all in agreement. While Salama (2003) concluded that there was no statistically significant relationship between corporate environmental reputation and financial performance, studies by Hart and Ahuja (1996), Waddock and Graves (1997), King and Lenox (2000) and White and Kiernan (2004) all found support for a positive link between environmental or corporate responsibility performance and financial performance.[4] The more positive of these studies support the idea that analysis of SEE issues would be worthwhile, but do not cast any light on whether enhanced analysis can actually deliver investment performance improvements.

Despite the weaknesses in the published literature, there appears to be a general consensus that the effective management of social, ethical and environmental issues can enhance shareholder value. For example, a recent survey of European fund managers, analysts and investor relations officers found that 78% of the fund managers and analysts that responded to the survey were of the opinion that the management of environmental and social risks has a positive impact on a company's long-term market value (CSR Europe *et al.* 2003). However, only 32% of the respondents indicated that environmental and social risk management significantly impacts market value over a shorter (3–12 months) time horizon.[5] While these types of survey should not be considered as providing proof that investment outperformance will result from focusing on social, ethical and environmental issues, such beliefs are important drivers for activism (see further the discussion in Chapter 13). Furthermore, the survey results increase the likelihood that investors will explicitly focus on such issues in their investment processes, and may be willing to pay more for companies that perform well.

2   It is pertinent to note that a number of recent studies have shown that there are significant benefits to listed companies from higher standards of corporate governance (Gompers *et al.* 2003; Deutsche Bank 2003, 2004).

3   There is also a significant literature on the portfolio performance of negatively (and, to a lesser extent, positively) screened funds (useful overviews are provided in Sparkes 2002: 252-53 and CIS and Forum for the Future 2002: 21-23). The balance of empirical evidence suggests that negatively screened funds do not materially out- or underperform the market. However, screened fund data are not directly relevant to discussions around enhanced analysis and integrated investment decision-making because: (a) there are significant inconsistencies in the manner in which screens are applied (Hawken 2004: 15-17); (b) screening processes may bias funds towards or away from specific sectors, with the consequence that performance may be a reflection of company or sector exposure rather than social, ethical or environmental performance (Bauer *et al.* 2002); and (c) the majority of the screened funds analysed in the literature are actively managed funds which makes it difficult to attribute fund performance to the specific screens or to the specific investment style (Camejo 2002: 60-61).

4   Care is required when analysing these studies as the published studies consider a broad range of environmental governance factors and an array of financial factors, making it difficult to attribute the effect of individual environmental governance measures to specific financial performance measures (White and Kiernan 2004: 10).

5   Similar results were found by Just Pensions in a survey of member-nominated trustees of UK pension funds (Gribben and Olsen 2003).

How can investment performance be enhanced?

Two distinct approaches to integrated investment decision-making have emerged in the institutional investment market. The first is an evolution of conventional approaches to the fundamental analysis of expected company earnings, where additional research is conducted into, for example, how expected environmental regulations or patterns of social change will affect earnings expectations in the future. The second is a more radical set of approaches, with analysis being driven primarily by data on SEE performance rather than by typical financial indicators. These can include ratings approaches (where factors such as quality of management are used to identify companies that are likely to outperform over the longer term), best-in-class approaches (where portfolios are weighted towards companies that perform best against their sector peers) and screened approaches (where certain companies or sectors are included or excluded on the basis of their performance against specified ethical criteria).[6]

Enhanced fundamental analysis

Chapters 5, 6 and 7 provide examples of how fund managers have sought to identify and/or better analyse SEE issues and, thereby, directly enhance investment analysis. Chapter 5 presents a case study of how major policy developments (in this case, the EU's proposed Registration, Evaluation and Authorisation of Chemicals [REACH] Regulation) may be overlooked or under-analysed by analysts, and how this presents an opportunity for investors to benefit from identifying an issue in advance of the market and/or better analysing the financial impacts of such changes. The case study illustrates that there are potentially a series of market inefficiencies associated with such regulations. These include analysts' reliance on companies to communicate information to the market (which can mean that the information is received too late to allow individual investors to benefit), and the inadequacies in the cost–benefit assessments conducted by companies, governments and industry associations. Chapters 6 and 7 describe how two fund managers, Morley Fund Management and Insight Investment respectively, explicitly analyse corporate responsibility issues as an integral part of their investment processes. Both chapters provide a description of 'mainstream' investment processes (focusing on equities and bonds respectively) and discuss how performance can be enhanced through an explicit focus on SEE issues.

Chapters 8, 9 and 10 discuss the practicalities of analysing the financial or business implications of SEE issues. Chapter 8 focuses on the financial implications of HIV/AIDS for mining companies in South Africa. The analysis shows how, when an issue is reasonably well understood, it is possible to analyse systematically the economic implications of an issue across a sector and draw conclusions on whether or not these will be significant for companies. The case study also shows that certain impacts (e.g. the

---

6   As discussed in Chapter 1, screened approaches have struggled to become more than a relatively small part of the institutional investment market, in part because of the perception that such screening is a higher risk than conventional investment approaches (see also footnote 3 on the previous page). From the perspective of encouraging companies to improve their corporate responsibility performance, a blanket refusal to invest in a specific company means that investors are likely to have limited ability to encourage higher standards of corporate responsibility.

longer-term impacts of HIV/AIDS on labour availability) are very difficult to assess. Chapter 9 draws together two distinct pieces of analysis. The first is research identifying the new generation of major oil and gas projects—research that concludes that the ability to manage extremely complex social and environmental issues is likely to be a key determinant of the successful delivery of these projects. The second is an assessment of the quality of management of the international oil and gas companies. By combining these two pieces of analysis, the authors demonstrate that it is possible to use information on the quality of corporate responsibility management to draw conclusions on the likelihood that companies will be able to ensure the delivery of these projects. Finally, Chapter 12 describes a collaborative project between fund managers and sell-side analysts to identify the material SEE issues for a range of sectors, focusing on how these issues can impact on short-term and long-term drivers of investment value.

SEE-driven analysis

While the first six chapters in this section discuss how standard investment processes can be enhanced through explicitly focusing on SEE issues, Chapters 10 and 11 describe investment approaches that aim to add value through adopting a specific view or philosophy relating to corporate responsibility issues. Chapter 10 describes Innovest's approach to investment and their view that focusing on key sustainability drivers and the quality of management of these issues allows for a richer and deeper analysis of companies' performance over the longer term.[7] This approach recognises that the benefits of such an investment approach may take 24–36 months to appear in financial metrics. Chapter 11 describes how SAM Group identifies companies who are best positioned to take advantage of the opportunities and manage the risks posed by SEE issues. In both chapters (as indeed with the section of Chapter 6 which describes Morley's sustainability matrix), the authors emphasise that analysis of corporate responsibility issues should not be seen in isolation from financial analysis. That is, their view is that an explicit focus on SEE issues should be seen as an enhancement to, rather than a substitute for, detailed financial analysis.

References

Bauer, R., K. Koedijk and R. Otten (2002) *International Evidence on Ethical Mutual Fund Performance and Investment Style* (Maastricht, Netherlands: Maastricht University, November 2002).

Blacconiere, W., and D. Patten (1994) 'Environmental Disclosures, Regulatory Costs and Changes in Firm Value', *Journal of Accounting and Economics* 18.3: 357-77.

Camejo, P. (2002) *The SRI Advantage* (Gabriola Island, BC, Canada: New Society Publishers).

CIS (Co-operative Insurance Society) and Forum for the Future (2002) *Sustainability Pays* (Manchester, UK: CIS).

7   It is worth noting that Kiernan also discusses how Innovest's analysis can be used as a supplement to fundamental analysis. In this case, Innovest's approach could be seen as another form of enhanced analysis.

CSR Europe, Deloitte and Euronext (2003) *Investing in Responsible Business: The 2003 Survey of European Fund Managers, Financial Analysts and Investor Relations Officers* (Brussels: CSR Europe).

Deutsche Bank (2003) *Beyond the Numbers: Corporate Governance: North America* (London: Deutsche Bank AG, 4 December 2003).

—— (2004) *Beyond the Numbers: Corporate Governance in the UK* (London: Deutsche Bank AG, 18 February 2004).

Gompers, P., J. Ishii and A. Metrick (2003) 'Corporate Governance and Equity Prices', *Quarterly Journal of Economics* 118.1: 107-55.

Gribben, C., and L. Olsen (2003) *Will UK pension funds become more responsible? A Survey of Member Nominated Trustees* (London: Just Pensions).

Gunthorpe, D. (1997) 'Business Ethics: A Quantitative Analysis of the Impact of Unethical Behavior by Publicly Traded Corporations', *Journal of Business Ethics* 16.5: 537-43.

Hamilton, J. (1995) 'Pollution as News: Media and Stock Market Reactions to the Toxics Release Inventory Data', *Journal of Economics and Environmental Management* 28: 98-113.

Hart, S., and G. Ahuja (1996) 'Does it pay to be green? An Empirical Examination of the Relationship between Emission Reduction and Firm Performance', *Business Strategy and the Environment* 5: 30-37.

Hawken, P. (2004) *Socially Responsible Investing* (Sausalito, CA: The Natural Capital Institute).

King, A., and M. Lenox (2000) *Does it really pay to be green? Accounting for Strategy Selection in the Relationship between Environmental and Financial Performance* (New York University Stern School of Business Working Paper).

Knight, R., and D. Pretty (2001) *Reputation and Value: The Case of Corporate Catastrophes* (Oxford, UK: Oxford Metrica).

Salama, S. (2003) 'A Median Regression Analysis of the Relationship between Environmental Reputation and Corporate Financial Performance: Empirical Evidence on UK Firms', paper presented at the *Rensselauer Polytechnic Institute Conference*, New York, October 2003.

Sparkes, R. (2002) *Socially Responsible Investment: A Global Revolution* (Chichester, UK: John Wiley).

Waddock, S., and S. Graves (1997) 'The Corporate Social Performance–Financial Performance Link', *Strategic Management Journal* 19: 303-17.

White, A., and M. Kiernan (2004) *Corporate Environmental Governance* (Bristol, UK: Environment Agency).

5

Integrated investment analysis
INVESTMENT IMPLICATIONS
OF THE REACH REGULATION

Steve Waygood

Insight Investment, UK

Steffen Erler, Walter Wehrmeyer and Harish Jeswani

Centre for Environmental Strategy, University of Surrey, UK

In order to obtain an accurate valuation of a company, material governance, social, ethical and environmental (GSEE) issues must be identified and factored in to the analysis. If specific GSEE issues have not been identified and/or properly valued by the market, a potential inefficiency arises that investors may be able to exploit. Using the example of an analysis of the proposed EU's Registration, Evaluation and Authorisation of Chemicals (REACH) Regulation, this chapter examines whether and how investment managers can generate outperformance when focusing on GSEE issues.

The chapter begins with an overview of the REACH Regulation and the implications for chemical companies operating in the EU. A description is then presented of how Insight Investment, in collaboration with the Centre for Environmental Strategy (CES), evaluated the implications of REACH for Insight's investment portfolio. The chapter concludes with a discussion of the added value to Insight of this analysis, and the lessons learned for future analyses of this type.

Setting the scene: about the REACH Regulation

Chemicals provide countless benefits to society. However, there is a lack of data on chemical hazards and chemical contents of products on the EU market (CEC 2001). To prevent risks becoming evident only after damage to human health or the environment has occurred, the European Commission has recently proposed legislation for a 'no data, no market' approach to chemical control (CEC 2003a). Anticipated to begin in 2006, any chemical produced or marketed in quantities of more than one tonne per annum (tpa) in the EU will be subject to the REACH Regulation. The Regulation will be progressively implemented over 11 or more years and will, ultimately, lead to the creation of a complete inventory of chemicals on the EU market.[1] With around 30,000 substances included in its scope, the Regulation potentially covers several hundreds of thousands of intermediates, over one million formulations and, conceivably, well in excess of one million finished products.

REACH seeks to reverse the 'burden of proof' from regulators having to identify chemical risks to the companies having to demonstrate the safety of chemicals. Industry must generate chemical risk assessments which must be registered with a newly created European Chemicals Agency (ECA). Together with EU Member State regulatory authorities, this agency will review and evaluate the submitted data. The primary responsibility for complying with the Regulation falls on chemical producers and importers. However, REACH will also place a general demand on manufacturers to notify chemical uses to their suppliers. Downstream users will have the option of withholding use information from their suppliers—owing, for example, to commercial confidentiality—but the users must then register the chemical application directly with the ECA if the use has not already been registered. Data-sharing mechanisms will be established to safeguard intellectual property, group multiple chemical applications under a single use, minimise animal testing and reduce duplicate chemical registrations.

Any unregistered chemical use will be banned, thereby eliminating general disincentives often created by current chemical legislation against companies conducting detailed testing of chemicals (Hansson and Rudén 2003). If the information supplied by industry proves insufficient to demonstrate the inherent safety or safe use of a chemical, regulators may request the provision of further risk data or may restrict certain chemical uses. Chemicals deemed to be of 'very high concern' to human health or the environment will also be subject to a use-specific authorisation process.[2]

---

1   It is proposed that chemicals will be phased in to REACH according to volume. Chemicals produced or marketed above 1,000 tpa will be registered during an initial three-year period, together with chemicals currently classified as carcinogenic, mutagenic or reprotoxic. Registration will, in the following three years, be extended to chemicals produced or marketed between 100 and 1,000 tpa. In the subsequent five years (i.e. years 6 to 11 of REACH), all substances above 1 tpa will require registration. Some exceptions will be applied to certain categories of chemicals (e.g. food additives, biocides, R&D chemicals) (CEC 2003a).

2   The authorisation process can apply to chemicals classified as carcinogenic, mutagenic, reprotoxic, very persistent and very bioaccumulative, persistent bioaccumulative and toxic, endocrine disrupters and other chemicals identified as presenting high-level risks to human health or the environment (see Christensen *et al.* 2003). The actual number of hazardous substances that will undergo the authorisation process will depend on the administrative resources available to the ECA and to EU Member State regulatory bodies.

A major aim of the policy is to stimulate the application and development of 'safer substitute' chemicals. Known as the 'substitution' principle, which already exists under EU occupational health legislation, a company should give strong preference to the least hazardous alternatives when selecting chemicals for a specific use. Although substitution will feature in regulatory decision-making under REACH, the increased availability of risk information is anticipated to provide demand-side incentives to companies marketing safer substitutes as a result of downstream users (including retailers) re-evaluating their work practices, manufacturing processes and product lines (Lohse *et al.* 2003). In this respect, REACH should also be regarded as a response to recent studies that report a serious lack of compliance with legislation concerning the classification and labelling of hazardous substances and information contained in safety data sheets (SDSs) (Spelt 1999; CLEEN 2004). Any improvements in the chemical risk and safety information provided in SDSs will have important implications for protecting human health and the environment across international supply chains (Agam 2004).

Overall, REACH represents a major challenge to the chemicals sector. In addition to compliance administration and managing compliance-related costs through supply chains, chemical companies will face the following management issues:

- Re-evaluation of existing product portfolios based on new risk information

- Communication of risk and safety information through supply chains, as well as to a wider set of stakeholders

- Leadership to identify and implement appropriate changes in business strategy

- Identification and development of new strategic partnerships (with upstream suppliers and downstream users)

- Redirection and, if necessary, reinvigoration of innovation capabilities

The chemicals industry has repeatedly expressed concern that compliance costs will be prohibitive to business and will undermine EU competitiveness. The assessments of the financial costs and benefits of the legislation vary to such an extent across 36 key regulatory impact assessments that, according to the EU Enterprise and Industry Commissioner Günter Verheugen, 'it is scarcely possible to come to [any] conclusions' (EurActiv 2005). The direct costs to the chemicals industry have been estimated to be €2.3 billion (CEC 2003b), which may appear negligible when compared to the EU25 sector's annual turnover of around €430 billion (Sura 2004).[3,4] However, the impacts will vary significantly between companies based on factors such as their product ranges, earnings and compliance resource availability. Many chemical companies will incur price increases for input materials, while also contending with an unpredictable mar-

---

3   Based on 2001 data. This figure excludes the manufacture of pharmaceutical, rubber and plastic products.
4   Manufacturing in the EU15 accounts for approximately 95% of the total EU25 chemicals sector turnover (Sura 2004).

ket resulting from bans on chemical use and the potential withdrawal of 1–2% of the 30,000 substances currently marketed (Canton and Allen 2003).[5]

Insight's preliminary analysis of REACH

Insight Investment is the fund manager for Halifax Bank of Scotland (HBOS plc), with approximately £75 billion of funds under management, including significant holdings in European chemical companies. Although Insight had identified the potential for REACH to impact significantly on company valuations, by the middle of 2003, sell-side[6] company brokers had not communicated the implications to buy-side[7] financial analysts. Following a series of internal discussions, Insight identified the main earnings implications of REACH as relating to:

- **Market loss.** The 'no data, no market' principle proposes that, without acceptable data, chemicals cannot be marketed. Therefore, it is possible that certain chemical lines will have to be discontinued

- **Input material loss.** Companies that depend on the output from primary chemical manufacturers may find that certain raw ingredients or processing chemicals are no longer available

- **Potential to stimulate innovation.** The 'substitution' principle should benefit companies with research and development (R&D) programmes that are able to systematically develop and commercialise 'safer substitutes'

- **Litigation risk.** REACH may increase litigation risk to the sector, as it proposes a greater level of public access to testing data

Even though implementing the Regulation will be bureaucratically burdensome to businesses, Insight concluded that REACH should be regarded as a welcome initiative for the listed chemical companies for a number of reasons. First, the chemical industry suffers from a view among some stakeholders that it is a 'dirty' sector due to historically weak regulation. By shifting the burden of proof onto chemical manufacturers, REACH should go some way towards alleviating concerns regarding human health and environmental impacts arising from poor regulation. Second, increasing the burden of chemical evaluation on companies raises barriers to entry and favours established market incumbents. Finally, the chemical industry has a poor record for innovation. The REACH principles of 'substitution' and the 'no data, no market' requirement was seen as

---

5   Product rationalisation is primarily anticipated due to prohibitive compliance costs, although some product withdrawal may occur from the identification of (potentially) high-level chemical risks (RPA and Statistics Sweden 2002; RPA 2003a).

6   'Sell side' refers to institutions that sell equities to investors for a percentage commission, and provide research analysis in order to attract investors to their share-brokering services.

7   'Buy side' refers to institutions that buy and hold securities in the expectation of a return on investment.

providing opportunities for product development and the creation of new markets for versatile manufacturers.

Insight's discussions with UK sell-side brokers in mid-2003 revealed that, despite the potentially significant impacts of the Regulation, none had formed a detailed research-based view on the implications of REACH for the EU chemicals sector. Most suggested that this was because the Regulation was in draft format, and was unlikely to be passed in its then current form. Others referred to the time horizon for the impact of REACH being too far off to affect current valuations.

Insight concluded that, while REACH was a highly relevant factor to its assessments of the European chemicals sector, the market did not appear to understand the business implications of the Regulation. Therefore, Insight also concluded that this was an area where further detailed research on the company-specific impacts of REACH could enhance investment returns. As a first step in this process, Insight's analysts began to introduce questions on REACH at company meetings in order to assess company preparedness. However, the responses were so divergent that Insight decided to conduct a more systematic sector-wide survey.

Initial Insight company survey

In early 2004, Insight surveyed 17 chemical companies in the UK and continental Europe, including BASF, Bayer, BOC Group, ICI and Yule Catto. The companies were requested to submit quantitative and qualitative information on how REACH might impact their business. Specifically, Insight asked companies to address the main potential earnings drivers of REACH and to provide corresponding financial assessments. Insight received responses from 13 of the 17 companies, although some responses were received only following multiple requests. The need for multiple requests was factored into the subsequent analysis as an indicator of lack of preparedness.

The quality of company responses varied significantly. Most companies were not in a position to give estimates of the financial impact but, nonetheless, asserted that the impact would not be material. Interestingly, these assertions ran counter to the statements of industry trade bodies who had argued that the costs to the industry would be very significant. The few companies that did offer cost estimates varied significantly in their assessment of the likely impact (even when taking into account differing product types), and only two recognised opportunities to establish market share through the innovation of 'safer' substitute chemicals. Insight concluded that, with a few outstanding exceptions, many companies were unprepared for the introduction of REACH. In addition, it was clear that the financial impacts of REACH were very poorly understood. As a consequence of the identified uncertainties around the financial impacts of REACH, Insight engaged the Centre for Environmental Strategy (CES) to work with Insight's analysts to develop a better understanding of REACH. CES was commissioned to perform the detailed company-specific business impact assessments because of its detailed knowledge of REACH and its ability to account for the many uncertainties regarding the future evolution of the Regulation.

CES study methodology

The CES research included both quantitative and qualitative elements. The quantitative part involved a desk-based analysis of the product ranges for the 19 chemical companies covered by Insight's UK and European Sector Fund Managers.[8] This quantitative study enabled CES to estimate company-specific REACH compliance costs for registration and increased processing costs.[9] The estimated costs for the 11-year duration of REACH were expressed as percentages of annual company turnover, earnings and R&D expenditures. The qualitative element aimed to use information on product portfolios, market sales and production locations to assess the wider business impacts of changes to chemical markets resulting from REACH. It also sought to compare company preparedness to implement the legislation and combined responses to the initial Insight survey with information from the companies' SDSs to develop a proxy for preparedness.

As a final step, the quantitative and qualitative data were combined to create a total picture of company business impacts. Business indicators were developed to assess the relative ability of companies to internalise costs, pass costs onto downstream users, overcome market obstacles, realise new market opportunities and maintain international competitiveness.

Assumptions

Costs were assessed based on the most probable regulatory demands. Only costs resulting from the registration of chemicals under REACH were quantified, including increased costs in raw materials and processing chemicals. Compliance costs directly resulting from regulatory bans or restrictions on chemical uses were assumed to apply to a small subset of highly dangerous chemicals and, consequently, were expected to be much lower than registration costs.

Given the difficulty in assessing the economic effects of such a complex regulatory regime, it was necessary to devise a set of simplifying assumptions. Average registration costs (rather than upper/lower estimates) were used to account for variations in costs within product or use-specific ranges. As each of the surveyed companies produces, markets and/or uses a large number of substances, the level of aggregation used in estimating the volume of chemicals produced, marketed or used by a company was considered unlikely to affect the overall findings significantly.

Other key assumptions made were:

- The development of more simplified and use-targeted risk assessment processes in future technical guidance documents produced by the European Commission will reduce registration costs

---

8   The study surveyed the following 19 companies: Air Liquide SA, Akzo Nobel NV, BASF AG, Bayer AG, BOC Group plc, BP Chemicals Ltd, British Vita plc, Ciba Specialty Chemicals plc, Clariant plc, Degussa AG, DSM NV, ICI plc, Givaudan SA, Johnson Matthey plc, Linde AG, Shell Chemicals Ltd, Solvay SA, Syngenta AG and Yule Catto & Co. plc.

9   Based on information available on company websites, product portfolios were compiled using a matrix of use, volume and product categories. Company-specific cost estimates were then calculated using data available from previous European Commission business impact assessments (RPA and Statistics Sweden 2002; Canton and Allen 2003; RPA 2003a, 2003b).

- The companies surveyed have a significant amount of chemical risk data necessary for registration already available and will benefit from registering multiple substances. In particular, 30% of specialty substances comply with recent chemical legislation and are considered 'automatically' registered

- Product formulations typically comprise of five substances, which are often produced and listed as substances by the same company

- In cases when product information is not available, production estimates can be read across from companies producing similar product ranges, using market sales as a proxy

- In the short term, product rationalisation within a company portfolio will be limited to low-volume and low-value fine chemicals. As a consequence, the volumes of high-volume or high-value chemicals produced will not be significantly reduced

- Increased processing costs arising from price increases for input chemicals will apply only to products produced in the EU. Market sales are used as a proxy for production location when production location data is unavailable. Registration costs apply to a company's entire product portfolio, however, even if the product is manufactured outside the EU

- The production and input chemicals used by the surveyed companies are mostly produced at higher volumes

- Cost estimates include the production or use of intermediates subject to the Regulation but exclude chemicals used for R&D. The positive business impacts arising from exemptions for R&D and substances produced below 1 tpa were excluded from the study on the basis that they are too difficult to predict accurately

- REACH will not create new litigation risks for the surveyed companies, as these companies are assumed to already be in full compliance with existing chemical legislation

- Commonly used higher-volume polymers will be included in the final legislative demands with lower registration requirements than most substances. However, monomers will be subject to similar requirements as for other substances

Scenarios

Three basic alternative scenarios (see Box 5.1) were developed to account for companies submitting joint chemical registrations. Under the current REACH proposal companies producing the same chemical will be able to share costs through consortia formation. However, not all of these cost savings will be realised as joint registrations are likely to frequently require more in-depth testing due to the larger number of combined uses. Participation in consortia will also be hampered by companies needing to manage confidentiality or other competitive issues (RPA and Statistics Sweden 2002; RPA

Scenario 1. Costs were calculated with the assumption that all companies register their substances individually

Scenario 2. Medium costs for medium- to high-tonnage substances resulting from a high degree of consortia formation were used based on five companies participating in each consortium

Scenario 3. Low costs were predicted for higher-tonnage substances resulting from a system of 'one substance, one registration'. Cost increases were, however, expected to be incurred for lower-volume substances resulting from the complexity of managing the system

Box 5.1 Policy scenarios considered in CES study

2003b). Scenario 1 therefore calculates costs assuming that all companies will submit individual registrations, whereas scenario 2 anticipates a mid-level of consortia formation. The third scenario reflects the adoption of a 'one substance, one registration' system which has been proposed by the governments of the UK and Hungary (Defra 2004). Although this approach (scenario 3) would avoid the potential for duplicate chemical registrations and would ensure a high level of data sharing between companies, the complex legal issues and management of confidential data compromises its potential implementation. There is clearly a range of alternative outcomes but, at the time of writing,[10] scenario 2 appears to be the most likely of the three scenarios.

Product portfolios

Information on product portfolios was also used to evaluate the wider business impacts of REACH on the surveyed companies. Product categories and production volumes were used to describe a company's comparative ability to pass costs on to its customers and to compete internationally. Sales 'impact categories' were devised to predict potential changes in chemical markets. For instance, product uses resulting in high chemical exposures to human health or the environment are more likely to be discontinued. Product portfolios are subject to constant review and change.

10   May 2005. Although the UK Presidency of the European Council of Ministers is maintaining a focus on a 'one substance, one registration' system (scenario 3), as of November 2005 scenario 2 still appears the 'most probable'. Amendments to the legislation adopted by the European Parliament in November 2005 to reduce registration demands appear broadly supported by the UK Presidency. These developments are consistent with the CES study assumption on registration costs based on levels of data necessary for compliance.

Company preparedness

Company preparedness to implement the new Regulation was also evaluated. Corporate responses to the Insight survey, combined with the information content and direct accessibility of chemical SDSs available on company websites,[11] were used to develop a qualitative ranking of preparedness. The ranking took account of factors such as the information provided on REACH compliance costs, the level of detail on the number of chemicals potentially impacted by REACH, the evidence of structured management systems that may facilitate responding to REACH and the availability of SDSs on company websites. The data underlying this analysis were based on information that was available at the time of the study. Clearly, such comparative levels of evaluation are subject to change over time.

CES study results

Quantitative assessments

The specific impacts of REACH will be highly dependent on company product portfolios. Companies producing base petrochemicals or gases will have the fewest number of substances that must be registered under REACH. In comparison, the production of fine chemicals generally involves a large number of substances at low tonnages, even when considering R&D exemptions. Specialty chemical portfolios typically consist of a large number of medium-volume substances spread across diverse product ranges.

As indicated in Figure 5.1, most of the surveyed companies produce between 500 and 2,000 substances that will be subject to REACH, with one company producing around 6,000 substances. Figure 5.1 also shows the volumes of each substance produced. For most of the companies surveyed, products exempt from REACH, such as active ingredients in pharmaceuticals or plant production products, often correspond to between 10% and 90% of company sales. However, chemicals subject to REACH may often be incorporated into the products or used during manufacturing.

With around a quarter of all EU chemical production consumed within the chemicals industry (OECD 2001), a substantial fraction of registration costs may remain within the sector. Companies heavily reliant on petrochemicals or naturally derived inputs[12] will be an exception, as these companies are likely to produce many of their secondary raw materials or even their own processing chemicals. Any company using input chemicals produced below 100 tpa can be expected to incur relatively elevated cost increases per tonne of substance. That is, REACH will offer advantages to companies operating at economies of scale. Following the assumption that product rationalisation will be limited to low-volume and low-value products, costs resulting from product reformulation and process redesign arising from upstream product rationalisation appears negligible for most of the surveyed companies. The exceptions are: British Vita (which manufac-

---

11   BP Chemicals, Shell Chemicals, British Vita, Syngenta and gas suppliers (Air Liquide, BOC, Linde) were not reviewed as their positions in the supply chain and product ranges were not comparable to the other surveyed companies.

12   Examples of naturally derived chemicals include starches, sugars and biological enzymes.

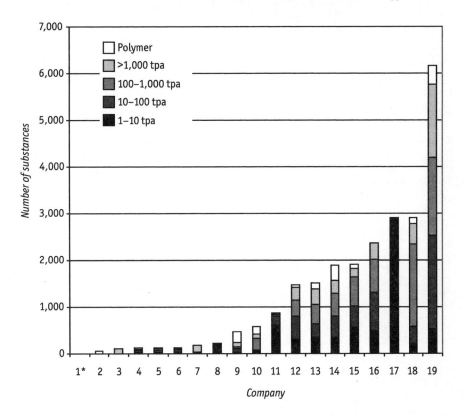

One company (indicated on the chart by *) produces only plant protection products and biocides. However, it is expected that this company will need to share the registration costs of formulation ingredients with its suppliers.

FIGURE 5.1 **Number of substances produced by each of the 19 surveyed companies (Q2/04)**

tures several finished products); Syngenta's plant protection products and biocides; and some BOC chemical formulations.

An overview of the projected costs for the surveyed companies is presented in Table 5.1. The projected costs are expressed here as lump-sum values based on a discounted cash flow of costs incurred over the 11-year-plus implementation period of REACH. Projected costs are based on the most probable regulatory demands and implementation scenario (scenario 2 as described in Box 5.1) and an 8% annual discount rate is applied. The present-day value of future cost is compared to the company's financial data for one year, yielding a worst-case indication of the potential effects that the Regulation may have on a company's cost base.

The findings broadly confirm the European Commission's and environmental NGOs' estimates that the direct costs of REACH will be around or below 1% of chemical company current annual turnovers (CEC 2003b; ChemSec 2004), even when considering

Costs and cost ratios	Air Liquide	Akzo Nobel	BASF	Bayer	BOC	BP Chem.	Brit. Vita	Ciba	Clariant	Degussa	DSM	Givaudan	ICI	JMAT	Linde	Shell Chem.	Solvay	Syngenta	Yule Catto
Registration (€ million)	3.0	25.6	54.5	125.1	2.7	7.3	3.3	19.5	26.2	16.5	9.0	0.6	22.0	8.8	2.8	9.4	7.3	5.6	3.7
Processing (€ million)	4.5	117.6	0	0	2.0	0	29.7	71.6	62.7	71.3	61.5	0.1	72.5	1.1	6.1	0	51.0	20.9	9.1
Reformulation (€ million)	0	0	0	0	0.2	0	3.2	0	0	0	0	0	0	0	0	0	0	1.7	0
Total cost/sales	0.1%	1.1%	0.2%	0.4%	0.1%	–	2.4%	2.1%	1.1%	0.8%	0.9%	0.04%	1.1%	0.1%	0.1%	–	0.8%	0.5%	1.5%
Total cost/earnings	0.9%	19.2%	3.2%	10.9%	1.2%	–	66.7%	34.6%	26.2%	19%	20.8%	0.5%	20.2%	5.4%	2.3%	–	13.6%	6.0%	34.5%
Registration/R&D	3%	2.9%	4.9%	5.1%	3.9%	–	62.6%	10.5%	9.1%	4.5%	1.9%	0.4%	10.3%	11.8%	1.6%	–	1.8%	0.9%	19.8%

TABLE 5.1 Projected REACH registration, processing and reformulation costs (scenario 2) (Q2/04)

single lump-sum figures that include processing costs. However, the total registration and processing costs, when expressed as lump-sum figures in present-day value, typically represent between 10% and 30% of annual earnings.[13]

As registration is anticipated to place significant demands on company R&D resources[14] (CEC 2003b), registration costs were compared to current yearly company R&D expenditures. This cost–resource ratio is generally above the Commission's estimated 3% average (CEC 2003b), and is as high as around 10% in four companies (Ciba, Clariant, ICI and Johnson Matthey), 20% in one company (Yule Catto) and 60% in another (British Vita). If reformulation also requires considerable R&D resources, this could increase the percentage for BOC, British Vita and Syngenta.

Production volumes provide an indication of how costs will be distributed over the 11-year registration period. The differences in the potential impacts on earnings between companies become more pronounced when considering the distribution of costs over the 11-year implementation time-line. Figure 5.2 illustrates how the anticipated yearly costs (reflecting the three registration phase-in periods) vary between a typical specialty chemical producer and a fine chemical producer, with the fine chemical producer (as a consequence of smaller production volumes) incurring most costs in the final five years of the REACH scheme. Figure 5.2 also shows the cost variations between the three possible implementation scenarios (i.e. depending on degrees of consortia formation).

It should be emphasised that REACH is in draft format and the above figures are estimates based on a series of assumptions. Furthermore, the figures do not include the benefits to market incumbents associated with, for example, the increased barriers to entry into chemicals manufacture that REACH represents. However, if the above cost estimates prove accurate, implementing the REACH Regulation may significantly affect the cost base of some companies and affect future valuations. REACH therefore appears to pose a material threat to some of the surveyed companies.

As illustrated in Figure 5.2, adopting a 'one substance, one registration' system for implementing REACH (scenario 3) is predicted to reduce processing costs by over one-half for most of the surveyed companies compared to scenario 1. However, the specific implications of increased processing costs depend on whether the implementation of REACH results in price increases for chemicals across international markets. As this study considers only processing cost increases for companies manufacturing in the EU, any global price increases per tonne of chemicals in reaction to REACH may result in lower price increases within the EU. In turn, this has wider implications for the future competitiveness of EU manufacturing and the ability of an EU chemical company to pass costs down the supply chain.

---

13   Lower percentages are predicted for gas producers and suppliers, as well as BASF, Johnson Matthey, Givaudan and Syngenta. Costs for implementing REACH were not assessed for the entire BP or Shell groups.

14   For most companies, it is anticipated that R&D departments will be charged with conducting a significant portion of the necessary compliance assessments required under REACH.

(a) Specialty chemical producer

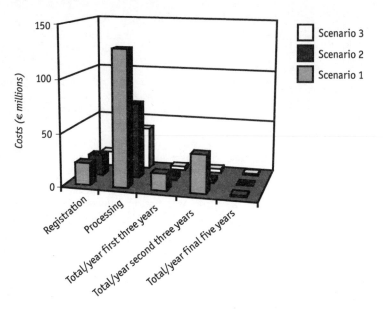

(b) Fine chemical producer

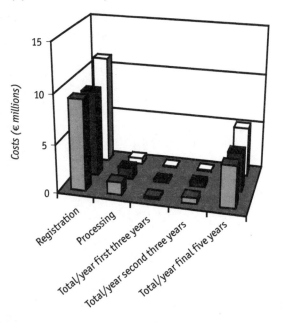

FIGURE 5.2 Example of total registration and processing costs and yearly costs for a company primarily producing (a) specialty chemicals and (b) fine chemicals

Qualitative evaluations

Information on product portfolios, market sales and production locations was used to qualitatively predict the wider business impacts of changes to chemicals markets resulting from REACH (see the methodology discussion above). In our analysis, we recognised that areas of concern regarding the potentially negative business impacts of REACH may also correspond to market opportunities. For example, companies could develop new markets by innovating or supplying safer 'substitute' product alternatives. Companies might also benefit by providing compliance-related assistance to downstream users or offering 'REACH-compliant' products. One company identified new business opportunities associated with the provision of consultancy services, and anticipated that this part of its business would grow to account for in excess of 5% of revenues during the first phase of REACH.

REACH is likely to increase the supply chain costs to the industry from above the current 8–10% averages of EU chemical company turnovers (Cefic 2003). Suppliers in close contact with downstream users will find themselves in a strategic position to provide REACH compliance guidance and assistance, as well as managing cost increases through supply chains. Both a chemical company's preparedness and its product end-markets will influence its ability to pass on costs to downstream users and to overcome any market obstacles arising from newly identified chemical risks. In particular, it is anticipated that it will be more difficult to pass costs onto customers for fine chemicals than specialty or industrial products, especially at lower production volumes. Maintaining international competitiveness may depend on the extent to which sales or production occurs outside the EU and the effect of costs on a company's earnings. Cash flow linked to product sales outside the scope of REACH is predicted to further influence a company's ability to internalise costs.

As REACH will grant companies time periods of between three and five years to register their products, company preparedness for implementing REACH resulting in early product registrations may prove crucial for those companies seeking to benefit from changes in the EU chemicals market. Preparatory measures include establishing REACH governance committees, creating central databases, reviewing product portfolios, screening dangerous substances and establishing new communication networks with suppliers and customers. From the data provided by the surveyed companies,[15] Ciba appears the most prepared for REACH. BASF, Bayer and Degussa also obtained high scores, closely followed by Clariant, Johnson Matthey and Yule Catto.[16] Increasing corporate attention to improving company preparedness may be particularly important for Johnson Matthey, Akzo Nobel, DSM, Givaudan, ICI and Solvay. Of course, comparative levels of preparedness are constantly subject to change.

---

15   Due to differences in product ranges, it was not possible to evaluate the preparedness of gas producers (Air Liquide, BOC, Linde), polymer producer British Vita or petrochemical companies BP Chemicals or Shell Chemicals.

16   Although Clariant and Yule Catto appear relatively prepared in terms of corporate governance and management structures, there is limited availability of SDSs directly accessible on the company websites.

Company abilities (comparative; 10-point scale)	Akzo Nobel	BASF	Bayer	Ciba	Clariant	Degussa	DSM	Givaudan	ICI	JMAT	Solvay	Yule Catto
Cost internalisation	5	8	8	3	3	3	7	10	5	5	5	3
Pass on costs	4	9	9	9	7	8	7	4	7	4	7	7
Overcome market obstacles	3	8	8	10	8	10	5	3	5	7	5	8
Realise new markets	6	7	7	8	7	8	4	8	6	4	7	6
Maintain international competitiveness	7	9	8	5	6	6	8	7	5	7	8	5

TABLE 5.2 Business impact indicators (Q2/04)

Combination of quantitative and qualitative data

Combining the quantitative cost data with the qualitative descriptions of the company profiles and company preparedness enabled the final assessment of business impacts. Transposed to a ten-point (qualitative) scale, the comparative business impact indicators are provided in Table 5.2, with lower scores (highlighted in grey) leading to higher concern.

The findings illustrate the wide difference in management issues that companies face with regards to implementing REACH. The business impacts of implementation will depend largely on a company's ability to either control or respond to the factors included in Table 5.2. Analysing the data in Table 5.2 reveals that various business impacts could have an overall 'balancing' effect within a company. For instance, while Ciba may experience difficulties with its ability to internalise costs, it appears able to pass costs on to its customers due to its specialist high-value products. In comparison, Givaudan's potentially limited ability to pass on costs may not prove financially significant since it has a high ability to internalise costs resulting from a low cost–earnings ratio and a large proportion of market sales exempt from REACH.

Company preparedness has been factored in to three of the business indicators—a company's ability to pass on costs, overcome market obstacles and realise new markets. Improvements in company preparedness may, however, significantly reduce compliance-related administration, which could account for up to 50% of registration costs for some chemicals (depending on scenario). Managing costs through supply chains is also predicted to be indirectly affected by corporate preparedness and appears particularly relevant for Akzo Nobel, British Vita, Ciba, Clariant, Degussa, DSM, ICI, Solvay and Yule Catto.

Other factors that a company may seek to control include changes to its manufacturing processes or product portfolios, potentially via mergers and acquisitions.[17] Increasing production volumes can proportionately reduce compliance costs per tonne of substance. Similarly, consolidating product ranges can decrease overall registration costs. A company with a low ability to internalise costs or to pass costs on to its downstream users may deem it necessary to rationalise its product range to a greater extent than the study already assumes.

Stimulating R&D in certain product lines should prove to be a partial solution to managing the costs of REACH and benefiting from new market opportunities. Yet, as noted in the section describing the quantitative data, companies facing high cost–R&D ratios may experience particular difficulties with implementing REACH if the necessary skills to prepare the initial registrations are located in corporate R&D divisions. In the absence of further resources being allocated to R&D by these companies, REACH may negatively affect their long-term competitiveness. Future R&D resource dedication for REACH compliance is therefore expected to prove especially important for British Vita and several of the comparatively less prepared companies (Clariant, Johnson Matthey, ICI and Yule Catto).

---

17 Since compiling the company product portfolios presented in this chapter, the most significant change appears to be for Bayer following the split-off of the chemical business Lanxess and the sale of the aroma business Haarmann & Reimer.

Discussion

Previous studies have found that many large multinational companies could improve their 'horizon planning' for environmental legislation by ensuring longer managerial time horizons and having systematic processes to anticipate the impact of future regulation (ERM 2003; Wehrmeyer *et al.* 2004). From an investor perspective, relying solely on companies to provide information may create a market inefficiency, as corporate horizon planning may be inadequate to ensure that necessary information is provided to the market in a timely manner. In the case of the REACH Regulation, Insight responded to these challenges by conducting its own business impact assessment.

The analysis conducted by CES allowed Insight to assess the likely financial impacts of REACH on its investments in the European chemicals sector. From the analysis, the impacts of REACH are likely to vary significantly between companies, with the Regulation having the potential to affect the earnings of some companies significantly. By considering variations in the distribution of costs across an 11-year implementation timeline, Insight was able to make predictions about impacts on future company turnovers and revenues. However, the costs to the industry are still uncertain, depending as they do on final regulatory requirements and the level of any voluntary industry consortia formation for submitting joint registrations. The impact of REACH on company valuations will become clear only once there is regulatory certainty.

Several of the surveyed companies are already taking systematic organisational steps to respond to REACH, which may significantly reduce the administrative costs necessary for compliance.[18] Conversely, several companies did not appear either to be very knowledgeable or particularly concerned about REACH. In the case of the fine chemicals producer Givaudan, the business impacts do, in fact, appear to be minimal and the lack of concern justified. In comparison, the findings indicate that Akzo Nobel, DSM and ICI are likely to experience considerable negative business impacts, which could include a limited potential to benefit from new market opportunities, if improvements are not made to their levels of preparedness.

There are two possible investor responses to this research. The first is to adjust portfolio weightings according to the projected financial impact of REACH. The second is to engage with unprepared companies that are exposed to REACH and promote better practices regarding their REACH readiness. The extent to which an investor adopts either or both of these approaches will depend, *inter alia*, on the investment time horizons of the investor, the scale of the holding and its policy regarding active engagement.

At the time of writing, it was not possible to say whether the study (or, more specifically, the manner in which Insight used the information in its stock analysis and selection processes) led to Insight outperforming the market. The market has yet to react to a final version of the REACH Regulation. This highlights two important issues regarding investment research on regulatory business impacts. First, it is not enough for investors to know the likely impact of the Regulation in order to capitalise on the financial impact; they also need to be able to anticipate the timing of the market reaction. Sec-

---

18   Insight continues to track REACH. It has recently observed some companies improving preparedness in key areas, which include: R&D and REACH communication (ICI), REACH preparedness communication (Johnson Matthey) and upstream supply analysis (Yule Catto).

ond, company portfolios and preparedness change over time. In order to correctly predict impacts, the research needs to be maintained and updated as circumstances and company preparedness change.

Conclusion

What are the general implications of this REACH research for 'integrated investment' processes that explicitly consider GSEE issues? Given the continuing uncertainties with the final provisions of REACH, it is unclear exactly how the Regulation will play out across the chemicals sector. However, if the assumptions within the study and the scenario projections regarding REACH prove accurate, this research highlights that REACH *will* affect some company valuations. Overall, companies are likely to be presented with both costs and benefits from the Regulation.

This study is limited in scope as the long-term benefits to chemical market incumbents arising from increased barriers to entry have not been factored in to the model. Nevertheless, this study exemplifies how company preparedness can play a significant role in influencing the balance of these costs and benefits on companies.

Finally, the fact that sell-side analysts had not conducted similar company-specific studies indicates a potential structural inefficiency in the way that the capital markets analyse corporate performance on GSEE issues. Specifically, sell-side analysts may rely too heavily on under-prepared companies to provide them with financial projections of the impact of regulatory change. In such circumstances, buy-side analysts and fund managers may be provided with inadequate (either incomplete or too late) information on which to form investment decisions. Wherever market inefficiencies exist, investors can seek to outperform the market by integrating primary research on GSEE issues into their long-term financial analysis.

References

Agam, G. (2004) 'Are MSDSs Safe? Reflections at the MSDS's 20th Birthday', *Organic Process Research and Development* 8: 1,042-44.

Canton, J., and C. Allen (2003) *A Microeconomic Model to Assess the Economic Impacts of the EU's New Chemicals Policy* (Brussels: CEC).

CEC (Commission of the European Communities) (2001) 'White Paper: Strategy for a Future Chemicals Policy' (COM[2001]0088; Brussels: CEC).

—— (2003a) 'Proposal for a Regulation of the European Parliament and of the Council Concerning the Registration, Authorisation and Restriction of Chemicals (REACH), Establishing a European Chemicals Agency and Amending Regulation 1999/45/EC and Regulation (EC) [on Persistent Organic Pollutants] (COM[2003]644; Brussels: CEC).

—— (2003b) 'Extended Business Impact Assessment. Commission Staff Working Paper' (SEC[2003]1171/3; Brussels: CEC).

Cefic (European Chemical Industry Council) (2003) 'Cefic Consultation Contribution. Summary of Business Impact Assessments of New Chemicals Policy' (Brussels: Cefic, 8 July 2003).

ChemSec (International Chemical Secretariat) (2004) *REACH: What Does It Cost?* (Fact Sheet 2:04; Gothenburg, Sweden: ChemSec).

Christensen F., J. de Bruijn, B. Hansen, S. Munn, B. Sokull-Klüttgen and F. Pedersen (2003) 'New Assessment Tools under the New EU Chemicals Policy', *Greener Management International* 41: 5-19.

CLEEN (Chemical Legislation European Enforcement Network) (2004) 'European Classification and Labelling Inspections of Preparations including Safety Data Sheets: June 2004', www.cleen-eu. net/projects/past_projects.htm, accessed 1 March 2005.

Defra (UK Department for Environment, Food and Rural Affairs) (2004) 'One Substance, One Registration: A Joint Proposal from Hungary and the UK', www.defra.gov.uk/environment/chemicals/pdf/ osor-proposal.pdf, accessed 1 March 2005.

ERM (Environmental Resources Management) (2003) *Corporate Environmental and CSR Issues Management: An ERM Study* (Oxford, UK: ERM).

EurActiv (2004) 'EU Officials Seek to Make Sense of 36 REACH Reports. 3 November 2004', www.euractiv. com/Article?tcmuri=tcm:29-131725-16&type=News, accessed 14 February 2004.

Hansson, S., and C. Rudén (2003) 'Improving the Incentives for Toxicity Testing', *Journal of Risk Research* 6: 3-21.

Lohse, J., L. Lißner, S. Lundie, A. Ahrens and M. Wirts (2003) 'Never Change a Running Process? Substitution of Hazardous Chemicals in Products and Processes: Definition, Key Drivers and Barriers', *Greener Management International* 41: 57-76.

OECD (Organisation for Economic Co-operation and Development) (2001) *Environmental Outlook for the Chemicals Industry* (Paris: OECD).

RPA (Risk and Policy Analysts Ltd) and Statistics Sweden (2002) *Assessment of the Business Impacts of New Regulations in the Chemicals Sector. Final Report Prepared for the European Commission Directorate-General Enterprise* (London: RPA).

—— (2003a) *Assessment of the Business Impacts of New Regulations in the Chemicals Sector Phase 2: Availability of Low Value Products and Product Rationalisation. Final Report Prepared for the European Commission Directorate-General Enterprise* (London: RPA).

—— (2003b) *Revised Business Impact Assessment for the Consultation Document. Working Paper 4 Prepared for the European Commission Directorate-General Environment* (London: RPA).

Spelt, C. (1999) 'Solid Enforcement of New Substances', in *Proceedings the Fifth International Conference on Environmental Compliance and Enforcement, Monterey, California, 16–20 November 1998: Volume 1*, www.inece.org/5thvol1/5thTOC.htm, accessed 1 March 2005: 653-56.

Sura, W. (2004) 'The Chemical Industry in the European Union. Statistics in Focus: Industry Trade and Services 47/2004', epp.eurostat.cec.eu.int/cache/ITY_OFFPUB/KS-NP-04-047/EN/KS-NP-04-047-EN. PDF, accessed 12 December 2005.

Wehrmeyer, W., S. Erler and G. Johnstone (2004) *From Processes to Products: Regulation, Competitiveness and the Future of EHS. Final Report* (Guildford, UK: CES, University of Surrey, June 2004).

6

Morley Fund Management's approach to investment integration

Ronnie Lim

Morley Fund Management, UK

This chapter focuses on the issues and challenges that arise for asset managers when evaluating the impact of governance, social, environmental and ethical (GSEE) factors on the financial performance of companies, and outlines Morley's approach to integrating these issues into the investment process. The aim is to answer the following common questions:

- Why should investors integrate analysis of GSEE issues into the investment process?

- What are the challenges of this approach?

- How can GSEE analysis be integrated with 'mainstream' investment?

- Does GSEE analysis add or detract value from investment performance?

Morley's approach will be explained first by describing the in-house tools it uses to identify and analyse GSEE issues, and then by demonstrating how it uses these tools to deliver investment outperformance and influence corporate behaviour. Some case studies are presented to explain how this integration works in practice.

Background

Morley Fund Management is the fund management arm of Aviva, the UK's largest insurance group that was formed through the merger of Norwich Union, Commercial Union and General Accident in late 1999. Morley currently manages £135 billion of clients' assets[1] in equities, bonds and property, and has portfolios that include pooled and segregated funds, multi-asset investments, alternative investments, private equity and socially responsible investment (SRI).

Morley's SRI funds under management have grown from zero in 2000 to £700 million today. The range of SRI funds have also expanded to include retail or unit-linked funds, pooled funds and three segregated funds including a pan-European equity long/short fund. All of the funds are actively managed against appropriate mainstream investment benchmarks.

Morley has a strong history of supporting responsible investing. Its corporate governance team, set up in 1993, plays an integral and active part in Morley's approach to managing, protecting and enhancing the long-term value of the stocks in which it invests. In 2000, Morley further developed its commitment to responsible investment through the establishment of a specialist SRI team. Led by Clare Brook, who has 14 years' experience in SRI, the team joined from Henderson Global Investors where they had a long and impressive track record at the forefront of developing SRI in the previous decade. Prior to Henderson's, a number of Morley's original team worked at NPI between 1994 and 1999 where their top investment performance with the Global Care Funds proved that SRI funds (as a unique investment style) could generate top performance.

Today, the Morley SRI team consists of four fund managers and four analysts, who all sit together on the investment floor in London. The team has spent a number of years developing a range of investment tools that assist in stock selection, and has assembled evidence demonstrating that GSEE issues can be an important driver of investment performance. The investment philosophy is based on the premise that long-term, extra-financial issues are important influences on future economic growth (e.g. climate change, demographics, resource availability, etc.), but that these issues tend to be under-analysed by the market. Morley believes that analysis of these under-researched GSEE issues provides its fund managers with an information advantage when evaluating investments for active mandates.

Integrating SRI

Why integrate?

In contrast to passive or index investing, active investment necessitates original insights into drivers of stock prices. In simple terms, active investors aim to be either faster (with information) or smarter (with analysis) than their competitors. Morley is com-

---

1   As at 30 June 2005.

mitted to active fund management and, specifically, as described by its chief investment officer Katherine Garret-Cox, to: 'exploiting all market inefficiencies identified by our multidisciplined research capability'. This philosophy values multidisciplinary analysis, which includes tactical asset allocation, quantitative screening, analysis of corporate franchise quality, global investment themes and, last but not least, less conventional drivers of security prices: for example, intangible assets, regulatory trends, stakeholder management and behavioural finance.

Non-conventional drivers of equity prices are often under-analysed by market participants, usually because they are either deemed to be irrelevant, too uncertain, or too far away in the future. In many cases, where these factors are analysed, the outputs are often too subjective or qualitative to impact investment decisions. This under-analysis presents opportunities for investment managers that are able to identify, properly analyse and integrate GSEE issues into their research and investment decision-making processes.

The integration of GSEE analysis with financial analysis is vital, not only to inform the investment thesis but also to ensure that investors' engagement with companies remains legitimate (i.e. linked to enhancing or protecting shareholder value), and not simply a policy or social agenda masquerading as investment dialogue.

How do we integrate SRI with 'mainstream' investment?

Fundamental to Morley's investment philosophy is a focus on probability. Rather than aiming to analyse *all* environmental and social issues, Morley prioritises issues that are likely to affect investment outcomes. It evaluates how society's expectations of corporate responsibility are likely to impact a company's strategic positioning and operating performance and, by extension, the company's stock valuation.

Research inputs include factors such as geopolitical trends, regulatory developments, sector information, and corporate GSEE and financial data. Analysis is focused on convergent areas that are potentially under-analysed by investors, potentially significant to prevailing valuations, and where Morley can develop sufficiently plausible scenarios to be actionable in its investment universe. This is an iterative process that employs the following tools:

- Assessment of companies' exposure to GSEE risks and opportunities using Morley's sector guidelines and sustainability ratings/matrix

- Detailed sector and stock analysis using sustainability themes and a proprietary process—'integrated sustainable value'

- Quantitative valuation screening, portfolio optimisation and risk monitoring

Morley's sector guidelines highlight key GSEE issues and communicate its framework for evaluating companies for their sustainability ratings. The ratings process involves SRI analysts giving a two-part rating to existing and potential securities, based on analysis of how a company's products/services are positioned to benefit or suffer from a shift towards increased corporate responsibility—for example, waste-water recycling—and how that company's management's policies, processes and performance are progressive from a sector or industry perspective.

The resultant rating determines a security's position on Morley's sustainability matrix, which in turn establishes whether or not that security is investable for the SRI funds (see Fig. 6.1). Stock ratings, which position them in the darkest areas, are investable for Morley's retail SRI funds. Stocks rated in the mid-grey areas are investable for existing institutional SRI funds, which prefer a larger investment universe for increased risk diversification. Rigorous quantitative analysis and portfolio construction techniques then allow Morley to select a combination from these in order to deliver the optimal portfolio risk–return ratio.

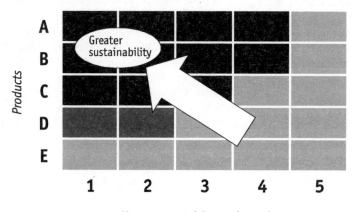

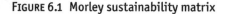

FIGURE 6.1 Morley sustainability matrix

Morley's analysts develop investment themes based on the GSEE issues that have been identified through research. Because the analysts focus on themes that are generally under-analysed by mainstream investors, valuation discrepancies can be acted upon in portfolio construction with objectivity and higher conviction. This impacts sector strategy and portfolio construction (e.g. by taking an over-weight position in a sector favourably positioned to an investment theme that is insufficiently appreciated by the market).

The analysts assess the impact of environmental, social and governance issues on drivers of shareholder value via a proprietary process known as 'integrated sustainable value' (Lim 2002). This uses scenario analysis to evaluate the incremental investment impact of specific GSEE issues or themes, explicitly integrating any qualitative analysis with established financial modelling techniques.

Each industry sector has specific drivers with different implications for modelling scenarios. For example, customer retention (via quality of sales) would be an important driver of cash flows for retailing. In the mining sector, costs would be a more important driver, as mining companies sell their output at prevailing spot prices. Where relevant, Morley would also evaluate the impact on balance sheets of individual companies (e.g. potential asbestosis liabilities).

Having evaluated the GSEE risks and opportunities a company is exposed to—arising from its business position and the management's ability to respond—the research analyst creates (or amends) a financial model of various scenarios using probability, significance and financial impact. Because many GSEE issues are uncertain and often long-term in nature, the financial impacts of various time periods can be discounted using an appropriate discount rate and an adjusted net present value computed and compared with other confirmed consensus estimates (such as from the Institutional Brokering Estimate Service [IBES]). Material valuation discrepancies will impact stock selection (see case study 1 below).

For Morley's SRI-screened funds, the investable universe of stocks is passed through its valuation and momentum quantitative screen—proprietary tools called Stockmap & Stockval. The screen contains a number of metrics designed to identify outperforming stocks, based on a combination of value, momentum and growth, using consensus data. This quantitative screen also identifies potentially attractive investment opportunities (both long and short), and those opportunities that may be suitable for a variety of Morley's range of equity funds depending on their style (e.g. value, growth), scope (geographic) and risk parameters. The highest-return, minimum-risk portfolio will then be constructed from these inputs using a portfolio optimiser. This process results in a broadly market-, sector- and style-neutral fund.

The ability to execute the above is enhanced by Morley's significant resources, both financial and human, and its commitment to support various disciplines and styles. Furthermore, this is leveraged by judicious use of external resources; thus, a significant proportion of total brokerage commission is allocated to incentivise service and ideas for SRI: for example, through bespoke analysis.

Case studies

The process outlined above is, essentially, a scenario-based approach to evaluating the incremental investment impact of GSEE factors on established drivers of shareholder value. The focus of this assessment is not general 'reputation risk' but, rather, direct financial impacts on revenues, operating costs, liabilities and cost of capital. To further demonstrate how the integration process works in practice, two historic examples of Morley's thematic research are provided below.

Case study 1: EU emissions trading scheme

The EU ETS represents the centrepiece of the EU's efforts to tackle climate change. Under the ETS, companies that exceed their allocation of carbon allowances will have to buy allowances on the market. If the allowances received exceed actual emissions, companies will be able to sell the excess on the market. Effectively, the scheme is designed to reward companies that pollute less.

Morley analysed the proposed legislation and deduced that the main burden of the ETS would fall on the utilities sector because it is the least exposed to international competition and has the highest energy consumption. The main drivers in the sector were analysed and the key ones isolated (in terms of which would have the biggest impact on incremental cash flows from the ETS). The two main drivers identified were:

- Cash inflows or outflows generated by the trading price of carbon allowances
- The expected rise in the level of wholesale electricity prices

Using standard economic forecasting methods, Morley assumed that all other endogenous factors remained relatively unaffected by these two drivers. It obtained data from a combination of public regulatory and corporate data, institutional brokerage reports and estimated CO_2 prices using various specialist providers. It then postulated various plausible scenarios, and used what it considered to be the most likely as the central scenario for the modelling exercise.

When Morley conducted its analysis in January 2004 (one year before the introduction of the ETS), it identified that the utility Scottish & Southern Energy plc (SSE) had one of the most efficient and clean power generation asset mixes in the UK, being the largest generator of renewable energy and with substantial capital expenditure plans (£200 million) for further new-build in this area. However, SSE was still a substantial emitter of greenhouse gases and this exposed it to tighter, or badly implemented, climate change policy with potential implications for its future revenue flows.

Morley's analysis predicted that utilities with the strongest commitment towards reducing their climate change impact—mostly through strategic planning for a cleaner fuel mix—would benefit from the ETS. Using these scenarios and discounted cash flow analysis, SSE was identified as being a clear beneficiary from the ETS, to the tune of 10% over consensus valuation as at January 2004, as shown in Figure 6.2. Finally, Morley compared the results of its assumptions and scenarios with prevailing market opinion (e.g. sell-side analysts, consensus forecast data and its fund managers' expectations). A few of the surveyed participants were aware of the ETS, but very few had explicitly incorporated the incremental impact of the ETS in their valuation of the impacted stocks.

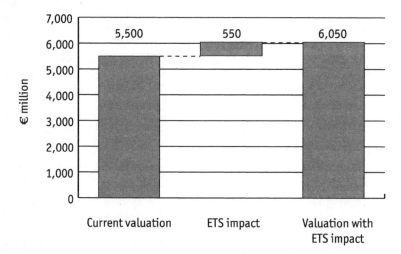

FIGURE 6.2 Expected impacts of ETS on SSE (as at January 2004)

Morley bought SSE, and the company subsequently outperformed both the market and its sector peers. Later, Morley considered its valuation to be excessive and sold the holding at the end of 2004.

Case study 2: corporate governance[2]

Sound corporate governance (CG) practices have become critical to stabilise and strengthen global capital markets and protect investors. They help companies to improve their performance and attract investment. CG enables corporations to realise their corporate objectives, protect shareholder rights, meet legal requirements and demonstrate to a wider public how they are conducting their business.

Does CG also represent an opportunity for investors? To explore this Morley has followed the methodology developed by some academics from Harvard Business School and Wharton Business School (Gompers *et al.* 2003) and analysed the relationship between CG and stock performance for the UK FTSE 350 during 1998–2002.

The study involved the following steps:

- **Definition of corporate governance.** 25 criteria were used to define 'good practice in corporate governance'. These criteria included minority shareholders' rights, board structure, compensation, takeover defences and disclosure

- **Portfolio construction.** Morley's definition of CG was used to build eight portfolios of stocks each with homogenous levels of CG. These portfolios were rebalanced every year when new CG data became available

- **Analysis of portfolio performance.** Using a multi-factor model of returns the value created (or destroyed) by CG was isolated and analysed

The study produced interesting results, the main one being that an investment strategy consistently buying the best CG portfolio and selling the worst CG portfolio would have earned an abnormal return ('alpha') of 6.8% per annum. This is illustrated in Figure 6.3, which also highlights two other important results from the analysis:

- The best CG portfolio outperforms the FTSE 350, and the FTSE 350 outperforms the worst CG portfolio

- The value of CG becomes more evident starting from March 2000, arguably because corporate scandals served as a wake-up call for many investors

Establishing a quantitative relation between CG and stock performance enabled CG to be further incorporated into Morley's research and investment processes. While CG was already an integral part of the Morley sustainability matrix (contributing to the 1–5 rating), the study created the conditions to incorporate CG into Morley's traditional financial analysis identifying relevant investment opportunities.

2 This section is adapted from Minerva 2005.

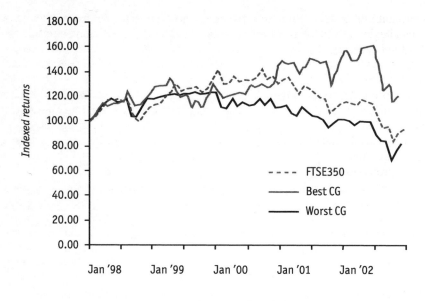

Performance of portfolio

FIGURE 6.3 Cumulative returns of extreme corporate governance portfolios compared
to the FTSE 350 index

Source: Morley Fund Management

Lessons learned

The emerging nature of much of the work on integration of GSEE factors into investment, and the multidisciplinary nature of the various processes to achieve this, means
that one of the biggest challenges SRI investors face is creating robust yet simple investment messages about fund philosophies. The retail market focus of many dedicated SRI
funds, combined with diverse screening methods and engagement overlays, have left
many (mainly institutional) investors and consultants with negative preconceptions
about the validity of SRI in the delivery of investment performance and the consequent
value of an explicit focus on GSEE issues in the investment process. As a consequence,
Morley recognises that the acceptance of its integrated investment process by mainstream investors depends not only on the credibility of its investment tools but also on
the performance of its funds.

In order to improve the credibility of SRI with mainstream investors and, ultimately,
to incentivise investors to consider GSEE issues, it is crucial that SRI 'grows up' and uses
the traditional language and processes of mainstream investors, in order to outperform. The more investors that take this approach, the bigger the market for responsi-

ble investment will be and, ultimately, the more likely it is that the investment community will begin to value responsible companies and management practices.

One of the key lessons learned is that effective integration is as much about people as it is about systems and processes. Morley's fund manager/analyst desk structure, which is replicated elsewhere in Morley's other equity teams, ensures that analysts support portfolio construction and stock selection by fund managers. SRI analysts also structure their coverage along industry lines, and they evaluate in greater detail the material GSEE issues that apply to those sectors. Idea generation and sharing occurs both formally via internal data tools and more informally across desks; the SRI team sits alongside the CG team and other equity desks. This enables a multidisciplinary team of investment professionals to debate and adopt investment ideas.

Morley's engagement with its investee companies takes several forms, including proxy voting, meeting company management and other communication. The primary aim of the investment team in having corporate dialogue is to obtain a comprehensive and updated view of a company's prospects, both in the short and the long term. The overarching objective is to converge Morley's principal responsibilities of investment performance, risk management and protecting shareholder value as a steward of long-term capital.

Morley takes the view that engagement with companies on environmental and social issues must be combined with active fund management in order for it to be effective in encouraging change in corporate behaviour. It therefore explicitly incorporates engagement as part of the investment process (i.e. engagement is informed by research). Engagement is prioritised on those issues that the research process has highlighted as most likely to have a financial impact. In addition, because engagement is combined with investment decision-making, where a company fails to respond to concerns, Morley is able either to vote against resolutions or divest from the stock to reinforce its engagement position.

Morley's voting policy applies across all its funds, not just the SRI funds. The policy requires companies to disclose 'sufficient' information on social, environmental and ethical risks. It states that Morley may abstain or vote against companies in the FTSE 350 that fail to disclose sufficient information. This is because the quality of data disclosed by companies is integral to the quality of analysis undertaken by Morley. In short, voting, engagement and research all combine to form an interdependent and crucial part of the investment process.

The SRI investment analysis and some themes are documented in Morley sector and company profiles, which are used as a basis for both informing investment decisions and improving corporate dialogue. These are communicated internally via email and a web-based stock information system, as well as through investment meetings. The SRI funds are all actively managed, and therefore have the potential to invest, divest or avoid stocks based on their ratings. This, together with the link to probable investment impact in Morley's thematic scenarios and combined with its significant size as an investor, gives real meaning to Morley's engagement discussions with companies.

Conclusions

The question of comparative investment performance of SRI versus non-SRI funds has been the subject of much academic study.[3] However, this is almost always a question of 'apples versus oranges' because SRI criteria are rarely judged in isolation.

Figure 6.4 shows the performance of stocks that were investable for Morley's SRI funds compared to those that were not for the period 1994–2004. There are many technical caveats with this demonstration of performance, which are not discussed here. Overall, however, Morley's view is that, over the longer term, a focus on GSEE issues will lead to outperformance.

FIGURE 6.4 Performance of investable portfolio versus non-investable portfolio

Source: Factset, Morley Fund Management

Integrating SRI with mainstream investment is currently more challenging than it should be. Various, often conflicting, investment philosophies, together with terminology obtained from non-related disciplines, has resulted in the 'mini-tower of Babel' that exists today.

The key drivers to integrating GSEE analysis with mainstream or conventional financial analysis are to:

3   See, generally, the references provided at www.socialinvest.org.

- Improve investment performance of active funds
- Differentiate Morley's approach from other investment styles
- Improve corporate dialogue

In this context, Morley's view is that the most credible way of achieving this is to assess the investment impact of GSEE factors on established drivers of shareholder value. This not only improves the odds of delivering investment outperformance for clients but also legitimises engagement with companies to improve corporate responsibility.

References

Gompers, P., J. Ishii and A. Metrick (2003) 'Corporate Governance and Equity Prices', *Quarterly Journal of Economics* 118.1: 107-55.

Lim, R. (2002) *From Values to Value: Transitions in Investors Assessment of Corporate Social Responsibility* (unpublished MSc thesis; University of East Anglia).

Minerva, L. (2005) 'Proving the Unprovable: Good Governance Pays', *Morley's Sustainable Future Newsletter* 6.

7

Integrating governance, social, ethical and environmental issues into the corporate bond investment process

Kerry ten Kate and Andy Evans

Insight Investment, UK

Historically, much of the attention on integration of governance, social, ethical and environmental (GSEE) issues into investment has focused on equities. However, bonds analysts regularly review a range of risks that include GSEE issues. In addition, several fund managers, including Insight Investment, explicitly apply policies on corporate governance and corporate responsibility to all their assets under management, including bonds. Indeed, the manner in which these issues are integrated into credit analysis and bonds fund managers' investment decisions are increasingly the subject of scrutiny by fund managers' institutional clients and the investment consultants who advise them.

This chapter will:

- Provide an overview of the nature of bonds (see Box 7.1)

- Discuss why GSEE issues are relevant to corporate bonds

- Describe how Insight Investment integrates GSEE issues into the bonds investment process

A bond is a debt security, similar to an IOU ('I owe you'). When an investor purchases a bond, it is lending money to central or local government, a government agency, a company or another entity known as the 'issuer'. In return for this loan, the issuer promises to pay the investor a specified rate of interest during the life of the bond and to repay the face value of the bond (the 'principal') when the bond 'matures', or becomes due at the end of its fixed life. In contrast to bond-holders, who effectively have IOUs from the issuer, shareholders are owners of the company they purchase. An investor can choose to invest in individual bonds, in bond–fund shares and in bonds unit investment trusts.

Traditionally, bonds pay a regular (usually annual) fixed rate of interest (or 'coupon', hence their alternative name of 'fixed-interest securities'), but the interest rates of some types of bonds ('floating-rate' bonds) are adjusted periodically according to an index, while others ('zero-coupon' bonds) do not make periodic interest payments but are sold at a considerable discount and redeemed for the full face value at maturity. Interest rates change in response to a number of factors. As interest rates change, so do the values of bonds, since a bond that was originally issued with a higher interest rate than is currently prevalent in the marketplace will be worth more than its face value and, conversely, if interest rates rise above those originally defined for the bond, the bond will be worth less than its face value. The 'yield' of a bond—its rate of return on the original investment—thus changes to reflect the price movements in a bond caused by the fluctuations in interest rates. After their initial issue, bonds can be bought and sold on secondary markets at their current market value.

The value of an investor's bond is affected not only by interest rates but also by the creditworthiness of the company issuing the bond. Should the company that issued a corporate bond face financial difficulties or, at its most extreme, go bankrupt, it would not be able to make all interest and principal payments in full and on schedule, thus jeopardising the value of the bond-holder's investment. Ratings agencies—such as Moody's Investors Service, Standard & Poor's and Fitch Ratings—assess bond issuers' creditworthiness and class bonds as 'investment grade' (those assigned to the top four quality categories by either Standard & Poor's [AAA, AA, A, BBB] or Moody's [Aaa, Aa, A, Baa]) or as 'speculative' investments, sometimes known as 'high-yield' or 'junk' bonds (all bonds with Standard & Poor's ratings below BBB and/or Moody's ratings below Baa). Bond choices range from the highest-credit-quality government securities—which are backed by the full faith and credit of the relevant government—to the most speculative junk bonds. Predictably, the lower-rated, more risky classes of bonds offer higher returns, while relatively safe investments offer relatively lower returns.

Box 7.1 About bonds

- Highlight some of the key issues for implementation of the process

- Outline some aspects of bonds engagement

- Draw some conclusions about the state of the art and future directions on GSEE investment integration and bonds

Why GSEE issues are relevant to corporate bonds

GSEE issues can be material to the likelihood of default by a company on its contractual obligations to bond-holders or other lenders. Poor-quality governance or an ineffective management response to the challenges posed by social, ethical and environmental (SEE) issues may increase the risk of corporate failure, thus impairing the company's creditworthiness. The management of GSEE factors is also a proxy indicator of quality of management overall, and therefore an indicator of management risk. GSEE issues are therefore considered in the corporate bonds investment process and will attract particular attention when they can have a material bearing on the likelihood of default. This generally involves consideration of aspects such as:

- **Litigation.** Harmful or unethical corporate activity has led to litigation that has cost companies, collectively, hundreds of billions of dollars. Examples include litigation relating to tobacco and other product liability issues, asbestosis and other health and safety issues, racial and other discrimination issues, and various forms of environmental pollution

- **Regulation.** Harmful or unethical corporate activity frequently gives rise to preventative regulation which prohibits the problematic business activity altogether (e.g. the production of chlorofluorocarbons [CFCs]) or which significantly raises the costs of doing business (e.g. consumer protection regulation in financial services)

- **Taxation and market instruments.** Increasingly, governments are using economic instruments such as the EU's emissions trading scheme (ETS) to deliver on their public policy objectives. These policy instruments can impose significant costs on badly positioned companies

- **Probity and governance.** The examples of Enron, WorldCom and Parmalat have demonstrated how ethics-related governance failures can destroy businesses

- **Direct impacts.** Some environmental issues have direct impacts on companies. For example, if climate change leads to rapid and unpredictable rises in insurance claims arising from storm-related damage, this will have a potentially severe impact on insurance companies

The integration process

An investor who buys a bond issued by a company is, in fact, exposed to several distinct and often uncorrelated sources of risk and return. Skilled corporate bond investors must disentangle these risks and decide whether the yield offered by an individual security offers an adequate return for the risks they will be exposed to. The bond investment process must therefore recognise and quantify these various components of risk and return so that a decision can be reached on the relative merits of each potential investment. Figure 7.1 illustrates the manner in which Insight categorises and analyses the components of risk and return. Some of these risks relate to macroeconomic factors such as expected movements in interest rates or exchange rates. These factors affect the government yield and currency risks associated with the bond. Other risks lie in the specific terms and conditions of the bond issue itself and are represented by the security yield component.

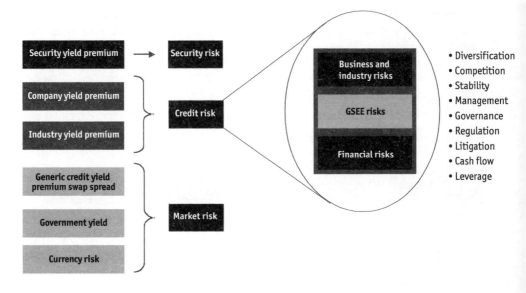

FIGURE 7.1 Components of corporate bond risk

A major additional component of the risk-and-return characteristics of a corporate bond (as opposed to a bond issued by the government) is 'credit risk'. This is the risk that the bond issuer defaults on the payments it is obliged to make over the life of the bond or that the probability of a future default increases. Corporate bond investors will usually lose money if a company defaults—say, in the event of bankruptcy or insolvency. Moreover, bond investors also lose money if the probability of default increases during the life of the bond. This deterioration in creditworthiness is often reflected in a downgrade in the company's credit rating and the market price of the bond will fall to reflect the higher yield required to compensate investors for the increased risk.

It is the job of a credit analyst to examine the sources of credit risk embedded in a corporate bond. GSEE issues form an important component of the analysis. Insight's credit analysts review any corporate bond contemplated as a potential investment, assessing the business and financial strength of the underlying company in detail and employing quantitative analysis techniques to identify attractive opportunities. The credit analysis framework identifies and examines key risks and drivers at both the company and industry levels, assigning an Insight credit rating to the company and an indicator of the trend in the company's creditworthiness. GSEE factors are an important source of risk in any corporate bond investment, to the extent that they can impact on a company's ability to meet its obligations to bond-holders and other creditors over time. These risks therefore need to be assessed as part of the credit analysis, for both industry allocation and company selection.

Industry allocation and strategy

Insight's industry allocation and portfolio strategy process incorporates the views of the credit analysts on a range of industries. Every industry is given a 'credit trend' score by the relevant analyst, representing his/her estimate of likely future changes in the credit risk characteristics of the industry sector as a whole. The members of the credit strategy team combine the industry credit trend score with an assessment of macro-economic factors and market valuations to arrive at a target portfolio allocation, as illustrated in Figure 7.2.

Combining fundamental and market views

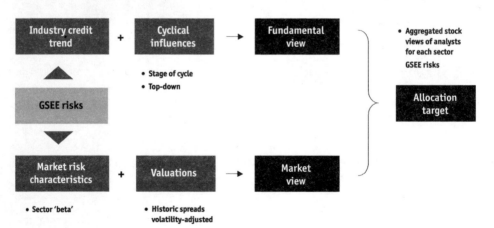

FIGURE 7.2 Industry allocation process

GSEE issues can represent an important dimension of the risk characteristics of certain industries. Insight's review process identifies current and future challenges facing an industry and gauges the extent to which these may impact on the default risks associated with corporate bond issuers within it. The industry risk analysis framework includes the identification and ranking of key industry 'credit drivers' in order to arrive at the overall credit trend score for a given industry. The implications of climate change for the insurance industry offer an example of an environmental issue that could have a bearing on industry allocation. Should current trends continue, levels of payments for claims arising from unpredictable changes to weather patterns could materially affect the insurance sector, and thus an investor's allocation of assets into this sector. Another example of a GSEE issue that bears on sector allocation is litigation in the tobacco sector (see Box 7.2).

The risk of litigation continues to affect the tobacco sector, particularly companies exposed to the US market which trade at a discount due to their perceived exposure. Insight's emphasis on monitoring risks associated with tobacco litigation lies in the US. Although some cases related to liability for damage to health from tobacco have come to trial in Europe, the long-standing issue of tobacco litigation is likely to apply only to companies with exposure to the US market, where juries can award punitive and compensatory damages in class actions. For instance, the award in the Engle case in Florida, to be reviewed by the Florida Supreme Court,* was $145 billion. The payments that companies are required to make under the Master Settlement Agreement (MSA) to individual US states, which cover healthcare costs, also run into billions of dollars. Tobacco companies offer the MSA as a defence against new litigation threats. Insight believes its success in this regard is likely to continue, and so we continue to invest in these companies. However, our analysts continue to monitor trends in the MSA implementation and tort actions closely.

Insight's allocation to the tobacco sector therefore takes full account of the litigation background, the impact on investor sentiment towards the industry and the likely market response to new developments. By being better informed on the likely outcomes and materiality of actions brought, fund managers can take advantage of market movements by adjusting industry allocation as appropriate.

* www.altria.com/media/press_release/03_02_pr_2004_05_12_02.asp

Box 7.2 Tobacco: an example of how GSEE issues affect industry allocation

Credit selection

Insight's credit analysts rank issuers in terms of their credit risk characteristics and expected market performance. Priority is placed on those issuers classified as potential sources of 'alpha', where a more in-depth analysis may be appropriate. The credit risk characteristics are ranked in terms of an internal credit rating and an 'outlook'. As part of the analysis, the analyst will also generate a score for a number of key risk factors, which we call the 'landmine checklist'. These key factors represent important downside risks which often result in sudden or unanticipated changes in a company's creditworthiness. For this reason, Insight's credit analysts pay particularly close attention to these factors. The landmine risks are:

- Liquidity
- Contingent liabilities
- Regulatory risk
- Litigation risk
- Governance and accounting
- Event risk

Examples of the types of landmine risks that would be identified and assessed in the credit selection process include:

- **Regulatory risk.** CO_2 emissions: the EU's ETS could rapidly change the landscape for European utilities. Taking effect in 2005, the scheme's objective is to reduce EU CO_2 emissions by 8% by 2010, relative to 1990 levels. This could substantially increase retail and wholesale prices. The rate at which gas displaces coal-fired power generation could also accelerate markedly, bolstering the gas industry and hurting the coal industry. Among utilities, the most likely beneficiaries include those focused on nuclear power, renewable energy and efficient gas generation. Gas utilities could also benefit from increased demand for the commodity. Major policy implementation issues remain, which make it too early to be prescriptive in investment decisions. The impact of climate change regulations is potentially, however, a major factor for utilities, and is therefore a specific regulatory risk for this sector

- **Litigation risk.** Welding rods: BOC is involved in litigation proceedings in the US concerning the use of manganese in the welding process. In the lawsuits filed, the allegation is made that manganese causes neurological injuries similar to Parkinson's disease. The potential claims on cash are currently estimated to be modest, with all juries so far providing verdicts in favour of the defendants. This will remain a significant area of risk in the future, as asbestos litigation is tailing off and the legal community may seek alternative potential causes of action, so the issue will need to be closely monitored. Currently, this is regarded as a significant negative in BOC's credit profile (particularly as no litigation issues are factored into BOC's credit rating); consequently, Insight has elected not to hold any BOC bonds

- **Governance and accounting.** Enron: poor corporate governance was a significant issue for investors long before it became apparent that Enron was experiencing financial difficulties. Insight's analysts had concerns about Enron after conducting a detailed interview with management and concluded there were risks in the business that were not priced into the bonds. As a result, Insight owned no Enron bonds at the time that the company's difficulties came to light

Insight's view is that a proper understanding of GSEE risks and, perhaps more importantly, the ability to understand how these play out in terms of 'landmines' such as liquidity, regulatory risk and litigation risk, helps deepen our credit analysis, through incorporating more data into the investment process and allowing us to fine-tune the risk scores, so that an accurate comparison can be made between different corporate bond offerings. This allows a better assessment of the expected performance of corporate bonds so that our clients' funds can potentially profit from market inefficiencies.

Issues for implementation

The process described above forms a routine part of the work of Insight's credit analysts and fund managers, who work together with the investor responsibility team (see Chapter 16) by conducting research to increase Insight's understanding of those GSEE issues that may be material to companies' performance; and by sharing information to ensure that research on the implications of GSEE issues is available to credit analysts and taken into consideration in bonds investment decisions. The manner in which the teams work together to improve the quality of Insight's decision-making on investment in bonds is illustrated in Figure 7.3. This is done principally through commissioning, conducting and assessing research, through use of Insight's research databases, and through staff meetings to review the implications of research for future investment strategy and particular bond issues, and to define future research priorities. Internal research forms 75% of Insight analysts' input, as it can be closely tailored to emphasise the risk factors and issues that are priorities for Insight and its clients. However, external research is valuable as a complementary source of information to supplement Insight's own analysis and enable it to draw on the findings of specialists in particular fields. Consequently, Insight also obtains a range of external research in the form of corporate governance analysis, company reports, sector reports, broker reports and press clippings.

The credit research team conducts in-depth credit analysis and modelling of corporate issuers, and also conducts ongoing surveillance of the corporate bond universe.[1] The analysts routinely take significant GSEE risks into consideration during the credit analysis process. The investor responsibility team adds specialist knowledge on GSEE issues, supplementing the work of the credit research team by drawing new GSEE issues to their attention and conducting in-depth research on particular issues. The investor

---

1   For further information, see www.insightinvestment.com/institutional/philosophy_and_process/philosophy_and_process_fixed_income.asp.

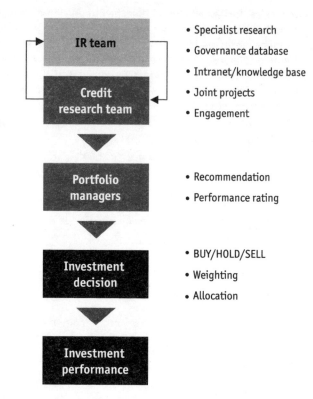

FIGURE 7.3 Improved decision-making

responsibility team conducts issue- and sector-based research on priority GSEE topics, selected through its own analysis or identified in meetings with the credit analysis team. The credit analysis and investor responsibility teams also conduct research together on issues jointly identified as 'priorities'. Recent examples include particular aspects of corporate governance and emerging corporate responsibility issues whose significance needs to be assessed (e.g. the implications of obesity for the food production sector and the implications of climate change for European electricity utilities). Issues are prioritised for research based on their potential materiality to Insight's portfolios (i.e. because of their potential financial significance to companies in which Insight's clients' portfolios have major holdings).

Another feature of Insight's process is the importance of sharing information and ideas. A research database enables bonds, equities and investor responsibility staff to record and share their analysis. In addition, the credit analysis team and the investor responsibility teams meet quarterly to update each other about emerging GSEE issues relevant to the bonds investment process and about the results from internal or external research, and to plan future research. Furthermore, individuals from the teams liaise regularly to discuss joint research, emerging trends and particular companies, and to identify issues that need to be raised in meetings with companies.

Above all else, Insight has found that the integration of specialist GSEE research input into the credit analysis process results in better-quality decision-making and hence better investment performance. By being better informed, bond analysts and fund managers are able to assess and quantify credit risks with a greater level of precision. Of course, some emerging GSEE risks may be considered immaterial (in financial terms) to the current credit standing of a company. However, Insight's credit analysts value the specialist research activities of the investor responsibility team as an 'early warning system' that helps them to identify long-term risks which can become significant relatively quickly (e.g. obesity). As such, Insight hopes to be one step ahead of the game when it comes to assessing and predicting how the corporate landscape is changing.

Engagement

Much of the discussion about engagement with companies on GSEE issues (see further Part III of this book) has focused on equities. Less attention has been paid to the question of whether or not it is possible to effectively engage on GSEE issues in the context of the corporate bonds investment process. We examine this issue briefly here.

The rights and responsibilities of shareholders provide an ongoing basis for institutional investors—on behalf of their clients—to engage with the companies in which their clients' funds are invested. As explained at the start of this chapter, bond-holders own an IOU, rather than shares, in the company issuing the bond. So, unlike shareholders, corporate bond-holders do not have the right to vote on ordinary resolutions, nor to file a shareholder resolution. Their formal sanction is simply through their market transactions, buying and selling bonds on the secondary market. However, if issues of concern arise once a bond has been issued, bond-holders can indicate to management that they would look upon new issues from this company less favourably in the future if the issues are not addressed: for instance, by signalling that a higher return would be required.

The examples presented in this chapter show the significance of good corporate governance and corporate management of GSEE risks and opportunities to bond-holdings, not only in high-yield but also investment-grade stocks. With this in mind, Insight engages with companies in which it holds or proposes to purchase bonds. GSEE issues are among those frequently discussed with company management. Traditionally, most of the interaction between company managers and credit risk analysts was at the time of issue of new bonds. However, companies are increasingly seeking opportunities to meet credit risk analysts even if they are not planning a bonds issue in the short term. Given the desire of companies to raise capital in the future, they have a strong incentive to meet the expectations of the capital markets with regard to GSEE issues. This provides significant leverage for investors to encourage good practice. Dialogue with corporate bond issuers also provides the opportunity for more detailed and in-depth discussions on GSEE issues than at the time of issue of new bonds. Fund managers are often shareholders in the same companies that are its large bond issuers. Engagement on GSEE issues in order to protect the interests of both bonds and equities clients can thus be conducted simultaneously.

Conclusions

GSEE issues can be material to the likelihood of default by a company on the bonds it has issued. Poor-quality governance and ineffective management of SEE risks increase the risk of corporate failure and thus represent a significant issue for investors. The issues that commonly merit analysis include: failures of corporate governance (e.g. fraud); litigation on harmful or unethical corporate activity, product liability issues, discrimination and pollution; regulation prohibiting certain kinds of activities or imposing additional costs to business; economic instruments such as carbon taxes and cap-and-trade systems; and environmental and social changes that will impose a direct cost to a company's operations.

A focus on GSEE issues as an integral part of the bonds investment process—in particular the ability to identify these issues before they manifest themselves as litigation, regulation, etc.—enables important sources of risk and return to be analysed and timely investment decisions to be taken. It is our view that an investment process that fully integrates consideration of GSEE risks can enable fund managers to spot risks and better assess the value of investments, delivering higher returns to clients. There is growing interest in the manner in which GSEE is integrated into fixed-interest investment processes. In the future, credit analysts will need to place greater emphasis on corporate governance and corporate responsibility, to seek timely meetings with the management of companies issuing bonds, and to work with sell-side analysts and rating agencies to encourage greater transparency on these issues.

8

HIV/AIDS
ECONOMIC IMPLICATIONS
FOR THE SOUTHERN
AFRICAN MINING INDUSTRY*

Simon Toyne
Dresdner Kleinwort Wasserstein, UK

Relative to global standards, mechanisation rates in the southern African mining industry remain relatively low, and workforce numbers high. The long-term availability and
stability of the labour force is therefore of paramount concern to the mining industry.
However, the prevalence rates of HIV/AIDS in southern Africa are the highest in the
world and, in the short term, are expected to grow further. As one of the largest employers in southern Africa, the mining industry is positioned to play a central role in com-
bating the epidemic, in its own commercial interest and as a matter of corporate and
social responsibility.

In this chapter, the potential financial and operational implications of HIV/AIDS in the
mining industry in southern Africa are assessed. The chapter describes the existing
scale of the epidemic in the population and workforce as well as the industry's
response, and assesses potential costs and longer-term outlook.

* This chapter (and the data presented) is based on a research report, *AIDS: Assessing the Financial
Impacts*, published by Dresdner Kleinwort Wasserstein in March 2005.

Overview of the AIDS issue

In sub-Saharan Africa, HIV/AIDS is one of the largest and most rapidly growing social problems. With 25 million people currently living with HIV, the area accounts for almost two-thirds of the global incidence of HIV infection. In South Africa, where mining in sub-Saharan Africa is concentrated, the proportion of the workforce infected with HIV can be one in four or higher, depending on the region. With the prevalence of HIV/AIDS on the increase, the long-term human infrastructure of the region is at risk of being substantially reduced as life expectancy potentially returns to late-19th-century levels.

A number of statistics highlight the potential severity of the problem in terms of the long-term impact on the labour force:

- The overall labour force in all but four African countries could be as much as 35% lower by 2020 due to AIDS

- It is estimated that AIDS will have claimed the lives of at least a fifth of the agricultural workforce by 2020, deepening already severe food shortages

- In Africa, studies suggest that at least 19%, and possibly as high as 53%, of all government health employee deaths are due to AIDS

- In the worst-affected countries of sub-Saharan Africa, if current infection rates continue and there is no large-scale treatment programme, up to 60% of current 15-year-olds will die before reaching 60 years of age

- Without antiretroviral therapy (ART), average life expectancy in Swaziland, Zambia and Zimbabwe could drop below 35 years. Only 7% of people in developing countries who need ART have access to it

- 15–24-year-olds account for nearly half of new infections worldwide, clearly a particular cause for concern with regards to the labour force

The potential social and economic cost of the HIV/AIDS epidemic is vast and is unlikely to abate of its own volition before the infection rate rises materially to a natural limit as the death rate increases. However, the cost of tackling the epidemic is daunting. It is estimated that US$12 billion by 2005 and US$20 billion by 2007 will be needed for prevention and care in low- and middle-income countries. This is more than double the current level of spending.

A cause for concern?

The mining industry is a major employer in southern Africa. Table 8.1 sets out a selection of the major players in the African mining industry, employing between them around 320,000 people in the region.

For these companies, the risks in the short term centre on the performance of the existing workforce, in particular the operational costs of the disruption caused by workers or their families falling ill due to HIV. Longer-term, the existence of an adequate

Company	Employees	% of total employees	Definition	Data correct at
Anglo American	139,000	69%	Excludes joint ventures (JVs) and associates	Dec 2003
BHP Billiton	14,000	32%	Excludes JVs and associates	Jun 2004
Lonmin	25,822	100%	Total complement in service	Sep 2003
Rio Tinto	6,083	17%	Includes JVs and associates	Dec 2003
Xstrata	9,379	53%	Excludes JVs and associates	Dec 2003
Goldfields	47,000	98%	Estimate based on group number; includes contractors	2004
Impala	31,500	100%	Whole group	May 2004
Harmony	52,000	97%	Estimate based on annual report	Jun 2004

TABLE 8.1 Numbers employed in Africa

Source: company data; DrKW equity research estimates

workforce and the labour cost inflation implications of a shrinking pool of workers are the key concerns.

The pressure on the mining industry is increased by the fact that the prevalence among its workforce is often close to 1 in 4 in sub-Saharan Africa, markedly higher than population prevalence rates, especially in South Africa. This is the result of a number of factors:

- The mining industry employs a large amount of low-skilled labour, where the prevalence of HIV/AIDS is higher

- Migrant labour is common; this results in miners living, often in single-sex hostels, away from their families for extended periods leading to a high level of promiscuity with sex workers, which increases the rate at which the disease is spread

Case study: Anglo American's response

As the largest stock on the Johannesburg stock exchange, and with a long heritage of diversified mining in South Africa, Anglo American's response to HIV/AIDS is one of the most comprehensive in the industry and serves as a useful case study to examine the measures corporations are taking to combat the epidemic.

The most significant recent change (announced in August 2002) in Anglo American's response to AIDS has been the free provision of ART to employees with AIDS when clinically indicated. This is the largest employer-sponsored AIDS treatment programme in the world.

However, the provision of ART is problematic. It is a complex treatment, which requires drugs to be taken at specific times. Interrupted or irregular therapy leads to the disease mutating into new and resistant forms. A salutary lesson to those beginning a course of ART in sub-Saharan Africa is that 10% of AIDS victims in the Western (or developed) countries are already resistant to at least one class of tablet. In addition, side-effects are common. These side-effects can reduce employees' effectiveness at work and can also compromise safety. For example, a common side-effect is peripheral neuropathy, where sufferers can lose sensation in their hands and feet.

As at the end of 2003, 1,048 Anglo American employees were receiving ART. One-third of these were at an advanced stage of the disease when treatment was initiated. Most subsequently returned to work and are leading normal lives. The treatment programme is still in its relatively early stages but, so far, 94% of employees on ART are back at work and 90% have reported adherence to the treatment regime, although this is yet to be demonstrated clinically. Twenty-eight per cent of employees receiving ART have suffered minor side-effects, but only 2% have suffered serious side-effects.

While the uptake of ART continues to increase, and the number of companies providing it is growing, the cost of ART and its inability to actually cure HIV means the industry focus is still on prevention. Anglo American is pursuing a variety of strategies to this end. The direct prevention measures adopted by the company include handing out free condoms, raising awareness through, for example, advertising on billboards, and education in the causes and consequences of HIV/AIDS as well as how to avoid it. This education is often carried out at social events by a specially trained member of the miners' peer group. A less direct measure to promote prevention, but at the heart of the company's response, is 'voluntary counselling and testing' (VCT). It is widely recognised that a key way of reducing the spread of HIV is to ensure that HIV sufferers are aware of their status, encouraging them to take personal responsibility for containing the spread of the infection. As yet, however, uptake of VCT at Anglo American has been disappointing—fewer than 10% of AngloGold and Anglo Platinum employers came forward for testing in 2003. This echoes the situation in Botswana where, despite free treatment programmes, fewer than 10% of the population have taken a test to determine their status. A key part of the reason for this is the stigma still associated with HIV/AIDS, which discourages testing. Efforts to eliminate this stigma play an important role in the education and awareness aspect of the corporate response to the epidemic.

For employees who test positive for HIV, Anglo American provides wellness programmes. These provide counselling, health advice and the offer of nutritional supplements, immune system monitoring, treatment of associated infections (especially tuberculosis) and ART provision where appropriate.

Finally, Anglo American is taking measures to involve the local community in its response. In October 2003, it formed a partnership with the non-governmental organisation (NGO) Lovelife, the key aim being to enhance HIV/AIDS services in government healthcare clinics. It has identified 38 government healthcare clinics for the initial effort, all in disadvantaged rural communities. Again, in addition to being consistent with corporate and social responsibility, such initiatives are aimed at containing the spread of the disease in communities that currently, and in the future, will provide the backbone of the labour force.

Financial impact

Using cost data released by AngloGold Ashanti and Anglo Platinum, the average annual cost of HIV/AIDS per southern African employee is ZAR1,571 (US$253).[1] The prevalence rates for these three companies range from 25% to 30%, so the annual cost of HIV/AIDS per infected employee is around ZAR5,788 (US$934). Costs include absenteeism, death-in-service benefits, medical treatment, and training and recruitment due to higher staff turnover.

	Rand per infected employee	Prevalence rate	Rand per employee
AngloGold Ashanti	4,993	30.0%	1,495
Anglo Platinum	6,583	25.0%	1,646
Average	*5,788*	*27.5%*	*1,571*

TABLE 8.2 Financial cost of AIDS

Source: company data; DrKW equity research estimates

In Table 8.3, we extrapolate the data from Table 8.2 to the major UK-listed miners with operations in southern Africa. The impact is clearly greatest for Lonmin whose operations are exclusively located in southern Africa, but is modest for all companies.

Company	Southern African employees	Estimated current annual cost of AIDS (US$ million)	EBITDA FY05E (US$ million)	Uplift as a % of EBITDA FY05E if AIDS excluded
Anglo American	139,000	30.1	7,527	0.4%
BHP Billiton	14,000	3.1	10,560	0.0%
Lonmin	25,822	5.7	344	1.7%
Rio Tinto	6,083	1.3	7,500	0.0%
Xstrata	9,379	2.0	2,682	0.1%

Note: EBITDA FY05E is DrKW's estimate of each company's earnings before interest, tax, depreciation and amortisation in each company's 2005 fiscal year.

TABLE 8.3 Financial costs of AIDS extrapolated across the mining sector

Source: company data; DrKW equity research estimates

1   Exchange rate of ZAR6.2/US$ in February 2005.

While the current cost is insignificant, the question is to what extent could it increase in the longer term. An increasing number of corporates are undertaking actuarial studies to model the potential evolution of the epidemic within their workforces over the next decade—Lonmin and Impala are examples. The key findings of Lonmin's study as it applies to its own workforce are as follows:

- HIV prevalence will peak around 2006 at 26% (2003 level was 25%)

- AIDS deaths will peak around 2011 (without ART), five years after the year of peak prevalence because of the long lag time between HIV infection and eventual sickness and death. By that time the actual prevalence will have dropped below 20%. With ART, the maximal death rate would occur in 2016

- The year of maximal cost including ART provision is 2011

For Impala, the results are similar. The peak cost is expected to occur in 2011 at ZAR86 million per year. However, this is highly dependent on the rate of new infection—halving this would almost halve the forecast maximum cost in 2011.

Based on the current number of employees at Lonmin and Impala the expected maximal cost of HIV/AIDS works out to be around ZAR2,800 per southern African employee per annum—78% more than the current level implied from AngloGold Ashanti and Anglo Platinum. Table 8.4 shows the potential EBITDA impact of HIV/AIDS on each of the UK mining corporations, compared to the disease not existing using the *maximal* cost estimates derived from Impala and Lonmin.

Company	Southern African employees	Estimated maximal annual cost of AIDS (US$ million)	EBITDA FY05E (US$ million)	Uplift as a % of EBITDA FY05E if AIDS excluded
Anglo American	139,000	53.5	7,527	0.7%
BHP Billiton	14,000	5.6	10,560	0.1%
Lonmin	25,822	10.1	344	2.9%
Rio Tinto	6,083	2.3	7,500	0.0%
Xstrata	9,379	3.6	2,682	0.1%

TABLE 8.4 Maximal financial cost of AIDS extrapolated across the sector

Source: company data; DrKW equity research estimates

Conclusion

Sub-Saharan Africa accounts for around two-thirds of the world's HIV-positive population and infection rates among the labour force can be one in four or higher. The corporate response to the epidemic has been comprehensive—the key recent development being the increasingly widespread free provision of ART. The focus remains on prevention through education and voluntary testing, but wellness programmes for those infected can materially extend useful working lives.

It is interesting that, even for a huge social issue such as HIV/AIDS, the current and potential future financial cost of HIV/AIDS is expected to be minimal even for a company operating exclusively in South Africa, such as Lonmin. Variations in commodity prices and/or currencies such as the South African rand are likely to continue to influence corporate earnings to a much greater extent than fluctuations (or a steady ramping-up as we expect) in the cost of coping with HIV/AIDS.

That said, it remains the case that the more bearish estimates of potential declines in life expectancy in southern Africa suggest that the longer-term impact could be greater than the financial analysis above suggests.

In terms of labour force availability, South Africa is arguably more able to sustain the higher death rate caused by HIV/AIDS because of its high unemployment rate—27.8% as measured in March 2004. However, some estimates suggest that the labour force could be as much as 35% lower by 2020 in all but four African countries due to AIDS. Even a less severe out-turn than this is likely to place upward pressure on labour inflation—already one of the key negatives for corporations operating in the country, where labour inflation is close to double digits in certain industries such as PGM mining.

Similarly, the longer-term impact on the general infrastructure of southern Africa is not factored into the financial analysis above. Notably, while the mining sector's response to HIV/AIDS is a comprehensive one that has evolved considerably in recent years, in other sectors, such as agriculture, this may not be the case—agriculture accounts for 24% of South Africa's GDP, 40% of foreign exchange earnings and 70% of its employment. Again, the impact of this in terms of food price inflation and the resulting levels of poverty and hunger, which affect the size of the labour force, is not a feature of the analysis carried out earlier.

Overall, the financial analysis presented in this chapter suggests that in the near term HIV/AIDS is not a key differentiating factor regarding the decision to invest in southern African mining versus the rest of the world. In the longer term, however, this may cease to be the case—HIV/AIDS will remain an issue that cannot be dismissed.

9
The Goldman Sachs Energy ESG Index
INTEGRATING ENVIRONMENTAL, SOCIAL AND GOVERNANCE FACTORS INTO ENERGY INDUSTRY ANALYSIS

Sarah Forrest, Anthony Ling and Jonathan Waghorn

Goldman Sachs, UK

There is growing pressure on brokers such as Goldman Sachs to demonstrate how it factors environmental, social and governance (ESG) factors into equity valuations. The drivers include the significant value of assets being managed under some sort of socially responsible mandates,[1] the expectations that investor interest in ESG issues will increase significantly (see, for example, Global Compact Financial Sector Initiative 2004; Mercer Investment Consulting 2005), and the expectation that an increasing proportion of brokers' commission will relate to the quality of their analysis on ESG issues.[2]

This chapter describes Goldman Sachs's attempt to systematically integrate ESG factors into its analysis of the oil and gas sector—the Goldman Sachs Energy ESG Index (Goldman Sachs 2005b). The focus was on how these issues may affect a key long-term

1 For example, a recent survey estimated that some €336 billion of assets are now managed according to some sort of socially responsible investment strategy, with approximately half of this being shareholder activism (Eurosif 2003: 10). This includes screened funds as well as funds where there is active engagement and/or explicit integration of ESG factors into investment analysis.

2 For example, the Enhanced Analytics Initiative (EAI), launched in London in November 2004, is a group of institutional investors and fund managers that have decided to allocate a minimum of 5% of their brokerage commissions to sell-side research that is effective at analysing extra-financial issues and intangibles. The EAI group expects this figure to be at least €5 million in 2005.

value driver for the sector: namely, the ability to access and operate new oil and gas resources.

The importance of the Top 100 projects

The key to changing underlying returns in the oil and gas industry in the future is the success of reserve development programmes; Goldman Sachs believes that the next generation of legacy assets, or new resources, will be the key differentiating factor. The report *100 Projects to Change the World* (Goldman Sachs 2005a) examined the economics of legacy assets under development in detail. These projects (see Figure 9.1a and b) represent 145 billion barrels of oil equivalent (boe), representing around 7% of global proven oil and gas reserves. The peak production from the 100 projects is expected to be 19.3 million boe per day in 2012, representing around 20% of current global oil and gas production. Among the Goldman Sachs's oil and gas company coverage universe (i.e. the companies covered by our research in this sector), 22% of planned capital expenditure from 2004 to 2008 will be spent on the Top 100 projects. The relative exposure of companies to the Top 100 projects varies and the impacts of these projects on individual companies will depend on the mix of materiality, profitability measures (such as internal rates of return and economic value-added), risk and the timing of cash flows. We believe that exposure to these projects will be a key driver of stock market performance over the next five years and beyond.

In June 2003, Goldman Sachs published a report *50 Projects to Change the World* (Goldman Sachs 2003a), the precursor to the Top 100 report. We have subsequently tracked the relative share price performance of the companies based on that report and have found that there has been a close link between companies' Top 50 projects relative exposure and share price performance since publication. As indicated in Figure 9.2, those companies that were identified as 'high risk–high reward' in the original Top 50 outperformed their peers by an average 11% since June 2003. We therefore expect relative Top 100 positioning—based on portfolio materiality, profitability, risk, timing of cash flows and execution success—to be a key driver of future stock market performance and subsequent corporate activity.

At a corporate level, the long-run returns for the oil majors range from 8% to 12%, with an average of 9.5%, while the gross asset life has averaged 21 years. Exploration and production (E&P) returns have been the highest, averaging 10% (compared with 9% for chemicals and 8% for refining and marketing), albeit with a slightly lower duration at just over 19 years (versus 21 and 22 years respectively). In comparison, the rate of return of the oil majors' top 100 portfolio (at a $20/barrel normalised Brent oil price assumption) is 12.5% (with a range of 11.5–14.5%), with an average duration (reserve life) of nearly 33 years, as shown in Figure 9.3. These new legacy assets are clearly attractive relative to existing corporate and upstream portfolios in terms of both returns and duration. This is why relative exposure to the Top 100 is, in our opinion, so important, as such projects offer the best chance of a sustainable improvement in returns.

The Top 100 projects are concentrated in nine key regions: Canada heavy oil, deep-water Gulf of Mexico, Venezuela's Orinoco belt, offshore Brazil, offshore West Africa, North Africa, the North Sea, the Middle East/Caspian and offshore Australia

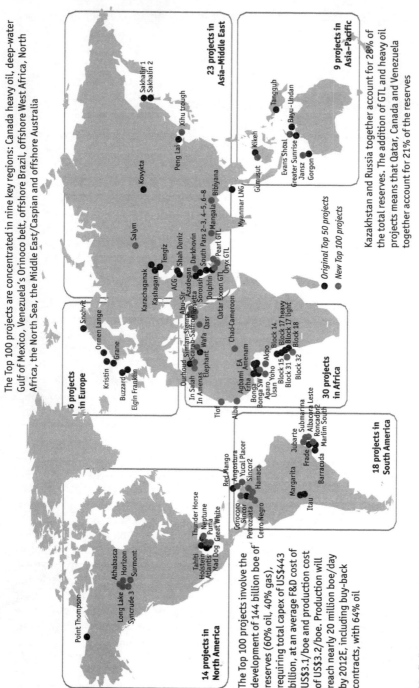

The Top 100 projects involve the development of 144 billion boe of reserves (60% oil, 40% gas), requiring total capex of US$443 billion, at an average F&D cost of US$3.1/boe and production cost of US$3.2/boe. Production will reach nearly 20 million boe/day by 2012E, including buy-back contracts, with 64% oil

Kazakhstan and Russia together account for 28% of the total reserves. The addition of GTL and heavy oil projects means that Qatar, Canada and Venezuela together account for 21% of the reserves

F&D = finding and development; GTL = gas-to-liquids

FIGURE 9.1a Map of the Top 100 projects

Source: company data; Goldman Sachs Research estimates

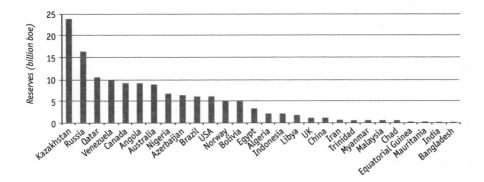

FIGURE 9.1b Top 100 oil and gas reserves by country

Source: company data; Goldman Sachs Research estimates

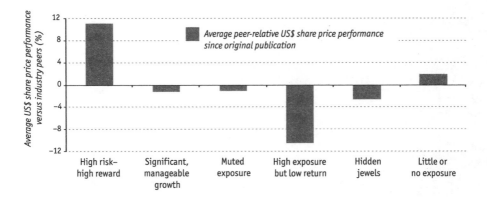

FIGURE 9.2 Share price performance since original Top 50 projects report (June 2003 to January 2005)

Source: Datastream; Goldman Sachs Research estimates

The Top 100 report, published in January 2005, introduced analysis of technical and political risks. This analysis indicates that the risk profile of the industry as a whole is rising, as shown in Figure 9.3. For the purposes of the analysis, political or country risk is determined by the ease of operating in different countries (assessed using Transparency International's Corruption Perceptions Index [Transparency International 2004]) and 'technical risk' which combines factors associated with the environment, stakeholders, technology and infrastructure. One of the important features of Figure 9.4 is that the country risk of the Top 100 projects is significantly greater than the average risk of the whole industry, and is also significantly greater than the historic risk profile of the industry. The oil and gas industry has traditionally had a high appetite for political and technical risk and it is the industry's willingness to take these risks that

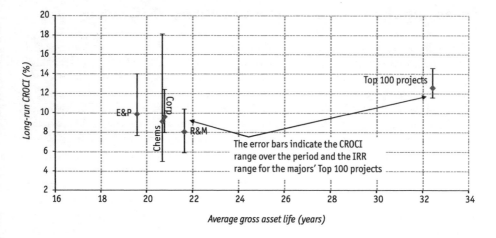

CROCI = cash return on cash invested; E&P = earnings and profits; IRR = internal rate of return; R&M = refining and marketing

FIGURE 9.3 Oil majors' cash returns and duration (1986–2004)

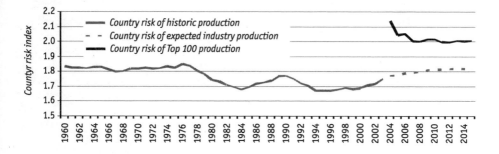

FIGURE 9.4 Risk profile of oil and gas industry

Source: company data; Transparency International; Goldman Sachs Research estimates

has provided long-term returns to shareholders. It is, however, important to understand that risk exposure is only one side of the equation. The other side is companies' ability to manage these risks. It is increasingly clear that a key element of companies' ability to manage risk is their ability to manage the ESG issues associated with project development and operation. Issues such as leadership, corruption, local communities, human rights, workforce management and environmental impacts are critical influences on companies' ability to develop projects and to operate them safely, securely and efficiently. In order to manage project political and technical risk, we believe that companies need to have the skills to manage these ESG issues effectively.

Assessing the industry's performance on ESG issues

In February 2004 we launched our Goldman Sachs Energy Environmental and Social (GSEES) Index (Goldman Sachs 2004) in response to an invitation from the Asset Management Working Group (AMWG) of the United Nations Environment Programme Finance Initiative (UNEPFI). The invitation was to identify the specific environmental and social issues likely to be material for company competitiveness and reputation in the oil and gas industry and, to the extent possible, to quantify the potential impact of these issues on stock prices. The report attempted to analyse not only historical issues but also those issues material to each company's future prospects.

In our view, economic return spreads are the key valuation driver for the market, across sectors and for the oil sector. Correlations of valuation to economic return spreads are very high for the market, across all sectors and for the oil sector. We find that no other valuation methodology comes close in terms of predictive power for share prices. The Goldman Sachs report *Director's Cut: Returns Win* (Goldman Sachs 2003b) argued that the bulk of the value (60%) of any company is determined by its long-run, or sustainable, returns; the next 20% by secular or cyclical change observed in the coming 12 months; and the remainder by longer-term growth or other issues. Thus, one-off ESG issues have a limited impact on share prices. However, ESG issues will, we believe, have an impact on share prices if they affect the long-term returns profile of a company. This concept is outlined in Figure 9.5.

Consequently, the analysis focused on those ESG issues that we saw as impacting on (or relevant to) long-term value drivers in the industry. Our ESG Index framework identified metrics in five categories (corporate governance, environmental and social management, social, environment and investment for the future) to quantify ESG performance with regard to the economy, market, society and the environment, and is applicable across all sectors. In total 42 metrics (performance measures) were developed for the Energy ESG Index. A worked example of one of the greenhouse gas metrics is provided in Box 9.1 to illustrate the methodology.

Strong relationship exists between ESG performance and the Top 100 projects

The Energy ESG Index is a composite index that comprises a number of different dimensions of corporate performance on ESG issues. For example, we recognise that performance on climate change issues is unlikely to be a key driver of companies' ability to deliver production from the next generation of legacy assets in the short to medium term, except in very specific circumstances such as the elimination of gas flaring in West Africa by 2008. On a longer timescale, however, climate change is likely to be a key driver of value, as it will help companies position themselves in relation to new legacy assets in a changing competitive landscape for the oil and gas industry, where limits could be placed on the volumes of oil and gas that are produced or sold. Given the regions that oil and gas companies must explore and in which they must operate

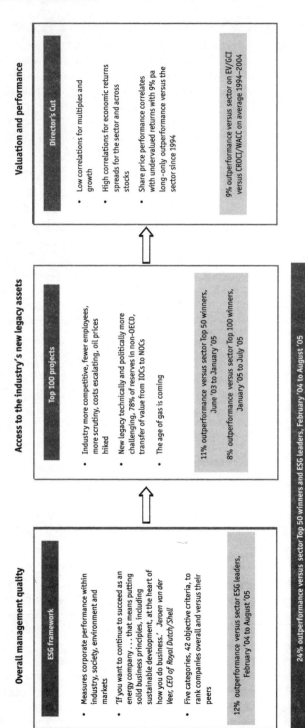

Overall management quality

ESG framework

- Measures corporate performance within industry, society, environment and markets

- 'If you want to continue to succeed as an energy company . . . that means putting solid business principles, including sustainable development, at the heart of how you do business.' *Jeroen van der Veer, CEO of Royal Dutch/Shell*

- Five categories, 42 objective criteria, to rank companies overall and versus their peers

12% outperformance versus sector ESG leaders, February '04 to August '05

Access to the industry's new legacy assets

Top 100 projects

- Industry more competitive, fewer employees, more scrutiny, costs escalating, oil prices hiked

- New legacy technically and politically more challenging, 78% of reserves in non-OECD, transfer of value from IOCs to NOCs

- The age of gas is coming

11% outperformance versus sector Top 50 winners, June '03 to January '05

8% outperformance versus sector Top 100 winners, January '05 to July '05

Valuation and performance

Director's Cut

- Low correlations for multiples and growth

- High correlations for economic returns spreads for the sector and across stocks

- Share price performance correlates with undervalued returns with 9% pa long-only outperformance versus the sector since 1994

9% outperformance versus sector on EV/GCI versus CROCI/WACC on average 1994–2004

24% outperformance versus sector Top 50 winners and ESG leaders, February '04 to August '05

CROCI = cash return on cash invested; EV = enterprise value; GCI = gross cash invested; IOC = international oil company; NOC = national oil company; OECD = Organisation for Economic Co-operation and Development; WACC = weighted average cost of capital

FIGURE 9.5 Integrating ESG framework into energy industry analysis

Source: Goldman Sachs Research

Greenhouse gas (GHG) emissions relative to gross cash invested (GCI) is one of five metrics used to indicate a company's performance on climate change. The data needed to calculate this metric are the GHG emissions in metric tonnes of CO_2 equivalent, and the GCI in US$, which is equal to the sum of gross tangible and intangible assets. GCI is generally found in the company's annual report and accounts on an equity basis. GHG emissions are typically in the environmental data disclosures, and may be reported on an equity or operated basis. Due to lack of disclosure we have not been able to obtain equity data for all companies and acknowledge that this may have an impact on the calculations for this metric. Table 9.1 shows the raw data for this calculation for the companies in our coverage universe along with the final results and rankings from 1 to 5, where 1 is the worst score (for companies with no disclosures) and 5 is the best score (for those companies in the lowest quartile of GHG emissions relative to GCI).

Overall results

For each of the 42 metrics we ranked the companies in our research universe relative to each other and gave them scores from 1 to 5. By aggregating the scores we created the Goldman Sachs Energy Environmental and Social (GSEES) Index. We did not attempt to score the industry against other industries. Most of the information came from primary data sources such as company annual reports, ESG reports and websites. Companies were given the chance to check the data and over 60% responded to our request. Most of the ESG information disclosed is not audited and there were some inconsistencies across the companies: for example, environmental data reported on an equity or operated basis and workforce data reported on full-time employee or contractor basis. In addition, many companies with Energy ESG Index scores below the average published limited information on their ESG performance.

  We found significant differences in performance across metrics and categories, but some companies scored consistently well, notably BP, Statoil, BG and TOTAL. There are a number of distinct groupings within the Energy ESG Index as ExxonMobil, Chevron, Hydro and Royal Dutch/Shell score on average 5% lower than the top four companies. Petrobras lies between the first and second quartiles, outclassing its EM peers with double their average score. The second quartile is tightly grouped with little between BHP Billiton, Cairn, ENI, Marathon, ConocoPhillips and Repsol, on average 15% lower than the first quartile. Table 9.2 shows the relative positioning of all the companies analysed.

  While the Energy ESG Index provides a ranking, it does not provide an explanation for the reasons why individual companies received these scores. A number of factors likely to be at play are:

Box 9.1 Greenhouse gas emissions relative to gross cash invested
(continued on page 120)

Company	GHG emissions 2004 (million tonnes CO_2e)	GCI 2004 (US$ million)	CO_2e/GCI (kg/US$)	CO_2e/GCI score (min = 1; max = 5)
Amerada Hess	5.6	17,420	0.32	4
BG	5.6	19,263	0.29	4
BHP Billiton	52.0	44,037	1.18	2
BP	81.7	239,881	0.34	4
Cairn	0.1	1,063	0.09	5
CEPSA	n/a	11,394	n/a	1
Chevron	62.5	103,736	0.60	2
CNOOC	n/a	10,753	n/a	1
ConocoPhillips	53.0	82,821	0.64	2
EnCana	3.9	39,930	0.10	5
ENI	60.5	132,613	0.46	3
ExxonMobil	137.0	239,963	0.57	2
Gazprom	n/a	151,195	n/a	1
Hydro	8.8	38,144	0.23	4
Lukoil	n/a	41,035	n/a	1
Marathon	19.4	24,749	0.78	2
MOL	4.7	10,796	0.44	3
Murphy	n/a	6,584	n/a	1
Occidental	9.4	23,277	0.40	3
OMV	7.9	22,127	0.36	3
Petrobras	33.5	58,180	0.58	2
PetroChina	n/a	92,904	n/a	1
Repsol	21.5	69,209	0.31	4
Royal Dutch/Shell	112.0	217,376	0.52	2
Santos	4.5	6,979	0.64	2
Sibneft	n/a	15,319	n/a	1
Sinopec	n/a	65,479	n/a	1
Statoil	9.8	62,564	0.16	5
TOTAL	69.4	163,491	0.42	3
Unocal	9.0	21,232	0.42	3
Woodside	1.3	6,480	0.20	5

TABLE 9.1 Worked example of calculation of score for GHG emissions relative to GCI

Source: company data; Goldman Sachs Research estimates

	Energy ESG Index (based on 2004 data)						
	Company	**Corporate governance**	**ES management**	**Social**	**Environment**	**Investment in the future**	**Overall**
1st quartile	BP	34	20	58	43	13	168
	Statoil	32	23	50	45	11	161
	BG	39	17	48	42	14	160
	TOTAL	39	14	52	35	17	157
	ExxonMobil	34	15	61	30	12	152
	Chevron	37	18	57	27	10	149
	Hydro	30	19	50	39	11	149
	Royal Dutch/Shell	35	19	49	34	10	147
2nd quartile	Petrobras	39	17	44	27	14	141
	BHP Billiton	30	19	42	32	13	136
	Cairn	33	15	45	34	8	136
	ENI	33	14	37	35	13	132
	Marathon	38	17	47	21	8	131
	ConocoPhillips	30	19	41	25	15	130
	Repsol	26	16	44	32	12	130
3rd quartile	Amerada Hess	23	19	42	33	8	125
	Santos	32	18	37	27	9	123
	Woodside	23	18	37	27	8	123
	Unocal	30	18	43	22	9	122
	EnCana	30	17	36	26	9	118
	OMV	26	11	38	30	12	117
	MOL	17	19	45	24	9	114
	Occidental	30	13	38	16	6	103
4th quartile	CNOOC	28	9	28	12	8	86
	Gazprom	14	10	25	22	10	81
	Murphy	25	10	22	10	10	77
	PetroChina	10	11	25	15	11	72
	CEPSA	13	8	30	10	6	67
	Lukoil	18	10	17	13	8	66
	Sinopec	12	7	23	10	13	65
	Sibneft	12	11	18	10	10	61
	Average score	27.5	15.0	39.7	26.4	10.6	119.3
	Maximum score (possible)	45	23	70	50	20	208
	Weighting	22%	12%	34%	24%	10%	

TABLE 9.2 Company results on the Energy ESG Index

Source: company data; Goldman Sachs Research estimates

- Increased company size is likely to be positively associated with good performance (perhaps as a result of the greater resources available to the company)
- European and US companies are likely to face increased scrutiny from non-governmental organisations (NGOs) and investors in their home countries, and so are likely to invest increased resources in ESG management
- Companies with a diversified geographic base are likely to have developed some of the key competencies necessary to operate in a range of complex operating environments

Box 9.1 (from page 117)

new resources, as shown by the geographic distribution of the Top 100 projects, it is likely that corporate performance on issues such as corporate governance, workforce, safety, human rights, transparency, resource use, waste, investment in exploration, development and R&D and vision are to be the key determinants of their ability to deliver these projects in a safe and secure manner.

We observe strong correlations between companies with high ESG Index scores and the relative exposure to new legacy assets compared to existing asset base. The correlation between Top 100 reserves as a percentage of 2004 reserves and ESG Index is 47%, excluding the outliers Cairn, Murphy and Woodside. In February 2004 we found a similar picture. In short, the companies with the best ESG score dominate the area that is the key driver of incremental returns. We did not intend the Index to demonstrate (or imply) a causal relationship between GSEES scores and exposure to new legacy assets.[3] What the Index provides is an assessment of the ability of companies to respond to the challenges they are likely to face in a rapidly evolving energy industry, as well as a measure of companies' ability to deliver successful projects. The higher the score, the more confident investors can be (all other things being equal) that companies will deliver successful projects and be better placed to deliver higher returns in the long term.

Conclusion

A strong performance in social and environmental issues is no guarantee of stock market performance but, in an increasingly complex world, social and environmental issues are having an increasing impact on companies' future project slates. We believe

---

3   While oil and gas companies frequently refer to the importance of a good social or environmental record when gaining access to new projects, it is not clear what specific weight is attached to these competencies compared to other issues such as technical competency.

that this will have an increasing impact on future returns, and therefore on valuation and share price performance. The increased focus on issues such as climate change, human rights and corporate governance, together with the rise of money managed in a socially responsible way, active engagement of companies by investors and NGO activity, is taking place at a time when the energy industry is undergoing profound structural changes—the globalisation of the gas industry, the ability to invest on a truly global basis and the creation of a more competitive and complicated industry with the rise of a new world order of emerging market players. We believe the ability of companies to respond to these issues effectively will have a growing impact on performance and valuation.

The GSEES Index is one example of how investors can make robust assessments of corporate performance on ESG issues (at least in relative terms) using publicly available data. Of course there are limitations—the methodology may not correlate specifically with performance, the quality of published data is of variable quality and reliability, the index is not a precise (numerical or probabilistic) measure of risk management competence. However, given the challenges in assessing country- and project-specific risks (and the multitude of challenges faced by oil and gas companies), a relative risk ranking is useful for identifying good and poor performers and allowing investors to make a more informed assessment of the likelihood of long-term business success.

References

Eurosif (European Sustainable and Responsible Investment Forum) (2003) *Socially Responsible Investment among European Institutional Investors* (Paris: Eurosif).

Global Compact Financial Sector Initiative (2004) *Who Cares Wins: Connecting Financial Markets to a Changing World* (New York: The Global Compact).

Goldman Sachs (2003a) *50 Projects to Change the World* (London: Goldman Sachs, 19 June 2003).

—— (2003b) *Director's Cut: Returns Win* (London: Goldman Sachs, 11 September 2003).

—— (2004) *Introducing the Goldman Sachs Energy Environmental and Social Index* (London: Goldman Sachs, 24 February 2004).

—— (2005a) *100 Projects to Change the World* (London: Goldman Sachs, January 2005).

—— (2005b) *Integrating ESG* (London: Goldman Sachs, 25 August 2005).

Mercer Investment Consulting (2005) *2005 Fearless Forecast* (London: Mercer Investment Consulting).

Transparency International (2004) *Corruption Perceptions Index* (London: Transparency International, June 2004).

10

Sustainable investment research
INNOVEST STRATEGIC VALUE ADVISORS

Matthew Kiernan

Innovest, USA

Innovest Strategic Value Advisors is a global research firm, with a primary focus on 'non-traditional' drivers of both investment risk and long-term outperformance. Its approach is unique in the 'sustainable finance' field in that it seeks to adapt what are essentially the same analytical techniques, tools, rigour and quantitative sophistication of mainstream Wall Street and City investment houses to what are decidedly non-traditional performance indicators. This chapter will attempt to elucidate that approach, and will argue that its most compelling application is an enhancement of, rather than a substitute for, more conventional investment analysis.

Innovest's approach to sustainable investment research is predicated on a number of basic, core beliefs. The first is that the limitations of traditional, accounting-driven investment analysis are becoming increasingly apparent. Such analysis tends to provide only a static, retrospective picture of the *trailing* indicators of company performance. More dynamic, forward-looking analysis of companies' 'intangible value drivers' should provide much richer insights into companies' true risk profiles and competitive potential. Companies' performance on environmental, social and governance (ESG) issues are among the most potent of those emerging intangible value drivers.

The second core belief is that companies' ability to manage ESG risks and opportunities has already become directly relevant to their competitiveness and profitability, and will become increasingly critical for the foreseeable future.

Innovest's third bedrock belief is that companies' performance on a number of ESG issues can provide robust insights about the quality of its overall strategic management, organisational agility and responsiveness. Other ESG issues, on the other hand, (contraception or animal testing, for example), are more germane to the ethical values of the investor, but provide few, if any, insights about management quality. Innovest readily acknowledges that the dividing line between the two is both blurred and constantly shifting, but believes that it is nonetheless important to make a disciplined and concerted effort to distinguish between them. At Innovest, our primary focus is on the former set of issues—those that are of greatest relevance to an assessment of management quality. This, in turn, is likely to make them directly relevant to companies' competitiveness and financial performance.

The fourth working assumption is that the materiality of different ESG factors differs substantially with each industry sector. Any truly robust analysis must start with an in-depth assessment of the competitive dynamics, risks and opportunities in each particular sector. Factor weightings must therefore be customised for each sector; 'one size fits all' analytical frameworks, which are not sector-specific, are decidedly suboptimal.

Our fifth basic belief is that this type of analysis is most useful when it is combined with traditional financial analysis. It is highly unusual to find a single firm able to excel at both ESG analysis and traditional investment management. Moreover, the medium- and long-term investment insights available from ESG analysis must be tempered with an appreciation of shorter-term value drivers and price movements. For these reasons, Innovest's ESG analysis has been explicitly designed as an 'alpha overlay' which is intended to add value to traditional approaches rather than to replace them.

The key value drivers

Innovest's analysis typically addresses over 100 individual factors, all of them grouped under what we believe to be the 'four pillars' of sustainability, as indicated in Table 10.1. Innovest's research attempts to focus on those factors which contribute most heavily to financial outperformance. It is Innovest's view that certain—but not all—ESG factors can directly enhance shareholder value by contributing to competitive advantage, risk reduction or both. Therefore, ESG performance measures are used as leading indicators for management quality and long-term financial performance.

At a general level, it is by now reasonably well established that ESG factors (like many other, more widely acknowledged, value drivers) can contribute materially to companies' competitive advantage and profitability. They can do so in a multiplicity of ways: cost reduction through energy efficiency measures; the creation of new markets through differentiated, more 'sustainable' products and services; and a superior ability to attract, retain and motivate top talent, to name but three.

It is important to note, however, that not all ESG factors create these competitive benefits: nor do they do so all the time and in all industry sectors. It is for that reason that Innovest's analytics platform relies heavily on empirical, financial analysis to isolate and over-weight those factors that are actually building value at a particular time and in particular industry sectors.

Human capital	Environment
• Labour relations • Health and safety • Recruitment/retention strategies • Employee motivation • Innovation capacity • Knowledge development and dissemination • Progressive workplace practices	• Board and executive oversight • Risk management systems • Disclosure/verification • Process efficiencies ('eco-efficiency') • Health and safety • New product development
Stakeholder capital	**Strategic governance**
• Regulators and policy-makers • Local communities/NGOs • Customer relationships • Alliance partners • Emerging markets	• Strategic scanning capability • Agility/adaptation • Performance indicators/monitoring • Traditional governance concerns • International 'best practice'

TABLE 10.1 Innovest's four pillars of sustainability

The research methodology

At the heart of Innovest's analytical model is the attempt to balance the level of ESG-driven investment risk with the companies' managerial and financial capacity to manage that risk successfully and profitably into the future. Risk alone is only one-third of the equation; what is also crucially important to investors is how well that risk is likely to be managed and what, if any, upside profit opportunities might be identified, created and/or captured. The Innovest assessment criteria have been designed with these three parts of the equation in mind.

Innovest rates companies based on their performance on a variety of non-traditional risk factors, primarily related to strategic governance, environment, human capital and labour relations, and stakeholder capital. The ratings are modelled after bond ratings whereby Innovest rates the performance of companies within a given industrial sector using the following scheme:

Rating
AAA   Best-in-class
AA
A
BBB   Sector average
BB
B
CCC   Worst-in-class

In order to generate the ratings, Innovest's analysts evaluate companies relative to their same-sector peers in Innovest's database of over 2,000 global companies. This is accomplished through the completion of a proprietary, 100+ factor analytical matrix which is completed via review of a wide variety of information from the company, industry trade groups, government databases, research organisations, non-governmental organisations (NGOs) and, importantly, direct interviews of company personnel by analysts. Innovest sectors correspond to the well-established MSCI sectors, and the Global Industry Classification System (GICS) industry groups. The methodology by which Innovest conducts its company and industry analysis is summarised in Figure 10.1.

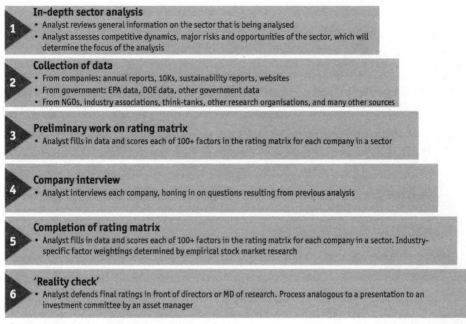

1 **In-depth sector analysis**
- Analyst reviews general information on the sector that is being analysed
- Analyst assesses competitive dynamics, major risks and opportunities of the sector, which will determine the focus of the analysis

2 **Collection of data**
- From companies: annual reports, 10Ks, sustainability reports, websites
- From government: EPA data, DOE data, other government data
- From NGOs, industry associations, think-tanks, other research organisations, and many other sources

3 **Preliminary work on rating matrix**
- Analyst fills in data and scores each of 100+ factors in the rating matrix for each company in a sector

4 **Company interview**
- Analyst interviews each company, honing in on questions resulting from previous analysis

5 **Completion of rating matrix**
- Analyst fills in data and scores each of 100+ factors in the rating matrix for each company in a sector. Industry-specific factor weightings determined by empirical stock market research

6 **'Reality check'**
- Analyst defends final ratings in front of directors or MD of research. Process analogous to a presentation to an investment committee by an asset manager

DOE = Department of Energy; EPA = Environmental Protection Agency

FIGURE 10.1 Innovest's company and industry analysis methodology

While this research methodology is similar to that used by mainstream investment houses in the City, Wall Street and elsewhere, it remains somewhat unusual in the world of socially responsible investment (SRI). The most conspicuous difference actually lies in what is 'missing'—the heavy dependence on questionnaires. Company questionnaires form the backbone of the methodologies of the majority of contemporary SRI research houses. This is despite the many limitations of such questionnaires, not least of which is the 'questionnaire fatigue' they have generated among responding companies. Even the best of questionnaires struggle to achieve a 50% response rate, and the veracity of the responses is—to put it diplomatically—open to question. Innovest's methodology eschews the use of questionnaires, relying instead on real-time, interactive interviews with company executives and officials, in addition to customers, suppliers, NGOs, industry associations, and other stakeholders.

The Innovest methodology is somewhat unusual in the SRI world in at least three further respects. First, it relies heavily on an in-depth analysis of the unique competitive dynamics, risks and opportunities of each industry sector. Innovest believes that this is the best way to contextualise and evaluate the strengths and weaknesses of individual companies: without such analysis, company assessments become much more arbitrary and almost journalistic and historical. Second, it places much emphasis on sector-specific factor weightings. Different industry sectors place differing premiums on the multiplicity of different sustainability factors. Environmental performance, for example, is clearly a better leading indicator of management quality and competitiveness in the oil and gas sector than it is in software. What is more, the potency of each factor also varies over time. The genesis of Innovest's factor weightings is ongoing, multi-year research and analysis of actual stock market performance. Third, and perhaps most importantly of all, Innovest's methodology relies heavily on analysts with experience in industry and investment management, as well as the various ESG issues themselves. Industry experience tends to enrich the company interview process immeasurably, and investment experience helps in the 'translation' of ESG analysis into actionable investment decisions and portfolio construction. Innovest analysts include alumni of such mainstream Wall Street/City firms as Bear Stearns, Morgan Stanley and Lehman Brothers. An extract from the 'risk' component of an Innovest company assessment 'work in progress' rating matrix for the global forest products sector is presented in Figure 10.2.

A parallel analysis is also undertaken on the other two 'meta-factors' in Innovest's analytical model: the robustness of the companies' risk management architectures, and their ability to identify and isolate strategic profit opportunities on the 'upside'.

The output

Individual company profiles are then drafted; an example for the Brazilian forest products company Aracruz Celulose is reproduced in Appendix 1 on page 349. The individual, factor-weighted company scores are then compared with international industry peers. Table 10.2 illustrates how Aracruz compares to its industry peers.

Integrating the research

Innovest's institutional investor clients tend to use Innovest's research in one or more of three different ways:

- As a source of additional information and insights, which are added informally to their existing investment research and analysis processes

- As background information and analysis to underpin a process of direct engagement with portfolio companies to discuss specific issues and concerns

- As an integral component of the investment algorithms for a specific 'sustainability-enhanced' investment fund or product

Industry / Category	Category %	Category %	% of 2000	% of 2000	Max points	Max points	IP International Paper Co. Paper and forest products			MODOB Holmen AB Paper and forest products			3861 OJI Paper Co. Paper and Forest Products		
							Raw score	Weighted score	Relative performance	Raw score	Weighted score	Relative performance	Raw score	Weighted score	Relative performance
Risk factors															
1) Historic liabilities															
A. Contaminated site liabilities	10.000		3.500		70		2.2	15	Bottom tier	8.0	56	Top tier	5.0	35	Middle tier
B. Other historic liabilities	0.000		0.000		0		0.0	0	Worst in class	0.0	0	Worst in class	0.0	0	Worst in class
Historic liabilities total		10.000		3.500		70	2.2	15	Bottom tier	8.0	56	Top tier	5.0	35	Middle tier
2) Operating risk															
A. Spills and releases	0.000		0.000		0		0.0	0	Worst in class	0.0	0	Worst in class	0.0	0	Worst in class
B. Regulatory compliance	0.000		0.000		0		0.0	0	Worst in class	0.0	0	Worst in class	0.0	0	Worst in class
C. Toxic emissions	20.000		7.000		140		6.7	94	Top tier	6.4	89	Middle tier	4.0	56	Middle tier
D. Hazardous waste	20.000		7.000		140		5.1	72	Middle tier	9.0	125	Top tier	6.5	91	Middle tier
E. Other	0.000		0.000		0		0.0	0	Worst in class	0.0	0	Worst in class	0.0	0	Worst in class
Operating risk total		40.000		14.000		280	5.9	166	Middle tier	7.7	215	Top tier	5.3	147	Middle tier
3) Leading sustainability/risk indicators															
A. Resource use efficiency/recycling	10.000		3.500		70		9.0	63	Top tier	8.0	56	Top tier	7.1	50	Top tier
B. Energy efficiency	10.000		3.500		70		8.0	56	Top tier	6.0	42	Middle tier	7.0	49	Top tier
C. Market risk	5.000		1.750		35		6.7	23	Middle tier	1.7	6	Bottom tier	5.2	18	Middle tier
D. Regulatory/legal risk	10.000		3.500		70		8.0	56	Top tier	10.0	70	Best in class	4.0	28	Middle tier
E. Global warming potential	5.000		1.750		35		10.0	35	Best in class	10.0	35	Best in class	7.0	25	Top tier
F. Other	0.000		0.000		0		0.0	0	Worst in class	0.0	0	Worst in class	0.0	0	Worst in class
Leading sustainability/ risk indicators total		40.000		14.000		280	8.3	233	Top tier	7.5	209	Top tier	6.0	169	Middle tier
4) Industry-specific risk															
A. Forestry risk	10.000		3.500		70		0.0	0	Worst in class	3.3	23	Middle tier	2.0	14	Bottom tier
B. Other	0.000		0.000		0		0.0	0	Worst in class	0.0	0	Worst in class	0.0	0	Worst in class
C. Other	0.000		0.000		0		0.0	0	Worst in class	0.0	0	Worst in class	0.0	0	Worst in class
D. Other	0.000		0.000		0		0.0	0	Worst in class	0.0	0	Worst in class	0.0	0	Worst in class
Industry-specific risk total		10.000		3.500		70	0.0	0	Worst in class	3.3	23	Middle tier	2.0	14	Bottom tier
Total score of risk factors	1		0.35	0.35	700	700	5.927	415.005	Middle tier	7.185	502.937	Top tier	5.220	5.395	Middle tier

The portion of the Innovest rating matrix shown here is itself an amalgam of a more granular, multi-factorial data set which underpins it.

FIGURE 10.2 Risk assessment: a partial matrix

Ticker	Company	Rating matrix		Rank
		Score	Rating	
MODOB	Holmen AB	1,583	AAA	1
SVCBY	Svenska Cellulosa AB	1,554	AAA	2
WY	Weyerhaeuser Co.	1,516	AAA	3
SEO	Stora Enso Oyj	1,440	AA	4
MESBS	M-REAL Oyj	1,404	AA	5
TBC	Tembec Inc.	1,385	AA	7
NF	Nexfor Inc.	1.385	AA	6
VCP	Votorantim Celulose e Papel S.A.	1,379	AA	8
IP	International Paper Co.	1,360	AA	9
AA6	Aracruz Celulose S.A.	1,359	AA	10
NSG	Norske Skog AS	1,317	A	11
KLBN4	Klabin S.A.	1,313	A	12
GP	Georgia-Pacific Corp.	1,271	A	13
SUZA4	Suzano Bahia Sul	1,237	A	14
CFP	Canfor Corporation	1,229	A	15
UPM	UPM-Kymmene Corporation	1,213	BBB	16
DTC	Domtar Inc.	1,213	BBB	17
MWV	MeadWestvaco Corp.	1,195	BBB	18
ABY	Abitibi-Consolidated Inc.	1,183	BBB	19
CENIBRA	Cenibra-Celulose Nipo-Brasileira S.A.	1,153	BBB	20
RPSA4	Ripasa S.A. Celulose e Papel	1,090	BB	21
BCC	Boise Cascade Corp.	1,083	BB	22
IP-BR	IP do Brasil	1,044	BB	23
LPX	Louisiana-Pacific Corp.	1,043	BB	24
TIN	Temple-Inland Inc.	990	B	25
PCH	Potlatch Corp.	981	B	26
3861	OJI Paper Co. Ltd	948	B	27
3893	Nippon Unipac Holding	875	CCC	28
PPX-AU	Paperlinx	617	CCC	29

TABLE 10.2 Comparison of Aracruz with its industry peers

Since the first two applications are relatively straightforward, this chapter focuses on the third.

It is important to reiterate in this regard that Innovest's analytics have always been explicitly designed to be used as an 'alpha overlay', not as free-standing investment recommendations. Nearly ten years of empirical stock market research tells us that the sustainability-driven risks and value opportunities which are the focus of our analysis often have an 'incubation period' of 24–36 months before they manifest themselves in improvements that can be captured by traditional financial metrics such as share price, return on investment, return on equity and others. For that reason, we believe that our analysis has its greatest value as an enhancement for traditional investment analytics, not as a replacement for it.

To illustrate with an example: Innovest's oil and gas sector team currently views BP as the top-rated company among 33 international companies in its industry sector. It is, therefore, our 'favourite' oil and gas company, the one we currently expect to be the strongest performer financially in 2–3 years' time. That does not, however, make it an automatic 'buy' today, as the company may be overpriced on a short-term basis. For that judgement, we rely on our traditional asset management partners, including State Street Global Advisors, ING and others. Combining their more conventional valuation methodologies with our own sustainability overlay, we reach a joint conclusion on what is an appropriate price to pay today to realise this additional value 'down the road'.

Since the Innovest analytics are designed to be superimposed on traditional approaches but not to replace them, our overlay can, in principle, be used as a complement to any number of investment styles and products. To date, the overlay has been used with the following investment products and styles: long-only active; enhanced index; 'active-quant'; and long/short equities, as well as more thematic funds such as 'clean technology' or 'low-carbon' funds.

Institutional investors approaching the 'sustainability space' for the first time (and even experienced players) seem to appreciate the opportunity to fine-tune the risk–return characteristics of the product to their precise specifications and investment style, rather than relying on the more binary approach of a number of more traditional SRI/sustainability offerings. With these other SRI approaches, individual stocks are screened either 'in' or 'out' of a portfolio, based primarily on the company's SRI characteristics. Any other investment characteristics of the portfolio—an 'over-weight' position in technology stocks, for example, or a bias towards (or away from) larger companies—become purely accidental by-products of the SRI choices. With an overlay approach, by contrast, one begins by constructing portfolios with the desired investment risk–return, style and sector characteristics, and then one superimposes a bias or 'tilt' towards sustainability factors. The degree of the tilt is primarily determined by two things—the client's tolerance of deviations from traditional investment benchmarks and the degree of 'sustainability purity' they wish to attain. Since Innovest's rankings are not absolute but relative to same-sector peers—Russian oil company Lukoil, for example, is currently rated 32nd out of 35 international oil and gas majors—the client may 'dial up' or 'dial down' the emphasis on each factor. This is clearly impossible with a binary 'in or out' approach.

The alpha overlay in practice: the Green Planet Fund

At the time of writing, Innovest is either sub-advising on or co-managing roughly US$1.1 billion in a variety of investment funds. It is an article of faith at Innovest to seek out mainstream asset management partners in each case. One of the most 'venerable' of those funds is the Green Planet Fund, started three years ago with IDEAM, a specialist quantitative manager formed by combining units of two French firms—Credit Agricole and Credit Lyonnais.

The Green Planet Fund is probably best described as a global active quantitative fund; active stock 'bets' are made, but within the context of some very tight and sophisticated risk controls to ensure a relatively low (2%) deviation or tracking error from its MSCI world benchmark. In the case of the Green Planet Fund, special care is taken to concentrate the active bets at the individual stock level; very little variance from the industry sector and country weightings in the benchmark is allowed.

The portfolio construction works as follows: all stocks in the MSCI world universe (roughly 1,600) are analysed and ranked in two separate processes, one using traditional financial factors and one using Innovest's sustainability assessments. In both cases, the comparisons are primarily made on a relative basis *vis-à-vis* industry peers. Companies receiving top-quartile ratings on both sets of criteria are over-weighted relative to their benchmark weights, but within the relatively tight constraints of the tracking error target. The sustainability and traditional financial assessments work together synergistically; to receive the maximum degree of over-weight allowed by the permitted tracking error, companies must score well across both dimensions.

This particular fund was designed to be relatively conservative, taking only limited 'sustainability bets' and striving to outperform its benchmark by a relatively modest 1–2%. Conversely, of course, if the sustainability bets failed, any losses would similarly be moderated. In the event, the fund has performed very strongly—over its three-year life, it has outperformed its benchmark by 2.2% annually, while exhibiting less volatility. The measure of the balance between a portfolio's outperformance and its volatility (risk) is called an information ratio. At the time of writing, the Green Planet Fund's information ratio was 2.7, which is considered extremely favourable.

Concluding remarks

Each sustainability or SRI research house has its own, idiosyncratic approach to analysing individual companies. In Innovest's case, that approach depends on four pillars:

- Focusing on those sustainability factors with the greatest anticipated impact on financial performance

- Placing the assessment of individual companies within the broader context of the competitive dynamics of the entire industry sector

- Conducting real-time, interactive interviews with a variety of company officials

- Combining Innovest's views on companies' medium-term prospects with the shorter-term valuation discipline of a traditional asset management partner

To date, that approach seems to have served our clients well. As the financial saliency of sustainability factors becomes more widely recognised by traditional analysts and portfolio managers, and as clients look increasingly to a longer-term investment horizon, it is our hope and expectation that Innovest's approach will gain even greater currency among the mainstream. Indeed, there are already strong indications that this will be the case. From the very outset it has been our objective to build both an investment discipline and an analytical team with a level of rigour that would be worthy of such investor confidence. As with all investment matters, however, the proof of the pudding must remain in the eating!

11

SAM's approach to measuring and valuing corporate sustainability performance

Gabriela Grab Hartmann and Thilo Goodall

SAM Sustainable Asset Management

Corporate sustainability, as defined by SAM, is an approach to business creating long-term shareholder value. The competitive position held by any market participant determines its share of overall value-added. Macroeconomic and sustainability trends and developments change the competitive environment. Sustainable companies are those that embrace change by seizing opportunities and by managing risks that macroeconomic and sustainability developments impose on each industry. By seizing the opportunities and effectively managing the risks, sustainable companies enhance their competitive position. Sustainable companies are thus better positioned to create shareholder value.

This chapter explains SAM's research approach to identifying companies that are: better than their peers at seizing opportunities and managing risks deriving from economic, environmental and societal developments; and are attractive investment opportunities.

About SAM

SAM Sustainable Asset Management (SAM) was founded 1995 as an independent financial services group specialising in sustainability investments. The company focuses on institutional asset management, investment funds and private equity. SAM is headquartered in Zurich (Switzerland), with branches and representative offices in Barcelona (Spain), Melbourne (Australia), Milan (Italy), Sonoma (California, US) and Stockholm (Sweden).

SAM's expertise stems from its own research as well as an active, worldwide sustainability network. With a research team of 18 analysts, SAM conducts research to identify successful companies that are good investments. It has developed a proprietary database collecting corporate sustainability performance data from more than 1,000 companies worldwide. Sustainability aspects are integrated into the entire investment process, providing a high degree of security, transparency and an attractive return for SAM's clients. An active research-driven investment approach is the foundation of all SAM products.

Today, SAM ranks among the world's leading institutions in the sustainability investing sector. Its clients include banks, insurance companies, pension funds, trusts as well as private investors. SAM offers financial products and manages individual mandates in areas such as global and European equity, corporate bonds, and energy and water technology. It offers both public and private equity funds. SAM currently holds over CHF2 billion (€1.3 billion) in assets under management.

SAM's research is the foundation of the first global family of sustainability indices, launched in co-operation with Dow Jones indices and STOXX Limited. These indices track the financial performance of the leading sustainability-driven companies worldwide. The Dow Jones Sustainability World Indices were launched in 1999, followed by the Dow Jones Sustainability STOXX Indices (DJSI) in 2001 and the Dow Jones Sustainability North America Indices in 2005. The indices provide asset managers with reliable and objective benchmarks to manage sustainability portfolios. Currently more than 55 DJSI licenses are held by asset managers in 14 countries to manage a variety of financial products including active and passive funds, certificates and segregated accounts. In total, these licensees presently manage €3.4 billion based on the DJSI.

Value proposition

Being based on the value-added impact of a company's approach to trends and developments, SAM analyses companies' strategic positioning within their industry and their ability to seize the opportunities and to manage the risks that arise from global and industry-specific developments. With a goal of generating superior risk-adjusted returns, SAM invests in companies that are leaders in corporate sustainability, and whose securities are priced favourably to their fair values. SAM's value proposition may thus be broadly divided into two parts. First, SAM adds value by identifying sustainable companies, which lead their peers in generating shareholder value. Second, SAM adds value by quantifying the impact of sustainability on the fair value of a company's securities to better exploit price–value discrepancies.

Research process

SAM's research process comprises three main stages. First, the trends and developments at the macro and industry level that potentially shape the competitive environment for companies are identified. This process includes analysing the factors that affect the level of competition (e.g. barriers to entry, the threat of substitutes). SAM's view is that sustainability trends and challenges must be linked to the competitive environment in which a company operates. Second, corporate sustainability performance is analysed, focusing on the company's position within markets, its degree of preparedness for the trends and challenges ahead, and its checks and balances to align management interests with shareholder interest. Third, the impact of the company's environment and its sustainability performance on its future financial performance and valuation are quantified. Each of these steps is discussed further below.

Analysis of macro developments and industry trends and challenges

Trends and challenges, be they sustainability-related or not, are likely to change the future competitive environment in each industry, shaping the context for each player within an industry. Some trends affect all industries in a similar manner. The demand for transparency, for example, driven both by regulation and investor pressure, is a trend affecting all industries in much the same way. Better reporting as well as corporate governance frameworks are consequences of this trend. In contrast, industry-specific challenges depend on the industry's characteristics. The challenges will differ depending on industry characteristics such as the degree of regulation, supply and demand structures, and barriers to entry. Some trends and challenges affect more than one industry, but not all industries alike. As an example, global climate change affects energy-intensive industries much more than others. The key challenges for the oil and gas industry, for instance, include energy resource scarcity and the environmental effects of greenhouse gas (GHG) emissions. These challenges are likely to create increased demand for clean, sustainable and competitive energy; recent high energy prices and high price volatility reinforce the importance of alternatives to fossil fuels. The development of alternatives will, in turn, be a key influence on the competitive positioning of energy companies.

Analysis of corporate sustainability performance

SAM has developed a series of criteria and indicators to measure a company's preparedness and ability to seize the opportunities and manage the risks that the trends and challenges pose. SAM also analyses the companies' positioning in the market to benefit from sustainability and other developments. A company's preparedness and positioning is not measurable in absolute terms, but it is possible to assess companies on a relative basis. Certain companies—the leading companies of an industry—are addressing risks and opportunities better than others. SAM thus applies a best-in-class approach targeted at identifying the companies that are expected to create more shareholder value. For example, in the energy sector, the assessment criteria used by SAM to judge a company's preparedness for global climate change are:

- The quality of the company's climate strategy

- GHG emissions

- Emission targets

- Emission trading strategies

- Reserve management for fossil fuels

- Strategies for alternative fuels and energies

Some companies position themselves in the alternative fuels market to benefit from the challenges that global climate change and energy resource scarcity pose. Vestas Wind Systems AS (Vestas), based in Denmark, is one of the leading companies in the alternative energy sector. Vestas's principal activities are the development, manufacturing, sale, marketing and maintenance of installations to use wind energy to generate electricity. Wind power is a clean, sustainable source of electricity. Wind power plants erected in areas with good wind conditions can compete with conventional energy sources such as coal, natural gas, oil and nuclear power. When externalities (such as pollution) are taken into account, wind power is even more competitive. At optimum sites, wind can be competitive with new coal-fired plants and, in some locations, can even challenge gas. Emerging markets such as India and China, which have the best conditions for distributed power solutions, have already started to install significant wind power capacity.

Vestas's strengths are also shown in other areas, combining its positioning in the renewable energy field with attention to all three dimensions of sustainability. Vestas's management capabilities in the environmental dimension are among the best in the industry. This is underlined not only by large parts of the management system being certified to ISO 14001 but also by Vestas's intention of introducing minimum environmental standards for all of its project sites. Environmental life-cycle considerations are an integral part of the product design processes. In workforce-related criteria such as human capital development and labour practice indicators, the company also scores above average.

Analysis of future corporate financial performance and company valuation

The third stage in SAM's research process is to measure and quantify a company's positioning and corporate sustainability performance, and to measure the impact of these factors on corporate financial performance and, ultimately, on shareholder value. From these quantitative results, conclusions relevant to companies as well as investors can be drawn. SAM invests in companies that lead their peers in terms of corporate sustainability performance, and whose securities are priced favourably relative to their fair values. SAM determines the fair value of a company's securities using its SAM Sustainability Discounted Cash Flow model. The model includes the impact of a company's sustainability performance, both in terms of preparedness and positioning, on the fair value of its equity and bonds. In other words, SAM explicitly considers the sustainability criteria in the valuation methodology as value drivers. The actual investment decision is then based on the discrepancy between security price and sustainable fair value, and on the portfolio risk characteristics of the company's securities.

By identifying and quantifying the transmission mechanisms from sustainability performance to financial performance, SAM includes corporate sustainability performances in the financial valuation of a company. The transmission mechanisms are quite simply formulated by dissecting the two determinants of shareholder value: free cash flow to the firm and weighted average costs of capital (see Figure 11.1). Generally speaking, seizing opportunities means that more profitable investments can be detected and made. This should lead to an increase in free cash flow to the firm. For example, if a company can manage risks better than its peers, it should be able to decrease production costs and/or lower its risk premium for financing. This leads to either an increase in free cash flow to the firm or a decrease in financing costs.

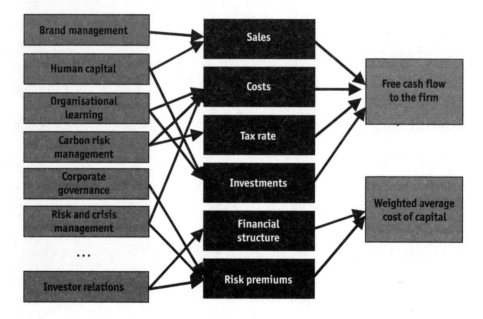

FIGURE 11.1 Sustainability and shareholder value

In SAM's model, management decisions regarding sustainability criteria are assumed to impact value drivers such as a company's resource efficiency, workforce motivation, innovation potential, reputation with stakeholders, and exposure to a variety of risk factors, both internal and external. The positive influence should, sooner or later, be measurable in the company's financials, such as revenues, costs or reinvestment rates.

The transmission mechanism for a company's market position runs along the same lines. For example, a good position in the provision of effective alternatives to fossil fuel may result in higher revenues and reinvestment rates and, in the end, to higher-than-average growth rates of free cash flow.

Returning to the example of Vestas, the company's position in the fast-growing alternative fuels markets provides a solid base for firm valuation. Based on estimates by the American Wind Energy Association (AWEA) and the European Wind Energy Association (EWEA), annual global growth rates for new installations is likely to remain as high as 25% for the period 2005–10.

Vestas currently has a global market share of 40%, and is well positioned in every world market. Sales growth rates for Vestas are expected to reach 20% over the short term and to remain at about 10% over the medium term.

Nevertheless, fast-growing markets attract new competitors. The market for wind power has few barriers to entry: any industrial company with basic knowledge in turbines and aerodynamics can enter. Indeed, in early 2005, Siemens announced its intention to enter the wind generation market to compete with the current major players Vestas, GE Wind and Mitsubishi. New entrants to the market can be expected to reduce potential profit margins for all competitors and, over time, these margins are expected to decline to earnings before interest and tax of about 5–6%. Even allowing for the effects of increased competition, Vestas's environmental management capabilities should increase its free cash flow by reducing the inefficient use of resources. As the company also scores above average on its approach to human capital development, its reinvestment rates and returns on investments should be enhanced through the efficient use of human capital.

Fast-growing markets require a high pace in production and investments, something that Vestas has not yet been able to demonstrate. Vestas's good human capital development should, in the end, allow it to increase its profits and achieve a stable profit margin, but the result will not be immediate. Vestas's decision to acquire NEG Micon was intended to increase Vestas's production facilities and strengthen its competitive position versus its main competitors. However, the acquisition has not yet delivered the promised potential. The increase in production capacity has not reduced quality concerns over its products. Such concerns increase costs and reduce profit margins, as well as triggering additional investments which can be a drain on free cash flow. The alleged cultural clashes between the two companies do not help in addressing quality issues.

Access to capital is a prerequisite in fast-growing markets, requiring Vestas to tap the capital markets. While Vestas performed a capital increase in 2004, which virtually made the company debt-free, its current growth rates mean that the company will need to return to the capital markets. Vestas's strong performance in the areas of environmental performance and investor relations, and its environmental product life-cycle considerations should reduce its risk premium on equity and bonds, thereby potentially allowing it to raise new capital at favourable rates. On the other hand, its performance in relation to corporate governance, codes of conduct and compliance is below average, which may weaken its ability to reduce its risk premiums.

Taking into account the industry's characteristics and challenges, and the impact of Vestas's positioning, preparedness, and checks and balances on its future financial performance, the SAM Sustainability DCF model calculates a sustainable fair value of DKK90–100 per share. Risk-adjusted variations of Vestas's share price from this fair value can act as the basis for decisions to hold or not to hold any shares of Vestas.

Conclusion

The competitive position held by any market participant determines its share of overall value-added. Macroeconomic and sustainability trends and developments may change the competitive environment, thus challenging a company's competitive position. SAM's sustainability investing approach is geared towards identifying those companies that will seize the opportunities and manage the risks better than their peers, thus creating more shareholder value than their peers.

This philosophy is different to investing according to ethical or ecological criteria. Such approaches are based on value sets and exclude entire industries or sectors that do not, or cannot, comply with a given value set. SAM, in contrast, tries to identify extra value-added in every sector and industry; ultimately, this promotes a best-in-class approach which identifies the sustainability leaders in each industry (i.e. the companies that seize the opportunities and manage the risks better than their peers and thus create a monopoly niche for themselves in a potentially competitive market). However, this type of analysis requires an understanding of how an industry operates and what management practices and processes can be considered best practice.

Sustainability research and investment is at a crossroads. Developments in the not-so-distant future will determine whether it will remain a niche, appealing to those with certain value sets, or whether it will make its way into mainstream research and investment approaches. To achieve the latter, three things are needed. First, the sustainability research community will have to improve its understanding of the common competitive forces and common trends and challenges that haunt market participants every day. Second, sustainability research and investment will have to find a way to integrate its findings in commonly used investment processes. Processes based on relative value investing offer the possibility of doing just that and there may also be other approaches that can be integrated. However, irrespective of the investment process, unless the value-added generated by sustainability research can be translated into investor value-added, the market for sustainability research will remain small. Third, and perhaps most importantly, the link between corporate sustainability performance and corporate financial performance and security performance needs to become visible. Without being able to show that there is value-added beyond servicing value sets (or the specific ethical values of individual investors), sustainability will remain an appeaser at best.

SAM's approach, being based on a link between corporate sustainability performance and corporate financial performance, requires a serious research effort and an in-depth understanding of how an industry operates, which strategic positions the competitive environment offers, and what management practices and processes can be considered best practice. Understanding and showing the link between corporate sustainability and financial performance is crucial for SAM's work. SAM believes that, with the approach it has adopted, it is in a position to serve mainstream investors as well as niche investors with specific ethical values.

12
Communicating risks to pension fund trustees
THE UKSIF SECTOR NOTES PROJECT

*Meg Brown**

UKSIF, UK

Between April 2003 and September 2005, a number of the UK Social Investment Forum's (see Box 12.1) fund manager members and affiliates contributed to a project to develop a series of sector notes to identify the potentially material social, ethical and environmental risks and their potential impact on shareholder value, for each of 11 sectors. The aim of the notes is to help pension fund trustees understand risks that lie outside the realms of 'traditional' financial analysis but that may nevertheless influence the performance of their investments. For each sector note, a series of questions that trustees could ask their fund managers was developed to assist trustees in understanding how effectively social and environmental risks are being incorporated into their fund managers' investment decisions.

The project has provided a number of important benefits. First, it demonstrated that, under the right conditions, it is possible for fund managers to collaborate. Second, it helped key socially responsible investment (SRI) analysts to reach a consensus on which risks to prioritise for each industry sector, thereby bringing focus to engagement with companies and helping build relationships with sell-side analysts. Third, the sector notes themselves provide trustees interested in exploring SRI within their fund with a useful resource to both challenge sceptics on their investment committee and to hold

---

* Meg Brown was the UKSIF sector analyst from 2003 to April 2005. The views expressed in this chapter are those of the author and do not necessarily reflect the views of UKSIF or UKSIF's members and affiliates.

The UK Social Investment Forum (UKSIF) is the UK's membership network for SRI. UKSIF's primary purpose is to promote and encourage the development and positive impact of SRI among UK-based investors. UKSIF believes that all material social, environmental and ethical (SEE) issues should be integrated into standard investment practice and that individual investors should be able to reflect their values in their investments.

The Forum was launched in 1991 to bring together the different strands of SRI nationally and to act as a focus and a voice for the industry. UKSIF's 250+ members and affiliates include retail and institutional fund managers, financial advisers, SRI research providers, consultants, trade unions, banks, building societies, community development finance institutions, NGOs and individuals interested in SRI.*

Just Pensions is a UKSIF 2002–2005 programme that aims to educate and influence UK pension funds and other institutional investors about the importance of international development issues in their practice of SRI. In addition to its education and awareness-raising activities, Just Pensions co-ordinates in-depth research to assess current practice, and works to address the barriers to the growth of SRI generally, and pro-poor SRI in particular. Just Pensions also provides SRI toolkits for trustees and engages with stakeholders on SRI best practice.†

* See, further, www.uksif.org.
† See, further, www.justpensions.org.

Box 12.1 About UKSIF

their investment managers to account as to how they are integrating social and environmental risks into everyday investment practice.

In this chapter, the inception, piloting and methodology for the development of the sector notes are described, followed by a discussion of the outcomes and an assessment of the benefits of the project to date.

Statement of the problem

Following an amendment to the 1995 Pensions Act (the SRI Pensions Disclosure Regulation which came into force in July 2000), the value of UK equities held under SRI mandates increased significantly (estimated at £80 billion of UK equity holdings in 2003 [Eurosif 2003: 17-26]). This expansion of the pensions market helped drive the expansion of a relatively new approach to SRI. Engagement with companies to identify non-traditional risks and to encourage improvement in the management of social and environmental issues, rather than screening out companies or sectors from the investment universe, is currently the dominant choice of pension fund trustees with proactive SRI policies. A small number of key players in the market now also offer 'engagement overlay' services to clients who do not want to move their assets from their existing fund manager.

During the summer of 2002, UKSIF started to receive anecdotal feedback from companies who were on the receiving end of this engagement activity that, while they appreciated this relatively new form of dialogue with investors, some of the topics being raised by SRI analysts did not appear to have obvious financial relevance, in contrast to the risk-based approach to assessing social and environmental issues more common in their boardrooms.

Responses to an UKSIF member consultation later that year indicated that SRI analysts were interested in collaborating on sector-specific research in order to narrow down the huge number of SEE issues relating to each company into a handful of risks on which they could focus. It was anticipated that this work would not only aid SRI practitioners in preparing for their engagement meetings, but would also help develop a more co-ordinated voice from the City regarding what issues investors were asking companies to prioritise in their corporate social responsibility (CSR) strategies.

The third driver for action was client demand. In conversations with pension fund trustees, UKSIF employees started to hear that many trustees who were interested in SRI were being put off raising the issue for discussion at meetings by investment consultants who considered that SEE issues were not material to business performance or share price. As a consequence, many pension funds, needing to comply with the Pensions Act amendment, simply wrote into their statement of investment principles (SIPs) that SEE issues were to be taken into account when material to the investment process, but then never followed this up with their investment manager. While trustees were convinced that some SEE issues were material to investment decisions, they also felt that they were not able to argue against consultants and advisors who were seen as being more experienced in investment management. These trustees indicated that some brief examples of how SEE issues interacted with the business model of key sectors would be helpful ammunition in raising the topic at their pension board meetings.

Chronology of the project

The sector note series was conceived in summer 2002, just as the proposals for the next phase of work by UKSIF's 2002–2005 institutional investment programme, Just Pensions, was being drawn up. Just Pensions' application to the UK Department for International Development (DFID) for funding was approved by Clare Short (the then Secretary of State for International Development) in autumn 2002. Clare Short expressed support for a sector-based research series that identified potentially material SEE risks and also highlighted issues of relevance to international development.

Once the funding was in place, UKSIF recruited an analyst to manage the project and carry out the research in collaboration with the organisation's fund manager members. A working group of fund managers (see Box 12.2) was assembled for the first note, which was to be run as a pilot on the pharmaceutical industry. Each fund manager agreed to contribute the time of the SRI analyst covering the pharmaceutical sector to support UKSIF in the research and preparation of the first note.

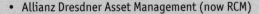

- Allianz Dresdner Asset Management (now RCM)
- Co-operative Insurance Society (CIS)
- Henderson Global Investors
- Insight Investment
- ISIS (now F&C)
- Jupiter Asset Management
- Morley Fund Management
- Schroders Investment Management
- Storebrand Investments
- Universities Superannuation Scheme (USS)

Box 12.2 Fund managers participating in the sector note pilot project

The methodology that was agreed during the pilot phase was, with a few amendments, used throughout the project (see Box 12.3). The aim was to understand sufficiently the financial drivers of companies within the pharmaceutical sector such that any SEE issue could be linked to the bottom line (and therefore considered a risk) or rejected from the list of issues under consideration. This test of materiality was an essential part of the process if the notes were to achieve their aim of meeting the expressed needs of pension fund trustees.

The research into the financial drivers of the pharmaceutical sector was undertaken through interviews with pharmaceutical equity analysts at UKSIF broker members HSBC, DrKW and West LB. Research into SEE issues surrounding the sector involved interviews with NGOs, SRI analysts and industry experts (including healthcare practitioners). A working group meeting was then held to shortlist those SEE 'issues' that could impact financial drivers and, thereby, become material to share price. Six themes were identified, with the materiality of each issue assessed over short (one year) and long (up to ten years) time-frames. The final stage in the preparation of the sector note involved working group members gaining input from their internal 'mainstream' pharmaceutical analysts to ensure the accuracy of the text as well as the integration of the themes into the investment process. Following the publication of the pharmaceutical sector note (see Appendix 2 on page 353) at the end of September 2003, the Trades Union Congress (TUC) distributed the note to its network of over 1,000 member nominated trustees (see further Chapter 25).

Having successfully completed the pilot note, the majority of the pilot working group was eager to continue the series (only one fund manager decided to withdraw from the working group). The general process followed is summarised in Box 12.3, and the complete list of sector notes that has been published is presented in Box 12.4.

1   **Research phase.** SRI analysts became involved in meetings with brokers to improve the working group's understanding of the financial drivers of the sector under consideration. The pool of brokers approached was extended beyond the three UKSIF members (HSBC, DrKW, West LB) to include those who did not have a track record in SRI research (including ABN Amro, Citigroup, CSFB, Goldman Sachs, Deutsche Bank, JP Morgan, Morgan Stanley, Lehman Brothers and UBS)

2   **Identifying SEE risks.** The working group increased their rigour in defining potentially material risks for inclusion in each of the notes through limiting the number of issues presented to those with a very strong link to a financial driver of performance

3   **Writing phase.** Liaison with leading (FTSE 100) companies in the sector was introduced to ensure accuracy in describing the detail of risks included and to increase company buy-in to the process

4   **Publication.** UKSIF's broker members hosted events at which leading companies in the sector were invited to respond to the note before an audience of SRI analysts. These events were often introduced by the equity analyst(s) who had been involved in the research phase of the note

5   **Dissemination.** The notes were distributed through the TUC's network of member-nominated trustees and through two annual mail-outs to purchased lists of employer-nominated trustees

6   **Composition of working group.** The working group was extended at the end of the first year of the programme to include a wider set of UKSIF fund management members and affiliates (Rathbone Greenbank Investments, Hermes Investment Management, SGAM, Cazenove Fund Management, Baillie Gifford & Co., Standard Life Investments, Gerrard). Each of these fund managers volunteered to be involved in up to two notes

Box 12.3   Process for developing UKSIF sector notes

1 Pharmaceuticals

2 Utilities

3 Media

4 Telecoms

5 Food producers and retailers

6 Tobacco

7 General retailers

8 Construction and building materials

9 Extractive industries (oil, gas and mining)

10 Beverages

11 Financial services

12 Questions to ask your fund manager

Box 12.4 Complete list of UKSIF sector notes

Discussion

The sector note programme could be considered a success simply on the grounds that it has achieved its basic objective—that of providing easily accessible information to pension fund trustees on the importance of holistic company analysis within the investment process. The sector notes make up a discrete pack which can be easily circulated around trustee networks due to the simple format and approachable layout of each note. However, the project has had a number of other important outcomes beyond the initial objective of trustee education. These include:

- **Improvement of research, through rooting SRI themes in financial drivers.** The explicit focus on 'materiality' at every stage of the process has helped to embed this concept into the research of a number of SRI analysts in their work for shareholder-value-driven clients. Having worked through a range of sectors, it was noticeable that the working group gained confidence in rapidly distinguishing between those issues that had a strong link to business value drivers, and those that they considered important solely from a moral perspective. At meetings with companies (timed to coincide with the publication of a note) analysts' questions have become both more numerous and more specifically related to business performance. This could help the integration of social and environmental risks into buy-side financial analysis as information from company meetings is more easily communicated back to financial analysts and portfolio managers in the language of shareholder value. The notes also help ensure that meetings between companies and SRI analysts speaking on behalf of shareholder-value-driven clients are focused on business risks, thereby tackling one of the key criticisms of the SRI community from corporates prior to this work being undertaken

- **Building relationships between SRI analysts and brokers.** Early on in the sector note series, Just Pensions realised that there was a significant amount of understanding of social and environmental issues within the sell-side research community that had not before been fully appreciated. Even the brokers themselves were not fully aware of their capacities in this area. When first approached by Just Pensions, a number of brokers were reluctant to be involved in the research as they believed they had nothing to offer. While it would be inaccurate to claim that most sell-side analysts are fully conversant with social and environmental risks, our interviews with this group often uncovered a deeper understanding than expected on the potential impact of some important SEE issues. While SRI analysts had been used to seeking advice from the two investment banks with specific SRI services (HSBC and DrKW), many had never before ventured into the world of 'mainstream sell-side analysis'. By encouraging SRI analysts to attend these meetings, preconceptions have been realigned and relationships forged between a number of buy-side SRI research teams and sell-side industry analysts which continue to feed SRI research in specific areas

- **Efficient use of collaborative resources.** To date there is no standard model for collaboration between the SRI teams of different fund managers. The approach used in this programme was for a full-time sector analyst to sit within the UKSIF office with access to resources from a broad cross-section of members. The time commitment from working group members was focused on key decision points in the process, with the opportunity for further involvement in the research stage on a more ad hoc basis. A challenging but achievable timetable for the two-year programme was published and carefully adhered to, thereby ensuring momentum through the project was sustained. The programme delivered each note on time and within budget, without members of the working group feeling overburdened by their involvement. This model of collaboration has enabled delivery of research of value to SRI analysts and has avoided the problem of high transaction costs experienced in other projects where considerable time was required from every participant

- **Prioritised sectors according to investment importance.** The sectors chosen for study were selected on the basis of their size in the FTSE 100, rather than their perceived impact on social and environmental issues. This led to the inclusion of sectors such as media and tobacco which had not previously been a focus of SRI analysis, despite their significant role in pension fund equity holdings. The sector note process was especially helpful for the media sector which had just formed an industry working group to look at these issues, and was interested in speaking with SRI analysts. The process of researching the sector for the note ran in parallel with the industry's own process, enabling the cross-fertilisation of ideas on this previously less studied sector. The prioritisation of sectors by significance in the FTSE also acknowledged that there are sectors that are not a major part of the UK investment universe (e.g. chemicals, automotive). UKSIF's sister organisation in Europe (Eurosif) has successfully fundraised to undertake similar work on these and other sectors that would be of interest to European investors

Critical analysis

It would be unrealistic to write about any project such as this without mentioning the drawbacks. While the overwhelming response to the work has been positive, I believe that there are a few key items which, had circumstances been different, could have significantly increased the impact of the work:

- **A mainstream organisation should have done this project.** If the overall aim is to integrate SEE risks into the everyday investment process across the City, an SRI organisation such as UKSIF may not have been the best base for the project. Had a mainstream investment organisation—such as the Investment Management Association, the UK Society for Investment Professionals, or even an investment bank's research department—undertaken this work, I believe it would have had a more profound impact on the mainstream investment community. A piece of work from an organisation perceived by some to be on the fringe of the investment community is always going to face an uphill battle to be universally respected and its advice accepted. While I do not believe that the contents of the notes would have been materially different had they been researched and published under the banner of an organisation at the heart of the City, their reception and distribution may well have been enhanced. However, UKSIF has a history of kick-starting projects that then move to other organisations, and a second iteration of the notes might well be managed from elsewhere

- **The necessary delay in dissemination made it difficult to improve the notes during the project.** While the format and process for researching and producing the notes was designed and tested during the pilot, and refined throughout the programme, the dissemination and associated evaluation processes were primarily conducted in 2005. Despite sending out over 1,500 copies of each note, the feedback from trustees has been limited to date. In addition, although *Professional Pensions* is the only mainstream industry journal through which the notes have been consistently communicated, seeking a media partner at the beginning of the project might have increased the depth of coverage and early feedback from trustees

- **The association of ethics with SRI hampered the risk-based approach.** The perception of many of those involved in the process (including sell-side analysts, companies and NGOs) was that SRI is based only on ethical criteria. This increased the hurdles that needed to be jumped; for example, meetings usually started with an explanation of what we did *not* want to talk about, to ensure that everyone understood the risk-based approach being taken. Interestingly, this was also an issue for some SRI analysts, as the government or NGO background of some analysts within the SRI teams meant that significant time needed to be spent on understanding the financial drivers of the various sectors before we could move on to relating the SEE issues to business value. One issue for the future of SRI is how these two, I believe, equally valid aspects of SRI can be differentiated and communicated more clearly both to the mainstream investment community and to pension fund clients

Conclusion

Are the notes being used? As noted above, this chapter has been written before the end of the project cycle so it is difficult to comment in full at this stage. It is also difficult to separate the impact of this work from other trustee-focused projects (such as the Just Pensions Trustee Toolkits, various fund manager training initiatives and the host of other organisations working to increase demand for SRI). However, since starting work on the sector notes project, I have noticed an increase in the demand for large fund management institutions to have 'someone' looking at SEE issues, feeding them into the investment process where material, and requiring that fund managers demonstrate that they are considering their ownership/voting responsibilities. However, the other outcomes of the project, such as increased rigour within the SRI research process, should help to ensure that this increase in demand for the assessment of social and environmental risks delivers meaningful benefits to the investment process.

Reference

Eurosif (European Sustainable and Responsible Investment Forum) (2003) *Socially Responsible Investment among European Institutional Investors* (Brussels: Eurosif).

Part III
Shareholder activism

13

Shareholder activism on social, ethical and environmental issues
AN INTRODUCTION

Rory Sullivan and Craig Mackenzie
Insight Investment, UK

Perhaps one of the most striking features of the past few years has been the manner in which institutional investors (fund managers and pension funds) have accepted a role in the governance of companies. This has been driven by the recognition of the potential financial benefits of activism, and by the growing consensus (at least among certain stakeholders and government) that institutional investors should play an active ownership role in the companies in which they are invested.

First of all, as discussed in Chapter 4, there is a general consensus that well-governed companies will tend to outperform over the longer term, and investors have indicated some willingness to pay a premium to invest in well-governed companies. This belief has been an important stimulus for shareholders to engage actively with companies to seek to improve their corporate governance and, to a lesser extent, corporate responsibility performance.[1] Hermes (one of the leading corporate governance activists in the UK) has argued (Melvin and Hirt 2005: 5-6) that there is:

---

1 It is important to recognise that this does not mean that all investors will engage with companies to encourage them to improve their performance. For example, as discussed in Chapter 2, short-term, relative-performance-focused investors in particular will probably have limited interest in shareholder activism.

convincing evidence for a link between active ownership (rather than the quality of corporate governance 'in itself') and improved performance of companies . . . That is, other things being equal, companies with active, interested and involved shareholders will tend to outperform those with passive shareholders.

Similar arguments have been made by other prominent shareholder activists (see, for example, the comments by Monks and Sykes [2002: 26-27] on Warren Buffett). This view on the importance of active ownership is supported by a number of academic and empirical studies. For example, in a seminal review of the activism conducted by the Californian Public Employees' Retirement System (CalPERS), one of the largest US pension schemes, Smith (1996: 251) concluded:

> Overall, the evidence indicates that shareholder activism is largely successful in changing governance structure and, when successful, results in a statistically significant increase in shareholder wealth.

Second, stakeholders—clients, beneficiaries, trade unions, non-governmental organisations (NGOs) (see, for example, Chapters 14, 21 and 25)—have actively encouraged investors to take a more activist approach to their investments. The motivations include both the potential financial benefits and the desire to address the specific concerns or values (e.g. labour or environmental concerns) of the organisation or the individual concerned. In the UK, as in many other countries, the government has played an important role in reinforcing these pressures by encouraging institutional investors to play an active ownership role. Perhaps the most important regulatory intervention in recent years has been the reform to the Pensions Act (see further the discussion in Chapter 3) which requires pension funds to state the extent, if at all, to which social, ethical and environmental (SEE) issues are taken into account in their investment processes. The government has also actively encouraged shareholders to be more activist. In March 2000, the Chancellor of the Exchequer commissioned Paul Myners to conduct a review of institutional investment in the UK. One of the areas considered by Myners was shareholder activism, where he recommended that trustees or their fund managers should engage with investee companies in situations where these companies are underperforming (Myners 2001). In December 2004, HM Treasury published a review of the implementation of the Myners principles (HM Treasury 2004). The review concluded that progress on activism had lagged behind other key areas. While the government has not, at the time of writing,[2] decided to legislate to require institutional investors to conduct activism, it has nevertheless clearly signalled its intention to legislate if institutional investors do not take a much more proactive approach to discharging their responsibilities as owners of companies.[3]

---

2 May 2005.
3 The government has indicated that it expects pension funds to voluntarily issue an independently compiled report on their implementation of the Myners Principles, including the principle relating to activism (HM Treasury 2004). This disclosure is expected to increase the pressure on pension funds to be more activist.

What is activism?

Shareholder activism occurs when shareholders use their unique power as the owners of companies to facilitate change. The starting point in many discussions around shareholder activism has been the importance of using the formal rights associated with owning shares, in particular the right to vote on resolutions at annual general meetings.[4] However, good ownership goes beyond simply exercising voting rights, important though this is (Butler and Lee 2004). For example, in his review of institutional investment in the UK, Paul Myners identified the need for good long-term shareholders to intervene at underperforming companies and engage with their boards to improve them and enhance investment returns (Myners 2001). These recommendations have been incorporated into documents such as the UK Combined Code on Corporate Governance 2003.[5] As an illustration of the range of strategies that could be considered under the general heading of 'activism', Box 13.1 presents the suggestions made by the International Corporate Governance Network (ICGN) on the actions that may be appropriate ways of giving effect to ownership responsibilities.

Activism and social and environmental issues

For the purposes of this book, it is important to be clear about the role shareholder activism plays with regard to environmental and ethical issues. To date, shareholder activism, in the main, has tended to focus on encouraging compliance with corporate governance codes such as (in the UK) the Combined Code on Corporate Governance. The Combined Code, in common with similar corporate governance codes in other countries,[6] focuses on creating structures and processes in the boardroom that align the interests of company executives with those of company shareholders and that establish an effective framework of internal control. The measures envisaged by the various codes include encouraging more independent directors, creating audit and remuneration committees with a majority of independent directors, separating chair and chief executive roles, ensuring that executive remuneration is based on long-term shareholder value creation, ending auditor conflicts and encouraging an emphasis on long-term risk management.

On the face of it, this kind of activity has little to do with the social and environmental impacts of companies. However, as discussed in Chapter 2, agency problems are a significant factor in causing harmful corporate social and environmental impacts, and in making it more difficult for governments to correct market failure effectively. Shareholder activism to correct agency problems by better aligning the interests of executives

---

4   See Mallin 2004: 70-71 for a brief overview of the variations between the UK and other countries in relation to voting rights and ownership structures.

5   www.fsa.gov.uk/pages/Doing/UKLA/pdf/lr_comcode2003.pdf

6   For a general overview of corporate governance codes in Europe, South-East Asia, South Africa, India and Brazil, see Mallin 2004: 123-206.

- Voting
- Supporting the company in respect of good governance
- Maintaining constructive communication with the board on governance policies and practices in general
- Incorporating corporate governance analysis in the investment process
- Stimulating independent buy-side research
- Expressing specific concerns to the board, either directly or at a shareholders' meeting
- Making a public statement
- Submitting proposals for the agenda of a shareholders' meeting
- Submitting one or more nominees for the board, as appropriate
- Convening a shareholders' meeting
- Teaming up with other investors and local investment associations, either in general or in specific cases
- Taking legal actions, such as legal investigations or class actions
- Outsourcing any or all of these powers to specialised agents: for example, where the institutional shareholder concludes that it does not have the necessary powers in-house
- Lobbying government bodies and other authoritative organisations
- Making appropriate statements regarding public policies affecting shareholder rights and corporate governance

Box 13.1 Activism approaches

Source: ICGN 2004

with shareholders and strengthening internal control can, therefore, help reduce social and environmental harm.

Can shareholder activism go further? In the US a number of institutional investors, particularly those associated with churches and religious orders, have been very effective at using proxy resolutions to encourage companies to respond to issues ranging from apartheid in South Africa, labour standards in developing-country supply chains and aspects of environmental management.[7] These investors have a substantial track record of success in using the shareholder resolution process to encourage change in companies. In Europe, this kind of religious, shareholder resolution-based activism has not been popular, due, perhaps, to the smaller scale of religious assets and the significantly greater obstacles in filing shareholder resolutions (see further the discussion in Chapter 3). However, as the following chapters indicate, since the late 1990s a number

---

7   Much of this work has been led by the Interfaith Center on Corporate Responsibility; see www. iccr.org.

of mainstream institutional investors have undertaken a significant body of share-holder activism on corporate social and environmental impacts. Like the more 'traditional' activism described above, some of this activism is oriented towards encouraging companies to adhere to codes of practice on SEE issues. While this is a relatively new activity for many investors, activism to encourage boards to set and enforce policies relating to standards of ethical behaviour and to ensure the effective management of SEE risks is clearly envisaged by traditional corporate governance codes. For example, Section A.1 of the Combined Code states: 'The board should set the company's values and standards and ensure that its obligations to its shareholders and others are understood and met.' Similarly, the Turnbull recommendations, which have now been incorporated into the Combined Code, require boards to establish effective systems of risk management relating to all the company's risks including, where relevant, those related to 'legal, health, safety and environmental, reputation, and business probity issues' (ICAEW 1999: 13). Harmful social and environmental impacts attract a range of government and social penalties for companies and, as a result, can be substantial business risks. It is also widely accepted by many business leaders that responsible corporate behaviour is essential in establishing strong relationships with customers, employees and other stakeholders, and in maintaining a strong brand and a good reputation. A number of investors, led by the influential Association of British Insurers (ABI), have sought to monitor corporate performance in this area and encourage change (ABI 2001). There have also been efforts to go beyond governance codes to draw on standards set by wider codes on corporate responsibility, such as the OECD Guidelines for Multinational Enterprises (Mackenzie 2002), but so far activism based on such principles has received limited support from investors.

Approaches to activism

In situations where investors decide to intervene with companies, there is a range of strategies that can be used. The specific strategies depend on factors such as the specific issue in question, the relationship between the investor and the company, the support from other investors and the relationship between the issue and financial performance. The strategies generally used by large institutional investors are:

- Dialogue (or engagement)
- The use of voting and other formal rights
- Collaboration with other investors
- Benchmarking
- Media communications
- The ability to influence share price through the buying and selling of shares

While these are reasonably well tested in the corporate governance arena, they remain somewhat less explored in the context of corporate responsibility issues.

First of all, companies will usually arrange to meet with their largest institutional investors (typically the top 30 shareholders plus the top 10 broker analysts) on a one-to-one basis in the course of a year. The issues that are typically discussed at these meetings include the firm's strategy, how the firm plans to meet its objectives, performance against objectives, the quality of the management and general corporate governance issues. These meetings are often complemented by meetings between investors and specialists within companies (e.g. corporate responsibility managers) to discuss specific issues of corporate responsibility and corporate governance. These various meetings allow investors to explain their views on SEE issues, and to assess how well these issues are being managed by the company. That is, these discussions can provide an indication of the manner in which company management is addressing the business risks and opportunities posed by SEE issues.

Second, institutional investors can use the formal rights granted to them as owners of companies, namely: to attend annual general meetings to ask questions; to propose shareholder resolutions; to exercising voting rights (e.g. on the adoption of the report and accounts or the re-election of directors); and to call an extraordinary general meeting (Green 2001: 8-11). While there has been a general increase in the level of votes against management and there have been some very high-profile voting controversies (e.g. the remuneration in 2002 of Jean-Pierre Garnier, Chief Executive of Glaxo-SmithKline [GSK]), there is a general consensus among large institutional investors that voting is just part of the process by which shareholders encourage higher standards of corporate performance and, thereby, enhance long-term sustainable shareholder value. Voting is generally seen as being most effective in the context of a range of other activities, including monitoring the performance of individual companies with regard to relevant corporate responsibility and corporate governance issues, discussions with board directors and other company executives, research on specific corporate governance and SEE issues in order to achieve greater understanding of the current shape and future direction of policy and practice, and working with other institutional investors and interested parties to pursue specific goals.

Third, investors collaborate on corporate responsibility issues, through formal coalitions such as the Carbon Disclosure Project, the Institutional Shareholders' Committee, the Pharmaceutical Shareowners Group, the Investors' Statement on the Extractive Industries Transparency Initiative and the Institutional Investors' Group on Climate Change,[8] as well as more informal arrangements where small groups of investors work together on specific issues. Investors also collaborate with trade bodies (e.g. the ABI, the UK Social Investment Forum) and, on occasion, with other stakeholders (e.g. environmental NGOs). Collaborative approaches allow investors to present a consistent and unified voice on corporate responsibility issues (thereby ensuring that companies are not facing competing and contradictory priorities from different investors) while also broadening the number of investors that work on a specific issue.

Fourth, investors have started to use benchmarks to compare company performance on different SEE issues. Recent examples have included studies on biodiversity management in the extractives industry and the sustainability performance of housebuilders (see Chapter 16). Investors have used the results of these benchmarking exercises to encourage companies to improve their performance in these areas. In addition,

---

8   A useful overview is provided in Global Compact Finance Sector Initiative 2004.

by making the results public, investors have allowed the media, NGOs and other investors to exert pressure on companies to improve performance. Other parties (e.g. NGOs) have also developed and published their own benchmarks, and have encouraged investors to engage with companies on the basis of these benchmarks (see, for example, Save the Children UK 2005).

More generally, investors also use the media to communicate their views on specific corporate responsibility issues. Articles in newspapers such as the *Financial Times* and magazines such as *The Economist* allow investors to communicate their views on corporate responsibility issues to company directors (executive and non-executive) and their advisors. Communicating through the media can be a very efficient means of communicating with these parties, as it is impossible for investors to meet all of these individuals on a face-to-face basis.

Finally, investors directly influence the share price or the cost of capital for companies. Depressed share prices or higher costs of capital are often an indication of lack of investor confidence in company management. Depressed share prices also increase the likelihood that the company will be taken over. The threat of takeover is widely recognised as having an important role to play in focusing management attention on shareholder value and has frequently encouraged management change and improved performance.

These strategies (which are used by large institutional investors) differ somewhat from the strategies that are used by smaller shareholders who tend to have less access and less direct influence over companies. For these investors, other approaches may play a more important part. These may include: establishing coalitions of like-minded parties to pursue specific issues with companies; more overtly negative voting strategies; critical public comment; and encouraging their fund managers to take action on their behalf. That is, through processes of targeted campaigning and collaboration, it is possible for smaller investors to exert influence that may be disproportionate to their actual holdings.

Case studies

While the preceding discussion has described the most widely used activism strategies, there has, as yet, been limited systematic examination of the manner in which activism is conducted on SEE issues. Five case studies are presented here to illustrate how activism on corporate responsibility issues can be implemented, the strategies that can be used, the outcomes achieved and the barriers to implementation. First, in Chapter 14, Peter Casson and David Russell describe how one of the UK's largest pension funds (the Universities Superannuation Scheme) has implemented activism through developing in-house capacity and through proactively engaging with other institutional investors in collaborative activism, engagement and research projects. Chapters 15 and 16 describe the approach adopted by two of the most activist UK fund managers (Henderson and Insight). Both chapters describe the philosophy and process underlying activism, the systems and resources used to implement activism and the outcomes achieved. Chapter 17, by Will Oulton, describes the manner in which the FTSE4Good

Index has been used to encourage performance improvements, both directly through FTSE4Good's own engagement activities and through stimulating investment managers to engage with companies that do not meet the FTSE4Good criteria. Finally, Steve Waygood (Chapter 18) describes perhaps the most important example of investor activism to date: namely, the work done by investors to improve access to HIV/AIDS antiretroviral medicines in Africa.

References

ABI (Association of British Insurers) (2001) *Disclosure Guidelines on Socially Responsible Investment* (London: ABI).

Butler, P., and P. Lee (2004) 'The Duties of Share Ownership', in *Global Corporate Governance Guide 2004* (London: Global White Page): 10-14.

Global Compact Finance Sector Initiative (2004) *Who Cares Wins: Connecting Financial Markets in a Changing World* (New York: The Global Compact).

Green, D. (2001) *Socially Responsible Investment and International Development: A Guide for Trustees and Fund Managers* (London: Just Pensions).

HM Treasury (2004) *Myners Principles for Institutional Investment Decision-making: Review of Progress* (London: HMSO).

ICAEW (Institute of Chartered Accountants in England and Wales) (1999) *Internal Control: Guidance for Directors on the Combined Code* (London: ICAEW; also known as *The Turnbull Report*).

ICGN (International Corporate Governance Network) (2003) *International Corporate Governance Network Statement on Institutional Shareholder Responsibilities* (London: ICGN).

Mackenzie, C. (2002) *Defining Global Business Principles* (London: Insight Investment).

Mallin, C. (2004) *Corporate Governance* (Oxford, UK: Oxford University Press).

Melvin, C., and H. Hirt (2005) *Corporate Governance and Performance: A Brief Review and Assessment of the Evidence for a Link between Corporate Governance and Performance* (London: Hermes Pensions Management Ltd).

Monks, R., and A. Sykes (2002) *Capitalism without owners will fail: A Policy-maker's Guide to Reform* (London and New York: Centre for the Study of Financial Innovation).

Myners, P. (2001) *Institutional Investment in the United Kingdom: A Review* (London: HM Treasury).

Save the Children UK (2005) *Beyond the Rhetoric. Measuring Revenue Transparency: Company Performance in the Oil and Gas Industries* (London: Save the Children UK).

Smith, M. (1996) 'Shareholder Activism by Institutional Investors: Evidence from CalPERS', *Journal of Finance* 51: 227-52.

14

Universities Superannuation Scheme
IMPLEMENTING RESPONSIBLE INVESTMENT

Peter Casson

University of Southampton, UK

David Russell

USS, UK

The Universities Superannuation Scheme (USS), established collectively by UK universities through a trust deed at the end of 1974, came into operation in April 1975. It is the main pension scheme for academic and academically related staff in the UK. The fund has total assets of approximately £25 billion, making it the second-largest pension scheme in the UK. The scheme is an immature fund in the sense that receipts in respect of active members and employers exceed payments to pensioners and other beneficiaries, a situation that is likely to continue into the next decade. The scheme's investment objective as stated in its statement of investment principles (SIP) is: 'to maximise the long-term investment return on the assets having regard to the liabilities of the scheme and the desirability of maintaining stable contribution rates'. In meeting this objective, USS has an investment policy of investing approximately 40% of its assets in UK equities (with both active and passive mandates), 40% in overseas equities, and the remainder in property and fixed-interest securities.[1] This reflects USS's belief that investment in equities will provide superior returns to other asset classes over the longer term. The assets themselves are managed by both internal and external fund managers.

---

1 More detail is available in USS's annual report and accounts; see www.usshq.co.uk/repacc2004/www.

The trustee of USS, USS Ltd, has a fiduciary duty to manage the scheme's investment assets for the benefit of members. Because of its size and investment policies, USS holds a diversified portfolio of assets. It therefore has many of the characteristics of what Hawley and Williams refer to as a 'universal owner' (2000a, 2000b, 2002a, 2002b; see further Chapter 19): that is, a fiduciary institution that holds, for the long term, a diversified portfolio of shares representing a broad cross-section of the economy. As a universal owner, USS is concerned both with the individual companies in which it invests and with the impact of investee companies on the economy as a whole. USS and its fund managers monitor and engage with those companies in which USS invests and vote on company resolutions. In addition, USS is engaged in responsible investment with a view to reducing the risk to long-term returns on its investment portfolio and to safeguarding the quality of retirement life of its members.

This chapter looks at USS as a universal owner. It begins by examining the concept of universal ownership and its implications for responsible investment before presenting an overview of USS and its investment strategy. Three projects are then considered in greater detail:

- USS's activities with the pharmaceutical sector and the public health crisis in developing countries

- USS's activities on climate change, in particular the Institutional Investors Group on Climate Change (IIGCC)

- The Enhanced Analytics Initiative (EAI)

Universal owners and responsible investment

Before examining the approach of USS to its engagement activities, it is useful to consider the work of Hawley and Williams on 'fiduciary capitalism' and the universal owner. As well as providing a framework for considering the activities of USS, there are indications that USS has itself been influenced by their ideas. Interestingly, Hawley and Williams (see further Chapter 19) use USS's work on climate change as an important example of the involvement of institutional shareholders in policy initiatives.

The term 'fiduciary capitalism' is used to describe the third stage of corporate capitalism in which the ownership of shares is concentrated in the hands of fiduciary institutions such as pension funds and mutual funds.[2] The term itself reflects the obligations of financial institutions to manage the funds for the benefit of investors or beneficiaries. Hawley and Williams argue that fiduciary capitalism represents more than a simple change in the pattern in the way in which shares are held. Not only are institutional shareholders seen as having different incentives and behaviour patterns to those of individual investors, but many institutional shareholders are also large and hold diversified portfolios that effectively represent a broad cross-section of the econ-

---

2 Hawley and Williams see the first phase of corporate capitalism as being one where the firms' founders hold significant stakes, and the second as being characterised by dispersed ownership and managerial control.

omy. They also often hold investments for the long term. The return on the investment for this type of fund is therefore dependent on the performance of the economy as well as on the performance of each individual company in the portfolio. These large institutional shareholders with diversified portfolios are referred to as universal owners. Hawley and Williams (2002a) suggest that this has two consequences:

- Universal owners should assess the impact of those companies in which they invest on the economy as a whole because, as owners, they capture the benefit of any positive externalities and are harmed by companies' negative externalities

- Universal owners 'come to occupy a quasi-public position as having an economic interest in the long-term health and well-being of society as a whole. The interests of universal owners extend beyond macroeconomic policy issues to include regulatory concerns and the provision of public goods such as health care and education.'

The universal investor concept is one in which the investor considers the interactions between various elements of its portfolio, particularly the negative and positive externalities generated by portfolio companies. This is considered appropriate for universal owners who should, in addition to normal monitoring and engagement with portfolio companies, have an interest in the policies and programmes that promote long-term superior economic performance. Universal owners also have an interest in encouraging companies to manage and minimise negative externalities and therefore have the incentive to be responsible investors.

Hawley and Williams (2002b: 168-69) write that:

> universal monitoring and the fiduciary nature of universal owners' perspectives suggests that they will continue to use a different language, and typically a different yet complementary approach to the SRI perspective. Universal owners will view many of these issues not as matters of ethics or morality as such, but in terms of sustainability and long-term portfolio-wide economic effects and financial performance.

They go on to note that large institutional shareholders usually cannot use screening and filtering but instead must engage, often in coalition with other institutions.

Unlike traditional socially responsible investors, who screen and thereby filter companies, sectors or issues on a case-by-case basis, universal owners hold shares in diversified portfolios which include shares in those companies or sectors that are often excluded by traditional socially responsible investors. Instead of screening and filtering, universal owners may engage with offending companies (or sectors) with a view to influencing their activities. Although, collectively, institutional shareholders hold a large proportion of the shares of listed companies, the holdings of each institution are usually small. Therefore, in order for universal owners to be effective in intervening, it is necessary to form coalitions of institutional shareholders. Universal owners are interested in both the performance of the companies in their investment portfolios, and in wider issues that affect long-term performance of the economy. Their engagement is, as a consequence, likely to be both at the level of the individual company and sector, while on broader social and environmental levels it is also likely to involve other institutional investors.

The work on universal investors is mirrored in a concept developed by Amalric (2004) who views pension funds as 'civic investors'. He identifies the following three reasons why they should be interested in extra-financial issues such as sustainability and the externalisation of costs:

- Pension funds' ability to meet their future liabilities is linked to the trajectory of societal change

- Pension funds influence that trajectory through their investment decisions

- Pension funds should aim to influence the economy and to promote those trajectories of societal change that will maximise their expected ability to meet their liabilities

In addressing these issues, Amalric suggests that pension funds should adopt the following strategies:

- Monitor how societal changes and emerging societal problems put their investments at risk

- Facilitate and promote state intervention by raising members' awareness about the issue at hand, engaging in political lobbying, and monitoring corporations' political influence and lobbying work

- Support the emergence of new forms of governance by raising corporate alertness and responsiveness to stakeholder expectations and encouraging the intensification of stakeholder engagement

USS, in the development and implementation of its responsible investment strategies, has incorporated these broader responsibilities in terms of generating the returns required to honour the fund's liabilities. USS is not unique in finding these concepts useful. For example, Hermes (the fund manager owned by the British Telecom Pension Scheme) specifically states as one of its ten principles that: 'Companies should support voluntary and statutory measures which minimise the externalisation of costs to the detriment of society at large.'[3] Commenting that investors are widely diversified, Hermes acknowledges that it makes little sense for it to support activity by one company that is damaging to overall economic activity, noting that:

> The ultimate beneficiaries of most investment activity include the greater part of the adult population who depend on private pensions and life insurance. It makes little sense for pension funds to support commercial activity which creates an equal or greater cost to society by robbing Peter to pay Paul.

3   Hermes Principle 10; see www.hermes.co.uk/pdf/corporate_governance/Hermes_Principles.pdf.

USS as a universal owner

The USS SIP sets out the scheme's policies on responsible investing. Generally, USS Ltd aims to be: 'an active and responsible long-term shareholder of companies and markets in which it invests'. It sees a policy that encourages responsible corporate behaviour as also one that protects and enhances the value of the fund's investments. More specifically, USS Ltd requires:

> its fund managers to pay appropriate regard to relevant corporate governance, social, ethical and environmental considerations in the selection, retention and realisation of all fund investments. The management committee expects this to be done in a manner which is consistent with the [USS Ltd's] investment objectives and legal duties.

Following from this, USS's fund managers (both internal and external[4]) are required to use their influence to promote good practice both in the companies in which they invest and the markets in which they are significantly exposed.

In addition to direct engagement by its fund managers, USS has a responsible investment strategy and a team of three responsible investment specialists who support both the internal fund managers and implement the responsible investment strategy. Consistent with being a universal owner, the responsible investment strategy is based on engagement rather than screening. The overall strategy is summarised as follows:[5]

> Our strategy is based on active engagement with the companies whose shares we hold. This involves dialogue about acceptable standards of corporate governance, environmental, ethical, and social performance. This dialogue is professionally planned and when needed, robust. Engagement also involves work to shape the context in which company-specific discussions take place . . . Apart from the moral issues involved, proper assessment of the reputational impact of the company's performance on these wider fronts is increasingly material to investment considerations.

An outline of the approach taken by USS Ltd is provided in its SIP. The SIP first includes a requirement for the management committee to review and, where appropriate, update the company's policies on corporate governance, social, ethical and environmental (now referred to as extra-financial issues [EFIs]) to ensure that they are consistent with good institutional investor practice. Second, USS's fund managers are expected to monitor the policies and practices of the companies in which they invest, or may possibly invest, on material corporate EFI issues. Third, USS Ltd expects its fund managers (internal and external) to collaborate (where this is likely to be effective) with other institutional investors to encourage the managers of companies to address these issues appropriately. Finally, as a part of the engagement strategy with companies, USS Ltd indicates that it will use its voting rights 'in a prioritised, value-adding and informed manner'.

---

4 USS utilises both internal and external fund managers. As at the fund's last annual report (April 2004), approximately 58% (50% securities, 8.4% property) was managed internally by USS Ltd's London Investment Office, with the remaining 42% divided between five external fund managers.

5 'USS and Socially Responsible and Sustainable Investment: An Overview'; see www.usshq.co.uk/special_interest_groups_index.php?name=SPECIAL_INTEREST_GROUPS.

Like other institutional investors, USS's internal managers routinely analyse information concerning those companies in which USS invests, and have meetings with company managers. Thus, USS monitors and engages with companies in much the same way as other institutional investors (as described by Stapledon [1996]). This engagement can, for convenience, be divided into routine and extraordinary actions. Routine actions include the analysis of information concerning companies and meetings, and dialogue with their managers. It also includes voting on resolutions presented at companies' annual general meetings. The shares held in both internally and externally managed funds are voted in accordance with the wishes of USS. USS uses Manifest, a voting proxy specialist, to manage its voting of shares in UK companies. USS has developed a voting template which Manifest uses for voting; resolutions that are in line with USS's voting policies are supported and others are referred to USS for consideration. A resolution that is inconsistent with the voting policies may nevertheless receive support. Not only does the use of the Manifest service minimise the operational problems associated with voting, it also serves to screen resolutions and frees time to focus on contentious issues.

In addition to the routine monitoring of, and engagement with, companies, USS may take extraordinary actions. These are usually triggered by share price performance, with either a company performing poorly relative to the sector or a sector performing poorly relative to the market. Actions can also be triggered by perceived poor governance or by poor management of other extra-financial issues. In such situations, attempts are first made to understand the reason for the poor performance, either through discussions with the fund manager(s) and/or broker, and/or through meetings with the company.

In the late 1990s, USS faced direct questions as to how it responded to the responsible investment challenge. Ethics for USS[6] was founded in 1997 by some members of the fund along with People and Planet, a national student campaigning group. Ethics for USS challenged the fund to adopt a socially responsible investment (SRI) policy, particularly one that screened out certain sectors or companies. Based on formal legal advice, USS's trustee board decided that it was not appropriate for a fund of the type and scale of USS to screen out investments on non-financial grounds, instead adopting the engagement approach as a more appropriate response to addressing these issues.

While Ethics for USS was undoubtedly an important influence, other drivers included the personal interest of particular directors and impending disclosure requirements for pension funds. Since then, the fund has taken a proactive role in interpreting what SRI or responsible investment means for a pension fund based on the professional advice of the in-house team and the commitment of its governance bodies to be at or near best practice standards for the sector.

USS's programme of responsible investment activities includes work with other institutional shareholders to ensure companies operating in Myanmar (Burma) are fully aware of the risks and comply with best practice, engagement with oil and gas companies on a variety of social and environmental issues, and the development of corporate governance policies for UK and US companies. It also includes work on pharmaceutical companies and the public health crisis in emerging markets, and on climate change. Both these projects are considered in detail below. In addition, USS focuses on areas

6   www.fairpensions.org.uk/act_now/uss.htm

where market failures could contribute to potential risk to the fund's performance: an example of such a project, the EAI, is also provided below.

Pharmaceutical companies and the public health crisis in emerging markets

One of the first sectors to be examined by USS following the appointment of its responsible investment team in 2000 was the pharmaceutical sector. This coincided with the launch by Oxfam in 2001 of a campaign focusing on increasing the access of poor people, primarily those in poor countries, to drugs and medicines. In that year, ISIS Asset Management (now F&C) co-ordinated a meeting between about ten institutional investors (including USS) and GlaxoSmithKline (GSK), the UK-based pharmaceutical company, a meeting also attended by Oxfam. These discussions and USS's concerns regarding the sector led, in 2002, to the fund establishing a project on the pharmaceutical sector. The objective of the project was:

> To encourage the [pharmaceutical] sector to address the risks associated with public health crisis in poor countries/emerging markets and to raise awareness among the sector's investors/analysts of the importance of this debate about affordable access.

USS's position was that the public health crisis in poor countries poses a threat to the business model of the pharmaceutical sector, which relies on patents to protect investments in risky R&D projects, and so to the long-term performance of companies in the sector (see also Chapter 18 by Steve Waygood). This model could be threatened if governments in developing economies, for example, weakened the protection provided by patents in emerging markets or imposed caps on the price of pharmaceutical products.

The project, which initially involved USS and ISIS Asset Management (later extended to include other institutional investors with the formation of the Pharmaceutical Shareowners Group[7]), had a number of strands. A key element was the development of a framework of good practice for pharmaceutical companies in relation to public health issues in poor countries and emerging markets. This focused on encouraging companies to disclose in their annual reports an assessment of the risks or opportunities arising from the public health crisis, and of the effectiveness of their systems for managing these. It is noted that investors 'particularly want to understand the rationale for companies adopting specific policies or approaches (e.g. differential pricing and donations versus voluntary licensing)'.[8] The framework also provides examples of good practice in areas such as pricing and patents, public–private partnerships and R&D.

---

7   www.pharmashareownersgroup.org
8   See the press release 'Investor Statement on Pharmaceutical Companies and the Public Health Crisis in Emerging Markets', 24 March 2003, www.pharmashareownersgroup.org and an updated statement at www.usshq.co.uk/downloads/pdf/all_sections/ri/PSG%20Press%20Release%2020 Sept04.pdf.

The importance of the framework is that it provides guidance on what information should be included in annual reports, thereby reducing the costs for institutional investors in collecting information and encouraging companies to adopt best practices. The Pharmaceutical Shareowners Group made the framework available to other investors and analysts, and encouraged its wider use. The group also had a programme of engagement with the large pharmaceutical companies. This included a letter, written in March 2003, to 20 top pharmaceuticals companies, including GSK, AstraZeneca and Novartis, in which the group outlined the steps it believed are required to be taken in order to reduce reputational risk to the industry. USS's work on the sector has also evolved and the fund is now part of Pharmafutures,[9] a collaboration between institutional investors and pharmaceutical companies to examine just how the sector's business model should develop.

A number of significant elements can be identified from the pharmaceutical project about the way in which USS engages as a universal investor:

- Rather than selling shares on the grounds of corporate responsibility failures, USS attempts to change policies and strategies at sector and company levels

- Intervention is justified by USS on the basis of the long-term financial and operating performance of companies rather than on social/ethical grounds

- USS develops relationships with other institutional investors to develop a shared approach

- USS engages with companies as part of an alliance of institutional investors rather than on its own

- USS and its partners develop a framework that enables both effective monitoring and encourages good practice

Some of these elements emerge again in USS's work on climate change, described below.

Climate change

Climate change is an issue of global significance; the scientific consensus[10] is that human-made emissions of CO_2 and other greenhouse gases (GHGs) are contributing to changes in the atmosphere that will cause significant changes in global temperatures. While there are uncertainties around the specific impacts, the predicted changes (e.g. rising sea levels, flooding, droughts) pose a threat to social and political stability and to businesses. Action by governments and business (for example, programmes to reduce carbon emissions) may contain the risks associated with climate change. As changes in the climate could have major effects on the quality of life and on the economy, issues

9   See www.pharmafutures.org and Chapter 26.
10 See the Intergovernmental Panel on Climate Change: www.ipcc.ch.

related to climate change are legitimate concerns of pension fund trustees. USS has consequently included climate change on its list of responsible investment projects.

USS's involvement in climate change issues stems from a discussion paper it commissioned on the risks to institutional investors associated with changes in the climate in 2001 (Mansley and Dlugolecki 2001). This report analysed the risks and responses to climate change and its impact on institutional investors, identifying a set of ten action points to help institutional investors better manage the risks and opportunities associated with climate change. One of the action points was to involve other institutional investors to develop joint action and USS has subsequently played a important role in the establishment and running of the Institutional Investors Group on Climate Change (IIGCC).[11] Much of USS's activity on climate change has been directed through this group. Before examining the approach to climate change issues taken by the IIGCC, it is useful to examine in more detail the rationale for USS's involvement in this area.

USS identifies two reasons for addressing climate change as an issue. The first stems from USS's perception of itself as universal owner; the second is to meet the needs of its members and beneficiaries (see, for example, the views expressed by Sir Graeme Davies, Chair of USS Ltd, in Davies 2003). The first justification for pension fund involvement in climate change issues is reflected in the following extract from the USS discussion paper (Mansley and Dlugolecki 2001: 5):

> Climate change is a major emerging risk management challenge for institutional investors. Institutional investors, and pension funds in particular, aim to provide pensions and other benefits through long-term investment. They can also be seen as 'universal investors' in that, due to their size, they commonly invest across the whole economy. If climate change threatens economic development, and especially if there are many or significant impacts, it will also therefore be likely to undermine the ability of pension funds and other institutional investors to fulfil their aims, so it is in their interests to see that risks associated with climate change are minimised. While this responsibility is widely shared, institutional investors are uniquely suited to take particular actions.

USS therefore sees climate change as a potential threat to the increase in value of its assets, noting in particular the detrimental effects that arise when a company (or sector) externalises its climate change management costs to other companies or to society as a whole.

The other reason for USS's involvement in climate change issues has to do with the real needs of its members. USS recognises that 'if the issue of climate change is not addressed, there will be significant changes in the environment which are likely to be detrimental to the quality of life of our members when they come to retire' (Davies 2003: 3). As a pension fund, USS believes that it has a legitimate interest in the quality of members' lives when they retire, and so considers it appropriate to invest and engage in activities that help to ensure a safe and stable future.

Evidence to support this view is provided in research by Bender and Javin (2005) which has indicated that financial well-being is not the only factor that influences overall retiree well-being: while economic well-being, measured by income and wealth plays a role, so too do other factors.

---

11   Details of the activities of the IIGCC can be found at www.iigcc.org.

USS was instrumental in establishing the IIGCC, which provides a 'forum for collaboration between pension funds and other institutional investors on issues related to climate change'. The IIGCC aims to:

- Promote a better understanding of the implications of climate change among its members and other institutional investors

- Encourage companies and markets in which its members invest to address any material risks and opportunities to their businesses associated with climate change

At the end of 2004, there were 26 members of the IIGCC, representing in excess of £1 trillion in assets under management. The activities of the IIGCC, which are focused through four 'workstreams', are co-ordinated by a steering group, which was chaired by an officer of USS during 2003. The four workstreams are:

- Communications and organisational development

- Engagement with companies and investors

- Property

- Public policy

The communications and organisational development workstream, whose co-ordinator is also a USS officer, is concerned mainly with 'promoting the growth and development of IIGCC and increasing IIGCC's profile, reach and effectiveness'. At the end of 2003, the IIGCC organised a conference, Climate Change and Institutional Investors: Managing the Risks and Profiting from the Shift to a Lower Carbon Economy, in order to raise the profile of the implications of climate change for the investment community and to develop links with policy-makers. The keynote speakers at the conference were Margaret Beckett, Secretary of State at the Department for the Environment, Food and Rural Affairs (Defra), and Lord Browne, chief executive of BP.

Another significant project undertaken by this workstream has been the development of materials to train pension fund trustees on the investment implications of climate change.[12] Produced by Mercer Investment Consulting,[13] the pension fund consultants, with funding and input from the Carbon Trust[14] and the IIGCC, these materials outline why climate change is an issue for trustees and what they can do about it. Significantly, the material clearly identifies climate change as a fiduciary risk.

The aim of the engagement workstream is to increase understanding and awareness of the risks posed, and the opportunities provided, to institutional shareholders by climate change. The workstream has engaged with companies on a sector basis and has, to date, focused its activities on aviation, power generation and construction materials. Reports on these sectors, highlighting the problems of climate change, have been produced for the IIGCC by Schroder Investment Management, BNP Paribas Asset Management and F&C respectively. In addition, the workstream has written to a number of sell-

---

12   These materials are freely available from the websites of the organisations involved (see footnotes 13 and 14 below).

13   www.merceric.com

14   www.thecarbontrust.co.uk/carbontrust

side brokers to indicate the need for them to incorporate the possible effects of climate change in their assessments of company prospects.

The third workstream, on property, aims to ensure that climate change considerations are included in the management of property investment portfolios. The final workstream, concerned with public policy, has produced a position statement that identifies the need for institutional investors to ensure that the long-term needs of institutional shareholders are recognised by public policy-makers. As noted on the IIGCC website:

> Climate change is a product of market failure: the absence of appropriate incentives has led to individuals and companies externalising the costs associated with greenhouse gas emissions, generating significant risks to both the global environment and the global economy. As a result, public policy innovation is essential not only to minimise the damage caused by climate change, but also to maximise the opportunities from the transition to a low carbon economy. Without credible public policy frameworks, companies and their investors will be handicapped in planning how they respond to the climate change challenge. Moreover, a policy framework that fails to take account of the strategic nature of climate change could result in discontinuous change in the future, a sub-optimal outcome for long-term institutional investors.

The workstream has entered into dialogue with policy-makers and opinion-formers to enable investors and policy-makers to come to a better understanding of the relationships between climate change and finance.

Over 2005, the IIGCC itself has undergone significant structural changes that have strengthened the structures and outputs of the Group. The IIGCC has formed a strategic partnership by becoming a semi-autonomous programme within The Climate Group (TCG),[15] an organisation specialising in addressing climate change with companies and policy-makers. TCG has strong links to both major companies and policy-makers, thus providing an ideal partner for the IIGCC. The IIGCC retains its own Steering Committee and, as part of this restructuring, has employed a programme director to provide a central leadership role.

The approach taken by USS to climate change is clearly located within the framework of the universal investor concept. Climate change affects both the long-term returns on the scheme's investment portfolio, and also has an impact on the quality of life of scheme members. The strategy adopted by USS has been to collaborate with other institutional investors, and to play a major role in the IIGCC. The IIGCC has promoted awareness of issues associated with climate change, especially as they affect institutional shareholders, and has acted to promote policy changes both within companies and sectors and at a public policy level.

Enhanced Analytics Initiative

A simplistic view of the relationship between analysts and fund managers can be expressed as: companies talk to analysts, analysts provide research to fund managers and fund managers invest. Unfortunately, while there is increasing evidence that extra-financial and intangible issues can affect the value and performance of companies, this is often not captured in the research by the analysts. As a consequence, it is excluded from the investment process, potentially putting investors' money at risk. This should be of particular concern to long-term investors, such as pension funds like USS, as many of these extra-financial and intangible issues are likely to impact corporate performance over the medium to long term. To date, however, brokers and other research providers have had little incentive to focus on these issues given that their business model, and that of the vast majority of investors, is driven by benchmarks and mandates to focus on short-term financial issues.

With this in mind, in November 2004, USS and a group of other institutional investors established the EAI[16] to encourage sell-side and other investment analysts to better fulfil the needs of long-term investors and their clients/members. The basis of EAI is a commitment or research by members to allocate a minimum of 5% of their respective brokerage commission budget to sell-side or other researchers who are effective at analysing material extra-financial issues and intangibles. Based on the broker spend of the group in 2004, the potential amount to be allocated under EAI in 2005 is in the order of €8 million. The strength of the initiative is that it provides investment research providers with a commercial incentive to produce innovative and differentiated research that captures the value of intangibles or corporate performance on extra-financial issues and intangibles.

Conclusion

USS is an interesting case study on how the debate about responsible investment has evolved. At one stage, the debate was one between those members who wanted negative screening and trustees who, on the basis of detailed legal advice and a disinclination to adopt such an approach, decided not to take that route. A few years later, USS and its members have found some common ground. Early market research would seem to suggest that USS is doing things that satisfy the needs of the majority of its members (see Box 14.1). This approach, insofar as it is possible to predict anything in the investment world, should better protect the long-term financial position of the fund.

In a context where active shareholding has taken an increasingly important place in investment and political agendas, USS has adopted a more proactive approach to managing extra-financial risks than the majority of funds. Establishing an in-house responsible investment team was a significant commitment by the trustees. Some would say this was only possible because USS is a large fund and, in terms of its overall costs, the

16   www.enhancedanalytics.com

In 2004, USS undertook a survey of member knowledge of, and attitudes towards, USS's approach to responsible investment. Approximately 5% of USS's total membership replied. The results indicate:

- Over 80% of respondents either agree or strongly agree with the statement: 'I am aware of the responsible investment activities of USS'

- Over 90% of respondents either agree or strongly agree with the statement: 'It is important for a large scheme such as USS to have a policy on responsible investment'

- 67% of respondents either agree or strongly agree with the statement: 'The shareholder engagement approach is the most appropriate method for USS to encourage good standards of corporate governance'

Box 14.1 USS member survey 2004

spend on this activity is not that particularly significant. However, there are other funds of a similar size who have not taken this approach and so fund size cannot be the sole rationale. Rather, investment beliefs are important. If they wanted to, other pension funds, both large and small, could easily implement active cost-effective shareholding measures. Examples could include ensuring that the mandates of fund managers include requirements for active shareholding on extra-financial issues and ensuring that these parts of the mandates are monitored by pension funds' consultants. In addition, all pension funds can participate in collaborative groups. Working with like-minded asset owners, pension funds can, collectively, send strong signals to the market that an issue needs to be addressed. Through such collaborative action, whether on climate change, encouraging brokers to address extra-financial issues, or other subjects such as long-term mandates, pension funds and their trustees can protect their funds against long-term risks, thereby safeguarding the pensions that their members are entitled to. Not only is collaborative action likely to be more effective, it also means that the costs of achieving any change are shared.

For legal and other reasons, USS focuses the vast bulk of its effort on activities that are likely to provide the greatest financial rewards to its members. However, the fund has also taken the strategic decision that, by managing these extra-financial risks (which are often externalised by companies onto wider society), it can help make the world into which its members retire safer and more secure than it might be otherwise. USS's commitment to this approach is strengthened by the belief that, in so doing, it is also better managing absolute and portfolio-wide risks and so safeguarding, perhaps even enhancing, the long-term value of the fund. The logic of this investment approach is hard to fault, and it is noticeable that other funds have increasingly adopted aspects of this agenda for themselves.

Investment beliefs are normally validated by empirical financial evidence. However, this may be inappropriate in the area of responsible investment. If, as many pension funds believe, changes in company practices in response to the debates on, for example, corporate governance, human capital, climate change or HIV/AIDS are just as important, then action by investors sooner rather than later would be in the best interests of members. This poses an interesting challenge for those pension funds that have either rejected or, more commonly, not seriously considered the sort of approach adopted by USS: 'What is the right thing for pension funds to do for their members?'

References

Amalric, F. (2004) 'Pension Funds, Corporate Responsibility and Sustainability', Centre for Corporate Responsibility and Sustainability Working Paper 01/04 (Zurich: CCRS, University of Zurich).

Bender, K., and N. Jivan (2005) *What Makes Retirees Happy?* (Boston, MA: Centre for Retirement Research, Boston College, www.bc.edu/centers/crr/issues/ib_28.pdf).

Davies, G. (2003) 'Investing in a Changing Climate: A Pension Fund Perspective', paper presented at the IIGCC Conference, London, www.usshq.co.uk/downloads/pdf/all_sections/reportsandvoting/q42003/ri_report_q4_2003_appendix_i.pdf, 16 November 2003.

Hawley, J., and A. Williams (2000a) *The Rise of Fiduciary Capitalism: How Institutional Investors Can Make Corporate America More Democratic* (Philadelphia, PA: University of Pennsylvania Press).

—— and —— (2000b) 'The Emergence of Universal Owners: Some Implications of Institutional Equity Ownership', *Challenge: The Magazine of Economic Affairs*, July/August 2000: 43-61.

—— and —— (2002a) 'The Universal Owner's Role in Sustainable Economic Development', *Corporate Environmental Strategy*, 9.3: 284-91.

—— and —— (2002b) 'Can Universal Owners Be Socially Responsible Investors?', in P. Camejo (ed.), *The SRI Advantage* (Gabriola Island, BC, Canada: New Society Publishers): 151-71.

Mansley, M., and A. Dlugolecki (2001) *Climate Change: A Risk Management Challenge for Institutional Investors* (London: USS).

Stapledon, G. (1996) *Institutional Shareholders and Corporate Governance* (Oxford, UK: Clarendon Press).

15
Henderson Global Investors
ENGAGEMENT AND ACTIVISM

Rob Lake
Henderson Global Investors, UK

Henderson Global Investors is an international fund management company with £66.5 billion (at 30 June 2005) in assets under management worldwide. Its clients are pension funds and other institutions (45% of assets), retail (i.e. individual) investors (14%) and closed life assurance funds. Listed equities (i.e. shares in companies quoted on a stock market) represent 40% of Henderson's assets, while corporate and government bonds account for 51%. The remainder is made up of investments in property and private capital.

Henderson's approach to engagement and activism

The evolution of policy

Henderson's history of managing sustainable and responsible investment (SRI) portfolios is particularly relevant to an understanding of its approach to engagement and activism. Henderson has been managing funds on this basis since 1977, and currently has just under £1 billion in SRI funds. These are funds in which clients explicitly wish to exclude specified sectors from investment, to favour others with high sustainability potential and to give preference within 'mainstream' sectors to companies with the highest corporate responsibility standards. Analysing sustainability and corporate responsibility issues over the years for its SRI funds has enabled Henderson to build up experience of the ways that companies' responses to these challenges can be relevant to their business performance.

In summer 2000 Henderson therefore took the step of adding corporate responsibility issues to the overall corporate governance policy that applies to all its funds (i.e. not just its SRI funds). This coincided with the introduction of the legal obligation on UK pension funds to make a policy statement within their overall statement of investment principles (SIP) on social, environmental and ethical (SEE) matters. Henderson's broadened policy was initially still referred to as the corporate governance policy.

In October 2001 the UK government published *Institutional Investment in the UK: A Review* (known as the Myners review after its chair, Paul Myners [Myners 2001]). This wide-ranging analysis concluded that:

> the pension fund clients of investment managers have a right to expect them to have an explicit strategy, elucidating the circumstances in which they will intervene in a company; the approach they will use in doing so; and how they measure the effectiveness of this strategy.

Henderson then introduced a formal activism policy that addressed these key areas and covered activism on both traditional corporate governance issues and the corporate responsibility topics already covered by its broadened corporate governance policy. In its response to the Myners review, the government indicated that it was considering introducing a legal obligation on pension funds and fund managers to take an activist approach. In response, in October 2002, the Institutional Shareholders' Committee (ISC), which brings together the UK's main investment industry associations— the Association of British Insurers (ABI), the National Association of Pension Funds, the Investment Management Association and the Association of Investment Trust Companies—introduced a voluntary Statement of Principles on the responsibilities of institutional shareholders and agents (ISC 2002). The ISC code committed members of the signatory industry bodies to 'set out their policy on how they will discharge their responsibilities' in respect of investee companies. Henderson's activism policy already covered this ground. In 2002, Henderson's corporate governance policy and activism policy sat alongside each other. For the 2003 UK voting season the two were combined into a single activism and voting policy.

An integrated approach to responsible investment

In October 2003, in preparation for the 2004 voting season, Henderson changed the title of the document setting out the framework for its work on corporate governance, corporate responsibility and voting, across all funds, to the 'responsible investment policy'. This was more than a cosmetic change. The new title reflects an important principle for Henderson. Henderson views 'activism'—the exercise of influence over a company by a shareholder using the corporate governance relationship—as a means to an end, rather than as an end in itself. That end is responsible investment—an integrated approach that takes account of a wide range of governance, social, environmental and ethical (GSEE) factors alongside conventional financial dimensions of a company's performance, capabilities and prospects. This reflects Henderson's belief that (Henderson Global Investors 2004):

> good management of a range of responsibilities that companies have towards different stakeholders contributes to business success and long-term share-

holder value. This embraces: economic responsibilities to shareholders, and fair and legal behaviour in the marketplace, towards consumers, suppliers and competitors; responsibilities to minimise and manage environmental impacts; responsibilities towards employees; and responsibilities to the wider community.

This approach is represented in Figure 15.1. This illustrates that research and engagement (dialogue with companies) on GSEE issues form the link between the investment and ownership functions that a fund manager performs on behalf of a client. The analysis that generates the insights to inform investment decision-making is conducted, in part, through direct engagement with companies. For Henderson's SRI funds, a company is not eligible for investment unless its corporate responsibility standards meet a minimum threshold. For non-SRI funds, sustainability and responsibility insights flow into the overall pool of information on which fund managers draw in making decisions on whether to buy, hold or sell shares. The extent to which these insights influence investment decisions varies according to the sector, company and issue concerned. In some cases, a single issue will be significant in its own right (e.g. an energy utility's exposure to risks and opportunities flowing from the EU emissions trading scheme [ETS]) whereas in others, a company's aggregate performance on corporate responsibility will be more important (e.g. the overall capacity to protect and enhance the company's reputation by successfully managing a range of individual responsibility issues).

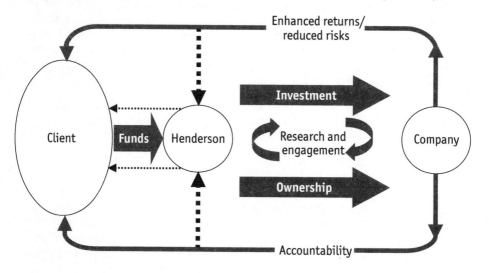

FIGURE 15.1 The responsible investment chain

Source: Henderson Global Investors

As well as generating analysis, this ongoing process of dialogue also serves to exercise influence. Here, the fund manager acts in a governance capacity as a representative of the ultimate (part-)owner of the company (the fund manager's client). Regular scrutiny of companies' handling of key responsibility and sustainability issues through dialogue with senior company management helps to ensure that companies' attention remains focused on maintaining and improving performance. Where this routine dialogue establishes that a company's management of a given issue is inadequate (and thus represents an unacceptable risk to the company and its shareholders), more focused influence can be exerted. Specific issues can also be raised over and above this ongoing process (see the engagement case studies below).

These twin processes of factoring GSEE issues into investment decision-making and the exercise of ownership functions are directly analogous to what investors do routinely on issues of corporate strategy and conventional business performance—understand the issues through research and direct contact with management, apply this intelligence to investment decision-making and voice concern where performance falls short of expectations. The close link between the investment decision-making and ownership functions also increases effectiveness in situations where Henderson seeks to exercise influence over companies. If changes in company practice that Henderson considers necessary are not made, shares can be sold.

As Figure 15.1 shows, the *purpose* of this approach to responsible investment for Henderson is to provide its clients with enhanced financial returns and reduced risk by means of improved investment decision-making, and to ensure that companies remain accountable to their owners through active share ownership.

Engagement without fund management

Some fund managers provide 'engagement-only' services, whereby engagement is carried out on behalf of a client without the fund manager concerned managing the underlying assets. Such an approach may be effective in exercising some influence over a company. But it is unlikely to allow the intelligence gained through engagement (e.g. on the quality of a company's risk management or on market opportunities associated with environmental or social issues in which the company has expertise and innovation capacity) to be utilised in the process of buying or selling a company's shares. While it may be possible for the 'engaging manager' to communicate such intelligence to the 'investing manager', it is unlikely that such communication will be as effective as that within a fund management house that is performing both functions. For Henderson, the link between investment and accountability is central to the concept of 'engagement'.

The nature of the investor's responsibility

It is also argued by some that there is a responsibility upon investors to seek to ensure that companies operate within commonly agreed standards of conduct (such as those set out in UN conventions), and that such a responsibility obtains independently of the extent to which a given form of corporate behaviour might be beneficial or detrimental in business terms. Even if such a responsibility in relation to 'public good' issues exists in principle, however, a commercial fund management company can only exercise this responsibility effectively to the extent that there is a business case for the companies in which it invests to take action to achieve the standards sought. To this extent, there is also a business case for the fund manager itself to engage in this way—companies that respond to efforts to exercise influence should, in due course, provide improved financial returns which will be in the interests of the fund manager and its clients. This is Henderson's approach. In this situation, the notion of 'investor responsibility' (other than the investor's responsibility to maximise its own returns) is effectively otiose. A commercial fund manager that sought to persuade an investee company to take action that was detrimental to that company in business terms might be breaching its fiduciary responsibility to its clients (unless it had a clear mandate from its clients to pursue objectives other than financial return, and at the expense of financial return).

A remaining area for discussion in relation to the concept of investor responsibility— albeit somewhat theoretically, perhaps—is whether the investor has a responsibility to promote changes in behaviour by investee companies that are neutral with regard to the company's financial performance but beneficial in terms of the public good (such as compliance with international labour standards). In this situation, a commercial fund manager might again need to be cautious. A strict interpretation of fiduciary duty towards its clients might suggest that resources should be devoted exclusively to activities with a clear prospect of delivering financial benefits. A clear understanding with clients of their expectations and requirements would appear essential.

Systems, processes and resources

Henderson has a team of six specialist staff for research and engagement on responsibility and governance issues. Team members have backgrounds in environmental management, sustainability policy, non-governmental organisations (NGOs) and corporate governance analysis. Priorities for issue-specific research and engagement, over and above the routine process of dialogue with companies on their overall approaches to sustainability and responsibility, are identified on a rolling basis. The aim in selecting priorities is, over time, to pursue a balanced range of issues across the dimensions in which Henderson's corporate responsibility analysis of companies is organised—corporate standards (covering ethics, governance and marketplace standards), environment, workplace, and social/community issues—and across sectors. Issues are identified as a result of ongoing monitoring of corporate responsibility trends through contact with a range of stakeholder groups, scanning of the media, involvement in specialist events, discussion fora, etc. Once an issue has been selected, the first stage of a project is to conduct further research to build an understanding of the issue at a technical level and of its implications for companies. This involves literature reviews, further discussion with specialist stakeholders and, in some cases, consultation with companies. Once the issue and its business implications have been clearly defined, the objectives of an engagement initiative are formally specified. This is sometimes done in a public position paper that sets out Henderson's analysis of the issue and its expectations of companies. This then forms the basis for approaches to selected companies to explore their response to the issues raised. These approaches are the start of a process of dialogue with the companies that may extend over a prolonged period. Once it is established that a company's position has formally changed, or that sufficient impetus has been given to the discussion of the issue within an individual company or among companies more generally, or if it becomes clear that significant change is unlikely to occur, the project is formally concluded. The activities involving contact with stakeholders and companies are recorded on internal systems to allow accurate and detailed reporting to Henderson's clients and for wider communications. This process is summarised in Figure 15.2. In practice, engagement is more fluid than this diagram suggests. For example the beginning and end of a project are, in Henderson's experience, considerably less clear-cut. Nonetheless, the diagram does serve to capture the overall shape of an engagement process.

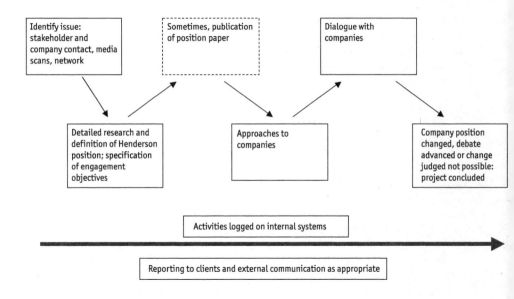

FIGURE 15.2 The engagement process

Engagement case studies

This section gives examples of issue-specific and sector-specific engagement initiatives Henderson has undertaken that have followed a path close to that set out in Figure 15.2.

Gender pay gap

1   **Identify issue.** Monitoring by Henderson of workplace issues identified continuing disparities between men's and women's earnings. Legislative change requiring employers to conduct gender pay audits and a series of legal cases for pay discrimination sharpened the business risk associated with the issue

2   **Detailed research.** Henderson researched the issue in detail by reviewing specialist publications and by consulting with trades unions and the Equal Opportunities Commission (EOC)

3   **Specify objectives and publish position.** *Closing Britain's Gender Pay Gap* was published in October 2002 (Henderson Global Investors 2002). Henderson held a seminar for companies and fellow investors, with speakers from the EOC, the Trades Union Congress (TUC) and Abbey National

4   **Approach companies.** Henderson subsequently wrote to 20 FTSE 100 financial and professional services companies seeking clarification of whether they had conducted a gender pay audit

5   **Dialogue with companies.** Dialogue with these 20 companies continued over a period of ten months

6   **Results and conclusion.** Forty-five per cent of the companies either had conducted an audit or planned to do so in the near future. Many of the remaining companies stated that their annual salary review process considered gender equality, but this was often conducted at a department level and did not provide the necessary overview obtained through an independent pay audit. Other companies questioned were in the process of developing human resource and pay systems that would enable them to collect and analyse the data necessary to conduct pay audits in the future. Companies were not prepared to indicate whether women's pay had, in fact, been increased as a result of pay audits, as this would effectively constitute an acknowledgement that unacceptable pay differentials had existed previously. Nonetheless, a number of companies did use phrases such as 'we are following up the findings of the audit' in their discussion with Henderson. On this basis the project was concluded in September 2003. Analysis of companies' approach to gender pay subsequently became a routine part of Henderson's ongoing corporate responsibility research, rather than a free-standing project

Business ethics in the pharmaceutical sector

1/2 Identify issue/detailed research. In this case the issue was identified through an overall review conducted by Henderson of corporate responsibility issues in the pharmaceutical sector. This exercise involved consultation with a range of stakeholders, including development and health NGOs, trade unions, investment bank researchers and pharmaceutical companies themselves

3 Specify objectives and publish position. *Fulfilling its Potential: Sustainability, Responsibility and Ethics in the Pharmaceutical Industry* was published in September 2003 (Henderson Global Investors 2003). This report identified five priorities for the industry: embedding corporate responsibility in governance systems; transforming business ethics performance and assurance; demonstrating leadership in addressing global health disparities; engaging with society on innovative genetic technologies; and establishing a common reporting framework

4 Approach companies. Henderson decided to focus on business ethics performance and assurance for detailed follow-up in the first instance on the grounds that the other issues highlighted in the review paper were either already being addressed through other initiatives in which Henderson was involved (e.g. global health disparities through the Pharmaceutical Shareowners Group) or less pressing in terms of immediate company performance and business risk. Henderson entered into detailed discussion with GlaxoSmithKline (GSK) on business ethics in the light of a series of incidents and allegations relating to the marketing of antidepressants and the publication of clinical trial results

5 Dialogue with companies. In discussion with GSK, Henderson proposed a series of indicators for business ethics reporting. The company decided at board level to include business ethics in its future corporate responsibility reporting

6 Results and conclusion. Henderson continued to monitor the issue, and to discuss other issues highlighted in the sector review paper with pharmaceutical companies

Tax, risk and corporate governance

1 Identify issue. There has been an ongoing discussion in some corporate responsibility circles relating to tax payments as a matter of social responsibility going beyond strict legal obligations. However, this issue had not featured prominently in what has become the 'mainstream' corporate responsibility debate. It is clear that from a financial perspective tax is extremely important for investors, given the implications of tax figures in company accounts for share valuations. In early 2004, Henderson became aware that the UK Inland Revenue and other tax authorities were increasing their scrutiny of companies' tax affairs. These agencies were suggesting that tax was a matter of corporate responsibility, not just law. Civil-society groups also began to raise tax more assertively, leading to increased media coverage of the issue

2   **Detailed research.** Further research into the issue, and framing of an appropriate approach to it from the investor's perspective, involved additional literature review, extensive discussion with Henderson's head of research (responsible for financial analysis) and the director of corporate finance and tax of Henderson's then parent company, HHG plc, and participation in a seminar for tax professionals organised by one of the 'big four' accountancy firms

3/4 **Specify objectives and publish position/approach companies.** In this case Henderson decided it would not be appropriate to make a public statement on the issue to 'launch' this work. Henderson framed the issue as a matter of risk management and corporate governance that should be addressed by company boards. In July 2004 Henderson wrote to the chairperson of every company in the FTSE 350 asking a series of questions about their approach to managing tax-related risks. In order to gain the trust of companies on such a sensitive issue so that information could be collected, it was important that Henderson's interest should not be publicly known.[1] Assurances were also given to companies that the information they provided to Henderson would not be made public

5   **Dialogue with companies.** A relatively small number of companies replied to Henderson's first letter. A reminder was sent in September 2004 and 162 responses were eventually received. Discussions were held with a number of companies to clarify their policies and processes

6   **Results and conclusion.** The findings of the survey were published in January 2005 (Henderson Global Investors 2005). The results were presented in such a way that no individual company could be identified. Henderson is aware from a number of sources (notably companies themselves and the major accountancy and tax advisory firms) that its initiative prompted considerable discussion both within and among companies, in professional tax circles and more widely. A number of companies intimated to Henderson that they had reviewed their systems and policies following the survey. Henderson received expressions of interest in this work from a wide range of sources, and the initiative appeared to contribute significantly to the developing debate in this area. At the time of writing Henderson is conducting follow-up discussions with companies to encourage formal board-level consideration of tax, risk and responsibility issues, and the adoption of board

---

1   In fact, Henderson's initiative became widely known very quickly. An article on it appeared in the *Sunday Times* three days after the letter had been sent to companies. Henderson had taken no steps whatsoever to publicise its work.

policies. While this evaluation is qualitative, Henderson is satisfied that the initiative was effective in focusing company attention on the management of tax risk and the links between tax and corporate responsibility

Evaluating and reporting effectiveness

A number of challenges arise in evaluating the effectiveness of engagement or 'activism'. While shareholders are particularly well placed to gain access to senior company management to voice concerns and to suggest improvements where needed, in most cases they are not the only influence to which a company is subject. Employees, NGOs, government and others may also be raising the same issue(s) as investors. Any suggestion that a given observed change in a company's practice came about because of a given shareholder intervention should therefore be made with extreme caution. Moreover, it is understandable that a company should not wish to state that any change it has made has been 'brought about by' the actions of a third party. An investor's ability to engage in the kind of dialogue that might contribute to such change depends on trust on the part of the company. The investor needs to retain this trust in order to maintain its relationship with the company so that productive dialogue can continue in the future.

Henderson therefore aims to measure and report the scale of the effort applied to a given engagement process—either ongoing dialogue on overall corporate responsibility matters or an issue-specific project—to assess whether change has occurred in relation to the objectives Henderson specified for its work; and to evaluate honestly the link between the two. We have a responsibility to report candidly to our clients on these three dimensions—our inputs, any change observed and an assessment of any causal link—while taking care not to attribute causality, or claim credit, where this is not legitimate. Where public communication is concerned, unsophisticated public statements on the impact of engagement could be both factually misleading and damaging to future effectiveness.

Reflections

Henderson's experience is that engagement has proved effective in contributing to changes in corporate practice in situations in which a clear case can be made that change is in the business interest of the company concerned and that it is also relatively straightforward in organisational terms. In the case of the gender pay project described above, for example, there were clear regulatory and financial risks to companies that did not conduct the required equal pay audits, so laying themselves open to being sued for discrimination by female employees. Carrying out audits is a technical exercise that is fully within the control of a company's management. As noted above, companies were not prepared to indicate clearly whether gender pay gaps had indeed been identified and closed as a result of audits. Nonetheless, companies that conducted audits, identified pay gaps and failed to address them would be open to litigation by female employees.

Henderson's work on business ethics in the pharmaceutical sector and on tax, risk and corporate governance also both relate to areas under the direct control of company management. In both cases there are indications that a clear link exists between Henderson's engagement and new steps taken by companies. The tax work also illustrates particularly well the way in which engagement can generate intelligence that is of value to investment analysis and decision-making. The direct financial implications of a company's approach to tax made the relevance of this work to Henderson's financial analysts readily apparent, and many of them were involved in follow-up discussions with companies.

In situations where companies face highly complex external circumstances over which they have incomplete control, engagement can perform a slightly different function. Henderson, working jointly with Insight Investment, has held extended discussions with Shell about its operations in Nigeria, which have been a source of widely publicised controversy as a result of community conflict and poor environmental and social performance. These discussions have taken place at both executive management and board level. However, the political, ethnic, social, economic and security complexities of the Niger Delta are such that 'solving' the problems that have plagued Shell is by no means a straightforward matter. Investors are poorly placed to offer specific practical suggestions as to how to address the situation on the ground. Nonetheless, it is a proper function of investors to seek assurance that the company board is itself discharging its governance responsibilities in ensuring that internal control processes designed to secure the implementation of company policies relevant to the situation are operating effectively—and to seek improvements in those processes if necessary. Sustained inquiries by shareholders seeking such assurance can help to ensure that companies' attention remains focused on the important issues.

However, it is important to acknowledge the limitations of engagement or 'activism'. The framework for this book is sustainable development. Measured against this yardstick, responsible active share ownership (and indeed the integration of social and environmental issues into the evaluation and selection of assets for investment) falls substantially short. Sometimes there simply is not a compelling business case for a company to pursue a course of action that would offer environmental or social gains. Current market frameworks (i.e. regulation and tax) allow, for example, levels of carbon emissions that are simply unsustainable in ecological terms (and will continue to do so even after the introduction of the EU ETS, despite the improvements this will bring). Companies with high carbon emissions want to protect and enhance their reputations. But this will not prompt action to reduce emissions to levels even remotely close to those required by the environmental and social imperatives of climate change. Similar 'brick walls'— points beyond which companies have no rational incentive to move no matter how engaged and active their shareholders might be—can be found in the case of many, even most, sustainability and responsibility issues. There is a gap between what is needed in sustainability terms or expected in responsibility terms, and what is rational for business within current policy frameworks. Engagement with companies can help to optimise business performance in environmental and social terms within the current paradigm. Such engagement can also (e.g. through encouraging companies to implement appropriate governance and management systems and processes) help companies to develop the capacity to respond effectively to changes in their business environment. However, it is only changes in public policy that can transform incentives for business to make more sustainable paths commercially rational.

References

Henderson Global Investors (2002) *Closing Britain's Gender Pay Gap* (London: Henderson Global Investors).

—— (2003) *Fulfilling its Potential: Sustainability, Responsibility and Ethics in the Pharmaceutical Industry: An Agenda for Change* (London: Henderson Global Investors).

—— (2004) *UK Responsible Investment Policy* (London: Henderson Global Investors).

—— (2005) *Tax, Risk and Corporate Governance: A Survey of the FTSE350* (London: Henderson Global Investors).

ISC (Institutional Shareholders' Committee) (2002) *Statement of Principles on the Responsibilities of Institutional Shareholders and Agents* (London: ISC).

Myners, P. (2001) *Institutional Investment in the UK: A Review* (London: HM Treasury).

16

Insight's approach to activism on corporate responsibility issues

Craig Mackenzie and Rory Sullivan

Insight Investment, UK

Insight Investment is one of the largest investment managers in the UK (see Box 16.1). On average, Insight holds approximately 1% of the issued share capital of FTSE-listed companies and is, typically, one of the ten largest shareholders in these companies. This chapter describes Insight's approach to shareholder activism relating to corporate responsibility. It sets out Insight's rationale for activism on this topic, its overall approach and the manner in which activism is implemented. The chapter also, using 2004 as an example, presents an overview of a typical year's activism activity, including a description of the major themes pursued and the outcomes achieved from this activity.

Insight's rationale for shareholder activism on social, ethical and environmental issues

In order to understand Insight's approach to shareholder activism, it is important first to recognise that Insight acts on behalf of its clients; Insight does not own the assets it manages. These assets are, in fact, owned by a variety of pension funds, life assurance funds and mutual funds. These funds, in turn, represent the savings of millions of individuals. In managing these assets, Insight is bound by a fiduciary obligation to serve its

Insight is the asset manager of the Halifax and Bank of Scotland Group (HBOS plc). Insight has approximately £79.1 billion of assets (including equities, property and fixed income) under management as at 31 March 2005.* Insight's client base includes pension funds, local authorities, charities and foundations, companies and insurance companies. These clients are predominantly located in the UK and Europe.

Insight has been a leading shareholder activist on corporate governance issues for over 20 years. In 2001, Insight decided to extend the scope of its activism to include activism on corporate ethics and environmental issues. Insight also decided to invest substantially in the area by supplementing existing expertise with a team of seven highly experienced staff. In 2002, Insight published a corporate governance and corporate responsibility policy† which applies to all of the assets it manages.

Insight also offers its activism services on a stand-alone (or 'unbundled') basis from its investment management activities. In 2004, Insight was appointed by the Wellcome Trust to provide a shareholder activism service on £3 billion of its UK equity assets.

---

*   Source: Insight Investment
†   www.insightinvestment.com/documents/responsibility/00292_SRI_Policy.pdf

Box 16.1 About Insight Investment

clients' interests. Even though the interests of clients are not all the same, the majority have fairly long-term investment time horizons: Insight is essentially charged with creating wealth for individuals over the longer term. Our shareholder activism is oriented to serve this long-term interest.

Insight believes that the long-term interests of its clients are generally served when companies behave responsibly by meeting the legitimate ethical and legal expectations of their customers, employees and other stakeholders.[1] This position is now explicitly accepted by many of our clients. Following the changes to the UK Pensions Act which required pension funds to state the extent, if at all, they take account of these issues in investment, many of our pension fund clients have adopted explicit policies (as part of their statements of investment principles [SIPs]) mandating Insight to conduct shareholder activism on these issues.[2]

Insight's view is that meeting the legitimate ethical and legal expectations of stakeholders is normally an essential element in the creation of long-term shareholder value; it is the basis for trusting relationships with customers and employees, and of a strong reputation with regulators and the wider business community. However, we

---

1   We accept that this subject raises a number of subtle issues. In particular, in situations of market failure the interests of a company and its shareholders may diverge from those of the wider public. In such cases corporate responsibility may not always pay. See Chapter 2 for a more detailed discussion of this issue.

2   In their SIPs, clients state that they (or their investment manager) will: integrate corporate governance and corporate responsibility issues into their investment decisions; and/or conduct shareholder activism on corporate governance and corporate responsibility issues. For a discussion of how Insight integrates SEE issues into its corporate bonds investment process, see Chapter 7.

recognise that a variety of market and organisational failures mean that companies often face significant pressures and temptations to act irresponsibly. As a consequence, the consistent delivery of corporate responsibility requires executive leadership and strong corporate governance, and it is the responsibility of the board of directors to ensure this happens. It is here that we, as shareholders, have an important role to play. Shareholders appoint boards to govern the company in their long-term interests. It is therefore important that investors support and encourage boards in their efforts to achieve the quality of leadership and corporate governance necessary to deliver corporate responsibility. It is also important that shareholders hold boards to account for doing so. Properly delivering this oversight role is in the long-term interests of our clients, and also helps deliver on shareholders' wider responsibility to society.

Insight's approach to shareholder activism

Insight's approach to shareholder activism is directed to support and encourage the boards of the companies in which it invests in their efforts to achieve the quality of leadership and corporate governance necessary to deliver corporate responsibility. It is important to be clear that we believe that shareholders' activism on corporate responsibility issues should be directed primarily at a company's board of directors, not at management. Investors appoint boards of directors to run companies. If they have concerns about corporate responsibility, or anything else for that matter, they should seek to raise them with the board.

Insight believes that effective board action on corporate responsibility is primarily a matter of boards establishing an effective approach to governance. Much of what is required for effective governance is set out in the Combined Code on Corporate Governance (FRC 2003). This provides the basis for our overall policy for shareholder activism. However, Insight's activism on corporate responsibility puts a particular emphasis on the following:

- **Standards.** The Combined Code requires boards to 'set the company's values and standards and ensure that its obligations to its shareholders and others are understood and met' (FRC 2003: Section A.1). Normally, we would expect this to entail the board approving a clear and complete policy statement that defines the standards of corporate responsibility the board expects the company's executive management to meet. We expect such policy statements to be consistent with generally accepted standards of business ethics, and with appropriate international codes.[3] It would be appropriate for boards to define high-level principles and require executive management to produce detailed policies consistent with these principles

---

3   Insight discussed the need for greater clarity about the nature of these principles in Mackenzie 2002.

- **Internal control.** Boards should ensure that there are effective systems to monitor and enforce adherence to company policy. This may involve establishing appropriate internal and external auditing and whistle-blower mechanisms. This aspect of internal control should be under the ultimate oversight of non-executive directors as, given the potential conflicts of interest, it is prudent for executives not to police their own behaviour. Many companies with large and complex social and environmental impacts have set up a separate committee of the board, comprised of non-executive directors, to fulfil this function. Below board level, internal control requires effective systems for management, internal reporting and audit

- **Risk.** Boards should ensure that there are effective systems to identify and evaluate risks associated with social, environmental and ethical (SEE) factors. Changes to corporate strategy or business models, and changes in the business environment will frequently expose companies to new risks. Boards should review significant risks that emerge and consider whether their current policy and internal control arrangements are sufficient

- **Incentives.** Boards should align performance management and executive remuneration systems with board policies. There are several aspects to this. Boards should ensure that executive management has incentives based substantially on delivering long-term, rather than only short-term, performance. This is important because, while there are sometimes short-term opportunities for companies to profit by irresponsible behaviour, these opportunities are scarcer over the long term (see further the discussion in Chapter 2). In some cases, it may also be appropriate for boards to assess performance against the company's standards of corporate responsibility. Where this is so, performance against these standards should be given due weight in performance-based remuneration

- **Reporting.** Boards should explain to shareholders their approach to addressing significant social and environmental risks. This should be addressed in the course of meeting the requirement in the Combined Code for boards to explain their approach to corporate governance, and the requirement in the new Operating and Financial Review legislation for boards to report information about social and environmental factors that are significant to understanding a company's position, performance and future prospects, as well as its risks and resources

Insight's shareholder activism: implementation

Resources

Insight's activism work is led by the eight company engagement specialists in the Investor Responsibility team. This team has specific expertise in issues such as governance, business ethics, environmental management and human rights, as well as considerable practical experience in investment, business, consulting and academia. One of the strengths of Insight's approach is that it is integrated with the activities of our equities and bonds investment teams (see Chapter 7) and draws heavily on the company-specific knowledge and relationships of these teams. This allows us to connect our shareholder activism on corporate responsibility issues with the financial analysis and investment activity conducted by the equities and bonds teams. This approach also allows us to address one of the common concerns expressed by companies (see, for example, Chapters 23 and 24) that the activities of analysts and shareholder activists are somehow divorced from one another. While there are inevitably differences in the specific questions that are asked, our close relationships allow us to communicate our interests in both short-term business influences (i.e. those aspects that drive short-term movements in share price) and longer-term value drivers.

Methods of engagement

Insight engages with company boards and management to support and encourage their efforts to deliver a high quality of governance with regard to corporate responsibility issues, in line with our understanding of best practice detailed above. In pursuing this agenda, we follow a range of strategies, including informal dialogue, voting, benchmarking and collaboration with other investors.

We generally prefer to engage companies in constructive informal dialogue in order to encourage change, rather than more confrontational, formal voting-based activism at the annual general meeting. We discuss issues of corporate responsibility with companies as a routine part of our analyst/investment meetings with chief executives and finance directors, and as part of our regular contacts with chairpersons and senior non-executive directors. Our analysts routinely attend these meetings, as they find these discussions help them develop a deeper understanding of companies' quality of management. However, if private engagement fails to lead to satisfactory outcomes, Insight will consider making its concerns known publicly and, where appropriate, will use the voting rights associated with the shares it manages.

Insight frequently conducts its engagement in collaboration with other institutional investors, whether through the Association of British Insurers (ABI) (of which it is a member) or through other relationships.[4] On many issues, effective governance with regard to corporate responsibility overlaps significantly with efforts by government and regulators to address these issues. Insight therefore engages regularly with relevant government departments and regulatory agencies to discuss corporate practice on social and environmental issues. In these discussions we focus on questions such as how voluntary corporate governance action on social and environmental issues can deliver better outcomes and, if regulation is deemed necessary, how it can be designed

---

4   Insight has actively participated in formal collaborative initiatives such as the Institutional Investors Group on Climate Change and the Pharmaceutical Shareowners Group. Insight has also worked on a bilateral basis with other investors. For example, we worked with Morley Fund Management on a research programme, including a series of seminars, to assess the corporate responsibility risks associated with operating in China and, in conjunction with Henderson Global Investors, we held extended discussions with Shell about the social and environmental concerns associated with Shell's operations in Nigeria.

and implemented in a manner that delivers its goals in the most dependable, efficient and acceptable manner.

Research

Insight organises its engagement with companies on both a sector and an issue basis. Many ethical and environmental problems are specific to particular business sectors. It often makes sense to compare the different approaches taken by companies across a sector in order to identify best practice. However, some issues (e.g. risks associated with poor labour standards in global supply chains) apply across many sectors. For such issues it makes sense to evaluate company approaches on an issue-specific basis. Insight's engagement is based on careful research of companies' approaches and performance relating to SEE issues, based on company reports, other publicly available information, and information gained from meetings and correspondence with companies, regulators and other experts. Normally, Insight will seek to compare the quality of a company's approach with those of its peers in order to identify whether it exceeds or lags behind best practice.

Measuring performance

It is important to Insight's clients that our engagement is demonstrably effective. However, it is frequently the case that Insight is only one of a number of stakeholders who raise particular concerns with companies. We also often find that companies are already in the process of addressing our concerns, and so deserve the majority of the credit for any change. The consequence is that it is difficult to establish where credit is due to Insight for changes in corporate practice, given the multiple other pressures and influences that also act on companies.

The Investor Responsibility team tracks all significant discussions with companies as well as any suggestions for improvement that we make. We then monitor corporate performance in these areas, recording any changes made. Where companies appear to have made changes in line with our suggestions, we look to see if there is any evidence that Insight played a significant role. It is frequently difficult to establish that we have had a causal role. Occasionally, however, we receive letters from company executives thanking us for our contribution to better governance, and sometimes our contribution is publicly acknowledged by companies.

It is important to note that companies often do not respond to our suggestions for improvement or take actions other than those that were originally discussed. We do not see this as a 'failure of engagement', as we recognise that companies are generally better positioned to decide on the actions that are in their best interests and that, on investigating a specific issue, they may identify more appropriate strategies for addressing the issue. In these situations, we engage with the company to understand the reasons for its action and to confirm that it is the best approach for it to take.[5]

5   This approach is similar to the 'comply or explain' approach that underpins most corporate governance activity, where the principles set out in documents such as the Combined Code are not intended to be followed slavishly but to provide a framework for informed management decision-making.

Reporting

There is growing acceptance that it is desirable for institutional investors to be more accountable for their shareholder activism. In Insight's case, this accountability is owed to pension, life assurance and investment fund clients, to the customers and beneficiaries who invest in these funds, and to the companies in which we invest. Insight produces quarterly reports for clients detailing its voting and engagement activities, as well as providing analysis of emerging issues.[6] These reports are made publicly available so that companies and other stakeholders can see what activities we have undertaken and can understand our views on a range of corporate responsibility issues. Given that some stakeholders have questioned whether engagement can make a significant difference to corporate responsibility performance we see this transparency as an important part of demonstrating the credibility of our shareholder activism.

Recent activity

To give a picture of what Insight's activism on SEE issues looks like in practice, the following is an overview of engagement activity during 2004. In this year Insight engaged with some 200 companies on a range of strategic issues and risks associated with SEE issues.[7] For the most part, the engagement was welcomed by the companies concerned and, in more than 30 cases, contributed to substantial policy and management improvements.

Benchmarking

Much of this work comprised of three benchmarking projects, assessing the performance of 70 UK companies on a range of issues against best-practice frameworks. The three topics were:

- Sustainability in the UK house-building sector

- Risks associated with labour standards in the supply chains of companies in six sectors

- Environmental risks associated with the operations of large extractive and utility companies

Each of the projects highlighted leaders and companies falling behind best practice. Insight subsequently held meetings with many of the companies included in these assessments, most of which committed to making changes to how they manage particular issues (see, for example, Box 16.2).

---

6   www.insightinvestment.com/responsibility/reporting
7   Engagement on SEE issues is just a part of our engagement with companies in general. We engage with companies on corporate governance issues, as well as regular meetings with management to review commercial performance and discuss strategy and prospects.

In January 2004, Insight and WWF, the global conservation organisation, launched a report of the results of a survey assessing how well 13 of the UK's largest listed house-builders manage their impacts on the environment and society. Following the release of the report, Insight met with several house-builders to follow up on the report. We discovered that all of the companies involved in the survey had made significant improvements in their practices. For example, Barratt Homes undertook a full review of its governance and corporate social responsibility (CSR) management, overhauled its risk management processes and produced a new statement about its compliance with the Combined Code. Barratt Homes also adopted a new CSR policy statement, established a team of senior managers led by an executive board member to oversee implementation of the policy and, in October 2004, published its first corporate responsibility report.

Box 16.2 Benchmarking UK house-builders

Primary research on new/emerging issues

Insight also conducted or commissioned primary research on critical and emerging corporate responsibility issues, and used that research to promote dialogue between companies, investors and other key stakeholders. Two of these reports are *Buying Your Way Into Trouble?* which was prepared on our behalf by the consulting company Acona and *Biodiversity Offsets: Views, Experience and the Business Case*, a joint report between Insight and the World Conservation Union. The former looked at the question of whether companies' buying and pricing practices create tension or, in some cases, directly conflict with their commitments to ethical sourcing. It found that the way companies incentivise their buyers has a significant affect on their ability to source ethically. The report has met with widespread interest and support from many companies. The latter report assessed the potential for 'biodiversity offsets' to be used by companies as a tool to manage their biodiversity impacts and associated risks. The report has been welcomed by several leading UK companies, and has informed the thinking of the International Council on Mining and Minerals on this topic.

Responding to events and issues

Not all of our company engagement can be planned in advance. Inevitably, we also need to respond to controversies and concerns as they arise. The sources of these vary but can include media reports of companies not behaving in an ethical or socially responsible manner, NGO campaigns or evidence that companies are lagging behind their peers in relation to specific corporate responsibility issues. In 2004, we responded to several important events and issues, including:

- Concerns regarding the human rights and environmental dimensions of the Baku–Tblisi–Ceyhan pipeline, a project led by BP. We facilitated extensive discussions between NGOs, investors and BP, and actively encouraged BP to address the issues raised by its NGO critics

- Concerns about Shell's Sakhalin II project in eastern Russian. We met with representatives of local communities and subsequently had a number of meetings with Shell about local environmental impacts, the impact of the project on the endangered gray whales and local benefit sharing. Because of the financial importance of this project, our oil and gas analyst also raised the issues with Shell's chief executive

- Concerns about Standard Chartered's oil-backed loan to Sonangol in Angola. We held a number of meetings with the company and other concerned investors. Widespread concern had been expressed about the damage such loans might do, given the history of corruption in Angola. In our meetings, the company assured us that its risk assessment process had taken due account of the potential reputation risks to the company

- The financial implications of Russia's decision to ratify the Kyoto Protocol and the introduction of the EU emissions trading scheme (ETS), which meant that greenhouse gas emissions now have tangible financial value. With a dozen companies (energy producers and major energy consumers) we discussed the expected costs to their business and their strategies for responding to these developments

- The high-profile media coverage of 'offshoring' (i.e. the practice of transferring jobs overseas), with the merits and shortcomings of the practice being debated in the press almost continually. We wished to ensure that any companies in which we invest that decide to pursue offshoring strategies adequately assess the implications for their domestic and overseas labour forces and manage any relocation of staff sensitively. We therefore developed a set of best practice principles and sent them to 43 UK companies in the banking, insurance, telecoms and software sectors. Some ten companies subsequently endorsed the principles

Public policy

It has become increasingly clear to Insight that shareholders' effectiveness in engaging with companies depends on a good understanding of the changing regulatory environment. Therefore, in 2004, Insight participated in a number of government consultations and proactively sought to build relationships with several government departments. For example, we actively contributed to the development and promotion of CHaSPI, the Health and Safety Executive's new Corporate Health and Safety Performance Index (see further Chapter 31) and we continued to encourage the government to effectively implement the OECD Guidelines for Multinational Enterprises (see Box 16.3). We also commented on the Department of Trade and Industry's proposals for the new Operating and Financial Review and on its CSR strategy. We strongly welcomed both initiatives, but had some concerns about the details, specifically around the question of whether they would encourage higher standards of corporate responsibility per-

The OECD Guidelines for Multinational Enterprises are one of the few comprehensive, internationally recognised and government-supported sets of principles for corporate responsibility. The guidelines allow NGOs and trade unions to raise complaints against companies, and impose a positive duty on governments to help resolve these complaints. Despite these strengths, the guidelines have been virtually ignored in discussions on the social responsibilities of corporations, reflecting the reluctance of governments to ensure their effective implementation.

In February 2003, Insight wrote to Stephen Timms MP (the minister then responsible for the National Contact Point [NCP]),* to raise our concerns about this lack of government support for the guidelines. We suggested that this was undermining support for the guidelines among business, NGOs and trade unions, and noted that 'in many respects the UK leads the world in CSR. It is therefore particularly jarring that many think that our NCP is not even in the first division in terms of its quality.' Insight subsequently met with the minister to discuss these concerns. He welcomed Insight's work on the guidelines and committed extra resources to develop a more robust UK NCP. He also initiated measures to ensure that companies are aware of the government's support for the guidelines.

Since that time, there has been some progress in improving the implementation of the guidelines: the NCP has convened a number of meetings with stakeholders (trade unions, investors, NGOs) and progress is being made on processing the complaints that have been lodged. However, NCP remains some way from functioning effectively. For example, the complaints process remains extremely slow, effective implementation relies on corporate parties willingly participating in the mediation and dialogue processes that underpin the guidelines, and the UK government has yet to provide the appropriate political impetus or support necessary for the NCP to function effectively. Insight has maintained an ongoing, active interest in the guidelines, and has continued to encourage the UK government to ensure that they are effectively implemented.

* For the OECD Guidelines for Multinational Enterprises

Box 16.3 Encouraging the effective implementation of the OECD Guidelines for Multinational Enterprises

formance. We held several productive meetings with the civil servants concerned, and with Stephen Timms, the minister responsible for CSR at the time.

Concluding comments

Insight's engagement with companies on corporate responsibility issues has confirmed our belief that constructive shareholder engagement can play a useful role in promoting higher standards of corporate responsibility, thereby serving the long-term interests of our clients. In our experience, companies have generally welcomed discussion of these issues from well-informed shareholders. We have also found that companies broadly accept that it is normally in their own self-interest to develop the strong executive leadership and corporate governance necessary to deliver corporate responsibility. In addition, our activity has received some support from government regulators interested in harnessing shareholders' influence to encourage more effective self-regulation by companies.

Our experience has indicated that a number of elements are important to our effectiveness. The first is the knowledge that we bring to company discussions as investors, with an understanding of the commercial realities of companies and their sectors. This knowledge of companies, of their sector peers and of other sectors, means that our analysis is often recognised as credible and, therefore, companies are willing to listen and, as appropriate, act on the issues that we raise. The second is that we are large institutional investors, with an active (as opposed to passive) investment management style. Our scale means that we have influence both formally through voting but, perhaps more importantly, through the access that our sizeable shareholdings give us to company boards. As active managers, our investment decisions can influence the share price of companies. Because of the close links between our investment analysts and fund managers and our Investor Responsibility team, information on corporate responsibility performance flows through into our investment analysis. The third is that we are willing to collaborate with other investors and parties. We have made our Investor Responsibility Service available to organisations (e.g. pension funds and other large institutional investors) that do not use Insight as their investment manager (see Box 16.4 for an example). This approach allows these organisations to take advantage of Insight's resources, in areas such as issue-specific research, engagement activities that take account of the organisation's priorities, voting, reporting and general research. Insight's view is that the combined and co-ordinated support for improvements which this approach offers enables such organisations to participate in constructive and effective shareholder activism.

One obstacle that we have is a lack of clarity about how, in practice, boards can take effective action in this area. While there is now in the UK a strong consensus between investors and companies about the nature of effective corporate governance in general, there is less clarity on the relationship between corporate governance and corporate responsibility. In order to address this, in 2005 Insight joined with FTSE and Business in the Community to launch a project looking at the role of boards and corporate responsibility. The first stage in this project involved consultation with board directors and other investors in order to identify best-practice principles leading to the publication of a major report—*Rewarding Virtue*—in November 2005. We expect this report will provide the framework for our future engagement on this topic.

The Wellcome Trust appointed Insight Investment to provide a shareholder activism service on governance and corporate responsibility issues for its £3 billion UK FTSE 350-quoted equity portfolio. The Trust's objective in issuing this mandate was to encourage more effective approaches to corporate governance in the companies in which the Trust invests, thereby increasing the long-term value of its equity holdings. Under the terms of the mandate, Insight will assist in drafting the Trust's activism policy, monitor the performance of individual companies, engage with the Trust's major holdings to encourage improvements to those companies' approaches to corporate governance and corporate responsibility, and vote the Trust's FTSE 350 equity holdings.

Box 16.4 Implementing activism for the Wellcome Trust

References

FRC (Financial Reporting Council) (2003) *The Combined Code on Corporate Governance* (London: FRC, www.asb.org.uk/documents/pagemanager/frc/combinedcodefinal.pdf).

Mackenzie, C. (2002) *Defining Global Business Principles* (London: Insight Investment, www. insightinvestment.com/Responsibility/project/global_business_principles.asp).

—— and S. Hodgson (2005) *Rewarding Virtue: Effective Board Action on Corporate Responsibility* (London: Business in the Community).

17
The role of activism in responsible investment
THE FTSE4GOOD INDICES

Will Oulton
CRG Advisory Services, UK

In July 2001, FTSE Group (FTSE), the global index company, created the FTSE4Good Index in response to the increasing attention being paid to responsible investment from a broad range of investors. In addition, an increasing number of FTSE's institutional clients were looking for customised benchmarks, reflecting particular concerns relating to a range of extra-financial factors. Since its launch, the FTSE4Good Index has become one of the most influential responsible investment indices, promoting a greater attention to, and disclosure of, corporate responsibility policies and management systems in some of the most well-known international companies.

What is the FTSE4Good Index Series?

FTSE is one of the world's leading index calculation, management and distribution vendors. The company is a joint venture, owned equally by the London Stock Exchange and the *Financial Times*. Each day, FTSE calculates, manages and distributes over 60,000 individual indices including the famous FTSE 100—comprising the UK's largest 100 listed companies by market capitalisation (see Box 17.1). FTSE also calculates indices for other stock markets including South Africa, China, Taiwan, Greece and Euronext.

The FTSE4Good indices comprise five broad-based regional indices (FTSE4Good UK, US, Europe, Japan and Global), as well as four fixed-number sub-indices (FTSE4Good

Stock market indices are used by investors and market commentators to describe the collective price performance of a group of assets be it stocks, bonds or any other tradable commodity. In the UK, the most widely published index is the FTSE 100. The FTSE 100 is simply the collective price performance of the UK's largest companies as defined by their market capitalisation (i.e. the number of publicly traded shares in the company multiplied by the share price). The index value moves throughout the trading day as activity on the stock market moves the price of each stock up or down. One characteristic of 'size'-based indices is that the same price movement in a larger company will affect a greater change in the index than would the same price change in a smaller-sized company. Investors tend to use market capitalisation (size) as one way of defining their investment approaches. Indices that are widely published and recognised tend to have many products linked to them.

For example, retail investors can invest in products that are linked to the performance of an index such as the FTSE 100 without needing to buy shares in each individual company within the index. This ease of market access, together with the fact that over extended periods investment managers on the whole tend to fail to outperform market indices has fuelled the growth of indices within the financial services industry.

Box 17.1 What are 'indices'?

UK 50, US 100, Europe 50 and Global 100). The key difference between these types of indices is that there is no limit to the number of companies that can be included in the broad-based indices, whereas the fixed-number indices are limited to the stated number of companies by reference to their market capitalisation.

The unique feature of the FTSE4Good indices compared to other FTSE indices is that to become a 'member', companies must meet a prescribed set of corporate social responsibility (CSR) criteria. Another unique feature of the FTSE4Good indices is that a relatively small number of companies are excluded by virtue of their business activities. These exclusions are companies involved in the manufacture of tobacco products, weapons, nuclear power plants and nuclear weapons systems. It is, however, FTSE's intention to remove these exclusions and replace them with meaningful criteria for these industries.

To be eligible for inclusion, a company must meet CSR criteria in three broad areas: human rights; environmental sustainability; and social and stakeholder issues, including supply chain labour standards. These criteria are designed to reflect a broad global consensus on what constitutes good corporate responsibility practice. This consensus is achieved by widespread market consultation, with the final criteria being drawn up by an independent committee of experts in the field of responsible investment and CSR. Box 17.2 presents the key objectives and features of FTSE4Good which inform the specific criteria that must be met by companies.

The FTSE4Good criteria have been set at a level that represents good practice standards for the majority, rather than best practice for the few. By setting challenging yet achievable criteria for the broad majority the FTSE4Good Index aims to encourage com-

Key objectives

- To provide a tool for socially responsible investors to identify and invest in companies that meet globally recognised corporate responsibility standards. These companies are best positioned to capitalise on the benefits of superior non-financial risk management and on the opportunities brought by good corporate responsibility
- To provide asset managers with a basis for socially responsible investment products (such as tracker funds and structured products), as well as setting a benchmark for all socially responsible investment products
- To contribute to the development of responsible business practice around the world

Key features

- Evolving selection criteria to reflect changes in globally accepted corporate responsibility standards and codes of conduct over time
- Criteria are challenging yet achievable to encourage companies to strive to meet them
- Higher-impact companies have to meet higher standards
- Transparent criteria and methodology
- Criteria based on respected codes and principles
- New criteria drawn up by experts following widespread consultation and approved by an independent advisory committee made up of experts within the field of corporate responsibility, governance and socially responsible investment

Box 17.2 FTSE4Good Index Series: key objectives and features

panies to address corporate responsibility issues, many for the first time. The inclusion criteria are drawn from a range of internationally accepted norms including:

- The Universal Declaration of Human Rights (UNDHR)[1]
- The OECD Guidelines on Multinational Enterprises[2]
- The UN Global Compact[3]

The aim is for the criteria to be regularly revised to ensure that they continue to reflect both standards of responsible business practice and developments in responsible investment. New index criteria are developed via a staged process of consultation and stakeholder engagement. The objective is that the criteria should be challenging but

1 www.un.org/Overview/rights.html
2 www.oecd.org
3 www.unglobalcompact.org

achievable. Once new criteria are defined and announced, a timetable is set for their implementation. This takes two approaches. First, companies affected by the change who are currently members of the Index are set a specific period of time in which to comply with the new requirements. Second, companies that are not in the Index at the time of the announcement of the new criteria are required to meet the criteria in full before gaining entry. This has the dual effect of minimising the volatility of the Index (i.e. where large numbers of companies are removed and then return to the Index shortly thereafter) and also of making the Index increasingly harder to enter. Companies therefore have to continually respond and meet the increasing threshold level to maintain their Index membership. FTSE4Good is unique in the socially responsible investment area due to this embedded constant improvement requirement for member companies. This also enables FTSE to measure the impact the Index is having on contributing to improvements in global standards of corporate responsibility behaviour and performance.

Case study: development of the FTSE4Good human rights criteria

In April 2002, FTSE announced a change in the requirements for companies in the global resource sector (i.e. oil, gas and mining) regarding human rights. The new criteria (see Box 17.3) had been developed over the preceding 12 months, following a process of focus groups with key stakeholders and an open public consultation.

Table 17.1 shows the status of 9 of the 23 companies affected by this enhanced Index requirement as of April 2002 and highlights areas of the policy, management system and reporting requirements that the companies did and did not meet.

The 23 global resource companies were required to meet the new criteria by the next Index review which took place in September 2002, (i.e. just five months after the public announcement of the changed requirement). At the meeting in September 2002, those companies that showed neither any response to meeting the criteria nor any intention of doing so were removed from the Index: nine companies met this fate. However a significant reaction was seen from the majority of companies, as illustrated in Table 17.2.

Who uses the FTSE4Good indices and how are they used?

Investors are using the FTSE4Good Index in index tracking funds, in active or enhanced index funds, as structured products and as a basis for engagement:

- **Index tracking funds.** In these funds, the companies in the index are bought in the same weighting as the Index and should therefore closely track the performance of the Index

Policy

The company has published policies covering human rights issues which are clearly communicated globally (in local languages where appropriate), the strategic responsibility for which rests with one or more board member(s) or senior manager(s) who report directly to the chief executive.

These policies must include:

- A commitment to respect all International Labour Organisation (ILO) core labour standards globally
- An explicit statement of support for the UNDHR
- Guidelines governing the use of armed security guards based on the UN Basic Principles on the Use of Force and Firearms by Law Enforcement Officials or the Code of Conduct for Law Enforcement Officials*
- A reference to respecting the rights of indigenous peoples

Management systems

The company has in place a management system to implement the policy. The management system must include:

- Training for employees globally in its human rights policy
- Evidence of a human rights impact assessment which includes the company identifying the major human rights issues it faces and integrating human rights concerns into its risk assessment procedures
- Consulting with independent local stakeholders in the countries of concern
- Monitoring the implementation of its human rights policy including the existence of procedures to remedy any non-compliance

Reporting

The company reports on its human rights policy and performance to the public in a published format.

* Signatories to the Voluntary Principles on Security and Human Rights meet this aspect of the requirement.

Box 17.3 FTSE4Good human rights criteria for resource companies

- **Active or enhanced Index funds.** In these funds, decisions are taken to over-weight or under-weight specific companies or sectors within the Index (i.e. only those companies that are included in the Index are considered for investment)

- **Structured products.** These work by capturing the upside performance of the Index with a 'guarantee' that the capital invested will be returned at the end

Name	Public policy communi-cated	Board or report to CEO	ILO/ UN GC/ SA8/ OECD	UNDHR	Guards policy	Indigenous policy	Implement policy and monitor	Employ-ment policy training	Local stake-holder consul-tation	HR risk/impact assessment	Report on hours
Cosmo Oil	Did not meet	Did not meet	Did not meet	Did not meet	Did not meet	Did not meet	Did not meet	Did not meet	Did not meet	Did not meet	Did not meet
Mitsubishi Corporation	Met	Did not meet	Met	Did not meet	Did not meet	Did not meet	Met	Did not meet	Met	Did not meet	Did not meet
Norsk Hydro	Did not meet	Met	Met	Met	Met	Did not meet	Met	Met	Met	Met	Met
Repsol-YPF	Did not meet	Did not meet	Met	Did not meet	Did not meet	Did not meet	Did not meet	Did not meet	Did not meet	Did not meet	Did not meet
Statoil	Met	Did not meet	Met	Did not meet	Met	Did not meet	Met	Met	Met	Met	Met
TotalFinaElf	Met	Did not meet	Met	Met	Did not meet	Did not meet	Met	Met	Met	Met	Did not meet
BG Group	Met	Met	Met	Met	Met	Did not meet	Met	Met	Met	Met	Met
Cairn Energy	Met	Met	Did not meet	Met	Met	Did not meet	Met	Did not meet	Met	Met	Did not meet
Lonmin	Did not meet	Did not meet	Met	Did not meet	Did not meet	Did not meet	Did not meet	Did not meet	Met	Did not meet	Did not meet

HR = human resources; ILO = International Labour Organisation; OECD = Organisation for Economic Co-operation and Development; SA = Social Accountability; UNDHR = United Nations Declaration of Human Rights; UN GC = United Nations Global Compact

TABLE 17.1 Compliance of companies against FTSE4Good human rights criteria as at April 2002

Name	Public policy communi- cated	Board or report to CEO	ILO/ UN GC/ SA8/ OECD	UNDHR	Guards policy	Indigenous policy	Implement policy and monitor	Employ- ment policy training	Local stake- holder consul- tation	HR risk/impact assessment	Report on hours
Cosmo Oil	Met	Met	Met	Met	Met	Met	Met	Met	Met	Met	Met
Mitsubishi Corporation	Met	Met	Met	Met	Met	Met	Met	Met	Met	Met	Met
Norsk Hydro	Met	Met	Met	Met	Met	Met	Met	Met	Met	Met	Met
Repsol-YPF	Met	Met	Met	Met	Met	Met	Met	Met	Met	Met	Did not meet
Statoil	Met	Met	Met	Met	Met	Met	Met	Met	Met	Met	Met
TotalFinaElf	Met	Met	Met	Met	Met	Met	Met	Met	Met	Met	Met
BG Group	Met	Met	Met	Met	Met	Met	Met	Met	Met	Met	Met
Cairn Energy	Met	Met	Met	Met	Met	Met	Met	Met	Met	Met	Met
Lonmin	Met	Met	Met	Met	Met	Met	Met	Met	Met	Met	Met

HR = human resources; ILO = International Labour Organisation; OECD = Organisation for Economic Co-operation and Development; SA = Social Accountability; UNDHR = United Nations Declaration of Human Rights; UN GC = United Nations Global Compact

TABLE 17.2 Compliance of companies against FTSE4Good human rights criteria as at September 2002

of the term. Most FTSE4Good products provide for, on average, 90% of the Index upside performance as part of the investments attraction. The average tranche size of this type of products is currently between £10 and £15 million. A number of investment banks operate in this sector providing the swap or hedge to the product's issuer to capture the Index performance

- **Engagement.** A number of investors use the Index's company membership as a proxy for identifying those companies that are clearly not addressing their non-financial risks and opportunities in a structured appropriate manner. These companies are identified by the fact that they are *not* included in the FTSE4Good Index and subsequently become targets for specific attention by investors who want to know why this is

Finally, FTSE4Good is also of use to companies as it helps them to both develop their own internal processes and to effectively communicate their social, environmental and ethical (SEE) business issues to their key stakeholders.

Changing corporate practices

As has already been mentioned, the Index criteria are not static. Unlike other similar products, the FTSE4Good criteria are continually evolving and becoming more challenging for companies to meet. Companies that are willing to engage with this process will continue to remain a member of the Index. Those companies that are not willing are publicly removed from the Index at one of its biannual reviews.

An important feature is that, when there is a change in the Index, the companies in the Index are given a detailed timetable of expected actions to comply with the required changes. During this period, FTSE develops a communications or engagement plan for all the companies affected by the change. This dialogue takes place at the highest level within the company and provides the directors of the business with the rationale and the business case for meeting the revised standards.

This proactive engagement process (and, possibly, the threat of adverse publicity if a company no longer meets the FTSE4Good criteria) has contributed to substantial changes in corporate practices. Companies from all over the world, including many household names, have positively engaged in this process and, as a result, have developed more robust policies, more sophisticated management processes and, in some instances, encouraging detailed corporate responsibility reporting. In this way, FTSE4Good has contributed to improved transparency, increased accountability for the delivery of corporate responsibility policy commitments, better governance of corporate responsibility and improved corporate responsibility.

There have been three major changes to the criteria since the Index was launched: tougher environmental requirements, more demanding human rights requirements and the inclusion of supply chain labour standards.

Inclusion in the FTSE4Good Index is evidence that a company has gone well beyond the statutory requirements laid out by governments by building corporate responsibility and sustainable business practices into the fabric of its operations. Companies in

FTSE4Good have developed a clear understanding of their social and environmental impacts, established policies, objectives and targets for improved performance, and have developed effective management systems to ensure that policies are implemented. The fact that their performance against their objectives and targets is monitored systematically, verified and reported to stakeholders is critical to ensuring the credibility of corporate actions in this area.

The role of FTSE4Good in the CSR debate

A number of factors have contributed to the effectiveness of FTSE4Good—peer-group pressure, media coverage, legislation, and transparency and disclosure. While disaggregating the specific effects of each of these factors is almost impossible, in combination they have been extremely important. Each is discussed briefly here.

In the early months after the launch of the Index, a number of well-known high-street brands were disappointed to find that their current corporate responsibility disclosures and practices were insufficient to meet the Index entry requirements, while their competitors across the 'street' were included in the Index. This competitive peer-group dynamic affected a number of leading companies across a number of sectors creating a 'race to the top' effect which drove standards and disclosure higher. In addition, the fact that companies excluded from the Index had a public relations issue to manage also contributed to companies taking action to ensure they were included in the Index. Indeed, media interest in CSR issues more generally has helped ensure that the debate around corporate responsibility has remained high, and has created a climate where a high-profile, well-managed index, such as FTSE4Good, is viewed as a key component of the industry's commitments to corporate responsibility.

The fact that many investors are planning to or being forced by legislation to take a much more active role in ensuring that companies are well run and employ sound business principles in order to protect their and their clients' investments has also propelled the issue higher on to the investment agenda. This has been fuelled by the entry into the market of government-sponsored institutional investors such as the Norwegian State Petroleum Fund and the FRR in France which have corporate responsibility as a significant part of their core investment strategy. This has not gone unnoticed by many companies.

Finally, increasing the standards and disclosure of CSR also provides a range of benefits and opportunities to companies, through increasing their (and investors') confidence that key corporate responsibility issues are being properly managed. FTSE4Good also provides investors with more information on which they can make an assessment of both the quality of a company's management and the future potential opportunities and risks it faces.

The role of indices in shareholder activism

Today, many codes of practice and, increasingly, legislation, provide a starting point for companies seeking to manage CSR issues. However, well-designed, -constructed and widely followed indices can provide the framework and encouragement for companies to adopt the good practices that codes of practice and legislation cannot.

Unlike asset management companies, index companies producing SRI indices do not enjoy the leverage of ownership to direct corporate behaviour. However, through the FTSE4Good Index, FTSE is making a significant contribution to raising the standards of corporate responsibility on behalf of investors and FTSE's clients.

Since the creation of the Index in 2001, increasing numbers of companies are meeting the challenges expressed in the FTSE4Good Index criteria. Many NGOs, investors and other followers of CSR are continually seeking answers to the question of how companies are responding to the demands of society. One process that can help is the future programme of developing and tightening the FTSE4Good Index criteria as this creates a compelling challenge of continual improvement for companies currently in the Index, and also helps define broader norms of corporate responsibility.

From an investment perspective, FTSE4Good provides investors with exposure to a broad range of companies that are doing more to manage their environmental and social impacts and that are capitalising on the benefits of good CSR practice. Through investing in FTSE4Good companies, investors enjoy the additional security of avoiding companies that are not addressing CSR issues, as these are the most at risk from potential environmental and social disasters. The FTSE engagement programme and the criteria development programme provide FTSE4Good investors with the mechanism to contribute to the encouragement of responsible and sustainable business practice around the world.

18

Measuring the effectiveness of investor engagement
GSK AND DEVELOPING-COUNTRY ACCESS TO ESSENTIAL MEDICINES*

Steve Waygood

Insight Investment, UK

One of the recurring questions with respect to investor engagement with companies is whether investors have sufficient influence over companies to motivate change in corporate responsibility policy. A related question is whether the effectiveness of investor engagement can be assessed (or whether changes in corporate behaviour can be attributed to investor engagement). This chapter reviews a specific case of investor engagement with a company—GlaxoSmithKline (GSK)—on a strategic corporate responsibility issue: namely, the threats to the industry's business models arising from the debates around access to medicines (in particular HIV/AIDS antiretrovirals) in Africa. The GSK case is one of the most high-profile and, in terms of the outcomes achieved, one of the most important examples of investor engagement on a specific corporate responsibility issue.

This chapter provides an overview of investor engagement with the company, placing the discussions in the context of ongoing non-governmental organisation (NGO) activity relating to access to medicines.[1] The chapter discusses investors' motivations

---

* The material in this chapter is based on research originally conducted for the author's PhD (Waygood 2004).

1 Over the past two decades, NGOs have significantly increased their attempts to use the influence of investors in company shares listed on the capital market in order to change corporate practices on a range of CSR issues. For example, Waygood 2004 identifies more than 30 NGOs making 70 substantive capital market interventions between 1990 and 2002.

for engaging with GSK and assesses the specific contribution of investors to encouraging the company to change its policies in relation to access to medicines.

Background

The provision of healthcare in developing countries is recognised as one of the key global public health issues. Oxfam estimates that '20% of the world's population does not have regular access to modern healthcare. One third does not have access to basic medicines. During the next year about 11 million people will die from infectious diseases . . . the vast majority will be poor' (Oxfam 2001a: 4). In 2001, Oxfam launched its Cut the Cost campaign, to encourage 'the world's pharmaceutical companies to do more to improve access to medicines in poor countries' (Oxfam 2001a: 1). Cut the Cost was part of Oxfam's broader campaign against World Trade Organisation's rules on patents (known as trade-related aspects of intellectual property rights or TRIPS). TRIPS enable companies to set prices over a 20-year period at the level necessary to make profitable returns on investment, by ensuring that others cannot copy their products and then sell them at a much lower price. While there are some provisions for countries to develop generic drugs (i.e. copies of patented drugs) in times of 'national crisis', Oxfam believed that the structure of the TRIPS system created too many barriers to ensuring proper access to drugs in developing countries.[2] Oxfam also argued that the reliance on profit-making companies to produce medicines had led to the under-provision of medication for diseases of the poor (Oxfam 2001a: 5):

> Of all annual health-related research, only 0.2% is spent on pneumonia, diarrhoea and tuberculosis—three poverty-related ailments which account for 18% of global disease burden . . . for many diseases of the poor, the potential market for even a patented drug is unlikely to be big enough to merit the investment.

Oxfam launched the Cut the Cost campaign at a briefing for City investors on 14 February 2001, with the intention of mobilising the support of large institutional investors. Oxfam decided to target institutional investors as it felt that its 'standard' campaigning tactics were proving ineffective at changing the behaviour of pharmaceutical companies. Oxfam called on institutional investors to use their influence to encourage GSK (in particular) to develop a policy setting out how it would meet its commitment to 'maximising affordable access [to medication] . . . within the first three months of the [newly merged] company's existence' (Oxfam 2001a).

The briefing was hosted by Friends Ivory & Sime—Oxfam's pension fund manager—which was then one of the largest socially responsible investment (SRI) institutions in the UK (Friends Ivory & Sime subsequently acquired Foreign and Colonial and became F&C Asset Management plc). Other investors present at the meeting included the Co-

---

2 See Kinley and McBeth 2003: 62-63 for an overview of the legal arguments for and against TRIPS in the context of developing-country access to medicines.

operative Insurance Society (CIS), Henderson, Hermes, Jupiter, Methodist Central Finance Board (CFB), Morley and the Universities Superannuation Scheme (USS). All of these investment institutions had previously made statements regarding the extent to which they were 'responsible investors'. Furthermore, a number had been monitoring the access to medicines issue for quite a while, and some had raised the issue with GSK in the preceding year.

Perhaps the most significant business (or financial) issue for investors was the potential for inappropriate corporate responses to the Oxfam case to increase the pressure for changes in intellectual property rules. Investors were acutely aware that pharmaceutical companies depend on patent protection to secure future revenue streams. The costs of developing medicines (e.g. R&D, safety testing, compliance testing) are so great that the industry has argued that it needs long-term patent protection to allow the industry to make commercial returns on its research and other activities. Consequently, any threat to the TRIPS regime would be seen by investors as being of strategic importance to the sector and, perhaps cynically, of greater interest than the purely ethical arguments around access to medicines. Oxfam argued that (Oxfam 2001a: 5):

> Pharmaceutical companies face a major reputation risk if they do not do more to promote access to life-saving drugs in the developing world. This is particularly important at a time of unprecedented scrutiny of the industry's record in this field . . . it carries with it the threat of more stringent government regulation . . . [It] is both ethically correct and in the company's self interest to ensure that those who own and control medical knowledge use all means at their disposal to stop preventable diseases from killing millions of people every year.

The City briefing also reviewed the risks to GSK's reputation arising from its involvement with the South African Pharmaceutical Manufacturers Association (SAPMA)'s case against the South African government, which sought to prevent the import of generic medicines. Oxfam also criticised GSK for appearing to defend patents on AIDS drugs in Ghana and Uganda.

Analysis

Viability and feasibility of investor engagement

GSK was an appropriate target for NGO campaigning and for investor engagement for six reasons:

1 The pharmaceutical sector as a whole was being targeted by NGOs. The NGOs presented strong arguments suggesting that the industry's approach to access to medicines was threatening the intellectual property rights regime (a critical component of the sector's business model)

2   GSK was newly formed from a merger of Glaxo Wellcome and SmithKline-Beecham and was, consequently, receiving a considerable degree of media and investor scrutiny

3   The newly combined entity was in the process of establishing Group-wide policies, which provided a timely opportunity to exert influence

4   The component parts of the Group had previously reported total sales of US$27.2 billion, including pharmaceutical sales of US$22.2 billion, giving it around a 7% share of the global market (Oxfam 2001a: 10). This market share rendered the company highly influential in its sector

5   GSK's chief executive had previously voiced his 'commitment to maximising affordable access to medicines in the developing world' (Oxfam 2001a: 8). It is likely that one of Oxfam's motivations was to encourage GSK to establish a new norm for the industry in relation to this issue

6   GSK was then the largest UK pharmaceutical company, with a market capitalisation of £107.3 billion,[3] and was a significant shareholding for many UK institutional investors—Oxfam's target audience

At the time, there were two factors that were seen as preventing GSK from offering cheaper access to medication in developing countries—'parallel importing' and 'reference pricing'. Parallel importing related to the risk that generic drugs produced in less-developed countries would be smuggled back into developed countries. Oxfam proposed a series of practical solutions, including more-stringent policing, tougher penalties and specific labelling. Oxfam also cited evidence from existing restrictions on parallel importing of branded products that allowed prices of patent-protected products to vary substantially among developed countries (Oxfam 2001b: 2). In relation to reference pricing, the concern was that developed countries would use the developing-country cost price as a reference point in negotiating their own contracts. Oxfam recognised that this relied on the political will of developed-country governments to refuse to use such negotiation tactics, and cited the UK government as an example of a country that had made such a commitment. The fact that Oxfam had recognised the potential barriers to its proposals and had proposed possible solutions helped reduce the extent to which investors viewed these factors as representing insurmountable limitations.

It should be noted that the pharmaceutical companies were aware of the business risks relating to the access to medicines issue and some had taken steps to address the matter. For example, GSK had been offering antiretrovirals on a not-for-profit basis for mother-to-child transmission since 1997, and was working with the Joint UN Programme on HIV/AIDS (UNAIDS) to distribute medication (GSK 2001: 2). The key question for investors was whether these actions would be sufficient to mitigate the risks to the business model.

---

3   Based on price per share of £17.32 at close of business on 8 January 2001.

Effectiveness of investor engagement

Following the launch of Oxfam's campaign, Jean-Pierre Garnier, chief executive of GSK, reportedly undertook to 'make the issue a priority' (*Financial Times* 2001a), and GSK subsequently published a policy on access to drugs (GSK 2001). The policy was cautiously welcomed by Oxfam. On 19 April 2001, SAPMA abandoned its case against the South African government. For GSK, this was a 'significant event . . . amount[ing] to a recognition that their legal battle in South Africa was a public relations disaster' (*Financial Times* 2001b).

As discussed above, a number of the investors attending the City briefing had previously engaged with the company on the question of access to medicines in developing countries. Following the City briefing, most of the attendees subsequently claimed to have raised concerns with the company. Friends Ivory & Sime, for example, had 'emphasised how important it [was] for GSK to protect its intellectual property rights . . . Failure to be seen to respond adequately to global concerns about the negative effects of the new . . . intellectual property regime could undermine the public case for patent protection.'[4] Such investor engagement typically took the form of one-to-one meetings with the senior management of GSK. In some cases this engagement was supported by written correspondence highlighting key issues and offering suggestions for GSK's policy on this issue. Some investors were also quoted in press reports on the issue.

Was this investor engagement effective? GSK itself confirmed that it had been influenced by investor concerns (*Financial Times* 2001a):

> Jean-Pierre Garnier, Chief Executive of GlaxoSmithKline, one of the pharmaceutical companies that led the industry's retreat from the case, which had become a public relations catastrophe, said he had been influenced by concerns from investors, shareholders and the public about access to medicines.

The *Financial Times* subsequently commented that: 'GlaxoSmithKline has bowed to pressure from institutional investors and health activists' (Dyer 2003). Oxfam also acknowledged the important role of investors. For example, Sophia Tickell, Oxfam's senior policy advisor on the public sector, had publicly stated that (EIRIS 2002: 3):

> We knew that if we could persuade investors of our arguments, this would have a powerful impact on the companies as [investors] are more influential [with companies] than non-governmental organisations.

These comments strongly suggest that GSK would not have changed its policy in this area were it not for investors' interest in the issue. This appears to confirm that investors do indeed have sufficient influence over companies to motivate change in corporate responsibility policy. However, to properly assess the outcomes from the NGO campaign and associated investor engagement requires that attention be paid to the question of whether or not this policy change actually led to an increase in access to medication. GSK's subsequent corporate social responsibility (CSR) report highlighted 'increased shipments of Combivir[5] to the developing world from 2.2 million tablets in

---

4   Personal communication by email from C. Mackenzie to Howard Carter, chief executive of Friends Ivory & Sime (unpublished), 20 April 2000.

5   An antiretroviral drug used in the treatment of patients with HIV/AIDS.

2001 to nearly 6 million tablets in 2002' (GSK 2003: 3). This increase approximately equates to an additional 2 million daily doses (or, expressed another way, approximately 5,500 more people per annum had access to 'affordable' Combivir). It is pertinent to note that, while this increase is significant, it would only make a small difference to the AIDS problem in the region given that 29.4 million people are thought to be suffering from AIDS in sub-Saharan Africa alone (UNAIDS/WHO 2002: 6).

Oxfam followed its Cut the Cost campaign with a broader initiative calling on the pharmaceutical sector in general to be more socially responsible when dealing with the developing world, and for investors to be active in challenging their policies. Oxfam, Save the Children and Voluntary Services Overseas (VSO) jointly developed a framework (Oxfam *et al.* 2002) to assess the responses of pharmaceutical companies to health problems in the developing world. The document proposed a set of benchmarks to assist investors in assessing the social responsibility of pharmaceutical companies, and surveyed GSK, Abbott, AstraZeneca, Aventis, Bayer, Boehringer Ingelheim, Bristol-Myers Squibb (BMS), Hoffmann-La Roche, Merck, Novartis and Pfizer. The benchmarks relate to company policies and practices in pricing, patents, joint public–private initiatives, R&D and appropriate use of medicines. In launching this report, Oxfam stated (Manifest 2002: 1):

> Twenty six people die every minute from infectious diseases. These deaths are avoidable. Drugs companies can and should do more. Investors too have a vital role to play as how they invest their money can have a positive influence on people's lives. There is a direct link between the City investor and an HIV-positive baby in Zambia.

This follow-up activity is highly relevant to the context of this chapter as two institutional investors—Friends Ivory & Sime (now F&C) and USS—later developed the framework into a broad collaborative investor initiative on access to drugs. This initiative was to become formalised as the Pharmaceutical Shareowners Group (PSG), 'with more than £454 billion of assets' and comprising 'six investment houses: Co-operative Insurance, Henderson Global Investors, Insight Investment Management, ISIS Asset Management, Jupiter Asset Management, Morley Fund Management and Schroders . . . [and] one pension fund: Universities Superannuation Scheme' (Gimbel 2003). The purpose of this collaborative endeavour was to benchmark all companies in the sector in order to help management, investors and analysts evaluate how pharmaceutical companies were responding to the risks related to the public health crisis in emerging markets (USS 2003: 1). In effect, the PSG institutionalised analysis of the issue—a significant outcome that further demonstrates the extent of investor engagement on this issue.

Regarding the relative distribution of costs and benefits, based on the GSK data cited above, investor engagement on this issue appears to have contributed to 5,500 more people in developing countries having access to antiretroviral medication in 2002—with further increases in subsequent years.[6] The previous annual cost of a course of Combivir in Africa was around £10,000 (GSK 2003). Consequently, the value of the

---

6　These further increases are not included here, as they are even more likely to have resulted from a range of other factors that cannot be solely attributable to investor engagement on this issue.

increase in access can be calculated as in the order of £55 million at previous prices. The campaign also resulted in the managers of more than £450 billion of capital expressing formal concern about the issue and institutionalising its ongoing monitoring and measurement.

Were these costs (or forgone revenues) material to GSK? Most of the costs associated with the campaign relate to GSK's loss of current and future profit from developing countries. Prior to the campaign, the region represented less than 1% of the company's overall profitability (an insignificant element of stock valuation). Similarly, in view of the lack of development in the region, GSK was unlikely to secure substantial revenue streams from the region over the 20-year lifetime of the Combivir patent. As a consequence, the costs incurred by GSK can be considered insignificant when compared to the long-term benefits to the pharmaceutical industry from having reduced the threat to the TRIPS system. This point, regarding a reduction in threat to TRIPS system, highlights one unintended consequence of Oxfam's campaign. That is, the decision by GSK to increase shipments of Combivir may have reduced Oxfam's ability to generate public outrage about the TRIPS regime.

Concluding comments

The chapter shows that investors can use their influence over companies to motivate change in corporate responsibility policies. Investors including the CIS, Friends Ivory & Sime, Henderson, Hermes, Jupiter, CFB, Morley and USS engaged with GSK regarding its policy on access to medication. The motivations for these investors to engage (at least those that were publicly expressed) related mainly to the strategic importance of the issue to the company's business model, and to the fact that these investors had published policy statements regarding the extent to which they were responsible owners.

From the evidence presented here, investor engagement with GSK contributed very significantly to changing the company's approach to the issue of access to medicines and has also generated further momentum (through the PSG) for further investor engagement on the issue. However, it is too early to assess whether investor involvement actually enhanced long-term shareholder value. While, as discussed above, GSK's actions may have reduced the threat to the TRIPS regime, campaigners have not changed their stance on the system and may yet be successful in their calls for reform of TRIPS. Ultimately, the shareholder value case for the policy change can be retrospectively assessed only in the light of any changes to public policy.

This case study highlights three important issues that are relevant to the broader themes of this book. The first is that, while there is clear evidence that investors played a key role in catalysing corporate action, it is not clear how much engagement investors needed to conduct in order to achieve these changes. Is there a certain level of investor activity or interest (either in terms of level of activity or number of investors interested in a specific issue) necessary for companies to take action on a specific issue?

The second, albeit related, issue is that investor engagement was conducted in the context of a broader NGO campaign. What would investors have achieved in the absence of such a campaign? Oxfam created a significant brand risk to GSK by allocating relatively significant resources to the campaign, providing well-researched business case arguments based on clear ethical principles, and focusing public attention through a concerted media campaign. Therefore, this case study does not necessarily indicate that investor engagement on corporate responsibility issues can be effective in the absence of an NGO campaign (after all, there was some evidence of investor engagement with GSK on the issue *before* the NGO launched the campaign). Conversely, it is not clear what Oxfam would have achieved in the absence of active engagement from institutional investors. The analysis suggests it is reasonable to hypothesise that investors did play a significant role in generating the outcomes achieved. However, given that GSK was already engaging with the issue, and had committed to further action, the extent of investor influence may have been limited to legitimising the business-case arguments set out by Oxfam and supporting the board of GSK in taking a decision to implement actions that incur short-term costs but aim to increase shareholder value over the longer-term.

The third is that the NGO–investor–company dialogue is not hermetically sealed. The challenges of providing adequate access to medicines will not be achieved by increased corporate action alone. For example, the governments of developing countries also have responsibilities in relation to purchasing or producing sufficient quantities of these medicines and providing the broader health infrastructure necessary for ensuring that these medicines are dispensed and distributed appropriately (see further Chapter 26).

References

EIRIS (Ethical Investment Research Service) (2002) *The Ethical Investor*, Spring 2002.

Financial Times (2001a) 'GSK', *Financial Times*, 16 February 2001: 12.

—— (2001b) 'Editorial', *Financial Times*, 20 April 2001: 19.

Dyer, G. (2003) 'GSK bows to pressure and halves price of top AIDS drug', *Financial Times*, 28 April 2003.

Gimbel, F. (2003) 'Ethical investors unite to strengthen initiatives', *Financial Times*, 4 August 2003: 2.

GSK (2001) *Facing the Challenge: June 2001* (London: GSK)

—— (2003) *The Impact of Medicines: Corporate and Social Responsibility Report 2002* (London: GSK).

Kinley, D., and A. McBeth (2003) 'Human Rights, Trade and Multinational Corporations', in R. Sullivan (ed.), *Business and Human Rights: Dilemmas and Solutions* (Sheffield, UK: Greenleaf Publishing): 52-68.

Manifest (2002) 'Drug Companies: Investors asked to assess firms on ethics', www.manifest.co.uk, accessed 15 September 2002.

Oxfam (2001a) *Briefing Paper on GlaxoSmithKline. Dare to Lead: Public Health and Company Wealth* (Oxford, UK: Oxfam, February 2001).

—— (2001b) *Implausible Denial: Why the Drug Giants' Arguments on Patents Don't Stack Up* (Oxford, UK: Oxfam).

——, Save the Children and VSO (2002) *Beyond Philanthropy* (Oxford, UK: Oxfam).

UNAIDS/WHO (2002) *Global AIDS Epidemic Update: December 2002* (Geneva: UNAIDS/WHO).

USS (Universities Superannuation Scheme) (2003) *Quarter 1 2003 Report* (London: USS).

Waygood, S. (2004) 'NGOs and Equity Investment: A Critical Assessment of the Practices of UK NGOs in Using the Capital Market as a Campaign Device', University of Surrey, unpublished PhD thesis.

Part IV
Perspectives on responsible investment

19

The universal owner's role in sustainable economic development[*]

James P. Hawley and Andrew T. Williams

Saint Mary's College of California, USA

This chapter briefly outlines one consequence of the sea change of equity ownership that has occurred in common-law countries in the last 30 years: the growth of the large, highly diversified and professionally managed institutional owner. What we term the rise of the 'fiduciary owner' (representing that large proportion of the adult population whose pension savings and investment are managed by fiduciaries) leads to a different and historically very new form of ownership. These large owners typically hold a cross-section of the economy as a whole.[1] This chapter explores some of the profound consequences of these developments as they intersect with growing global concerns about sustainable economic growth and development. The focus is on how negative and positive externalities are managed and accounted for, and how, more generally, institutional owners manage and account for political, reputational and market risk.

The first section outlines the rise of fiduciary capitalism and describes how fiduciary duties are defined and exercised. This is based on the growth of what is termed 'universal ownership'. From this understanding a form of what we call 'universal monitor-

---

* This chapter originally appeared, in a different form, in *The Journal of Corporate Environmental Strategy* in autumn 2002. This version expands and extends ideas in the earlier article based on events and reflection.

1 These ideas are developed more fully in our book, *The Rise of Fiduciary Capitalism* (Hawley and Williams 2000a).

ing' is discussed. The chapter then briefly examines sustainable development in general, and concludes with a discussion of how universal ownership and an expanded and deepened vision of fiduciary duty intersect: how this relates to past and current developments in corporate governance is also discussed.

The rise of fiduciary capitalism

One of the most striking characteristics of market capitalism in the US and Great Britain is the way that corporate ownership has evolved over the past hundred years. Early in the last century, for example, ownership in the US was concentrated firmly in the hands of founders such as Carnegie, DuPont and Ford, and their companies were identified with, and run by, them personally. But, as the 20th century progressed, important changes occurred as a multitude of individual shareholders came to replace the founders. This led to what Berle and Means (1967) famously characterised as the 'divorce of ownership from control'. Thus, for most of the 20th century, capitalism in America (and later in Britain) was viewed as 'managerial capitalism' in which the major decisions about the course of the corporation were made by professional managers hired to run companies within the constraints provided by big labour and big government and with minimal input from widely diversified shareholders, the nominal 'owners' (Chandler 1977).

Beginning in the 1970s, and accelerating through the remainder of the century, a reconcentration of ownership took place as fiduciary institutions—mutual funds, insurance companies and, most importantly, public and private pension funds—came to own a larger and larger fraction of corporate equity. As recently as the 1970s, the household sector owned about 80% of US corporate equity. By 2003 their holdings had fallen almost by half to 43%, while institutional holdings had risen to almost 45% (US Federal Reserve 2004). The trend is more pronounced in the UK where, in 2003, only 15% of equity was held by individuals. Institutional ownership, which peaked at about 60% in 1994, has since declined somewhat. This decline is due to increased equity holdings of non-UK individuals and particularly of non-UK (primarily US) institutions which currently stand at about 32% of the British equity (National Statistics 2004).

Fiduciary duties

This shifting pattern of ownership from individuals to institutions has a number of important implications, as institutional owners exercise almost all of the rights and responsibilities that normally go with share ownership. They decide to buy or sell the stock of individual companies. They vote and submit proxies, and they can directly lobby management for changes in the way companies operate. What the institutions cannot do is profit directly from their activities. Instead, these institutional owners are 'professional' owners. That is, they are hired by individuals to act as agents in certain specified situations. In the US, the UK and other common-law countries, these institutional owners are fiduciary institutions and, hence, their operations are subject to the very high legal standards of 'loyalty' and 'care' imposed on those who are responsible for managing other people's money.[2]

In the US, the duty of loyalty, often referred to as the 'exclusive benefit rule', requires a fiduciary to take only those actions that are to the exclusive benefit of the beneficiaries of the institution: for example, retirees and potential retirees of a pension fund. Institutional investors have often strictly interpreted the duty of loyalty to prohibit consideration of any factor other than those directly related to maximising shareholder wealth. Thus, they have rejected consideration of factors that are judged not to materially affect financial returns. Furthermore, they have been largely indifferent to the source of financial returns.[3] The companion duty, the duty of care, requires the fiduciary to act as a 'prudent person' in the exercise of his/her obligations. That is, to take only action that, after due consideration, a prudent person would take in a similar situation.[4] Until recently, social, environmental and ethical (SEE) issues were not, on the whole, seen as material to the value of a firm, and thus did not need to be disclosed to investors. However, this has been changing rapidly. In the UK, investment vehicles must now 'comply or explain' as to how and by what standards they screen their investments in publicly traded companies for SEE issues. In the US a far more limited mandate from the Securities and Exchange Commission (SEC) applies to mutual funds. Thus, the duty of care has come to include new forms of 'materiality' which are typically akin to market risk. As of April 2005, UK-listed corporations, as part of their annual reports, had to develop and complete an operating and financial review which describes both quantitatively and qualitatively (as appropriate to the specific business) all social, economic, environmental and ethical factors that might materially affect the firm's valuation.

These two duties (i.e. the duties of loyalty and care) have contributed substantially to the way ownership of US corporate equity is exercised. Just as the management of corporations became professionalised earlier in the 20th century, so the ownership of equity became professionalised late in the century. Professional owners are trained, typically in law or business schools, to exercise legal ownership on behalf of others and to fulfil their fiduciary duties. They are paid for performing these duties, and their performance is judged on how well they execute those duties. For example, professional owners are obligated to study and consider proxy proposals and the various SEC filings of the companies they own, or to delegate that responsibility to money managers whose performance they must monitor.

The US Department of Labor, through its famous 'Avon letter', has defined proxies as plan assets and, therefore, as something toward which institutions governed by the Employee Retirement Income Security Act 1974 (ERISA) must exercise their duties of

---

2   Fiduciary duties have a long standing in English common law. In the US, they have been codified in Section 1104 of the Employee Retirement and Income Security Act (ERISA).

3   There have been exceptions to this rule: notably the movement to divest investments in South Africa during the latter days of apartheid. However, such actions are taken reluctantly and only under unusual circumstances, since a strict interpretation of the duty of loyalty rejects any action that cannot be justified as enhancing shareholder wealth.

4   See Cogan 2000 for an excellent description of the fiduciary duties of loyalty and care. Note that the duty of care is sometimes cast as the prudent 'investor' rule rather than as the prudent 'person' rule. This is a higher standard of care and places a greater burden on fiduciaries to act in a thoroughly professional manner.

loyalty and care.[5] In 2002, the SEC issued what may become known as the 'super Avon letter', in which it extends the fiduciary duty to vote proxies to all investment advisors. In that letter, the chair of the SEC states: 'We believe . . . that an investment advisor must exercise its responsibility to vote the shares of its clients in a manner that is consistent with . . . its fiduciary duties under federal and state law to act in the best interests of its clients' (Lublin 2002). In 2003, the SEC went even further when it announced rule changes requiring mutual fund companies to report how they voted portfolio company proxies (SEC 2003). This important rule change was due in no small part to the actions initiated by Domini Social Investments and AFL–CIO trade union funds which led the charge calling on the SEC to mandate not just viewing proxies as assets, but the release of how each fund votes its proxies (Domini Social Investments 2002).

Universal ownership

While all institutional investors in the US are subject to the twin duties of loyalty and care, some institutions have grown to such a size or have adopted indexing strategies for such a large fraction of their portfolios that they have, in effect, become 'universal owners'. Because of their widely diversified portfolios, universal owners effectively own the economy as a whole by owning a small portion of almost every company with marketable equity. As such, their portfolios' performance—hence their ability to provide for beneficiaries—depends more on the overall health of the economy than on the fortunes of any particular company. Furthermore, many of these institutions should naturally adopt a long-term outlook when it comes to investing since they are pension funds with predictable liabilities stretching far into the future.

Contemporary examples of universal owners are the large state pension funds such as the California Public Employee Retirement System (CalPERS) and the CREF portion of TIAA–CREF[6] (the retirement system for academics in the US) and the Universities Superannuation Scheme (USS, the retirement system for academics in the UK). CalPERS had assets at the end of 2004 of approximately US$170 billion dollars, with most of the equity portion of its assets invested in index funds. USS is the one of the largest pension schemes in the UK while CREF, the equity portion of TIAA–CREF, is invested in over 4,000 different equity issues.[7]

Combined with the fiduciary duties of loyalty and care, the fact that the performance of a universal owners' portfolio depends on overall economic performance suggests that a universal owner should act in particular ways. In addition to performing due diligence with respect to individual firms and engaging in traditional forms of institutional

---

5   ERISA regulations generally apply to private employee pensions funds. Other fiduciaries in the US are subject to various state laws; however, the general thrust of fiduciary duties is supplied by ERISA.

6   TIAA–CREF is the acronym for Teachers Insurance and Annuity Association College Retirement Equities Fund.

7   About 20% of the portfolios of both CalPERS and TIAA-CREF are invested in the equity of firms outside the US. Thus, they are global investors in the terms Monks (2002) uses. Large mutual fund companies such as Fidelity Investments are also universal owners but, until the recent SEC action referred to above, they typically have not acted from this perspective. However, the Vanguard Group is an exception having an active proxy-voting programme based on detailed guidelines (www.vanguard.com).

investor activism centred on corporate governance issues, a universal owner should be mindful of the interactions between various elements of its portfolio—particularly the market failures represented by positive and negative externalities thrown off by portfolio companies. Thus, universal owners have a particular stake in superior macroeconomic performance—and in the policies and programmes that promote it.

This perspective stands in stark contrast to the traditional view where an investor picking individual stocks may profit by investing in companies that try to increase profits by shifting some production costs to other companies or to society at large in the form of negative externalities, such as pollution. Likewise, traditional investors may avoid investing in companies that generate positive externalities, such as education and training, because the firm captures only part of the benefit but bears all the cost.

In contrast, a universal owner is likely to experience lower profit from a portfolio company's negative externality since the externality will be transferred in whole or in part to other portfolio companies. In the same way, it benefits from positive externalities because its other portfolio companies are the beneficiaries. For example, the gains from a better-educated and more highly trained workforce accrue to all companies, even if the company making the investment cannot capture all of the benefits. These impacts are particularly important to universal owners, since the benefit of a negative externality in the form of lowered costs may be much less than the social cost it imposes on the rest of the portfolio. Likewise, the benefit generated by positive externalities may exceed the cost to the company generating it.

The costs and benefits are, of course, proportional to the universal owner's holdings in the firm generating the externality and in the firms being affected by the externality. Since universal owners have large diversified holdings, often holding 1% or 2% of outstanding equity, externality effects may be relatively large in monetary terms. However, in pursuing this programme, the goal is not to totally eliminate the externality. Rather, a universal owner should expend resources to internalise externalities up to the point where the benefit it receives from internalisation equals the cost it bears to bring about the internalisation. Coalitions of universal owners may be able to act together to reduce the cost of internalising some externalities. Furthermore, the duty of loyalty requires that the universal owner consider only those economic effects that materially affect its returns, even if there are costs or benefits conferred on society at large. Nevertheless, it is clear that these types of externalities have significant negative impact on firms in a universal owner's portfolio; that is, they are partially internalised.

While universal owners should only look at externalities that (as externalities) impact their portfolio, that does not mean they should ignore ones that may not directly impact it. For example, child labour in many developing countries results in concrete non-pecuniary externalities. A child who does not go to school limits the future productivity potential of that economy and is, therefore, an externalised opportunity cost. While US or UK investors may not internalise that type of externality in their portfolios, the firms in their portfolios may experience increased risk (e.g. market, political, regulatory, reputational) if they invest in companies that use child labour in their supply chains. So investors may be affected because of the indirect (or consequential) risks to their investments rather than by the externality itself.

Sustainable development

Sustainable development has many meanings. The classic Brundtland Report for the UN published in 1987 defines it as 'development that meets the needs of the present, without compromising the ability of future generations to meet their own needs' (WCED 1987). The Organisation for Economic Co-operation and Development (OECD) notes that: 'Economic growth is a fundamental driver of human welfare, and a key component of sustainable development' (OECD 2001: 16).

Clearly, sustainable development is a broad concept that includes multiple definitions and possibilities.[8] At its core, however, it suggests that human welfare is best served by being sensitive to the implications of current economic activity for both current and future generations. Because of their long time horizons, universal owners and, particularly, pension funds share the sustainable development movement's concern for husbanding resources while using them efficiently, in the broadest sense, and for taking into account the impact of current decisions not only on other actors on the current economic scene but on future generations as well. They are well positioned to appreciate the need to develop policies toward portfolio companies that encourage sustainable economic development. The over-production of negative externalities and the under-provision of positive externalities clearly undermine a society's ability to achieve sustainable economic development.

A universal owner's role in fostering sustainable economic development

Universal owners should adopt a comprehensive approach to their portfolios as part and parcel of their fiduciary responsibilities. Not only should they monitor the economic performance of particular companies—the traditional way to fulfil the responsibilities of the duties of loyalty and care—but they should also engage in 'universal monitoring' which attempts to identify important sources of positive and negative externalities. Furthermore, universal owners should also be aware of broader risks to the economic success of portfolio companies such as global warming (an externality with potentially massive consequences) and the reputational risk associated with, for example, the labour practices of suppliers. Some of these risks may not stem directly from traditional externalities (e.g. reputational risk) but, nonetheless, they should be the subject of universal monitoring. It is only by viewing their portfolios as a whole that universal owners can maximise investment returns for their beneficiaries.

---

8   See, for example, Férone *et al.* 2002: 87-125, 179-88. The authors make the important point that different cultures, nations and regional groupings define sustainable development in very different ways, emphasising very different aspects. For example, they note that Nordic countries tend to emphasise the environmental aspects of sustainability, while southern European countries tend to focus on the human capital and social relations aspects.

Universal monitoring

Universal monitoring can take a number of forms. Fiduciaries can articulate a position on an area such as worker education and training. This would be a natural area of concern for a university endowment fund. The institution can then communicate its position on this issue to portfolio companies as an expression of desired corporate behaviour. The fiduciaries can also survey portfolio companies as to their practices in these areas and use the results to develop a report on best and worst practices on an industry-by-industry basis. Highly ranked companies would get recognition and encouragement for their best practices, while some fiduciaries might find it useful to meet with poorly ranked companies in order to gain further insight into their poor performance while lobbying for improvements. Other fiduciaries might take a 'let the sun shine in' approach and simply publish the results.

In addition to trying to influence policies at portfolio companies, institutional investors, by virtue of their broadly diversified portfolios, and because their beneficiaries often represent a broad cross-section of the population, have a particular interest in fostering appropriate public policy in areas such as accountancy reform, education, health, tort reform, trade policy and environmental policy. As such, they are in an excellent position to form coalitions with other institutional investors with similar interests.

An example of investors focusing on environmental issues in investee companies is the recent decision by CalSTIRS (the large California teachers' pension fund, with assets of about US$90 billion at the end of 2004) to focus on two environmentally problematic industries—car manufacturers and electricity generation utilities. Both industries are major contributors to global climate change as well as other forms of pollution, and both have resisted state and federal regulatory pressures to reduce their emissions. The CalSTIRS type of approach argues that resisting higher regulatory standards through lobbying and legal actions are counterproductive and wasteful of shareholder assets.

An example of universal monitoring for risk (as compared to externalities) is CalPERS's decision to set standards for performance in emerging markets relating to issues such as political stability, market transparency and labour market practices (Engardio 2002). Clearly, many of these factors overlap with issues that are important to sustainable economic development. Under this new policy, CalPERS will abstain from investing in equities traded on exchanges in countries that fail to meet their standards.[9] In 2004, only 15 emerging market countries met CalPERS's standards, with economically important countries such as China, Russia and India being excluded from investment (CalPERS 2004). By making issues such as labour practices and press freedom, along with traditional issues such as transparency, trading costs and taxation, criteria for investment, CalPERS has taken a stand on broad public policy issues as viewed from a risk/opportunity perspective, and is acting as a universal owner.

A similarly important example of universal monitoring is a report, *Climate Change: A Risk Management Challenge for Institutional Investors* (Mansley and Dlugolecki 2001), commissioned by the USS.[10] The report argues that, since the fund holds both equity and property that would probably be drastically affected by global climate change, it

---

9 This decision does not affect overseas direct investment decisions by firms in which CalPERS holds stock.

10 Other institutional investors such as CREF are also deeply interested in this issue.

should develop analysis and policies in this area. The reason for this recommendation was that the negative externality of adverse climate change would probably force major costs on to portfolio companies and, consequently, a prudent stance on the part of universal owners is appropriate. To respond to these challenges the report recommended a number of measures that institutional investors should take, such as reviewing portfolios for risk, engaging with investee companies, etc. The report also states (Mansley and Dlugolecki 2001: 47):

> It is possible to argue . . . that long term universal investors have a substantial degree of common interest and purpose with the good of the economy as a whole. This implies that it may be in the narrow interest of institutional investors to press for actions that support the common economic good.

Thus, the report recognises that a universal owner's broad and long-term view place it in a unique position to both engage with firms it owns and to weigh in on public policy issues, acting as a 'bridge between public policy, corporate governance and the well-being of individuals (especially beneficiaries)' (Mansley and Dlugolecki 2001: 12).

In addition, the report notes that universal owners have an interest in assessing the impact of special interest lobbying and influence peddling of the firms they own. Activity in the public policy process on the climate change issue can help to offset such special-interest activity. Importantly, universal owners have the potential to 'stand above short-term and vested interests and could play a powerful role in supporting policy-makers to address climate change in the optimal economic and environmental way' and that, from a strategic universal investor perspective, 'there is a case for institutional investors to adopt a more strategic approach to climate change risk. This is to intervene in the policy debate [nationally and internationally] to encourage governments to take action to address climate change' (Mansley and Dlugolecki 2001: 23).

The traditional corporate governance approach

This approach to what we call universal monitoring is similar to the approach institutional investors have successfully taken on issues of corporate governance. Since the mid-1980s, major institutional investors led by CalPERS and the New York City funds as well as by state pension funds from states such as Florida, Wisconsin and Colorado, and TIAA–CREF (in the US), have actively lobbied for good corporate governance practices at portfolio companies. At times they have achieved a considerable measure of success.

Traditional corporate governance activism is motivated by the realisation that, when representative portfolio companies perform better financially, they will act as a model for other companies—and as a competitive prod as well (Hawley *et al.* 1994). The same motivation animates the concerns of a universal owner for whom superior economic performance depends not only on what happens at individually targeted companies but on the behaviour of the portfolio as a whole. Failures at firms such as Enron, Global Crossings, Waste Management, Parmalat, Ahold and others do not suggest that this corporate governance approach has failed, so much as they indicate that the lack of transparency (and, in some cases, outright fraud on the part of managers) calls for tighter and perhaps new methods of monitoring. For example, these 'high-flying' failures were apparently (and, typically, fraudulently) hyper-performers, and therefore not on the corporate governance radar screen which typically focuses on financial underperformers. Performing extraordinary due diligence on hyper-performers to determine whether their success is real or illusory should be one lesson learned from the Enron- and WorldCom-type scandals. That is, corporate governance monitoring should be focused on *all* outliers, both underperformers and super-performers.

A fiduciary's duties of loyalty and care require that an institutional investor has access to accurate, reliable information in a timely fashion about the companies it owns or is thinking of owning. Thus, both traditional institutional investors and universal owners have a deep, natural interest in transparency and accountability, an interest challenged by the Enron-type scandals that raises important questions about the independence of the public accounting profession and the completeness and accuracy of the information it provides to investors.

Conclusion

We have argued that a universal ownership perspective, implemented by universal monitoring, are logical extensions of fiduciary duty. Therefore, it is important to develop a clear idea of what universal monitoring should do (its scope) and how to accomplish each part of that task (e.g. analysis of interactive portfolio externality effects, monitoring for different aspects of risk in firms and industries). We have suggested some possible strategies, but we expect that as the issues presented by universal ownership are engaged other, possibly more effective, strategies will emerge.

Universal monitoring will not by itself solve the world's sustainability problems, nor is it meant to. It will, however, contribute to an understanding which should be reflected in a single financial bottom line of a universal owner. When there is a full accounting within large portfolios for pecuniary and non-pecuniary externalities, the long-term self-interest of the most significant global equity investors comes to overlap to an important degree with many sustainability concerns. Additionally, when various forms of risk (market, reputational, political) are taken into account as a matter of fiduciary duty, a more fully informed style of institutional investing may well emerge. In the absence of these critical elements of universal monitoring, institutional investors cannot pursue their long-term financial interests and, hence, cannot fully and adequately act on their fiduciary duty. Without full data transparency (e.g. financial, environmental) and a set of metrics to analyse that data, they are unable to factor into their financial analysis all of the risks that may impact a universal owner's portfolio.

References

Berle, A., and G. Means ([1932] 1967) *The Modern Corporation and Private Property* (New York: Macmillan, rev. edn).

CalPERS (2004) 'CalPERS announces 2004 emerging markets equity policy', press release, 18 February 2004.

Chandler, A. (1977) *The Visible Hand: The Managerial Revolution in American Business* (Cambridge, MA: Belknap Press of Harvard University Press).

Cogan, D. (ed.) (2000) *Tobacco Divestment and Fiduciary Responsibility: A Legal and Financial Analysis* (Washington, DC: Investor Responsibility Research Center).

Domini Social Investments (2002) 'Domini Social Investments continues push for increased corporate accountability', press release, 21 March 2002.

Engardio, P. (2002) 'The era of blind investment is over: CalPERS sets tough new governance and financial standards', *Business Week*, 11 March 2002: 50.

Férone, G., C. d'Archimoles, P. Bello and N. Sassenou (2002) *Le Développement Durable* (Paris: Éditions d'Organisation).

Hawley, J., and A. Williams (2000a) *The Rise of Fiduciary Capitalism* (Philadelphia, PA: University of Pennsylvania Press).

——, —— and J. Miller (1994) 'Getting the Herd to Run: Shareholder Activism at the California Public Employees' Retirement System (CalPERS)', *Business and the Contemporary World* 6.4: 26-48.

Lublin, J. (2002) 'Proxy voting is a fiduciary duty, SEC chief says in letter to Group', *Wall Street Journal*, 21 February 2002: C20.

Mansley, M., and A. Dlugolecki (2001) *Climate Change: A Risk Management Challenge for Institutional Investors* (London: USS).

Monks, R. (2002) *The New Global Investors* (Oxford, UK: Capstone Publishing).

OECD (Organisation for Economic Co-operation and Development) (2001) *Sustainable Development: Critical Issues* (Paris: OECD).

National Statistics (2004) *Share Ownership: A Report on Ownership of Shares as at 31st December 2003* (London: National Statistics; www.statistics.gov.uk/downloads/theme_economy/ShareOwnership2003.pdf, accessed 17 November 2005).

SEC (US Securities and Exchange Commission) (2003) 'Final Rule: Disclosure of Proxy Voting Policies and Proxy Voting Records by Registered Management Investment Companies. 200317 CFR Parts 239, 249, 270, and 274 Release Nos. 33-8188, 34-47304, IC-25922; File No. S7-36-02RIN 3235-AI64', www. sec.gov/rules/final/33-8188.htm, accessed 4 February 2005.

US Federal Reserve (2004) 'Flow of Funds Accounts of the United States, Annual Flows and Outstandings, 9 December 2004', www.federalreserve.gov/releases/Z1/Current/annuals/a1995-2003.pdf, accessed 4 February 2005.

WCED (World Commission on Environment and Development) (1987) *Our Common Future* (Oxford, UK: Oxford University Press).

20

Companies run in shareholders' long-term interests also serve society's long-term interests*

Robert Monks

Lens Governance Advisors, USA

Allen Sykes

UK

The reality of Anglo-American shareholder capitalism is that public corporations are no longer run primarily in the long-term interests of the shareholders. Most of the effective powers of shareholders over the last 40 to 50 years have unconsciously and unintentionally been relinquished to corporate managements. They have been able to maximise their own rewards, usually short-term ones, without delivering optimal long-term performance. The purpose of this chapter is to: show how this has come about; discuss, very briefly, how it can be remedied; and consider its relevance to corporate social responsibility (CSR). It is our contention that companies run in the long-term interests of shareholders also meet society's reasonable long-term goals and thus the reasonable aims of CSR.

For over 200 years, mainstream financial and economic theory has held that corporate performance is optimised when companies maximise the long-term discounted income of their owners (Jensen 2001). This is the fundamental tenet of market capitalism. The efficient working of market capitalism—which has far outstripped the wealth creation of any past or present economic system—requires the allocation of resources,

---

* This chapter is largely based on Monks and Sykes 2002.

either by the owners, or by their fully independent competent representatives working solely in the owners' long-term interests. This ideal position has been steadily eroded over the past four to five decades with the rise of institutional shareholders neutered by serious conflicts of interest. This has prevented corporate managements being held accountable to shareholders' interests.

We are seeking the reform of Anglo-American shareholder capitalism by ensuring that publicly quoted companies have a critical mass of effective, committed, knowledgeable long-term owners who will hold corporate managements fully accountable to the longer-term interests of their presently disenfranchised individual and beneficial shareholders. The almost total lack of such owners at present has handed effective power to corporate managements, particularly their chief executives. Investment institutions are neutered by conflicts of interest which they are powerless to overcome. Their individual incentives are too weak to achieve what is in their collective long-term interest. Once corporate managements are not required to maximise long-term returns to shareholders they immediately maximise something else (e.g. short-term earnings to maximise the value of short-term share options). All the relationships are distorted by this. This is evidenced by the fact that in Britain and America chief executive earnings have grown significantly year after year, often despite severely falling share prices and failing corporate performances. Failure is routinely rewarded. The main weaknesses have been left largely untouched by the numerous governance reforms over the last 12 years. This is not the result of free-market forces. Free markets reward only success. Rather, it is evidence of a serious systemic fault which can be overcome only by an effective external catalyst—the main thrust of our proposed reforms.

There is a clear link between companies run in their underlying owners' long-term interests and corporate social responsibility (CSR). 'To be successful in the long term such companies need the enthusiastic co-operation and long-term support of all their stakeholders—employees, customers, suppliers, etc. and the local communities where they operate' (Sykes 2000). Such companies have a vital long-term reputation to preserve with all these entities for it is in effect their 'licence to operate'. They will not want to pollute the environment, employ overseas labour in poor conditions, discriminate against minorities, cheat on taxes, etc. They will want contented, well-trained, loyal staff that are proud to work for their company. In sum, such companies recognise that it is in their interests to be good corporate citizens and to meet the reasonable needs of CSR. There is more to shareholders' values than 'shareholder value'. They do not need to be coerced on these points for it is in their long-term business interests (although government regulations will always have an important role to play).

It is important to remember who the real owners of Anglo-American corporations are. They are primarily the working populations saving for their retirement through pension funds, life insurance policies, unit trusts, etc. These indirect, beneficial owners are so widespread and representative that they are a good proxy for society's general interests. They want the companies they invest in to be good citizens. Decent pensions in a decent society require nothing less.

It should thus be apparent that the interests of the real shareholders and society at large are essentially congruent, but this will only occur if companies are run in shareholders' long-term interests. 'Slash and burn' capitalism has nothing to offer either shareholders or society. Contemporary share capitalism, however, must first be reformed to be run in the underlying owners' long-term interests. However, as long as

Anglo-American shareholder capitalism goes unreformed—and in all essentials, despite endless governance codes, new regulations, etc., it remains unreformed—CSR aspirations will make little real difference to most public companies. When a corporate management perforce must concentrate mainly on short-term performance to survive, while it may pay lip service to CSR concerns, they will simply not be a priority.

In the interest, *inter alia*, of achieving justified and reasonable CSR—and not every issue urged under that heading can be so described—the rest of this chapter is devoted to what is involved in understanding and achieving effective long-term corporate ownership.

The loss of shareholder control

In the US, for nearly 80 years lawyers and jurists—in particular, former Supreme Court Justice Louis D Brandeis—have taken the lead in expressing concern about the widening separation between shareholders and corporate management, and the resulting abuse of corporate power. The same concerns were expressed by Adolphe Berle and Gardiner Means. The prescient concerns of all these pioneers were well summarised by Hurst (1970: 89):

> Stockholder surveillance is the principal internal factor on which tradition relied to legitimate corporate power . . . The continued willingness of our citizens to have privately chosen corporate leaders make decisions affecting production, employment and quality of life has been countenanced because of the accountability of these leaders to the corporate owners. In our view, the practical erosion of stockholders' voting power undermines the very structure of private enterprise upon which our national economy and political system are based.

In Britain, similar concerns have resulted in six major official inquiries in 12 years. In both countries, there has been the involuntary, indeed largely unconscious relinquishment of powers to corporate managements. Both trends are consequent on the marked rise of tax-incentivised institutional investment. This has left an ownership vacuum at the heart of shareholder capitalism, resulting in the serious abuse of managerial powers and, inevitably, a serious backlash against business.

Investment institutions, lacking the ability to control corporate managements fall back on the strategy of holding a wide spread of shares combined with a high share turnover. Shares are regarded like betting slips on unforecastable races. Thus, shareholders have long been 'punters rather than proprietors' (*Economist* 1990). The most successful institutional shareholders, however, have mainly been long-term holders of small portfolios who have usually committed to an ownership role (e.g. Berkshire Hathaway).

The serious weaknesses

Market capitalism cannot allocate resources efficiently if shareholders—individual, institutional and beneficial—accept de facto disenfranchisement, leaving important decisions almost wholly to senior corporate managements with conflicting interests.

The major inappropriate powers of corporate management

Effective capitalism requires that corporate managements have wide executive powers and incentives to develop and execute strategies in the long-term interests of shareholders. To meet this requirement, the wider interests of customers, suppliers, employees and the community must be met, since shareholder profits are the residual after meeting the costs of these prior claims, be they labour costs (wages, salaries, pensions, training) or pollution costs, etc.

The rise of the institutionalisation of personal investment has perforce resulted in the transfer to corporate managements of major inappropriate powers resulting in serious conflicts of interest. They can, for instance, choose (or veto) their 'independent' non-executive colleagues' appointment and the appointment of independent auditors. Thus, those being monitored choose the two most important monitors. They also largely choose the remuneration consultants for the independent board remuneration committee who are usually the company's own remuneration consultants and so beholden to management. They also effectively choose their pension scheme fund managers who are not encouraged to be activist. There are almost no examples in the UK or the US of corporate private-sector pension fund activism. Such reciprocal passivity suits nearly all corporate managements.

The effective removal of these inappropriate powers is the litmus test for any worthwhile reform of shareholder capitalism. Some of these inappropriate powers are beginning to be addressed. In the US, the abuses of Enron, WorldCom, etc. are beginning to produce significant regulatory legislation—such as that on accounting regulation and reform—and are requiring chief executives to guarantee their financial statements. In the UK, reform began earlier. However, the proposed reforms in both countries still primarily address auditor integrity and independence. The other inappropriate powers are not yet widely appreciated or acted upon.

Deeply entrenched short-termism

If corporate managements have inappropriate powers, they also suffer from a major weakness (which they share with fund managers) that gravely handicaps their performance and damages the interests of shareholders. This is the market pressure to raise corporate performance, as measured by share prices, over unrealistically short periods of time, often over only two to three years.

This is manifested by the shortening average tenure of chief executives in major companies, now down to four years (and falling) in both America and Britain. The pressure—mainly from fund managers urged on by investment analysts—is itself the result of the increasingly short periods (typically three years in Britain and rather less in America) over which fund managers themselves are judged. Perversely, this is largely due to the terms imposed by corporate pension funds, despite such terms not being in the general interests of pension fund beneficiaries.

Such short-termism is unsuitable for most industries. It prevents managements and fund managers alike from playing to their long-term strengths—to the clear detriment of individual and beneficial shareholders who are saving mainly for retirement. In this matter, corporate managements have a fully justified and serious complaint. However, chief executive short-termism is powerfully reinforced by generous contractual termination payments and by the fact that share options usually vest if a merger or takeover occurs.

Absentee ownership, the double deficit

The essence of any successful system of governance is that those to whom power is entrusted must be accountable to those whom they serve. Shareholder capitalism in both Britain and America fails this test. Managements are not effectively accountable either to individual shareholders or to the investment institutions and fund managers who are the agents of the ultimate shareholders. Nor, in turn, are these intermediaries themselves effectively accountable to the ultimate stakeholders—the individuals who are pension fund members or policy-holders. There is thus a double accountability deficit which inevitably results from passive, absentee ownership. This is the fundamental weakness of Anglo-American shareholder capitalism. It must be effectively remedied for all other weaknesses to be resolved.

It is a fundamental tenet of free-market capitalism that owners choose how their assets are used to best advantage. It is thus particularly unsatisfactory that the largest single category of personal property—stocks and shares (including the beneficial interest held collectively via investment institutions, mainly to provide retirement income)—should lack effective ownership. Those who hold shares directly (50% of all shares in America, 15% in Britain) are individually so insignificant as to be virtually powerless. Those who own shares beneficially are, if anything, even more powerless. Only if shareholders could combine effectively—and in practice this applies only to institutional shareholders—would corporate managements be held accountable. It seldom happens save in a rare corporate crisis, by which time the damage has usually been done (as for instance with Marconi and Enron).

The investment institutions

The only interested parties who could realistically hold corporate managements accountable—the investment institutions and their fund managers—are organised somewhat differently in the US and UK.

In the US, the tradition of individual investment remains strong, with half of all shares owned personally. Most of the rest are owned by life assurance companies, mutual funds and defined benefit pension funds, through which companies invest to provide staff with pensions. Under tax incentives introduced in 1970 (the '401[k]' clause), US employers are switching to defined contribution schemes. Often their contribution to these funds is paid in the form of their own shares, such that many employees (as at Enron) held over 50% of their retirement funds in their own company's stock.[1] While a company is still growing, this may be acceptable but for employees' jobs and pensions alike to be tied to a rising share price is dangerously risky.

Increasingly, employee contributions to 401(k) schemes go into a wide spread of shares. Mutual funds compete heavily for this huge business. Their corporate governance activities will thus have a crucial effect. However, there is, to date, no real tradition of corporate pension fund or mutual fund governance activity comparable to even the occasional activity of some British investment institutions. The sole exceptions are some of the larger public-sector pension funds which are in no way beholden to corporate managements. Thus, in North America, opposition to very high executive remuneration—or to the routine re-pricing of share options—is almost unknown, and direct pressure on failing chief executives to resign is a delayed and sporadic process.[2]

In the UK, individual share ownership has long been much lower than in the US. As a percentage of all shares, it has fallen in 50 years from 50% to under 15%. Tax incentives for pension provision (half via individual policies held with life insurers) plus the benefits of professional fund management, have greatly favoured collective shareholding. Hence, British shares are held approximately 25% each by pension funds and life insurance companies, 10% by unit and investment trusts, and 20% from overseas (mainly by investment institutions). Increasingly, corporate pension provision is being switched to much less generously funded defined contribution (DC) schemes, with most major companies closing their long-established defined benefit (DB) schemes even to existing employees.

British investment institutions have occasionally been activist over the last decade or two, but they fall far short of being regularly activist, as important reports for HM Government by Paul Myners (Myners 2001) and the Company Law Review group (both issued in 2001) attest.[3] In part, this stems from their small size relative to that of the companies they invest in. British pension funds seldom hold more than 2–3% of any large company they invest in. Life insurance companies hold up to 3–4% and they only hold 2% or less in mega companies. In North America, the disparity is even greater. Individual holdings in the top 500 companies seldom exceed 1%, and they average 0.5% or less. The potential for individual investment institutions to influence policy is, thus, small in both countries, and particularly in the US. It is only the *latent* collective power of investment institutions that could give them real influence.

There are growing signs in the UK of institutional co-operation in limited areas, although this falls far short of general regular co-operation on the vast majority of the top 250 UK companies. For instance, a dozen institutions co-operate fairly regularly on CSR issues (predominantly public-sector or ex-public-sector pension funds). Further the Association of British Insurers (ABI) and the National Association of Pension Funds (NAPF) encourage their members to oppose serious governance abuses (e.g. grossly inappropriate chief executive remuneration schemes). These activities do not, how-

---

1   In many mega companies, such as GE and Coca-Cola, the proportion is 75%, and in Procter & Gamble the proportion is over 90%.

2   American chief executives frequently lose their jobs because they fail to meet the short-term performance targets required by institutions and fund managers, but this is due to market pressures not shareholder activism.

3   The leadership of the British Telecommunications Pension Fund and its investment manager, Hermes, provides a model for the industry, though it is not one that many have followed.

ever, constitute permanent ownership exercising alliances for the affairs of any major companies.

Corporate pension funds, controlled by corporate managements, have almost never been activist in either country. There is an implicit understanding that each company's pension fund will refrain from an activist stance in return for a reciprocal stance from all the others. As for life assurance companies, banks, mutual funds (unit trusts) and investment trusts, they tend to be in fierce competition with each other; hence co-operative action is rare. In addition, many are parts of bigger groups also seeking banking or insurance business. There is an explicit duty on all these institutions to be proactive investors on behalf of their beneficial shareholders—indeed, this is enshrined in trust law in both countries (albeit seldom enforced)—but the collective action which alone could be influential is rare; it is largely confined to gross underperformance over many years, or to very serious corporate management misconduct, by which time it is too late.

The fund managers

The same constraints that make investment institutions largely passive owners apply equally to fund managers. These specialists manage the funds of the investment intermediaries, particularly pension funds (few of which are managed internally). Over 75% of fund managers are owned, broadly equally, by investment banks and insurance companies. Most insurance companies usually invest not only their own very large funds (principally of policy-holders) but also corporate and public-sector pension funds, making them both direct institutional investors and fund managers.

Investment terms are always agreed with clients, but fund managers have the prime responsibility for choosing the strategy best suited to client needs. They unquestionably exercise great power in determining investment decisions. Their top managers and specialists are among the highest-paid people in the US and the UK, at least equal to most senior corporate managers. In Britain, management of the pension funds of the top 100 companies (over 75% of the UK stock market) is highly concentrated on the top ten fund managers. They thus compete fiercely to attract and retain major corporate business, inevitably reducing their willingness to co-operate to hold corporate managements accountable.

The reluctance of fund managers to hold corporate managements (their main direct or indirect paymasters) accountable causes them to seek risk diversification by holding widely spread share portfolios—the reaction of a 'punter' rather than a 'proprietor'. This is compounded by the fact that clients expect funds to perform well over relatively short periods: three years in Britain and rather less in America where competition is even fiercer. This highlights one of the most significant weaknesses of shareholder capitalism—the serious mismatch between the periods over which fund managers are judged and the longer periods (say five to six years) which would better suit most beneficiaries. Client pressure thus forces fund managers to favour shares expected to perform well over the short term; this has caused many commentators to blame fund managers for the share bubble and burst over the two and a half years to mid-2002.

There is a destructive process at work here whereby long-term corporate performance is damaged and with it the interests of most investors and the main stakeholders. There are very few incentives for either fund managers or corporate managers to take as long-term a view as their skills justify, yet fund managers blame corporate managements *collectively* for putting them under short-term pressures (and vice versa). Breaking this vicious circle is one of the most important challenges for corporate governance reform.

Fund managers are divided into 'active' and 'passive'. Active funds go in for ever-changing selective portfolios and asset allocations, whereas passive ('tracker') funds (now managing 30% of all funds) hold all shares in an index and charge much less. Since passive pension funds tend to perform well in bull markets, active funds have largely replicated their shareholdings (i.e. 'closet' indexing) because, given their inappropriate short-term benchmarks, there is safety in overlapping portfolios. With most fund managers holding most shares most of the time, they lack a compelling incentive to improve companies in their portfolios if any significant costs or risks are involved since to do so would be almost entirely for their competitors' benefit.

The systemic fault

Analysis of the investment institutions and their fund managers reveals that, despite their huge *latent* collective ability to enforce corporate management accountability for their beneficiaries, they quite fail to achieve it.

The institutions are not necessarily to be blamed for this because there is a *systemic* fault that prevents them. The fault is that shareholders, whether individual, institutional or beneficial, lack the necessary individual incentives. The fact that all would benefit from the introduction of full accountability and superior governance does not mean that it will come to pass. Unless the members of a group are few, or unless there is some kind of coercion, they will not, indeed cannot, act to achieve their common or group interest. There needs to be a sufficient *individual* incentive for enough of the players to make the effort and to bear the costs even though, if successful, non-contributors will benefit at no cost (the 'free-rider' problem) (Olsen 1971). Crucially, this type of problem cannot be resolved by market forces.

In the case of corporate governance, the position could hardly be less favourable to collective action. There is not just one large group that needs to act but several—individual shareholders, investment institutions, fund managers and beneficial shareholders. Each has little contact with most of the others and, in the case of the beneficial shareholders, none at all. It is this that explains why, despite many attempts at reform in the dozen years, little real change was effected in either the US or the UK and why so much more remains to be done. A handful of senior corporate managers in each country can prevail over the interests of the huge body of individual and beneficial shareholders. Effective action requires realistic, powerful individual incentives for effective countervailing power. We argue that the catalyst must be a modest but well-targeted government action to overcome the systemic fault and create a demand for market forces to provide effective corporate ownership.

The market forces in Anglo-American capitalism which are intended to hold corporate managements accountable to owners have broken down. This has occurred because of the failure of successive governments to enforce the basic law of trust which governs all pension fund trustees and investment institution fiduciaries as it relates to conflicts of interest. It is nonetheless essential that a way is found to enable the trustees of the underlying beneficial owners, the investment institutions and their fund managers, to discharge their responsibilities. Successful corporate governance reform may require more than this, but certainly not less.

In both the US and UK, public-sector pension funds are the most active fiduciaries because they have few conflicts of interest. However, their staffs generally lack business experience. The more knowledgeable corporate fiduciaries that could bring business expertise to bear are, as noted, mainly passive. Hence, institutional activism to date is easily derided as naïve.

We understand the reservations expressed about more regulation, especially given the excessive existing burden in both countries. However, if the analysis of a systemic fault is accepted, then change cannot occur without the involvement of an external catalyst. Senior managers are not going to propose reforms that reduce their own powers. Investment institutions and fund managers want to hold on to their major clients, to attract new ones and to avoid the reputation of a troublemaker. Plus, a conscientious institution would gain only a few per cent of any reward from holding a corporate management successfully to account, would bear 100% of the costs and may well lose business to more pliable competitors.

Hence, at present, passivity pays. Passive institutions gain 95% or more of the benefit from any successful shareholder action at no cost to themselves and with a real chance of winning business away from the more activist group. It is a no-win situation for conscientious institutions, and a no-lose situation for passive ones. This is the uncomfortable reality facing all who seek to improve corporate governance, and it explains why British institutions are fiercely resisting the essentially modest requirements for institutional activism in the Myners review (Myners 2001). Proposed reforms must be judged against this reality, which has been neglected by virtually all corporate governance investigations.

Board composition and accountability: the reality

The traditional view of publicly quoted companies is that they are run primarily in shareholders' interests by senior managers with closely aligned interests, under the control of independent non-executive directors. The truth is otherwise. Shareholders take no part in the nomination of directors. American shareholders have no powers of nomination, nor, effectively, do British individual shareholders. Moreover, British investment institutions resolutely refuse any such role, despite the strong recommendation of the 1992 Cadbury Report. Therefore, chairmen/chief executives nominate them since nobody else can or will become involved. Further, in North America, shareholder votes on directors are merely advisory and there is huge business resistance to a modest US Securities and Exchange Commission (SEC) proposal to allow shareholders to nominate even a single director in underperforming companies.

Nomination committees, consisting primarily of non-executive directors, increasingly recommend non-executive candidates. The critical point to note is that any appointment (and any renewal) nearly always depends on chairmen/chief executive agreement and is usually at their initiative. Non-executive directorships are generally prized, so how likely is it that the benefactors will be held regularly to account?

While current practice falls far short of the original intention, supporters claim that it avoids the disharmony of non-collegial boards. However, non-executives cannot fulfil their responsibilities if disagreement with chief executives (or even a board majority) is considered disloyal.[4] What credence can be placed on an 'independent' director who is under pressure not to act independently when required?

Shareholder responsibility for board nominations is very clear in Britain. It is the shareholders' obligation to ensure the services of an appropriate board of directors on a continuing basis, an obligation that is routinely delegated to chairmen/chief executives. However, shareholders retain a powerful reserve power. The UK Company Act permits the removal of directors by 10% of shareholders at a specially convened extraordinary general meeting. In North America, while the obligation is the same, implementation is virtually impossible. However, reforms now being discussed may one day permit the same simple activism mandate as in Britain.

The end result in both countries is much the same—there is only ever one set of nominations for directors, who are nearly always unanimously elected. Institutional investors usually give their consent in advance in the form of proxy votes, a process fairly described by Professor M.A. Eisenberg as 'coerced ratification'. The reality is thus of self-perpetuating boards without any ownership involvement. Hence, the oft-repeated dictum that shareholders 'appoint the directors' does not bear serious scrutiny. By definition, self-perpetuating boards cannot be independent.

The misconceptions

Careful analysis of what boards do (or can do) in a crisis is needed. British boards—with a non-executive chair and up to half of the board comprising senior executives—are better informed than US boards, where typically the chief executive is the only executive member. Nonetheless, non-executives typically devote only 10–15 days a year to board duties (sometimes a little more in the UK), which may not match their growing responsibilities. Boards seem to work to some degree of adequacy only when the demands are predictable and slender.

A window on the Enron board

Senator Carl Levin, chair of the Senate sub-committee on investigations, provided an authentic view into the nature of US boards at a hearing in 2002 with the five most senior directors of recently bankrupted Enron. These individuals were supposedly the 'flower' of US director culture. They had each served for 17 years; they chaired the most important committees—executive, finance, compensation and audit—three had doctorates, and all were paid a minimum of US$350,000 a year. They appeared voluntarily and at substantial personal inconvenience and legal hazard in order to articulate plainly and repeatedly that, individually and collectively as members of a board, they were not responsible in any way for the collapse of Enron or for the loss of investments, pensions and jobs.

Despite this, Senator Levin issued a formal report in which he insisted that blame lay at the door of the board. Peter Drucker provides the context: 'Whenever an institution malfunctions as consistently as boards of directors have in nearly every major fiasco of the last 40 or 50 years, it is futile to blame men. It is the institution that malfunctions'

---

4   Even Jack Welch, former chief executive of GE, made clear his 'ambivalence' about genuinely independent directors in a famous television interview on 13 September 2002.

(Drucker 1981: 110). The same comment applies to investment institutions and fund managers—it is all part of the systemic fault. Does the experience of Enron confirm Drucker's conclusion, that you can count on the board except when it is really needed? If so, there are very major policy implications.

Some characteristics of Enron's non-executives suggest caution. The unusually high pay, an average of 17 years' service and no board self-evaluation all suggest too little rigorous scrutiny of management. Without an independent chairman (an issue that was never raised), who was responsible for ensuring that the board covered its full responsibilities? In evidence, the non-executives felt they were widely misled, but insisted that they had no direct personal responsibility. For instance, when management set up the 'independent' off-balance-sheet entities to which corporate assets and debts were 'sold', the non-executives would not accept that this was a breach of Enron's conflict of interest rules since they had been given the chief executive's assurance that no harm would result.

The details revealed by the Enron hearings are essential in understanding the often fragile defences of corporate excess and misbehaviour in US boards. Perhaps non-executives are not able to discharge their responsibilities. If so, the investing public has been mightily misled.

As we turn to the very different situation in the UK, one question obtrudes—what were the lessons from the Marconi affair? The losses there, albeit without fraud, were just as egregious as with Enron. And what do we learn from the fact that there were no parliamentary or regulatory hearings on Marconi or on the governance of Railtrack, etc. etc.? Is this explained by the absence of any fraud? Or is it just a reflection of a more conformist culture?

In both the US and UK we are seriously misled by the language describing corporate governance. Why do we say shareholders elect the directors and auditors when they take no part? Why do we ignore blatant conflicts of interest? Why do we pettifog endlessly, trying to refine definitions of 'independence' which everyone knows to be untrue?

Alan Greenspan's remark in his March 2002 speech at New York University's Stern School, that North American corporations are essentially characterised by 'chief executive dominance', not only shocked the conventional wisdom but it challenged the US insistence on using the vocabulary of democratic institutions to describe corporate functioning. The whole subject of corporate governance needs similar frankness if a system that lives up to the sound principles of accountable shareholder capitalism is to be created.

In Britain, the accountability of corporate boards, owing in part to the split between the chairman and chief executive roles is better than in the US, while still falling short of what is desirable. The chief executive, however, is still the dominant figure. Boardroom revolts are still very rare, and resignations of even a single director on a matter of principle almost as rare. Plus, when they go, they just go quietly in the traditional British manner, despite the 1998 Hampel Committee's call for a public explanation.

In sum, the British system of governance and the greater accountability of its corporate boards may have something to teach North America. However, Britain still suffers from most of the same serious weaknesses and conflicts of interest, and it shares the same need for major reform.

Management remuneration abuse

Few subjects in shareholder capitalism attract more comment, most of it hostile, than the remuneration of chief executives and other executive directors. It is the 'smoking gun' of governance failure in both the US and UK.

High remuneration is defended as the necessary reward for the risk taking and high performance on which growth, prosperity, jobs and pension benefits all depend—a natural and key part of market-driven shareholder capitalism. As a result, from the mid-1980s, remuneration has accelerated many times faster than corporate performance and profits, and outstripped average earnings to levels unrecognisable to the preceding generation. Pay is determined by remuneration committees, usually advised by the company's own remuneration advisors—who are appointed by the management which determines their fees. Such committees consist mainly of chief executives of other companies appointed by the company's chief executive, with a group interest in rising levels of rewards. Investment institutions exercise almost no checks on behalf of their beneficiaries in America (Bebchuk and Fried 2004), and not many in Britain. For British remuneration (on average the highest in Europe, but less than North America) to be justified by reference to US levels, as it so often is, is highly suspect.

Executive remuneration, while high in both countries (compared with rival nations or the past), could be at least partly justified if it reflected very high sustained corporate performance; this is very far from the general case. There are almost no reputable studies in either the UK or US that have found any significant correlation between remuneration and corporate performance. There is, however, a close correlation with company size.

The consequence of management remuneration abuse cannot be overstated. It is the most worrying of all the serious corporate governance weaknesses since it undermines the whole basis of trust on which shareholder capitalism is built. Once corporate managements are mainly rewarded for anything other than longer-term corporate performance (which is the overwhelming requirement of direct and beneficial shareholders, and which is equally in the long-term interests of all key stakeholders such as customers and employees), then longer-term corporate performance will suffer badly. This is undeniably the outcome of the last 20 years or so. What has been maximised are:

- Unsustainable short-term share price performance

- The value of two- to three-year stock options

- Gross short-term earnings before tax, interest and depreciation, with no allowance for the cost of corporate capital employed

- Excessive takeovers and mergers the majority of which destroy shareholder value but increase corporate size and with it management remunerations

Only when chief executives in particular, and corporate managements in general, are incentivised mainly for longer-term (five-years-plus) sustainable corporate performance, and given, subject to safeguards, the expectation of a five-year tenure, will the interests of shareholders, corporate managements and stakeholders be properly aligned. Only then can shareholder capitalism efficiently discharge its historic function.

Since 1983, in both the US and UK, stock options have been by far the most important element in remuneration, massively larger than before. Unfortunately, they are a poor form of incentive—a risk-free, one-way bet. They correlate poorly with corporate performance and, if share prices fall, they are usually reissued at a much lower price. Option costs have not generally been shown in published accounts yet in the US, but they now account for about 12% of issued shares. However, after the abuses of recent years, it is likely that options in many companies will be costed in future with the main accounting institutes, the Financial Accounting Standards Board (FASB) and the International Accounting Standards Board (IASB), leading the way.

The implications of this are significant. Many top US companies would be trading at a loss if stock options were properly costed. Reliable estimates of the impact on earnings range from 9% to 20%, and up to 70% in IT companies. A recent US Federal Reserve study estimated that options meant large companies' annual earnings were overstated by 2.5% during 1995–2000 and reported that profits would have peaked in 1997, three years earlier than reported (Greenspan 2002). These are major information distortions and almost certainly fuelled the stock market bubble, but Wall Street was silent.

This puts into perspective the embarrassingly self-serving response of the American Business Round Table (BRT), an organisation comprised uniquely of chief executives, when FASB tried to require the value of stock options to be charged against earnings. Using its members' huge political power, the BRT forced the US Senate (by an overwhelming margin) to direct the FASB to back down. The FASB, with no independent basis of support, had no choice but to comply. This action, said Senator Fitzgerald at the Levin hearings, was the primary cause of the corporate value losses of 2000–2003 which affected most shareholders and beneficiaries.

Market forces were undermined by this, but investment institutions and analysts were silent. The British story is little better, but it matters less as options still comprise only 2–3% of issued shares.

Transparency is insufficient for reform

Britain has its own dismal record of openness over directors' remuneration. The 1995 Greenbury Committee wanted to show the full—but hitherto hidden, and often very high—costs of corporate pension fund contributions to directors' remuneration. Business and management organisations, fearing a 'fat cat' backlash, opposed disclosure fiercely and forced a compromise. Companies could choose between partial disclosure of relevant facts or full disclosure. Fears of adverse publicity, or hopes of credit for openness, were equally unfounded, however, because the investment institutions and their fund managers showed no interest either way in how companies reported. Little will change until institutions are required to protect their beneficiaries' interests. Information transparency alone will not overcome neutered governance structures.

Proposed reforms

Space precludes setting out in any detail our reform proposals to overcome the entrenched systemic conflicts of interest.[5] The essence of the proposals is for modest but

---

5   Comprehensive proposals can be found in Monks and Sykes 2002: Section 5.

highly catalytic government actions to remove the conflicts of interests for investment institutions and to free-market forces to provide superior corporate governance. The overwhelming need is for the government to enforce trust law so that pension fund trustees and investment institutions are required to have regard solely to their beneficiaries' interests for the exclusive purpose of maximising their benefits. The conflicts of interest will of course remain, so most investment institutions and many, perhaps most, pension fund trustees will choose to delegate their ownership (governance) responsibilities to new entities that are not in conflict and are ready to discharge those responsibilities. The July 2004 assignment to Hermes by the British Coal Pension Fund of its £6 billion equity portfolio is a rare contemporary example of this process. Another is the assignment by the Wellcome Trust of its £3 billion UK equity portfolio to Insight Investment (see further Chapter 16). Both fund managers are in receipt of enquiries from more potential clients.

The demand for such services would become commonplace if government really enforced trust and fiduciary law. Once public companies have effective long-term owners, there would be more independent non-executive directors. Corporate managements would be generously incentivised but only for longer-term (five-years-plus) performance. Chief executives, subject to safeguards, would be given expected tenures of five years or so, sufficient to run their companies on a five-year-plus basis. Equally, subject to safeguards, fund managers would be given five-year-plus expected mandates, and thus would be able to adopt a wide variety of investment strategies. All the inappropriate powers of chief executives (the effective selection of non-executive directors, auditors, remuneration consultants to board remuneration committees, etc.) would be withdrawn. Corporate managements would be free to concentrate on their prime responsibility, long-term performance, relieved of all inappropriate powers. Fund managers would equally be freed to concentrate on their main skills of maximising longer-term investment returns. Auditors, recommended to shareholders only by independent directors, would no longer be pressurised by chief executives to report short-term earnings in the most favourable light. Finally, with companies run on a long-term basis, CSR would be a significant component of corporate policy.

Conclusion

Anglo-American shareholder capitalism is prevented from delivering its optimum performance by strongly entrenched and destructively reinforcing weaknesses and short-term restrictions on corporate managements and fund managers. Together, these comprise major systemic faults. It is the unintended and unforeseen consequence of the decline in influential shareholders (who aligned the longer-term interests of owners and managers) and their replacement by essentially passive institutional shareholders who lack the means and incentives to hold corporate managements accountable. Power has gradually been relinquished to such managements who have inevitably used it in no small part for their own gain. They have usually concentrated on much shorter-term gains for themselves, often at investors' expense. Further, corporate managements have gained undue and undesirable power over auditors, investment institutions and fund managers. The governance system is riddled with serious endemic conflicts of interests which would not be tolerated in other walks of life. A decade of major investigations and reports in the 1990s has produced mainly apparent rather than real governance. The resultant checks and balances introduced fail far too often. They are usually in evidence only after a company and its shareholders are already severely damaged, by which time it is far too late, as in the cases of Marconi, Enron and so many other major companies on both sides of the Atlantic. The need is to establish effective governance reforms along the lines we have set out; then companies would have every incentive to meet society's long-term interests. This indirect approach would best meet the reasonable and justified aims of CSR.

References

Bebchuk, L., and J. Fried (2004) *Pay without Performance: The Unfulfilled Promise of Executive Compensation* (Cambridge, MA: Harvard University Press).

Drucker, P. (1981) 'The Bored Board', in *Towards the New Economic and Other Essays* (New York: Harper & Row).

Economist (1990) 'A Survey of Capitalism: Punters or Proprietors?', *The Economist*, 5 May 1990.

Greenspan, A. (2002) Speech at New York University Stern School, 26 March 2002; www.federalreserve. gov/boarddocs/speeches/2002/200203262/default.htm.

Hurst, J. (1970) *The Legitimacy of the Business Corporation in the Law of the United States, 1780–1970* (Charlottesville, VA: University of Virginia Press).

Jensen, M. (2001) 'Value Maximisation, Stakeholder Theory, and the Corporate Objective Function', *European Financial Management* 7.3: 297-317.

Monks, R., and A. Sykes (2002) *Capitalism without owners will fail: A Policy-maker's Guide to Reform* (London/New York: Centre for the Study of Financial Innovation).

Myners, P. (2001) *Institutional Investment in the UK: A Review* (London: HM Treasury).

Olsen, M. (1971) *The Logic of Collective Action* (Cambridge, MA: Harvard University Press).

Sykes, A. (2000) *Capitalism for Tomorrow: Reuniting Ownership and Control* (Oxford, UK: Capstone Publishing).

21

Why socially responsible investment requires more risk for companies rather than more engagement

Peter Frankental

Amnesty International UK

This chapter, written from the perspective of a human rights NGO, outlines a decade of progress in putting human rights on the agenda of companies. It argues that the socially responsible investment (SRI) movement has served as an amplifier of the concerns of campaigning groups, reinforcing their attempts to generate public and political pressure around business practices that have adverse social and environmental impacts. It also points to the inherent limitations of the SRI industry arising from the mandate and fiduciary responsibilities of fund managers.

The chapter argues that the large SRI funds have been established primarily as a branding exercise designed to increase the appeal of their companies' products and to differentiate them from those of their competitors. It also criticises the 'engagement' approach for its over-emphasis on managing risk and safeguarding reputation, and for the lack of any tangible threat behind it. The conclusion is that a 'carrot and stick' approach is needed if engagement between SRI funds and the companies they invest in is to become anything more than an inconsequential dialogue.

A decade of progress

During the 1990s, Amnesty International's engagement with companies was very limited. We would write to companies asking for a meeting, and those that agreed probably did so more out of courtesy and curiosity than for other reasons. At that time there were a number of questions that companies would ask us. 'What do you mean by human rights?' was a frequent opening line, as if they thought that human rights were an invention of Amnesty International. What most companies were ignoring at that time was the whole development of human rights architecture that had taken place within the UN system over the previous 50 years. UN treaties, conventions and protocols are the fundamental building blocks of human rights, embodying widely accepted principles and definitions. Most of them have been ratified by an overwhelming majority of member states. Indeed, in the case of the International Labour Organisation (ILO) conventions, companies have been actively involved in their drafting.

Ten years later, by the end of 2004, over 1,200 companies had become signatories to the UN Global Compact, which requires them to support the protection of internationally proclaimed human rights within their spheres of influence, and to ensure that they are not complicit in human rights abuses. Signatories to the Global Compact are also required to operationalise principles relating to freedom of association, the elimination of forced labour, the abolition of child labour, as well as non-discrimination in employment practices. Many companies across a whole range of sectors have also incorporated specific references to international human rights standards into their business principles and policy statements.[1]

The relevance of international human rights standards for business has been further clarified in the UN Norms on the Responsibilities of Transnational Corporations and other Business Enterprises with Regards to Human Rights, developed within the UN Sub-Commission on the Promotion and Protection of Human Rights. The process of articulating the human rights responsibilities of business now rests with the Office of the High Commissioner for Human Rights. The fact that these initiatives have a growing profile and are being contested by businesses, governments and NGOs means that it is unlikely that we would get asked the question today: 'What do you mean by human rights?'

Another line that some companies would take a few years ago is that: 'We already have a human rights policy', pointing to their policies on issues such as equal opportunities, health and safety, environment, anti-corruption and community affairs. Companies at that time tended to subsume human rights within other policy areas. Today, many companies realise that they cannot integrate human rights into their global functions and operations without first making human rights an explicit area of policy, with dedicated resources and designated responsibilities at senior management level.

Other companies we approached would try a different line, arguing that: 'Promoting and protecting human rights is the responsibility of governments, not of companies. We are politically neutral. We don't want to interfere.' The reluctance of businesses to

---

1 For perhaps the most comprehensive database and research resource on business and human rights issues, including details of corporate commitments to the protection and promotion of human rights, see the Business and Human Rights Resource Centre, www.business-humanrights.org.

accept responsibility for their human rights impact was understandable. It stemmed from the view that nation-states alone have the obligation to further human rights, a perception that is underpinned by the development of international human rights law within the UN system since 1948. It is states, not companies, that ratify UN conventions and protocols, and which are accountable for compliance. However, the notion of neutrality was strongly challenged in Nigeria during the mid-1990s when Ken Saro Wiwa and eight other Ogoni activists were sentenced to death. Shell's policy of non-interference and their silence was widely interpreted as complicity, causing the company considerable reputational damage and leading to some soul-searching within the company and to a subsequent change in direction (see further Human Rights Watch 1999; Eide *et al.* 2000; Lawrence 2002). More recent research (see, for example, Amnesty International and International Business Leaders Forum 2002) has highlighted that most or all major transnational corporations have, due to the geographic diversity of their operations and supply chains, significant exposure to human rights issues. Today, many companies would acknowledge that there is a human rights context to their operations and that the protection of human rights is their responsibility within their legitimate spheres of influence. At issue now is not whether business has any responsibility for human rights, but where the boundaries should be drawn.

A conduit between pressure groups and business

Clearly there are a number of drivers of change that have unlocked thinking within companies on social and environmental issues, and that have led to changes in attitude, perception and policy. The SRI industry has played a key part in this by continuously challenging companies to take these issues more seriously. One of the most significant challenges has been presented by the launch of the FTSE's series of ethical indices, FTSE4Good, which has sent clear messages to companies of what is expected of them regarding human rights management systems (see further Chapter 17). Also of significance is the fact that some major fund managers, such as Morley, Henderson, F&C and Insight, have developed a SRI strategy for their mainstream funds. A main plank of this strategy is a willingness to engage with the companies they invest in with regard to their social and environmental impacts. Another important development has been the Association of British Insurers (ABI)'s *Disclosure Guidelines on Socially Responsible Investment* (ABI 2001), which have helped put issues such as human rights on the radar screen of their member companies. Such developments are all reflections of how concern about the social and environmental impacts of companies is no longer restricted to pressure groups but has become mainstreamed within the investment community.

From the viewpoint of NGOs such as Amnesty International, the SRI movement as a whole has served as an amplifier of our concerns, reinforcing our attempts to generate public and political pressure around business practices and projects that have adverse impacts on human rights. Parts of the SRI industry have also backed some of the regulatory changes called for by NGOs and, on some occasions, fund managers have come together to make public statements on human rights issues or to support hostile annual general meeting resolutions at the behest of campaigning organisations. SRI fund managers have also served as a good conduit of issues between pressure groups and business; they have better access to companies than NGOs, they can speak the language of business and can frame issues in a way that is more likely to evoke a positive response.

Limitations of engagement

At the same time, the SRI industry has inherent limitations that are not always apparent behind its self-serving and self-sustaining hype. Perhaps the most fundamental limitation arises from the fund managers' mandates and fiduciary responsibilities which make it difficult for investment decisions to be taken other than on financial grounds. This is compounded by the fact that human rights issues are rarely material to a company's performance or earnings.

Another limitation arises from the purpose of the SRI operations of the mainstream fund managers. These are not established as a philanthropic gesture by the major financial institutions but, primarily, as a branding exercise, designed to increase the appeal of their products and to differentiate them from those of their competitors. Their purpose is not to rock the boat of global capitalism or to bring about systemic change in the behaviour of companies. This places limitations on the kind of shareholder activism that they are prepared to engage in. For example, actions such as supporting hostile shareholder resolutions at annual general meetings or disinvesting from a company on ethical grounds are viewed as 'nuclear options', to be used only as a last resort in the most extreme of circumstances. By withholding their most powerful weapon, fund managers are using only a small part of their leverage over companies. In doing so, they are failing to match their rhetoric with effective action.

This calls into question whether their strategy of engaging with companies on social and environmental issues has much substance to it. The proponents of an engagement strategy argue that it is more consequential than one based on screening and disinvestments, which is only relevant to a niche market of investors. In reality the two approaches should be viewed as complementary and mutually reinforcing: in essence, a carrot and stick. Those fund managers that rule out the option of disinvestment on ethical grounds are disarming themselves and, in doing so, are undermining the effectiveness of their engagement. If there is no tangible threat behind a fund manager's engagement with a company, then there is a danger of the engagement becoming an inconsequential dialogue between inconsequential actors. In effect, a charade is being played out between peripheral SRI teams and peripheral corporate affairs managers of the companies in which they invest. Key decision-makers are not involved in this dialogue, which inevitably means that the issues raised will have little traction.

In contrast to this low-key approach to engagement on social and environmental issues, fund managers have shown that they can exert real influence over companies when the issues at stake are perceived by them to be fundamental to their interests. On 12 November 2004, the *Financial Times* ran an article headed 'Business and Fund Chiefs in Fresh Talks on Governance' (*Financial Times* 2004). This article reported that the chief executives of some of the UK's leading financial institutions were about to engage with their counterparts in industry on issues of common concern to both parties—the impact of new accounting standards, the implications of the requirement for companies to publish an annual operating and financial review, and the revised Combined Code on corporate governance. This contrasts starkly with the approach taken to human rights issues, where the discussion between business and investors is often pitched at a level that ensures little will happen. In fact, NGOs are sometimes able to pitch their human rights concerns to companies at a much higher level than those companies' own major shareholders are able to. At issue here is how far do matters of this kind raised by investors reach the company's key decision-makers? What kind of engagement is necessary to have traction at board level?

Another limitation of the engagement approach is its over-emphasis on managing risk and safeguarding reputation. Most major corporations are very good at managing the risks attached to their adverse impacts on human rights as part of their wider political and financial risk strategies. Such an approach often revolves around the functions of public relations and stakeholder engagement. In some cases, companies will develop policies and take action that will lead to improvements in their human rights impacts, but human rights are always secondary and supplementary to financial considerations. They are never equal components. The vast majority of companies would view an effective risk management approach as one that ensures that, whenever there is a clash between commercial imperatives and human rights, it is commercial imperatives that will prevail with as little downside to reputation as possible. Such an approach to human rights does not encourage companies to change their behaviour any more than they need to in order to avoid the threat of litigation or of reputational damage. The reputational dimension of a company's human rights policies and practices tends to be overplayed by the SRI industry. The barometer of reputation moves according to the willingness of the media to expose corporate malpractices, and according to the ability of pressure groups to generate public campaigns against a company. It is only when both these things happen that the force of consumer pressure may come into play. Given the fickleness of the media and of consumers, and given the lack of capacity of NGOs, the prospect of reputational damage related to human rights impacts is a remote one for most companies.

The engagement approach also assumes that, if only companies had a better understanding of the human rights context of their operations, then their behaviour would change. Accordingly, the SRI industry puts the emphasis on stakeholder engagement as a means of awareness-raising. But this premise is a weak one. The main barrier to companies improving their human rights performance is not a lack of understanding of their adverse impacts but the ease with which business can externalise the costs attached to these.

This is where the mainstream SRI fund managers find themselves in an impasse. No amount of engagement with companies will bring about significant changes in behaviour unless such changes are rewarded and unless the failure to change is penalised. This would require a significantly higher level of risk than companies face at the moment. But the SRI industry does not view its role as creating risk for the companies it invests in or as advocating a tougher regulatory regime that will impose costs on companies that get things wrong. While the mandate and fiduciary responsibilities of fund managers might discourage such an approach, the SRI industry will not be able to maintain its credibility in the longer term unless it pushes at these boundaries. SRI engagement with business on human rights issues will have to bear more fruit to remain credible.

References

ABI (Association of British Insurers) (2001) *Disclosure Guidelines on Socially Responsible Investment* (London: ABI).

Amnesty International and International Business Leaders Forum (2002) *Business and Human Rights: A Geography of Corporate Risk* (London: Amnesty International UK and International Business Leaders Forum).

Eide, A., H. Bergsen and P. Goyer (eds.) (2000) *Human Rights and the Oil Industry* (Groningen, Netherlands: Intersentia).

Financial Times (2004) 'Business and fund chiefs in fresh talks on governance', *Financial Times*, 12 November 2004.

Human Rights Watch (1999) *The Price of Oil* (New York: Human Rights Watch).

Lawrence, A. (2000) 'The Drivers of Stakeholder Engagement: Reflections on the Case of Royal Dutch/Shell', *Journal of Corporate Citizenship* 6 (Summer 2002): 71-84.

22

SRI analysts
IS IT TIME TO BRING
THEM IN FROM THE COLD?

Ralph Edmondson and Adrian Payne
British American Tobacco, UK

To what extent should socially responsible investment (SRI) analysts be treated as a special group or be brought in to mainstream investor dialogue? Are the portfolio managers and the SRI analysts just too diverse to be brought together in the same room? At British American Tobacco (BAT), the Head of CSR and the Head of Investor Relations (IR) work together on the same management team with shared goals for recognition as a responsible tobacco company. Where is the evidence that the investment community takes the same common approach to dialogue with companies? This chapter reviews how BAT has aligned its corporate social responsibility (CSR) programmes with its IR communications.

About British American Tobacco

BAT is the world's most international tobacco group, with brands sold in 180 markets around the world. We are the only international tobacco group with a significant interest in tobacco leaf growing, with 22 leaf programmes in 22 countries and working with some 250,000 farmers worldwide. The Group's subsidiaries have 65 cigarette factories in 59 countries, with a further 13 factories producing other tobacco products; it purchases some 520,000 tonnes of leaf; and has a global volume of 685 billion cigarettes a year. Our companies, including associated companies, employ over 90,000 people worldwide.

The key features of the Group are its strongly multicultural workforce and its devolved structure, with each local company having wide freedom of action and responsibility for its operations. Decisions are made as close as possible to the local stakeholders of each business, within a framework of principles, standards, policies, strategies and delegated authorities.

Our Group vision is to achieve leadership of the global tobacco industry through strategies focused on growth, productivity and responsibility supported by an ethos of a winning organisation. By growth we do not mean 'selling smoking', but growth in our share of the global market, growth in profit and continuing growth in shareholder value. By productivity, we mean using resources smartly, enabling additional money to be generated for reinvestment to strengthen our competitive position and performance. Like many companies, we recognise that, by running our business well, we help to drive the engine of economic development, which in turn helps to achieve social and environmental development. Accepting corporate social and environmental responsibilities, and contributing in the ways that a business can, make good business sense. Business cannot deliver every solution, and companies can rarely act alone. Partnerships are vital, and almost all our contributions involve working constructively with partners.

Group companies in 34 countries are now engaged in social reporting based on stakeholder dialogue. Taken together, these companies account for two-thirds of our global sales volume. Both the dialogue process and all our companies' social reports are measured against the AccountAbility AA1000 standard through rigorous independent review and assurance. We use the Global Reporting Initiative (GRI) guidelines as a framework for reporting against economic, environmental and social performance indicators.

In 2005, BAT was again selected as an index component of both the 2006 Dow Jones Sustainability World Index (DJSI World) and 2006 Dow Jones STOXX Sustainability Index (DJSI STOXX). Launched in 1999, the DJSI tracks the performance of the leading sustainability-driven companies worldwide.

Not everyone will invest in tobacco . . .

BAT has been present on the London Stock Exchange for more than 90 years. For a period in the 1990s, when Gallaher Group was part of US-based American Brands and Imperial Group was part of Hanson Trust, the BAT business, as part of B.A.T Industries, was the sole constituent of the UK tobacco index. During the 1970s through to the late 1990s, B.A.T Industries diversified into other sectors, but tobacco always generated at least 50% of Group profitability. If an annual general meeting can be taken as a litmus test of the public's interest in the controversial nature of a company's business, prior to 1998 it was the insurance businesses of B.A.T Industries that generated the most hostile response from pressure groups and aggrieved shareholders.

By 1995, the message from our major shareholders was that tobacco and financial services should be separated. The demerger of financial services and listing of British American Tobacco Plc in 1998 coincided with growing interest among large financial institutions in SRI.

We have always assumed that certain investment funds would be precluded from investing in tobacco because of the health risks posed by our products. While it would be difficult (and pointless) to quantify the proportion of the capital markets closed to tobacco stocks, we have assumed it is relatively small. In terms of engagement, we do not expect to receive requests from ethical fund managers to meet with BAT senior management. However, we would be receptive to such requests to demonstrate that BAT manages its business to the highest international standards. We are less receptive to suggestions that we should exit tobacco and invest in other industries because this is not what our shareholders want. If BAT cannot find investment opportunities for the cash generated, that cash is returned through the share buy-back programme and dividends. In addition, our shareholders have supported our strategy for shareholder value through growth, productivity and responsibility, supported by a winning organisation. This is a strategy that has delivered handsome returns to shareholders in recent years. We are proud of our leadership position in the tobacco industry and fully committed to meeting society's reasonable expectations of how a responsible tobacco company conduct itself in the 21st century.

What are we trying to achieve through our dialogue with investors?

BAT's investor relations strategy primarily aims to:

- Engage large shareholders who have a significant interest in the company and give them an opportunity to engage in dialogue with management on a regular basis

- Assist investors in recognising the value in the business

- Identify large investors who are under-weight in the stock and offer meetings with management with a view to encouraging demand for the shares

- Broaden the geographic diversity of the shareholder base to widen demand for the stock and enable stability in the event of a situation where UK-based investors may be forced to sell

- Broaden recognition among investors that BAT is a responsible tobacco company, thus improving long term business sustainability and achieving above-average earnings growth. Such recognition should be reflected in the company's market rating and deliver shareholder value

Who are our investors?

With the exception of the former holders of Rothmans, R&R Holdings SA, the BAT shareholder base does not have any other shareholders with more than 4% of the shares. Most of the names on the share register holding 500,000 shares or more are names found on the registers of most upper-quartile FTSE 100 companies. In terms of large international investors, there are some that have chosen not to invest in tobacco: the best known is the California Public Employees Retirement System (CalPERS). CalPERS took the decision in the late 1990s to divest tobacco stocks in the light of intense hostility in US when state governments were seeking medical reimbursement from tobacco companies. The states' claims were settled in 1998 and several state retirement schemes are now present on our share register.

The rise of the SRI analyst

More recently, we have seen large UK-based financial institutions establishing SRI teams who are seeking active dialogue with management. Compared to the resources available to sell-side and some buy-side analytical teams, the SRI analyst may have a vast portfolio of sectors under coverage with no time to look at individual companies in depth or read and analyse the social and environmental reports that many companies now produce. While, perhaps, understandable in view of the time constraints, it is frustrating given the effort that is often put into producing these reports. As a result, surrogate SRI teams, together with independent SRI/CSR research firms and compilers of screened indices, have placed significant demands on limited internal resources to respond to questionnaires. Some of these questionnaires are neither relevant to the sector nor acknowledge that the data is in the public domain through published reports. Furthermore, unlike financial reporting, there are no internationally recognised standards and each questionnaire seems to differ from the next.

An initiative by the London Stock Exchange (the so-called Corporate Responsibility Exchange) to make available to all investors on a centralised database completed questionnaires required by Business in the Community, FTSE4Good and Sustainable Asset Management, has obvious attractions for companies. This initiative could cut down the amount of resources expended by companies and lead to the development of non-financial reporting standards that could be applied to all companies. However, such an initiative would work only if it received widespread support from the CSR/SRI community, which is unlikely.

From a company's point of view, prioritising the demands of the SRI analysts can be extremely burdensome and can lead to frustrations on both sides. At BAT, we have taken the view that the SRI community fall within the responsibility of the IR team and should not be treated differently from conventional portfolio managers. For instance, when our management embarks on roadshows in the UK, the IR team will contact the relevant SRI analysts at the institutions to be visited. Unfortunately, there are too many meetings where SRI analysts are not represented or, if they are in attendance, they miss out on the opportunity to raise issues with senior management. These meetings are important opportunities for management to hear the concerns of key shareholders.

Investor concerns

More than many other sectors, tobacco has been at the centre of public issues such as health, environmental issues through leaf growing, litigation, regulatory and excise issues. From the point of view of investors, tobacco share prices have been sensitive to some of these public issues, particularly litigation, so it is no surprise to management that these issues are raised in meetings with portfolio managers. We do not see a natural boundary where certain issues fall either on the portfolio managers' side or the CSR/SRI analysts' side. In 2002 and 2003, when the Group's former investment in Myanmar was the subject of public scrutiny, we met separately with SRI analysts from several UK institutions and exchanged points of view. However, the debate was no more or less constructive or intense than the discussions we held with portfolio managers from the same institutions during that period.

The SRI community stepped back from insisting that BAT divest its interest in Myanmar but has chosen to focus on reputational risk. In other words, would conducting business in a territory, for whatever reason, constitute a risk to the company's reputation that far outweighs the financial rewards? This is a very fair question which should be considered before a company decides to invest in a new market. It is more difficult to take action if international opinion in relation to a specific regime changes and an existing investment gives rise to reputational risk. Management's function is to balance the risk versus reward but it would be foolish to do so without listening to the views of a broad spectrum of stakeholders first. However, we have found our meetings with SRI analysts useful and have adopted new procedures into our corporate governance process to monitor human rights in all of our markets.

Investor engagement

Engagement with our larger institutional investors has been open and productive since B.A.T Industries had to defend a hostile bid in 1989. Since that time, the Group has maintained an active IR programme ensuring that senior management has the opportunity to meet with institutional shareholders on a regular basis.

During the past ten years or so, investors have sought to influence management over only a handful of issues: the Group's investment in financial services; the business in the US at the height of litigation concern; and management's approach to share buyback. On the whole, investors have been supportive of strategy, management's handling of litigation and public smoking issues and shareholder returns.

In terms of corporate governance, BAT has participated and contributed to the debate since the days of Greenbury and Cadbury through to the recent Higgs Report. We have not always been in full agreement with all the proposals at various times but the nature of the tobacco business and our focus on strong financial controls have ensured that the Group has been at the vanguard of best practice. The development of CSR in recent years has been seen as a natural extension of corporate governance and has enabled our CSR committees to be modelled on the audit committees that have existed in the Group on a global basis for decades. The aim of the CSR committees is to support the embedding of CSR principles across all our companies, including those that do not produce social reports. They enable our companies not only to address issues of importance globally but also issues of relevance to particular local societies.

Since 2001, the Group has engaged in stakeholder dialogue with a view to producing annual social reports at the British American Tobacco plc level and locally. Several stakeholder groups are invited each year to participate in dialogue including investors for the British American Tobacco plc report. Institutional shareholders, in 2004, were represented by SRI analysts rather than portfolio managers. Despite the significant resources committed to CSR within the Group, we receive few comments on the social report from sell-side and buy-side analysts. Most responses come from NGOs, special-interest groups and the SRI/CSR community. In 2005, the number of SRI analysts who participated was rather disappointing. Once more, this may be due to the time pressures on SRI analysts rather than a conscious decision not to participate.

Dialogue is a two-way process with stakeholders and has enabled BAT to develop and endorse with third parties its statement of business principles, which is focused on 18 'core beliefs'. In subsequent dialogue sessions, stakeholders have been asked to explore what is expected of our business in order to live up to these beliefs and to highlight any perceived inconsistencies between them and our current practices. This process has also enabled management to identify those issues that are of paramount importance to stakeholders and to develop the way forward in addressing those concerns. We continue to be receptive to the views of our investor base in terms of overall strategy, business and financial performance and our progress in all areas that fall into the area of CSR. At BAT, the IR team and CSR team endeavour to work seamlessly to offer a unified approach to investor engagement. We believe that this area of stakeholder engagement would be more productive for investors if institutional investors could provide a similar unified approach, where the views of portfolio managers and their SRI counterparts may be heard in the same meetings.

We do not believe that CSR and shareholder value are inconsistent. In fact, for a tobacco company, the uphill task of being recognised as being responsible is a fundamental step in demonstrating that our business is sustainable and will continue to generate shareholder value. Responsibility should not be compartmentalised and treated as a stand-alone issue. There is still much to do to bring responsibility into the mainstream discussions with investors. While we will continue to do our part, we also expect our major shareholders to do theirs.

23
Exerting influence
ENGAGEMENT OR BEST-IN-CLASS?

*Andy Wales**

Severn Trent plc, UK

Severn Trent plc is a leading FTSE 100 environmental services group providing water, waste and utility services. The Group, which includes Severn Trent Water, Biffa Waste Services, Severn Trent Services and Severn Trent Laboratories, generated revenues of £2.081 billion in 2004–2005 and employs more than 15,000 people across the UK, the rest of Europe and the US.

Severn Trent is among the leaders in the water and waste sectors in understanding and integrating sustainable development into business practices. We have publicly reported our environmental impacts since 1992 and publish an annual corporate responsibility report ('Stewardship') alongside a comprehensive corporate responsibility section on our website.[1]

Corporate responsibility (CR) issues are managed as part of our core business activities—the water and waste industries have significant environmental impacts—while excellent performance on workplace issues such as health and safety is crucial in terms of responsibility to our employees. CR issues are therefore built into the management procedures of individual business units and into the bonus targets of their managing directors. Some parts of our CR programme also deliver significant revenue, such as our renewable energy generation activities.

Severn Trent's CR performance has been recognised through it being the leading global utility in terms of socially responsible investment (SRI) rankings. The Group is a member of FTSE4Good and has been named leading utility in the Dow Jones World Sus-

* I would like to thank Julian Wais (Severn Trent plc), Matt Gorman (BAA) and Dunstan Hope (Business for Social Responsibility). However, the views expressed here are those of the author.
1 www.severntrent.com/corporateresponsibility

tainability Index for the last five years. We have received the top ranking for our industry from many rating agencies and investors including: AAA by Innovest; B1 by Morley; A by CoreRatings; and 'best-in-class' by Storebrand.

History of CR within Severn Trent

Throughout the 1990s, Severn Trent was a UK leader in corporate environmental performance, putting in place a Group-level environmental management system certified to ISO 14001, heading indexes such as the Business in the Environment Index and winning a number of awards. Towards the end of the 1990s, our environment report developed into a broader 'Stewardship' report which included performance on community and workplace issues. We also developed and launched a Group-wide code of conduct. The Group now publishes a comprehensive CR report which includes a 'marketplace' section, detailing our supply chain improvement programmes, our relationships with customers and our interaction with socially responsible investors. In 2004 we expressed support for the UN Global Compact and we report regularly on our performance against the Compact's ten principles.

Corporate responsibility performance is overseen by the corporate responsibility committee, chaired by the Group chief executive and including the managing directors of the four main businesses in the Group. The CR committee meets quarterly and discusses CR performance in detail, as well as considering upcoming issues the Group should respond to, such as the human rights agenda. The committee also discusses the Group's interactions with SRI investors. In addition, the main board is provided with periodic updates on SRI performance and SRI investments in Severn Trent through investor relations reports.

The Group's CR strategy is built around managing and improving our performance in the principal areas of environmental and social impacts that are core to the performance of our businesses. The three central environmental issues we focus on are climate change, resource management and biodiversity. Severn Trent generates around 0.3% of the UK's greenhouse gas emissions, but also produces 5% of UK renewable electricity (equivalent to around 60% of our own electricity use). In terms of resource management, Biffa recycles over one million tonnes of waste each year, while Severn Trent Water has a major focus on reducing water leakage rates from pipelines and other infrastructure. Finally, Severn Trent plc has a significant land portfolio; therefore, managing ecosystems responsibly is also a priority.

Turning to social issues, the Group's workplace focus includes programmes to improve health and safety performance, work–life balance, diversity, and training and development. Our community activity is strong, particularly in terms of employee volunteering, and we have featured in the top 20 of *The Guardian* newspaper's annual 'giving list' for a number of years. In terms of 'marketplace' issues, we have established the largest utility trust fund in the UK—the Severn Trent Trust Fund assists vulnerable customers struggling to pay their bills. The fund aims to help customers re-establish economic control over their lives and, as such, will assist in paying other bills such as rent or buying essentials.

The SRI context

Severn Trent has responded to SRI questionnaires for a number of years, as evidenced by the awards and rankings discussed above. In particular, the Group has performed well in the various best-in-class rankings that have been compiled over the last five years. The Group has been able to demonstrate that it understands the key issues the sector faces, that it is dealing with them at an appropriate level in the business and that it has delivered major improvements.

More recently, we have seen greater evidence of mainstream (as opposed to specifically ethical or screened) investors using an 'engagement approach'. Over the last three years, the Group has hosted a number of SRI investor roadshows and one-to-one meetings to discuss our CR performance in more detail and to answer analysts' questions. The feedback from these sessions has been very positive and the Group plans to undertake more such events.

Both best-in-class rankings and engagement have encouraged the Group to improve its CR performance further. It is the latter that has the best opportunity to connect SRI thinking into how mainstream-sector analysts perceive the Group; when that happens, SRI will really have come of age. The relative merits of the two approaches are discussed below.

In the author's experience of a number of businesses, investors come a close third behind regulation and customers in driving change on CR issues within companies. Senior executives take investor opinion seriously, including that of SRI investors; thus, the issues SRI investors choose to focus on when engaging a company are likely to feed through into an action programme, especially if a number of investors make the same points. However, the connection between SRI engagement and mainstream investment is still perceived as weak. Unless the main-sector analysts engaging on behalf of mainstream investments start to ask more questions regarding CR issues, then SRI will remain an investment niche. The real bottom line for SRI investment (best-in-class or engagement) is whether, over time, companies can expect to see a significant proportion of their stock held by those who use SRI criteria in their decision-making. If we get to a point where companies begin to perceive that this is not and will not be the case, then internal interest in SRI may wane.

Best-in-class

Senior executives in the Group understand the value of perceived CR performance to SRI analysts in terms of both corporate reputation and (in theory) improved levels of niche SRI investment by those who use best-in-class filters for investment. In particular, high-profile indices such as the FTSE4Good Index and the Dow Jones Sustainability Index (DJSI) are discussed at the CR committee level. New areas of assessment for these indices are noted, with programmes put in place to ensure that good performance continues. The annual timing of many of these indices, and the public profile attached to them, may result in them receiving a higher level of internal attention than is, perhaps, warranted, in comparison to the 'engagement' approach.

The best-in-class approach is effective at identifying minimum expected standards for an industry on a particular issue and highlighting those that do and those that do not reach that standard. FTSE4Good's human rights criteria, introduced in 2004, is a good example of such a baseline. The effect of the FTSE4Good's human rights criteria can also be seen outside of those industries that were required to respond immediately, with other companies seeing the move as an indication of where such indices might go on this issue in the future.

From a practitioner perspective, while responding to best-in-class questionnaires can be a useful process, it can also be a taxing experience. The more high-profile questionnaires such as those from the Ethical Investment Research Service (EIRIS) and DJSI are well constructed and the analysts seek to understand the sector's issues. Generally, the profile or ranking that comes out of the process reflects the business's performance fairly well. Established teams that provide analysis for their own investments, such as Innovest and Morley, also engage with the Group in a sensible way and gain a good understanding of the challenges it faces and the performance they should expect from a large company in this sector. However, the many smaller indices, rankings and company profiles that have grown up over the last few years pose a new set of problems. With some notable exceptions, these questionnaires are often administered poorly, with last-minute requests to comment on poorly compiled research, questions that ask for Group-level data but are really interested only in one Group company and analysts who clearly do not understand the sector at all. Such weaknesses lead to serious doubts about the usefulness of these questionnaires.

One emerging issue is the increasing global spread of SRI questionnaires. Severn Trent now responds to questionnaires not only from the UK but also from France, Germany, the US, Scandinavia, the Netherlands and other countries. Questionnaires from the less established SRI markets generally make the same mistakes as the early movers in the UK and US, with poorly designed questionnaires, lack of understanding of the sector and inconsistent performance ranking. It is frustrating that the newer entrants to the field do not seem to have built on existing best practice.

For all of the best-in-class approaches, including those that are well administered, there are some crucial issues going forward:

- How many investors actually use these indices to inform investment decisions? If SRI investment does not follow index performance over the long term, will the buy-in to such indices from within companies diminish?

- Useful analysis can be difficult when an index return does not allow for a full explanation of a change in business strategy or business conditions that lead to a change. An example could be an increase in environmental impact as a result of an acquisition

- How to rank issues that defy ranking (e.g. diversity)? When each company has a different level of 'background' diversity (e.g. the level of ethnic minorities in its employment catchment area, or the male–female ratio in the core professions that form the backbone of key employees in that sector), it can be difficult to judge performance objectively. In relation to these sorts of issues, companies can be given credit for introducing schemes that improve diversity, but providing an objective quantitative score can be much more difficult

The London Stock Exchange's Corporate Responsibility Exchange (CRE) is a good idea, bringing together the questionnaires to allow more rapid completion of some very similar sets of questions. Severn Trent will be testing the CRE over the coming year to see how well it streamlines the process. However, CRE needs both commitment and flexibility from the various rating companies to ensure that it gains a critical mass.

The engagement approach: Severn Trent's experience

Severn Trent's experience of the engagement approach to SRI stretches back three years and includes roadshows in Paris and London attended by over 30 different institutions, one-to-one conversations with analysts on particular issues initiated either by the Group or by the investor, and joining SRI and company partnerships to explore the impact of a particular issue on a sector, such as climate change or biodiversity. Severn Trent has received very good feedback from investors regarding these interactions. In particular, investors refer to the fact that roadshows are often fronted by the chief executive or another senior executive and that over time the Group has established an approach that builds much of the presentation around questions from the previous sessions. In general these events are held at six monthly intervals in London but we are considering running them annually in other key locations such as Paris. The interest of the Group chief executive, the management team and the investor relations department in the developing SRI field has been central to Severn Trent's willingness to present such regular and detailed updates.

Face-to-face meetings are a more useful form of interaction than questionnaires because they are usually more challenging for the business—there needs to be substantial preparation and it is also likely that if a company provides too simplistic an answer to questions then the analyst will push the issue harder until they get a satisfactory response. The Group has valued these meetings as a means of sharing some of its progressive work with SRI investors, such as a recent carbon management project which included a scenario projecting the Group's likely greenhouse gas emissions to 2020. SRI investors found the information very helpful in terms of understanding business risk and intend to ask Severn Trent's competitors for similar information. Feeding back such a message within the Group demonstrates to senior management the importance of such a programme.

The Group has also faced challenges with regard to its performance. In 2002–03 its health and safety record was raised during SRI meetings. While performance was good in the context of the industry sector as a whole, it had nevertheless deteriorated against Group standards as new acquisitions had taken time to integrate into the businesses. SRI investor interest in this area reinforced the Group's serious internal concern on the issue. A range of new programmes has been put in place across the Group to address the problem, and in 2003–2004 and 2004–2005 performance improved.

SRI analysts in general ask perceptive questions which can be a significant driver for a company to improve its performance in a particular area, or to highlight an issue that the company has not considered in depth. Certainly the non-governmental organisation (NGO) background of many SRI analysts is a strength as they are not shy to ask the tough questions. SRI analysts seem the most thorough and professional users of good CR reports and, increasingly, CR reports are designed for this audience.

The maturing of the SRI engagement field means that companies can develop longer-term relationships, resulting in a better understanding on both sides and a more valuable engagement. More and more 'engagement' is essentially a good-quality conversation regarding management's approach to CR risks and opportunities. Those companies with a strong CR ethos understand the risks they face and have programmes in place to deal with them, generally finding SRI engagements positive.

While our experience of SRI investor engagement has generally been very positive, there are a number of areas where the engagement process could be improved. Most importantly, the engagement process is still largely confined to SRI analysts. Only in a minority of cases has Severn Trent experienced an SRI analyst sitting in on a mainstream investor meeting, or a mainstream-sector analyst sitting in on an SRI meeting. Without this visible connection, it is hard to avoid the conclusion that SRI does not really affect the overall investment decision. It may well be that mainstream analysts really get interested in SRI analysis only when things go very wrong and that their lack of interaction on CR issues shouldn't be taken as a lack of interest. However, this argument is difficult to prove. One factor that does assist this debate is the widespread coverage of SRI in the mainstream investment media, including the *Financial Times* and the *FT Fund Management* supplement. Coverage of projects such as the Enhanced Analytics Initiative (see further Chapter 14) also brings credence to the argument that mainstream investors are interested in these issues when the connection to future financial risk or business opportunity is clearly made.

It is important that SRI analysts devote significant resources internally to getting their concerns heard by their own mainstream-sector analysts. At one recent SRI engagement meeting, Severn Trent's Group chief executive was asked to push CR issues harder in meetings with an institution's mainstream-sector analysts, despite the fact that mainstream-sector analysts from that institution had shown little interest in CR issues when they had been previously mentioned. SRI staff need to do their own internal lobbying. Where the Group does see a particular issue as a financial opportunity or risk that mainstream analysts would be interested in, such as the revenue from renewable energy generation, then it is presented at mainstream meetings and generally receives a good degree of interest.

In common with mainstream investor presentations, larger SRI investor engagement events are also hampered by very different levels of understanding around the table. Analysts from different institutions are at different stages of understanding and, in our view, a 'one size fits all' presentation is reaching its limits. Going forward, the Group is considering splitting its larger presentations into two types—a general introduction to CR issues within the Group and a more detailed presentation on a specific issue, such as carbon management or climate adaptation, in order to engage with the most progressive analysts.

For senior management and mainstream investor relations staff presenting at SRI engagement events there is an interesting challenge around divergent questions. Our experience has been that meetings with mainstream-sector analysts tend to include 80% similar questions (generally revolving around finance and strategy), but meetings with SRI analysts often bring very different and sometimes unexpected issues into the discussion. This often seems to be linked to the individual analyst's background and can raise questions of how the raising of these diverse issues creates a valuable insight into the company's future performance and risks, or whether they are just nice bits of information to have.

The materiality of SRI questioning is an important issue of credibility for SRI analysts going forward, both within their own institutions and with companies. There are plenty of stories of companies being questioned in detail on an issue that is not a significant impact for their business—and equally one or two stories where businesses have had to work hard to convince SRI analysts that a particular issue should be considered as more important for their sector. In particular, the operating and financial review (OFR) is an opportunity for SRI analysts to demonstrate their value to mainstream-sector analysts within their own institutions.

Cultural considerations are also relevant for SRI engagement. The Group's experience of conducting SRI roadshows in Paris was that French investors had a different set of priority issues to British investors, including a greater focus on detailed workplace and social measurements as well as a different perspective on some environmental issues. Reconciling these competing priorities can be difficult. Companies may need to state their own priorities more strongly and accept that, in some SRI contexts, this may harm investors' perceptions of them.

Finally, it is interesting to ask why there are so few SRI analysts who have worked within industry and who therefore understand what the view looks like from a company perspective. More career movement between companies and SRI investors would bring substantial benefits to both sides of the dialogue process.

Going forward

The best-in-class approach is important because, on key issues, it can set a baseline for what would be considered the expected CR practice of a sector. However, it seems unlikely that best-in-class SRI funds will grow rapidly. The better opportunity for SRI to influence company performance will be through mainstream-sector analysts being convinced of the materiality of CR issues by SRI analysts within their own institutions. Equally importantly, companies need to better articulate which issues they consider material to future business success and which are more peripheral. The new requirements for companies to prepare OFRs will help this process, but both CR staff within companies and SRI analysts must ensure they are fully involved in drafting and evaluating OFRs.

There also seems to be a helpful trend developing where one or two SRI investors will take a lead on understanding a particular issue for a particular range of sectors, such as biodiversity in the extractive, manufacturing and environmental services sectors. This approach allows analysts to understand more of the detail of an issue and leads to more meaningful engagement with companies.

In conclusion, SRI is an important driver for improved corporate performance on CR issues. However, in my view, it has a limited amount of time to prove its worth in adding to mainstream investment analysis before it loses some of its current momentum. The OFR provides an important opportunity for both CR and SRI teams to test the materiality arguments within their organisations, and to more fully establish the business and investor case for improved CR performance.

24
Engaging with investors
FROM VALUES TO VALUE

Chris Tuppen
BT, UK

In 1990 I became BT's first environment manager. Stepping out of the ivory towers of academic research into the very different culture of the company's communications department was quite a shock to the system. In my new role I started coming into contact with a wide range of the company's stakeholders. Notably absent though was the investment community.

In those early days BT received a small number of questionnaires from very niche ethical funds, but compared to today my interaction with 'the City' was negligible. On one occasion in the early 1990s, I hosted a meeting of environment managers from large FTSE companies to discuss the apparent lack of City interest in such matters. BT's then head of investor relations came along to the meeting (the first time I had ever met him) and told it like it was. 'In my experience,' he said, 'our investors are just not interested. They see no link between environmental management and shareholder return.' In some ways, since then, a lot has changed but, in others, the message is just the same.

Today, I make regular presentations to socially responsible investment (SRI) investors on BT's corporate social responsibility (CSR) programme. I go on investor roadshows similar in nature to those made by our chief executive and Group finance director when discussing the company's commercial strategy. We receive multiple and detailed questionnaires from investors and rating agencies. And our investor relations team has someone assigned specifically to support our SRI engagement programme.

However, speaking at the UK Business in the Community annual conference in 2004, Ben Verwaayen, BT's chief executive, mused on the fact that he had recently met over a hundred mainstream telecoms analysts and not one had asked about the company's social, environmental or ethical (SEE) performance. And, when the Dow Jones Sustainability Index placed us at the top of our industry sector for the fourth year running, our head of investor relations passed his congratulations on to the CSR team. In an interesting postscript, though, he said he longed to see the day when such an announcement made even a flicker of difference to the share price. It is still a sad fact of life that, however well a company performs in matters of sustainable development, there is no significant impact on share price. The best it seems that can be said is that even though getting it badly wrong can be damaging, getting it particularly 'right' is not seen as a negative.

SRI teams: do they always put the shareholder first?

Today, pretty much every institutional investor has an SRI department. However, while SRI teams increasingly talk to their mainstream counterparts, they are still predominantly in separate departments and engage separately with the companies.

Over the past few years there has been an interesting mix of people moving into SRI positions. Some have financial backgrounds while many have company CSR backgrounds and others have come from non-governmental organisations (NGOs). This leads to an interesting and eclectic range of conversations. Much of the analysis that takes place is grounded in sensible risk assessment—seeking to minimise legal and financial liabilities, as well as risks to reputation and brand value, arising out of SEE issues. Where risk management gives rise to opportunity to deliver direct value to the bottom line—for example, through new revenue generation or cost savings—then this also becomes a useful part of the conversation.

Given their passion for the issues, it may not be surprising to see some SRI teams almost seeking to create change, not as a reaction to external societal forces but rather because they, as people, believe change should take place. Not surprising, one might think, given some of their backgrounds. Sometimes SRI teams identify a *potential* risk to the future prospects of a business sector and then go on to highlight it in the public arena, publish reports, benchmark companies and push the matter through their engagement processes. In so doing they actually increase the level of risk that, from a shareholder perspective, one is trying to minimise. Let me offer two examples.

The electronics industry has not, until very recently, been subject to concerns about working conditions in its supply chain. Towards the end of 2003 some campaign groups, such as Cafod (2003), had begun to be a bit more vocal about these matters. At around the same time, the SRI industry also started to get involved in these debates. For example, Insight Investment worked with AccountAbility on its *Gradient: Promoting Best Practice of Supply Chain Labour Standards* report which had a chapter on supply chain issues in the telecommunications industry (Insight Investment and AccountAbility 2004). It may have occurred anyway, but I am sure that this SRI intervention has actually accelerated the manifestation of this risk for the information and communication technology (ICT) industry.

On another occasion, I was asked by one of our big London investors what BT was doing to address digital divide issues in the developing world. There is clearly a huge economic gap opening up as a result of the international digital divide, which is why it was especially mentioned in the UN's Millennium Development Goals. However, the investments required to connect a large proportion of the Earth's population to modern Internet-based networks are huge, and the current so-called 'bottom of the pyramid' business models are far from sufficient. BT's commercial strategy, which was well known at the time, was to concentrate on business-to-business activities outside the UK. When asked the question, I wondered if the investor was asking because it wanted to encourage a change to our commercial strategy or if it was concerned we were shifting position, so I queried the motive behind the question. It was clear from the stumbled response that I had been asked because it was an important global social issue, and not because the investor had thought through the link between its investment in BT and what it expected the response to be.

These examples demonstrate the important societal issues we are dealing with, and I have every sympathy with a desire to improve things. But how far into the campaigning space should SRI teams go, and what impression does this leave on their mainstream colleagues when they overstep that mark?

The elusive business case

In trying to find a link between sound sustainability performance and increased shareholder value, companies are often their own worst enemy. Many corporate presentations to SRI analysts are based on policy commitments, charitable good works, awards and management processes. Few attempt to put hard financial figures to the business benefits of their CSR programme. This is, generally, not because they are reluctant to divulge that information, but because it is really difficult to find the proof points. It's much easier to talk about corporate values than corporate value. This is an area we must all work hard to improve.

I am not for a minute suggesting we dismiss corporate values or that business should not have a sense of ethical responsibility. I am, however, arguing that values-driven action must be consistent with the commercial strategy of the business. This is where the all-so-elusive CSR business case comes in. If one can succeed at both levels, then I believe CSR really builds stakeholder trust and respect, *and* delivers shareholder value. For example, BT's own activities on the business case have led to quantification in a number of areas, in particular:

- Linking CSR performance to customer satisfaction and loyalty
- CSR risk assessment based on likely impacts on profits over a three-year time horizon
- Cost savings from BT's environment programme
- Degree of employee motivation from CSR activities
- Number of graduates considering CSR when deciding to join BT
- Value of BT bids for new business with customer CSR requirements

Judging performance

Although a sound business case is critical for investment decision-making it is not, on its own, sufficient. The investor needs to know how, and how well, the company is minimising its risks and maximising its opportunities. This comes in part from the engagement process, but more often than not involves some form of questionnaire—either directly or via a rating agency. We get flooded with questionnaires, some good, some challenging, many asking questions that we have already answered via our sustainability reporting website,[1] and far too many simply offering a series of box-ticking options. In my view, those seeking to achieve a true insight to a company's sustainability performance via a box-ticking questionnaire are misguided. It takes a much more detailed assessment process. It requires inputs from other sources (such as the media, opinion formers and NGOs), it needs a sector-specific approach, and it needs a real investment in time and resource. Very few ratings achieve this. Those that do not only provide value to the investor but are also extremely useful to the company being evaluated. Those that don't add to company costs and, if they get out of proportion, could well incite a muted backlash from the corporate community. 'Muted' because what company will want to turn away potential investors?

Hopefully, we will see a reduction in low-quality baseline questionnaires. This may take place via consolidating web-based portals or via advanced Internet technologies such as XBRL. Indeed, it is very encouraging to learn that the Global Reporting Initiative (GRI) is working on the development of an XML/XBRL taxonomy. However it happens, it will still need to offer companies a way in which they can communicate their messages to reflect their corporate persona, as well as offer a more cost-effective approach than today's models provide.

Future forward

Since my first engagement with SRI in the early 1990s, things have come a long way. SRI teams have grown, CSR professionals in companies are gradually learning to talk the language of investors, and business cases are becoming more robust. Mainstream analysts have moved from a position of no interest to one of guarded interest. They feel they need to know more, and they increasingly recognise that how well a company manages its stakeholder relations (which is what CSR is really all about) could actually be a very good indicator of long-term value. The new investment manager, Generation Investment Management (set up by Al Gore and David Blood), may well be a sight of the future. Here, there is no distinction between SRI and mainstream—they are completely blended together. Quite possibly, by 2025, SRI will have disappeared and will simply be integrated into investment models.

On a recent roadshow in Paris, my investor relations colleague and I were in discussion with an SRI analyst and the mainstream telecoms analyst. We were talking about ADSL broadband roll-out in the UK, under the topic of *la fracture numérique* (the digital

1   www.bt/com/betterworld

divide). 'But this isn't SRI,' the telecoms analyst said, 'it's mainstream.' The rest of us looked at each other, laughed, and said: 'That's exactly the point.'

References

Cafod (2003) *Clean Up Your Computer: Working Conditions in the Electronics Industry* (London: Cafod).

Insight Investment and Accountability (2004) *Gradient: Promoting Best Practice of Supply Chain Labour Standards* (London: Insight Investment).

25

Workers' capital
PROMOTING TRADE UNION CONCERNS THROUGH INVESTMENT

Tom Powdrill

Trades Union Congress, UK

This chapter provides an overview of the attitude of trade unions in the UK towards shareholder engagement and outlines the activity undertaken by the Trades Union Congress (TUC) to promote responsible investment. The chapter explains the 'workers' capital' perspective on investment, describes the TUC's work with pension fund trustees and its analysis of fund managers, and concludes with a discussion of responsible investment in the UK at present and the role of the labour movement within it.

Workers' capital perspective

The 'workers' capital' movement can be seen as being based on several basic ideas (see, generally, TUC 2002). The first is the assertion of ownership. The money in pension funds and insurance policies comes largely from employees, many of whom are trade union members. It is workers' capital that is being invested. Professional City firms may manage the money—but it belongs to employees and, as such, unions have a legitimate interest in making sure it is invested in a responsible manner.

The second idea is the need to ensure that workers' retirement savings are not used to their detriment. Pressure from institutional investors for short-term increases in investment returns has often had a detrimental effect on employees, pushing companies into behaviour that has damaged the interests of union members—lay-offs, reductions in R&D and training, needless merger and acquisition activity, international job flight, and so on. So the workers' capital movement seeks to ensure that, where possible, members' own financial assets are not used against them.

The third idea is more positive—to try to use workers' capital to promote high standards in investee companies. The point is often made that companies associated with poor standards (for example, the use of sweatshop labour) can suffer reputational damage which can affect their share price. Certainly, at least in some cases, analysts now look to quantify the potential financial liabilities of behaviour that has negative social impacts. Increasingly, unions see activist investing as an additional tool to help drive up standards.

Workers' capital in the UK

Uniquely among the variety of groups that have looked at pension fund investment as a way of influencing company behaviour, UK trade unions have considerable potential to bring about change. In the UK, a minimum of a third of the trustees of a pension scheme must be nominated by the membership of the scheme, and the government has recently announced its intention to move to require half of trustee boards to be member-nominated trustees (MNTs). Many of these MNTs are trade union members, and the TUC is in direct contact with several hundred of them.

The TUC Member Trustee Network, a support service for MNTs, has approximately 1,000 participants, including representatives from many of the largest pension funds in the UK. We estimate that the assets of all funds where there are network contacts exceed £260 billion. With the move to 50/50 trustee boards we expect both the influence of MNTs and membership of the network to increase. It is important to stress that the network is a service to support trustees on questions about all issues, whether they be legal, concerning benefits or relating to investment.[1] Through the network we are trying to encourage trustees to take a more proactive role in shareholder activism. In a quarterly newsletter we provide suggestions on questions that trustees can ask their fund managers in relation to their views and decisions on topical governance or corporate social responsibility (CSR) issues, and news items on shareholder activism. We also distribute the sector notes produced by Just Pensions to advise trustees on CSR issues in particular industries (see further Chapter 12). The TUC also provides free trustee training, within which there is a session on shareholder activism.

Aside from our activity through the network we have also sought to develop relationships with institutional investors. Over the past three years the TUC has built up contacts within the pensions and investment industry in order to ensure that our views and policies are widely understood. We frequently consult with industry contacts to ensure a regular dialogue.

There is also a more direct element to our work. Each year, the TUC carries out a number of shareholder voting campaigns. These have mainly focused on executive remuneration—for example, at Vodafone, HSBC and GlaxoSmithKline (GSK)—although we have also addressed wider governance issues at companies such as Corus and BSkyB. In

---

1   See further the section of the TUC website devoted to the MNT network: www.tuc.org.uk/trusteenetwork. The TUC publications cited in this chapter can also be found at this location.

addition, we have supported labour-oriented shareholder resolutions at Rio Tinto and Unocal. In each case we send an alert to the network explaining how we believe shareholders should vote on the item in question. Our position is also communicated to corporate governance staff at fund management house and to the various proxy voting agencies. The TUC does not, at present, expect to be able to influence voting outcomes significantly, but we are aware that in some cases trustees do follow our position, and, more importantly, that such campaigns serve to prompt useful discussions between fund managers and trustees.

Aside from these campaigns, the TUC's most high-profile intervention in the field of investor activism is the annual Fund Manager Voting Survey (TUC 2003, 2004). This asks fund managers for information both on voting policy and on practices, and monitors their voting decisions on 50 key votes. The questionnaire is sent direct to fund managers and to trustees. The completed survey is distributed to all network participants. The aim of the survey is to give trustees more information on this important element of share ownership. While pension funds may receive corporate governance reports from their own fund managers, these can vary in detail and quality. In addition, without the survey trustees would not have comparable information to see how their manager voted in relation to others. The second voting survey, published in 2004 (TUC 2004), saw a markedly improved response rate from fund managers. Voting data was obtained for 26 different investors, representing tens of billions of pounds worth of assets. We hope to see the number of responses increase further in future years.

The TUC recognises the need to work constructively with the fund management industry. As such, we ensure that examples of good practice are highlighted in the survey and we stress that trustees should recognise the commitment to transparency that those fully participating managers have made. As an incentive to participate, contact details for managers that disclose fully are listed in the published survey. Non-respondents are also listed so that trustees can identify which fund managers are not willing to be transparent.

Providing comparable data on shareholder voting has increased both transparency and fund manager accountability to their clients. In one case, it was through the process of obtaining voting data for the survey that one pension fund became aware that one of its managers voted only where it held 3% or more of an investee company's stock. In addition, in 2004, we were able to show that one fund management firm, which had managed to garner itself a reputation for activism was, in fact, the only manager in the sample that supported management in every one of the 50 votes analysed. The survey has also highlighted the wide variations in positions taken by fund managers in relation to voting. Some regularly vote with management, others are more likely to abstain or oppose over controversial issues. The TUC firmly believes this variation is grounds for trustees to take a close interest in how fund managers exercise ownership and, more broadly, for fund managers' voting records to be publicly disclosed.

The most important outcome from the survey has been to empower trustees. At a basic level, the questionnaire gives the opportunity for trustees to engage with their fund managers on an important area of share ownership. But going beyond this it is important to recognise that the survey represents member trustees from many different schemes collectively pooling information on fund managers' corporate governance activity. In this sense, it is probably unique as an example of trustees working together.

Extending the focus from corporate governance to SRI

To date, the TUC's work around shareholder activism has focused predominantly on corporate governance issues. There are some strategic reasons for this. First, there are clear mechanisms for governance activism. Items of importance to shareholders, such as board appointments, remuneration, appointment of auditors and so on, are put to the vote at company annual general meetings. Second, it is now widely accepted that governance issues are of legitimate shareholder concern and there is an almost universally accepted set of standards to work towards in the Combined Code. However, it has always been the TUC's longer-term aim for our shareholder activism work to address wider issues than governance. Ultimately, we want to ensure that CSR issues, particularly those of importance to the labour movement, are taken seriously by companies. Hence, it is worth sketching some of the TUC's views on socially responsible investment (SRI).

Along with others, we have been disappointed by the lack of take-up of SRI strategies by pension funds, although this it is not a complete surprise. Compared to corporate governance, the acceptance of the legitimacy of shareholders raising CSR issues with investee companies is more limited, and there is no one, widely accepted framework of standards equivalent to the Combined Code. More fundamentally, SRI is seen as having an impact on underlying investment decisions in a way that governance does not, and many misconceptions about its financial impact persist. Many people, including trustees, still assume it must involve some trade-off with returns and, as such, is in conflict with fiduciary duty. This view is clearly based on an understanding of SRI as a screening approach, where companies with a poor CSR rating are excluded or those with a positive profile are included. The TUC believes a screening approach is defensible, as screened funds have sometimes outperformed. There will also, no doubt, continue to be demand for screening. It is understandable for values-driven organisations such as churches, charities and trade unions to want to ensure that the way they invest their own assets does not conflict with their principles. Ultimately, this may lead them to exclude certain investments. However, in the wider world of corporate pension funds it is quite clear that there are significant barriers to screening and, consequently, engagement is likely to be the most commonly used approach to responsible investment.

Engagement has two major advantages over screening. First, it is clearly more likely to have influence with the investee company. By continuing to hold shares, and therefore having ownership, the investor retains leverage. In contrast, if the disinvestment route is taken, then ownership, and with it influence, is given up. And, in any case, the sold shares will merely be bought by another investor. The act of selling shares could also depress their price. Second, and more importantly for trustees, because there is no disinvestment the underlying portfolio is unchanged. This means trustees can implement an SRI strategy without having to face the accusation that they are sacrificing returns.

Another interesting facet of engagement is that it is now offered as a stand-alone service by some fund managers. Both the mineworkers' pension schemes and the Wellcome Trust have recently awarded engagement-only mandates. This is a significant development as it gets away from trustees having to hope that the manager they pick for a particular mandate is also committed to engagement. Instead, they can introduce the investment strategy required and apply an engagement mandate across the whole fund. Trustees can choose the managers they believe are best suited to manage particular asset classes and, separately, the organisation they believe has the best skills for carrying out shareholder engagement without compromising on either element.

This is not to say that engagement is a perfect solution. The whole concept of engagement is still rather nebulous. There is currently no independent quantitative or qualitative analysis of the engagement carried out by fund managers. This matters as, in the current environment, managers know they are under political pressure to be seen to take their ownership responsibilities seriously. As a result, many managers report that they 'engage' with investee companies. However, the quality and depth of this engagement must vary significantly between fund managers. Some employ a team of people to work on governance and CSR issues; others employ, at best, only one person. As such, engagement is so loosely defined that it can be used to describe both a one-off meeting with a company that leads nowhere or a prolonged period of interaction that brings about change. In short, there is a clear need for standardised benchmarking and reporting, so that trustees and their advisors can tell what is going on, and which managers are really putting the effort in. Not only would this improve trustee decision-making, it would also start to tackle the issue of free-riding.

Trustees also need to be reassured that engagement is worth spending time and money on. Research carried out by Just Pensions in association with the TUC found that among the most common reasons for trustees not being more active on SRI were cost and resource implications, combined with uncertainty about the benefits it would bring (Gribben and Olsen 2003). Fund managers have many anecdotal examples of the positive results of engagement, but systematic evidence of their effectiveness is very limited. This information again needs to be far more standardised in order that trustees can see that the service they are paying for is bringing about results. In response to the lack of reliable information, the UK Social Investment Forum has initiated a project to develop a set of guidelines to enable fund managers to report voting and engagement activity (see further Chapter 12).[2] The TUC believes that these guidelines could play an important role in tackling the assessment of engagement.

What about labour issues?

Ultimately, of course, unions want to see pension funds giving labour issues proper weight in their SRI strategies. Finding a causal link between a company's behaviour in relation to a particular issue and share price performance is the Holy Grail of the SRI community, but remains notoriously hard to prove. What might be termed 'labour' issues are no different to any other in this regard. However, health and safety looks as though it could become a breakthrough issue for trade unionists interested in advancing the workers'-capital idea. There are several reasons for this. First, there have been a number of recent examples where health and safety problems at companies have resulted in sharp falls in share price. Second, it is easier for mainstream investors to see health and safety as a 'common sense' issue as opposed to a political or moral campaign. Finally, investor interest in health and safety is being encouraged by the development of a specialist index developed by the Health and Safety Executive (HSE). The Corporate Health and Safety Performance Index (CHaSPI) is intended to provide investors and other interested parties with an indicator of how various companies are managing health and safety (see further Chapter 31). Ultimately, CHaSPI will give participating companies a score which can be compared across its peer group. In developing the index, the HSE has sought to involve companies, investors and union representatives. As such, it is hoped that CHaSPI will be seen as a reliable and useful tool for mainstream investors which will, in turn, encourage companies to give health and safety proper consideration.

One of the questions that has been raised about shareholder activism is whether trade unions can legitimately raise questions as investors without compromising their fiduciary duty as trustees. It therefore needs to be stressed that trade unions will not undertake any kind of activity that damages either returns or investee companies. Given the high position of pensions on the trade union agenda, we simply have no interest in subverting the function of pension schemes.

Conclusions

In fact, if there is a criticism to be made of the SRI movement to date it is that it has sometimes appeared as if its proponents believe that corporate governance and social, environmental and ethical issues are the only thing that trustees should be concerned about. Given the problems that have befallen occupational pension schemes over the past three or four years, the focus for trustees has clearly been elsewhere. So the slow process of encouraging more pension funds to become responsible investors must be underpinned by an understanding of how funds typically invest and the myriad other issues that face them. This is patently a more constructive approach than trying to 'shame' pension funds into action.

To conclude, in this early phase in the development of investor activism, there is no alternative to the long hard slog of building up the intellectual case in favour, providing guidance and advice on how to implement policies, attempting to develop widely accepted standards and benchmarks, and then working directly with trustees to try to convince them to be proactive.

Unions were perhaps slow to respond to the opportunities presented by responsible investment, and the TUC recognises that some of the more committed fund managers are considerably ahead of most trustees in terms of their understanding of, and belief in, the potential of shareholder activism. However, we now have a few years' experience in the union movement of what can work in this field. Our activities will continue to grow and we aim to work constructively with others to develop a more long-term and responsible investment culture among UK pension funds. Through our links to pension fund trustees, we hope we have the capacity to bring about real change. There will be no overnight transformation of pension fund investment. Realistically, we can probably expect governance and CSR issues gradually to become more common as items on the trustee agenda. In this way, client pressure on fund managers to take such issues seriously will build slowly. But, while the sometimes glacial nature of change can be frustrating, it is worth remembering the scale of ambitions of investor activists. It is nothing less than bringing proper accountability to company boards and seeking to improve standards of corporate behaviour.

References

Gribben, C., and L. Olsen (2003) *Will UK pension funds become more responsible? A Survey of Member-nominated Trustees* (London: Just Pensions).

TUC (Trades Union Congress) (2002) *Working Capital: Institutional Investment Strategy* (London: TUC).

—— (2003) *TUC Fund Manager Voting Survey 2003* (London: TUC).

—— (2004) *TUC Fund Manager Voting Survey 2004* (London: TUC).

26
Pharma Futures
INVESTOR ANALYSIS OF THE FUTURE OF THE PHARMACEUTICAL SECTOR*

Sophia Tickell

Pharma Futures, UK

The Pharma Futures scenario planning project was convened in early 2004 by three pension funds—Algemeen Burgerlijk Pensioenfonds (ABP, the Netherlands), the Ohio Public Employees Retirement System (OPERS, US) and the Universities Superannuation Scheme (USS, UK). As long-term owners in the pharmaceutical sector, these pension funds recognised that they have a substantial interest in the continued profitability of a sector that had created considerable shareholder value during the 1980s and 1990s. At the same time, they acknowledged the very serious challenges facing the industry's business model.

The project sponsors were aware of the limited utility of the traditional tools available to manage risk: namely, bottom-up stock-picking or under-weighting the sector, especially when they took a portfolio-wide and absolute risks–returns perspective. Hence, they sponsored the Pharma Futures project to facilitate a considered, informed discussion between the industry and its owners about the future of a sector with a vital role to play in the development and manufacture of innovative therapies, improving public well-being and contributing to economic growth. At the heart of the project was a desire to better align the goal of profitability with society's need for improved access to affordable healthcare, including innovative and life-enhancing prescription drugs.

---

* The material in this chapter is based on the Pharma Futures report, *The Pharmaceutical Sector: A Long-Term Value Outlook*, published in December 2004.

Underpinning the project was an assumption that such an alignment is at the heart of any durable business model for the sector.

Pharma Futures brought together 15 informed private-sector stakeholders (pension funds, sell- and buy-side analysts, pharmaceutical executives from ethical/branded and generic firms) to review how the sector might develop over the next 10 to 15 years. Their deliberations over a 12-month period were enriched by interviews with 30 external experts and a website discussion forum. The group discussed a range of issues relevant to a successful, long-term pharmaceutical industry, including: innovation; adaptive leadership; emerging markets; access to medicines in developing countries; intellectual property protection; marketing; information and advertising; pricing; societal expectations; government health provision; and demographic changes.

The project created an opportunity for participants to do some long-term thinking in a way that was not easy to do in the context of their various 'day jobs'. It also allowed them to interact in a collaborative and creative way with people who had very different types of expertise with regard to the sector. All participants accepted the project's starting premise: namely, that for industry and its investors to act successfully on the challenges facing the sector, some adaptation of the sector's business model will be needed.

Rationale for the project

Pharma Futures was set up in response to the serious challenges facing the pharmaceutical industry and, in particular, the dilemma of needing to convince investors of ongoing profitability while simultaneously meeting growing societal expectations that, on the one hand, innovation will continue to yield new medicines and, on the other, that at least some medicines should be widely available to people on limited incomes in all markets. Other challenges include an imminent wave of patent expiries without commensurate compensating new drug approvals (see Figs. 26.1 and 26.2); demographic changes (see Fig. 26.3); pressure on governments to reduce health expenditure; corporate pressure to reduce health insurance costs; calls for price reductions; challenges to intellectual property rights; unmet health needs in emerging markets and poor countries; and media and societal anger at corporate priorities and behaviour.

The project was based on an understanding that existing market structures do not currently provide the right incentives and disincentives for pharmaceutical companies to place adequate priority on meeting a wide range of societal expectations (including responsible marketing, affordable pricing, ethical scientific practices, etc.). At the same time, institutional investors and other industry commentators continue to have high expectations of the profitability of pharmaceutical companies. These expectations translate into powerful mechanisms to reward or penalise management and thus help to provide incentives to the sector to continue with its current business model.

There is, therefore, a growing imbalance between the short-term benefit that industry provides to shareholders and the productive research that these shareholders and other stakeholders want from the industry in the long term. The result is serious tension for the industry in mature markets. This is exemplified by a range of public initia-

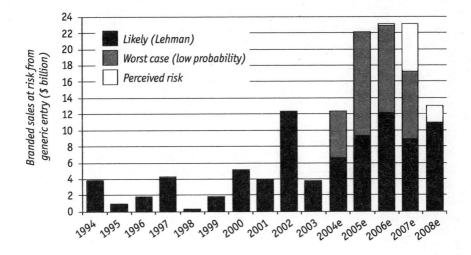

FIGURE 26.1 Annual sales of US brands facing potential generic competition

Source: US Orange Book; Lehman Brothers estimates

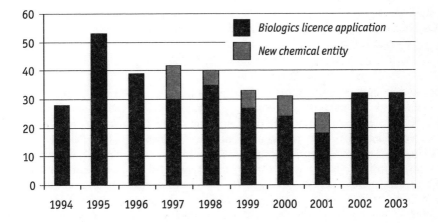

FIGURE 26.2 FDA new drug approvals

Source: US Food and Drug Administration, Center for Drug Evaluation and Research, 'New Drug Approvals', 2004; see www.fda.gov/cder/da/da.htm

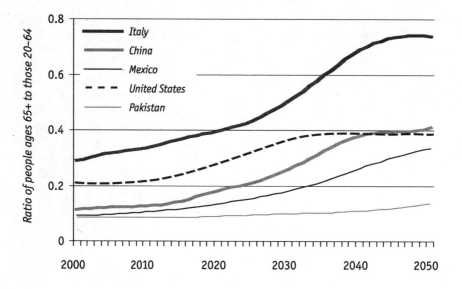

China's pattern is unusual because of the country's birth policy. The other four countries represent, in broad terms, the patterns evolving in the other countries of the world. Pakistan represents the least-developed countries. Mexico represents a set of countries in middle stages of development where fertility rates have dropped significantly over the past couple of decades. The US represents a set of developed countries where fertility rates have not totally caved in and where there is some immigration (e.g. Australia, Canada, the UK and France to lesser degrees). Italy represents a set of developed countries where there is not much immigration and where fertility rates are around or below 1.35.

FIGURE 26.3 Age–dependency ratios for selected countries 2000–50

Source: UN Population Division, World Population Prospects 2000

tives. For example, the US Maine Rx legislation mandates the same price discount to uninsured individuals as the largest state purchaser of medicines is able to obtain. In parallel, a growing number of states are permitting the reimportation of less expensive drugs from Canada, despite the fact that this practice is presently against federal law. Price or reimbursement controls continue to operate in Europe and Japan while similar cost control disciplines are creeping into many US states. Also in the US, private responses are increasingly visible and include concerted efforts by large employers and consortia of such organisations (e.g. Business for Affordable medicines) to cap medicine prices. The recently approved US Medicare drug bill is unlikely to solve the pricing problem. Indeed, some argue it may even make the situation worse as it offers limited drug coverage and makes it probable that employers who currently pay for retiree drug coverage will cease to do so. Furthermore, it transfers a growing proportion of the US drugs bill to the government, making price regulation much more likely.

The industry faces internal pressures as well. Innovation faces high failure rates, there is a decreasing scope for obtaining high prices for 'me-too' drugs in the face of wider choice from a rapidly growing list of generic alternatives, and there are more pressures from regulators leading to more trials and larger patient groups for those trials. The loss of confidence in Cox-2 inhibitors has led to growing pressure for long-term studies on all chronic use drugs and thus to a situation in which regulators may require clinical trials to compare new drugs with best current treatment, rather than the present practice of comparing them to a placebo. The same loss of confidence is likely to lead to greater government and public scrutiny of the professional and financial independence of the regulators. Marketing is under scrutiny for a range of reasons, ranging from ethics, legality, reputation and diminishing returns from the traditional 'share of voice' marketing strategies (see Fig. 26.4). In manufacturing, regulatory requirements are proving difficult to keep up with and companies are being challenged on efficiency grounds. There is also growing concern about the sector's political (and therefore regulatory) influence as a result of its substantial and partisan approach to political donations.

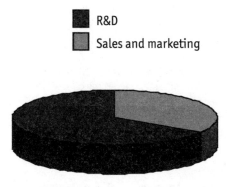

Note that a proportion of the R&D expenditure (possibly between 5% and 10%) could be phase IV studies which could be classified as sales and marketing expenditure.

FIGURE 26.4 Relative expenditures on R&D and marketing for the European pharmaceutical industry in 2003

Source: ABN; AMRO

In emerging or developing-country markets, there has been a high-profile debate about access to antiretroviral treatment for HIV/AIDS. This debate can only intensify as the macroeconomic effects of this illness are better understood. Furthermore, as the incidence of other communicable and non-communicable diseases increases, the debate will involve more companies and become more complex. The situation is likely to be exacerbated by the increase in chronic diseases such as diabetes, cardiovascular disease and hypertension. Many recent therapies for the treatment of these diseases are still under patent and in the least-developed countries and emerging markets are therefore likely to be unaffordable for the majority of the population. Unlike many of those with HIV/AIDS, some of the new 'health-poor'—particularly those suffering from chronic diseases—will be articulate and empowered middle classes in countries with growing political influence (e.g. Brazil, Russia, India and China). Poor infrastructure and lack of delivery mechanisms in poor countries will continue to be a serious problem.

Pharma Futures acknowledged that pharmaceutical companies cannot and should not be expected to provide the solution to chronic under-investment in healthcare resulting from poverty or governmental neglect. Despite this, popular concern about globalisation, the nature of global communications and high levels of profitability all combine to mean that the sector will inevitably be drawn into the firing line with other stakeholders as the market's failure to meet expressed health needs in poor countries becomes apparent. The sector's involvement, directly or via trade representatives of sympathetic governments, in the debate about generics and patents further exacerbates these risks since it tends to position the sector with some audiences as neither interested in solving the problem nor in stepping aside and letting public policy-makers and others get on with the challenge. The outcome of these pressures is likely to place unsustainable pressure on an industry that created considerable shareholder value for investors in the 1980s and 1990s.

The sector has responded assertively to these challenges in the expectation that innovation will be delivered and that this will remove the threats. This holding strategy has worked more or less, but it is unclear how long it will continue to do so or what will be the long-term cost in terms of reputation and ability to adapt.

Pharma Futures was created to facilitate a new kind of dialogue that emphasised creative and problem-solving engagement by industry practitioners, long-term investors and their analysts, and those who reflect the views of government and societal players. A solution that excludes any one of these groups is unlikely to lead to a satisfactory resolution to the major problems facing the industry.

Project methodology: the use of scenarios

Pharma Futures chose to use scenarios as the tool to identify existing trends that will change the shape of the global pharmaceutical industry between now and 2015. The scenarios are neither predictions nor strategies. Instead they are descriptions of different possible futures designed to highlight the risks and opportunities inherent in each one. As such, they are a useful tool to help overcome anxiety about the lack of hard data regarding the future. The point of using scenarios is to explore and understand more deeply a number of different possibilities in order to make better reasoned choices among them.

The Pharma Futures report outlines three plausible scenarios (see Box 26.1). The first highlights a likely shift of pharmaceutical production to developing countries, such as India and China. The second sees a future driven by knowledgeable patients demanding transparency and value for money. The third describes a future in which governments negotiate with the industry in setting R&D priorities for acute and chronic diseases.

Themes arising from the scenarios

Although the Pharma Futures scenarios are not predictions, the stories they tell are nevertheless built on existing trends which will be responsible, at least in part, for changes to the global pharmaceutical industry between now and 2015. For this reason, the Pharma Futures report outlined possible implications of each scenario for three key

Scenario 1: producers' scenario

The absence of new drugs continues to cause mounting cost pressures. Efficiencies are sought in marketing, manufacturing and research. Former employees return to the emerging markets of India and China which see a growing concentration of manufacturing and marketing expertise, increased patient demand and government support for research initiatives. Investors see the potential for making money on volume. Western pharmaceutical companies are challenged to deepen existing relationships with emerging-country firms. Southern governments become more powerful and obtain technology transfer arrangements and favourable interpretation of intellectual property rights (IPR) agreements. All these changes result in more competition and increased accountability in the global pharmaceuticals market.

Scenario 2: the patients scenario

The genotyping of disease propensity advances, but there are no commensurate drug breakthroughs. Individuals assume greater responsibility for their health. Health spending shifts away from drugs and towards diagnosis/prognosis and early treatment intervention. Pharmaceutical companies seek non-conventional sources of medicine, opportunities in emerging markets and herbals, while also revisiting the existing library for novel indications. Investors signal a willingness to accept greater risks in exchange for potential rewards. Patient groups form an effective, educated lobby with greater awareness of the risks and benefits of therapies, and successfully call for increased transparency in clinical trials and post-marketing surveillance.

Scenario 3: the politics and public health scenario

A global flu outbreak causes public outrage about the lack of investment into new antibiotics and vaccines. Governments assume a more active role in directing R&D priorities first for acute and then for chronic diseases. Over time elements of a social business compact become clear, including: government commitment to expand access; sophisticated purchasers who negotiate price on value-for-money calculations; higher rewards for innovation in exchange for more secure IPR agreements; patients' agreement to a healthy living package as part of insurance and pension plans; pharmaceutical company agreement to less aggressive pricing in exchange for volumes; and reward for true innovation.

Box 26.1 The three Pharma Futures scenarios

stakeholders in the industry: institutional investors, pharmaceutical executives and governments.

It is worth clarifying that the Pharma Futures process began with a close examination of a 'business as usual' future, one in which the industry manages to 'muddle through' tomorrow much as it has today and yesterday. It looked at a range of things that would have to happen, simultaneously, to permit the current business model to continue to operate as it currently does. If looked at individually, it is easy enough to see these trends continuing into the future. However, if considered as a group—along with the assumptions underlying each one—this 'muddling through' future collapsed under its own implausibility.

First, there would need to be more consolidation to deal with issues of pipeline productivity and revenue pressures. Second, and in spite of accelerating healthcare costs and downward pressure on their budgets, governments would have to be prepared to accept increases in the costs of prescription drugs. Third, more effective marketing would have to provide a counterweight to pricing pressures. Fourth, there would need to be a growth in the availability of and demand for new therapies for chronic and degenerative diseases. Fifth, the introduction of pharmacogenomics and more highly personalised treatments would need to open up additional disease states to more efficacious (but expensive) treatment. Sixth, developing-country demand for access would need to be managed with just enough incremental concessions to keep at bay reference pricing pressures, intellectual property challenges and other major disruptions to current business practices. Finally, the expansion of biotechnology resulting in new hybrid products and companies, would need to expand the market overall. While some mixes of these eventualities are highly likely, the working group found it implausible that they would all happen simultaneously.

In addition to the scenarios and a discussion of their implications, the working group identified the following cross-cutting themes and trends relevant to all the scenarios and, indeed, any likely future:

1 The impacts of emerging markets on the global pharmaceutical industry appear to be significantly underestimated at the present time. These impacts may take many forms. They may offer larger markets than is assumed to be the case, they may generate unexpected models of innovation which could be turned into an advantage or a disadvantage for traditional pharmaceutical companies and they have the potential to disrupt current trade agreements (see point 6)

2 The speed and scope of new science in bringing innovative therapies to market will be critical in determining the fortunes of the industry. In the absence of new drugs, the risk of downward valuation of industry is likely to continue and societal pressure for change is likely to increase

3 The industry faces a period of transition that requires a step change to a more adaptive, flexible and open-minded leadership. This leadership needs to signal to investors the need for change. Some of the industry winners of the next decade may not yet be on the radar screen, and investors need to find new ways to identify these new winners

4 Any major change to the business model will require a company to embrace the risks and benefits of being the 'first mover'. At present, financial markets are more likely to punish rather than reward adaptive first-mover behaviour. Informed by 'thought leaders' from within the sector, investors need to develop their own understanding of what constitutes adaptive leadership and create market-based incentives that reward this behaviour

5 Trust is a key issue for this highly regulated sector and is under serious threat. The lack of trust between many of the stakeholder groups and the industry could lead to balance-of-power shifts including, in the US, from producer to government, thus impacting industry margins and returns. In addition, there is an erosion of investor confidence in the sector's ability to deliver durable shareholder value. As society needs a thriving pharmaceutical industry, all stakeholders need to work to re-establish an equilibrium that acknowledges their inter-dependence

6 Market-based solutions are unlikely to systematically meet the access needs of people in the least-developed countries due to extremely low per capita health expenditure. Continued commitment to overseas development aid is therefore likely to be necessary. Since it seems plausible that aid from Organisation for Economic Co-operation and Development (OECD) countries will remain insufficient to meet this need, increasing pressure for access to affordable medicines can be expected to persist and will inevitably impact on the sector and its shareholders. It will be important that relationships with key stakeholders are well managed

7 The growth of the 'patient-consumer' lobby is a discernible trend that is likely to become more pronounced. The likely increase in patient co-pays (out-of-pocket contributions to health costs) in all markets, combined with more patient information, will further contribute to the transformation of patients into more critical consumers. While this offers long-term benefits in terms of patient empowerment and marketing advantages, it is also likely to lead to greater awareness of the risks and benefits of therapies, including an increased understanding of possible harmful side-effects, a greater demand for value for money and calls for increased transparency on clinical trials and post-marketing surveillance

Conclusion and its implications for investors

The Pharma Futures project concluded that fundamental change to the way the pharmaceutical industry is run is inevitable. It explains why muddling through by fire-fighting each existing challenge is not an option. In parallel, it argues that it is possible to manage this change and come out profitable and successful. To achieve this outcome, however, both investors and industry will need to make fundamental changes to their behaviour. There is no prescription dictating precisely where to start, but investors can (and are already beginning to) address the fundamental question of how to develop better metrics to measure extra-financials in the pharmaceutical industry.

The pension funds that sponsored the Pharma Futures process fully acknowledge the difficulties faced by any public company wishing to challenge sector norms, and the near impossibility of doing so without the support of its key investors. These investors judge companies against others in the sector, meaning that individual companies can only take a more proactive role if far more proactive approaches become the norm for the sector. In turn, the sector as a whole will be best able to respond if a broad group of institutional investors make clear that they understand and are ready to accept new ways of working. To come to the best judgement, these investors will need to understand and acknowledge that key stakeholders have the power and, increasingly, the incentive, to effect significant changes to the regulatory environment in which the industry operates.

To date, the highly regulated pharmaceutical sector has adopted a compliance mentality with regard to stakeholder demands, explained, perhaps, by the assumption of societal approval arising from the social benefit of their product. The outcome has been a marked tendency to frown on first-mover behaviour that goes beyond this compliance. The temptation to avoid being the first mover must be resisted if the challenges facing the pharmaceutical sector are to be addressed. Individuals and institutions with a stake in the industries' future will need to take a lead in setting new norms and this leadership will be vital in determining how successfully the industry manages the transition. The stakeholder base for the pharmaceutical industry is very wide, encompassing pharmaceutical executives and their consultants, institutional investors and financial analysts, government regulators, purchasers, individual patients and patients' groups, doctors, pharmacists, insurance firms, media and other commentators. All these groups have an interest in how the sector evolves.

The Pharma Futures report poses many question, some directed at the industry and others its owners. How, for example, will investors recognise and reward positive change? Specifically, what incentives might investors provide to encourage pharmaceutical executives to restructure remuneration packages to focus more on R&D productivity and to develop some credible indicators of improved relationships with key stakeholders, thus moving away from the current focus on earnings per share? Investors and pharmaceutical companies are also challenged to respond to a situation in which a wider range of products are sold at volume over price. What should investors and companies do, respectively, to accommodate this trend? As a key driver of this change is likely to be the situation in emerging markets, both supply (growing production and manufacturing capacity) and demand (the growth of domestic markets), what should investors consider to be good management practice in this field? Investors and pharmaceutical companies are challenged to decide whether these changes can be achieved through competition between companies or by developing a new set of agreed standards to guarantee a level playing field. Although phase one of the Pharma Futures project has closed, a number of initiatives have already begun to address some of the questions it asks. Some institutional investors are working on issues raised in the report; for example, the links between remuneration, innovation and post-marketing surveillance on chronic disease medication. In addition, the question of how to improve the quality and reliability of financial reporting has generated interest in some audit firms. These and other initiatives, if more widely supported, could ensure that investors are able to shape the changes they consider desirable, rather than simply being on the receiving end of changes that take little or no account of the long-term interests of the real owners of these companies: namely, the members of pension funds and the customers of insurance companies.

Other questions are posed to governments. What, for example, would appropriate government incentives to promote more energetic research into new antibiotics look like? What changes need to be made to clinical trials to encourage innovation: for example, moving quickly to clinical trials that compare new drugs with best available treatments rather than placebos, as at present? Finally, the Pharma Futures project poses questions to the millions of people whose futures are tied to healthy returns from pharmaceutical shares and also to healthy and comfortable lives facilitated, in part, by access to medicines.

The Pharma Futures project analysed a particular sector and many of its findings are, therefore, peculiar to that sector. However, the methodology that encouraged a longer-term investment view and the findings that relate to relationships between owners of capital and industry executives are also applicable to other problematic sectors. It may not be coincidental that it was the really long-term investors—the pension funds—that were able to raise fundamental questions about business models. The project highlighted the importance of understanding the obstacles that stand in the way of fund managers adopting this longer-term perspective and moving beyond simply under-weighting a failing sector. Pharmaceuticals is a vital sector, important for health, well-being, jobs and research. It is too important for the tyranny of the benchmark to prevail.

27

Evaluation and research of SRI managers

Emma Whitaker

Mercer Investment Consulting, UK

In 1999, the UK Pensions Act legislation was amended to require pension schemes to state their policy on 'the extent (if at all) to which social, environmental or ethical considerations are taken into account in the selection, retention and realisation of investments'. This raised the profile of social, environmental and ethical (SEE) considerations among the UK investment community and, for many funds, it resulted in a decision to integrate SEE issues into their investment process. The amendment also increased the profile of socially responsible investing (SRI), which had traditionally been the domain of retail and charity investors rather than something considered by pension funds.

In advance of this legislation being passed, Mercer Investment Consulting (Mercer IC) formed a team dedicated to researching SRI, operating as part of Mercer IC's wider, global investment manager research. The team's remit is to research SRI in the UK in terms of investment management teams and products offered and to monitor SRI trends within the UK pension fund market, although Mercer IC's view is that this research will progressively become more global in its scope. This chapter gives a brief introduction to Mercer's role as an investment consultant, its view of SRI and its approach to SRI research.

Mercer Investment Consulting

Investment consultants are organisations or individuals who are qualified to give investment advice (as defined by the 1995 Pension Act) to trustees and other responsible bodies. The advice can range from the appointment of investment managers through performance measurement to asset allocation. However, investment consultants are not involved in the management or trading of securities.

Mercer IC is a leading global provider of investment consulting services, offering customised advice at every stage of the investment decision, risk management and investment monitoring process. We have been dedicated to meeting the needs of clients for more than 30 years, working with the fiduciaries of pension funds, foundations, endowments and other investors in some 35 countries. With over 200 full-time staff dedicated to investment-related issues in the UK, we are the largest UK investment consulting organisation. Globally, we have over 640 interdisciplinary staff members, making us the largest investment consulting organisation in the world. Our resources include a research team dedicated to monitoring and evaluating investment managers.

Mercer creates value by applying our extensive knowledge to solving investment challenges. Our consultants provide customised guidance at every stage of the investment process, from governance and investment strategy through to short- and medium-term performance monitoring. Mercer's investment risk management process helps investors through each stage of the investing planning cycle by:

- Setting appropriate investment objectives and developing a statement of investment principles (SIP)

- Deciding on the long-term strategy of the portfolio

- Deciding on investment manager structure and roles

- Searching and selecting managers

- Monitoring the results against the objectives set through performance evaluation of both the managers and overall portfolio

Another aspect of investment consultants' roles is education—ensuring clients fully understand the trends and developments within any asset class and the potential implications of these. For many trustees, SRI still conjures up visions of negatively screened funds with an 'ethical agenda' to pursue, a view being reflected in the comparatively small amount of institutional assets under management. SRI has changed considerably over recent years and this is no longer an accurate perception. Consequently, both fund managers and consultants should ensure that trustees remain appraised of these developments in the marketplace and related opportunities.

Confusingly for trustees, corporate governance-related issues are increasingly being included under the SRI/SEE banner (and vice versa). While there are undoubtedly areas of overlap between the two, they cannot necessarily be regarded as being the same thing. Given that the approach to SEE/governance varies widely within the investment management community, Mercer IC's research has been structured to be flexible enough to allow a clear understanding of a manager's approach to both areas. In addition, Mercer IC also undertakes specialist research into corporate governance.

Researching and assessing investment managers

Mercer believes its global and comprehensive manager research capability is fundamentally important to its role as consultants in an increasingly globalised investment management market. We strongly believe that helping to identify and select those investment managers most likely to meet performance objectives is a vital part of our client service.

We combine understanding of our clients' needs with research-driven knowledge to recommend potential candidates. The aim is not simply to provide clients with a choice of good investment managers but also to identify managers who are likely to form good working relationships with our clients.

Mercer's manager research consultants are engaged full-time in interviewing managers, analysing portfolios and conducting original research. The research process involves a combination of on-site visits to investment managers, statistical analysis and the direct experience of the consultants responsible for establishing Mercer's view on each asset management house. Mercer's research process combines quantitative and qualitative analysis. The factors considered at research meetings with managers are:

- Evidence of any sustainable competitive advantages that should give a manager above-average prospects for future outperformance

- Evidence of any significant potential weaknesses that may impact the prospects for future outperformance or give rise to an above-average risk of future underperformance

In most cases, these factors are weighed up against each other in the final assessment.

Adapting this approach to researching and assessing providers of SRI products

To date, Mercer's SRI research in the UK has not sought to produce specific product ratings for SRI funds (unlike for mainstream asset classes), as the range of products is too disparate for a 'like-for-like' comparison to be made. Instead, it seeks to provide clients with information about the teams and products currently available to the UK institutional market: for example, their strengths, weaknesses, general approach and philosophy. Research findings and views are then used to provide clients with informed advice as to which manager or products would best meet their needs. While the research focuses on a range of areas, the following considerations are particularly important to this asset class (although these factors are not equally weighted when assessing a product but are, instead, adapted by the researcher as necessary):

- How committed is the house to SRI/SEE/activism? This involves consideration of the resources employed, the profile of SRI and activism within the organisation and the organisation's future plans in these areas

- What is the investment manager's general stance with regards to SRI/SEE/ activism and the link with corporate governance? Is SRI/SEE/activism an integral part of the investment approach of the house or does it stand alone?

- What is the size of the team? Is the team dedicated solely to SRI/SEE work or do those involved have other responsibilities?

- Does the investment manager use external research providers? Is there an in-house research team? If so, how much original research work do they carry out?

- What is the investment manager's product range? Is the same investment process used to manage SRI/SEE funds as mainstream funds? If not, what are the differences and who manages the funds?

- What are the investment criteria? Investment consultants should help clients identify funds that match their requirements and beliefs. In particular, when looking at screened funds, clients should be aware of the exact criteria of the fund and the implications for the investment risk–return profile of the fund. For example, depending on the specific criteria used, and/or the manner in which these are interpreted, the effect of a screen that endeavours to exclude one or two specific sectors may actually have the effect of excluding rather more

- What is the fund benchmark? There are as yet no widely accepted benchmarks for SRI/SEE products. Performance evaluation requires extreme care. Particular attention should be paid to the specific benchmark/performance universe being used, as many track records are relatively short

An increase in engagement products, both stand-alone and as an overlay, has presented new research challenges. While many of the above points still apply (in particular, the amount of resource dedicated and the remit and scope of the engagement work, in terms of resource and market coverage), product-specific issues should also be investigated. As engagement products have developed, so has the quality and depth of reporting. However, to date there is no engagement standard or benchmark against which trustees and consultants can judge the effectiveness of the engagement work. This is something some in the industry are seeking to address and the publication of the UK Social Investment Forum (UKSIF) guidelines[1] is a first step (see further Chapter 12). Similarly, the list of factors above would need to be adapted if seeking to assess a mainstream manager's approach to these issues.

Since Mercer's SRI research work began in the UK, several asset management firms have been investing heavily in building large teams dedicated to SRI. These teams have launched a range of products and each has a different approach to the market, both in terms of what they believe to be the key SRI/SEE considerations and the products they offer. For example, some houses still firmly believe that specific funds are the best way to achieve their aims while others seek to operate wide-ranging engagement programmes.

---

1   www.uksif.org

As SRI product ranges grow (driven both by the potential for added value as well as client-specific demand, in particular public and national funds), a trend in the development of SRI is the increasing integration of SEE and wider governance research resources into mainstream buy-side research. SRI teams are now far more likely to work with their mainstream analytical colleagues, be regarded as part of the same team and attend the same company meetings. No longer are SRI teams the 'green team' in the corner. In addition, there appears to be a trend for investment managers (who do not have stand-alone SRI teams) to explicitly incorporate SEE/governance considerations when evaluating companies. This also presents new challenges for manager research work, which Mercer is currently seeking to address.

Rather than expanding our current level of coverage of SRI (or screened) products (an area for which there is only a limited interest), we are presently focusing our efforts on developing a methodology to assess how mainstream fund managers behave in terms of shareholder engagement, and how they incorporate non-financial criteria into their investment approaches. Such information can be used by Mercer consultants with interested clients, either in relation to incumbent managers or as a consideration in new manager searches. This methodology, which is currently in development, will consider three main areas: corporate governance issues; corporate social responsibility (CSR); and the extent to which managers take non-financial criteria into account when making investment decisions.

Mercer IC's policy

Many clients have, to date, decided not to take an active stance in respect of SEE/SRI considerations. As advisors it is not our role to dictate to pension fund trustees what stance they should adopt in respect of SEE considerations. Instead, we aim to provide them with sufficient information to ensure that they remain abreast of latest developments and thinking. For those pension fund trustees who wish to implement a specific policy, we will work with them to achieve this.

Mercer IC encourages fund managers, where appropriate, to incorporate consideration of SEE factors into their investment research, as anecdotal evidence suggests that companies with well-developed SEE policies will perform better than their peers who pay less regard to these issues. As with governance and activism-related issues, managers should be allowed to determine and manage their own policies in this area to reflect their investment approach and their clients' needs. Where managers do decide to incorporate SEE-related issues they would be expected to explain how this works in practice and to provide examples of where it may have resulted in a change of investment decision. Ideally, they should ultimately be able to assess what impact the consideration of SEE (and governance) issues has had on the performance of mainstream products.

Many pension fund trustees will be content to adopt the same corporate governance and CSR policies as their managers, and to incorporate these policies into their SIP. Mercer IC recommends that trustees review their SIPs periodically, and request regular update reports from their managers to ensure that there has been no change in the manager's policy that may conflict with their views. In addition, where trustees decide to offer an SRI investment option to members, they should periodically review the appropriateness of the investment. Trustees may also wish to incorporate a review of SEE issues into their manager selection process. For clients who wish to take a more active stance in this area, either through engagement or more traditional SRI investments, Mercer IC will work with the appropriate specialist providers to structure the clients' portfolios accordingly.

The future?

The world of SRI and activism is evolving apace, and it is important that Mercer's research approach follows suit. The launch of the Enhanced Analytics Initiative (EAI)[2] (see further Chapter 14), continued debate on SEE, governance and activism and their links to improved company performance, together with discussions as to appropriate benchmarks for both funds and engagement programmes, present challenges for the investment community. Benchmarking, in particular, remains an issue that has yet to be entirely resolved. The launch of the UKSIF guidelines is a first step but it is currently too early to tell what the uptake of the guidelines will be by the fund management community. The one certainty is that SRI will not go away. It seems entirely reasonable to expect that consideration of SEE and associated issues will become part of mainstream investing and will impact on analysts/managers' assessment of companies' future prospects. For investment consultants, this means that SRI and activism capabilities will become a standard part of the investment manager assessment process.

28

Why should investors care about responsible investment?

Yusuf Samad

Hewitt Bacon & Woodrow, UK

Terms like 'responsible investment' and 'engagement' have attracted a great deal of media and industry attention. Unfortunately, far too much of this attention has, often incorrectly, focused on single issues or overheated activism. In simplifying issues to such concepts, the reasons why the investment community should care have become obscured. It is important to consider governance of companies in the round. What links all of these terms—activism, engagement, corporate governance, socially responsible investment (SRI), etc.—is the desire to consider more than a company's financial performance and take a longer-term view of a company's value and the factors which may impact this.

It is simplistic to think that good corporate behaviour results from ticking the boxes to comply with, or disclose against, numerous market codes. Nor should it be assumed that good behaviour will result in better share price performance. First and foremost, the goal of good governance is to mitigate the risk of loss to owners and to ensure that they get their fair share of the value created by a company over time. In its purest sense, good governance refers to the interaction of managers, directors and shareholders to direct and control the company, ensuring that a company's earnings and assets are equally distributed to all financial stakeholders. In recent times, the control over corporate value and destiny has shifted in favour of management over labour and capital. If there ever was a time for shareholders to exercise their rights and achieve a better balance, it is now. Encouraging companies and fund managers to consider where improvements can be made in current processes will protect shareholders' interests and, ultimately, mitigate against negative impacts on invested capital. Investors and their agents should adopt a more sustainable approach than simply voting with their feet. In a two-way market the buyer simply inherits the problem and thereby perpetuates the risk—a process that in the end benefits no-one.

To some extent, the onus is on us, the investment consultants. As advisors, we need to highlight the merits of active ownership to the trustees of pension schemes and assist them in the exercise of their rights as owners of companies in order to preserve the value of their investment. After all, we are concerned with the owner's interest, and participation in the governance of the company may protect this.

Investment approaches

Why is it that corporate governance has come into such sharp focus to the extent that certain fund managers and index providers now offer it as a specialist or stand-alone product? If poor governance can cause investment losses, then fiduciaries and their managers should have already been paying considerable attention to prevent erosion of present wealth and future. However, in reality, shareholders have grown progressively more distant from their investment as delegating investment management has become the norm (see further Chapter 20). This raises the question: 'Why is it that most managers appear to be either apathetic and/or to see a focus on good governance as a special effort in their investment process?'

The extent to which a manager will try to protect against the risk of loss due to poor management depends on his or her style. Some managers eschew classical fundamental analysis of the Ben Graham and Warren Buffett stable (i.e. the focus on understanding a company deeply within the context of its economic environment and industry, where they get to know the management well and dig hard into analysing the business and its financial position covering all risks including regulatory or environmental issues). If something can hurt the business they, like an owner-manager, want to know about it.

More recently, fund management styles have evolved that apply quantitative analysis to fundamental data about the company but do not contemplate qualitative inputs such as meetings with company management. The rationale for such an approach is that it reduces the risk of introducing bias into a quantitative process. Even more removed from classical fundamental analysis is the domain of technical analysis which focuses on the price and volume data related to a security to extract information and value.

It is difficult to say that there is one right way to manage money. All these styles have validity at some time. The distinction one can make reflects an underlying philosophy identified by Lord Keynes. He appropriated the term 'speculation' for the activity of forecasting the psychology of the market, and the term 'enterprise' for the activity of forecasting the prospective yield of assets over their whole life. Keynes warned that, as the organisation of investment markets improves, the risk of the predominance of speculation is likely to increase.

What should pension funds do?

So, should pension funds with a long-term time horizon invest in an approach based on forecasting the psychology of the market? An approach focused on fundamental analysis and understanding of the enterprise is more suited to long-term investors. Pension funds are now being enticed to invest in strategies that enhance value through active engagement—but what proof is there that this works?

There are several studies that have attempted to measure the relationship between stock price performance and a governance feature or quality. The right to govern is deemed by the market as valuable, which explains why shares with voting rights trade at a premium to non-voting shares. With that said, direct relationships between performance and governance are difficult to prove. Several studies have attempted to establish a link between specific features of governance—such as the independence of the board and share price performance—but these remain difficult to prove and have actually become a distraction from the tenet: 'When managing for upside always protect against the downside'. However much value a manager can add to investment capital, the basic objective of active ownership is to protect wealth from the financial impact of mismanagement, fraud and poor governance of the company. The very basic aim is to avoid a catastrophe such as at Parmalat. There is also reasonable evidence that active ownership can improve an underperforming company (Caton *et al.* 2001). Think of it as a 'profitability improvement'—a watchful eye on your investment is better than ignoring it.

The majority of pension fund trustees are not in a position to undertake the role of active owners themselves and, as a result, the obvious course is for this function to be delegated to a fund manager. At Hewitt, we believe that managing investments to avoid the risk of loss due to mismanagement of capital, poor strategy, ill-advised acquisitions, fraud or excessive remuneration is as much a responsibility of the fund manager as buying and selling securities at the right price. We believe that the market is, and will continue to be, increasingly of this view. At Hewitt, we organise training sessions designed to increase our clients' understanding of the key risk areas, such as: board structure; audit; strategy; and alignment of management interests. We also assist in the assessment of the fund manager in their control of these risks, both at the time of appointment and on an ongoing basis.

In March 2003, one the UK's largest pension funds, the Universities Superannuation Scheme (USS) and Hewitt Associates sponsored a global competition for managing pension fund assets described, 'As if the Long Term Really Did Matter'. The competition was based on a hypothetical mandate for a global consortium of pension funds and the judges were senior decision-makers from major institutional investors around the world that all supported the competition's aims. Central to the idea behind the competition was a shared concern that the structure of investment mandates, and the process of managing and measuring them, encourages a short-term mind-set. This short-term perspective means that institutional investors looking at investment opportunities have not been giving sufficient priority to strategic issues and longer-term risks. Ultimately, the objective of the competition was to encourage and stimulate longer-term thinking by investors and, in turn, more responsible actions by managers who are appointed to direct pension fund investment capital. The competition challenged existing mainstream fund management perceptions and prompted the fund management community to consider the value, and risk, inherent in non-financial issues in order to come to a sustainable, long-term investment view. Interestingly, in most of the entries to the competition, the 'responsible' element clearly played second fiddle to the 'long-term' part, suggesting that investing responsibly is still broadly viewed as a niche activity. As part of the competition the judges were looking for the manager to demonstrate a relationship with investee companies designed to influence responsible corporate behaviour (i.e. active engagement implemented with an understanding of appropriate costs and benefits). In this sense the competition not only provoked a debate about what fund managers could and should do but also raised important challenges for trustees and investment consultants. These challenges have been further highlighted by the Myners review (Myners 2001) and the Treasury's post-Myners review (HM Treasury 2004) and include issues such as investment time horizons and shareholder activism.

The future direction of activism

Integrating and measuring the impact of a responsible investment strategy as part of the investment process is clearly challenging. However, a longer timescale means that making a significant impact becomes a more realistic prospect. Moreover, taking a longer-term view necessitates it. Pension fund clients are becoming more and more focused on all of the issues this touches—longer-termism, responsible investment, corporate governance, CSR and sustainability. A good example of this is the Marathon Club, a direct follow-up project to the USS competition. The Club was established to continue what the competition started in stimulating longer-term thinking among pension funds, endowments and other institutional investors and their agents. This places more emphasis on being responsible and active owners, with a view to increasing knowledge about how investment strategy and process can improve the long-term financial and qualitative buying power of fund beneficiaries.

This is just one example of asset owners actively trying to affect change; we believe it will not be the last. The best institutions have already responded, or are in the process of responding, to this by putting in place sufficient resources and measures committed to this task, and by recognising that the greatest benefits are gained by those funds that fully integrate active ownership into the investment process.

Trustees should expect the fund manager to actively engage with the company management in advance of issues being put to a vote and exercise voting rights on their behalf. To be effective, this needs to be closely integrated with the economic decision-maker (i.e. the person closest to the company), not a voting service within the same institution that has no context on which to base these decisions.

At Hewitt, we firmly believe that trustees will in future expect managers to demonstrate, through records of their engagement and voting decisions, that they have taken an active interest as owners. As such, we support an increasing tendency for managers to include their key voting and engagement activity related to the client's portfolio within their periodic performance reports. Despite this, we also recognise that the degree of effective engagement that is possible, and the influence that can be exerted, depends on the relative size of the holding that an owner or its agent controls. Of course, for fund managers the size of the holding in a company on behalf of their entire client base is entirely relevant. The cost of implementing good governance both in the UK and in foreign markets may outweigh the benefits, particularly for small holdings. It is important to remain realistic about what is achievable. For us, the task is to explain to clients that active ownership is important for mitigating the risk of loss from poor company management and thus preserving the value of their assets. After all, what homeowner would allow cracks to appear in their property only to watch them spread without acting or calling in a trade specialist? The same principle applies to medium- and long-term investments.

Finally, companies should not be concerned about active ownership. There is no suggestion that owners should become day-to-day managers. It is not easy for owners, or fund managers, to second-guess professional business managers' views on strategy. Perhaps most importantly, the dialogue between investors and companies should not be a question of applying arbitrary principles or codes. The value of a company can be destroyed by management action or inaction in many ways—internal controls failing, an ill-advised acquisition or disposal strategy, inadequate succession planning, inappropriate remuneration levels, capital structure decisions or just plain inertia in the boardroom. Investors must be close enough to the business in which they are investing to recognise the risk as early as possible and act accordingly. Co-operation between institutional shareholders and the companies they invest in can yield benefits to all parties. An environment that promotes dialogue between the management, the non-executive board and the agents of the company's owners is not just desirable but should be viewed as a necessity of long-term sustainable financial markets.

References

Caton, G., J. Goh and J. Donaldson (2001) 'The Effectiveness of Institutional Activism', *Financial Analysts' Journal* 57.4: 21-26.

HM Treasury (2004) *Myners Principles for Institutional Investment Decision-making: Review of Progress* (London: HMSO).

Myners, P. (2001) *Institutional Investment in the United Kingdom: A Review* (London: HM Treasury).

29

A critical perspective on activism
VIEWS FROM A PENSION
FUND PROFESSIONAL

*Raj Thamotheram**

USS, UK

Investor activism (or engagement, as most pensions funds prefer to call it) has fast become accepted as a tool for safeguarding, if not improving, investment returns over the longer term. It is also close to being accepted as an obligation that goes hand in hand with the rights that come from being a shareowner. The rate of progress has been such that few institutional investors, at least in the UK, would now admit to not doing it, and none would say, in public at least, that it was a bad idea—arguing in favour of absentee ownership does little to build client confidence! Together with changing beliefs about the materiality of extra-financial issues, this represents a sea change in investment beliefs.[1] It is noteworthy that, in a recent survey of over 220 investment

*   The views expressed in this chapter are those of the author and do not necessarily represent those of USS. I would like to thank Jane Ambachtsheer, Frank Curtiss, Paul Hodges, Keith Johnson, Terry Raby, David Russell, Dan Summerfield and Helen Wildsmith for their comments. However, I take responsibility for all judgements and any errors.

1   Extra-financial issues are best described as fundamentals that have the potential to impact companies' financial performance or reputation in a material way, yet are generally not part of traditional fundamental analysis. Extra-financial issues typically include, but are not limited to: future political or regulatory risks; alignment of management and board incentives with durable long-term company value; quality of human capital management; risks associated with governance structure; related party transaction conflicts between management and shareholders; environmental liabilities; public relations risks; fraud/ethical culture exposure; product obsolescence; and similar concerns. They may be specific to a company, an industry or cut across several industry groups. Academic analysis indicates that a substantive part of a company's value over the long term is related to matters outside the scope of traditional financial analysis.

managers from around the world, professionals in all markets bar one consider that these issues will 'become a common component of mainstream investing within ten years' (Mercer Investment Consulting 2005). As illustrated in Figure 29.1, the exception appears to be the US, where a majority of investment professionals consider these issues will 'never' become material.

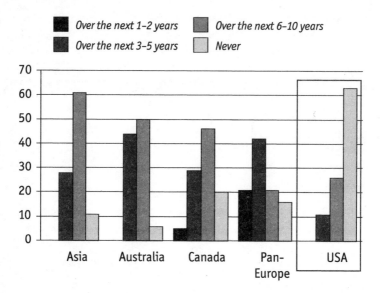

FIGURE 29.1 When will extra-financial issues be a common component of mainstream investing?

Source: Mercer Investment Consulting 2005

From the perspective of a pension fund that has a diversified portfolio and whose members have a wide range of political and ethical beliefs, engagement is most useful when it meets three fundamental principles (see Box 29.1).

Standing in the way of these principles being better known and more widely practised are five challenges (see Box 29.2). The purpose of this chapter is to provide a 'critical perspective' on how these challenges could be overcome.

Sending stronger signals that engagement is important

If pension funds support the case for greater engagement, they also need to be proactive in ensuring that this investment belief is put into operation—holding the belief will, in and of itself, have little positive impact given how the investment supply chain currently operates. Pension funds have four main control points in their relationship with fund managers: the selection of managers; the initial contract; the (investment)

1 **Optimise long-term value.** Risk-adjusted returns are what matter most. Hence the goal should be to 'optimise' rather than simply 'maximise' returns. Similarly, long-term creation of value is more important than stimulating short-term share price movements

2 **Encourage good standards of corporate governance (CG) and corporate responsibility (CR) (or, at least, not create disincentives for such developments).** When interpreted pragmatically, it is reasonable to expect that this approach to responsible investment will promote better enterprise risk management and so safeguard and enhance value, especially over the long term*

3 **Affect the whole portfolio.** While a focus on high-profile cases/issues may, to some degree, be unavoidable, it can be a poor use of limited resources. It can also arouse concerns that engagement is primarily a marketing and customer relationship management tool or, worse, that there is an 'underlying agenda'. In contrast, a portfolio-wide approach has an inbuilt presumption in favour of sector-wide change and pragmatic standards, as well as collaborative action between like-minded investors and between these investors and change agents in companies

* Most large pension funds consider responsible investment to mean some mix of engagement (to encourage good standards of CG and CR) and integration of extra-financial issues into investment decision-making. Such funds generally consider exclusion of companies and sectors on ethical grounds to be prohibited by current definitions of fiduciary duty. See, for example, the comments by John MacNaughton, the president and chief executive officer of the Canadian Pension Plan Investment Board (MacNaughton 2004).

Box 29.1 Principles for 'pension fund-friendly' engagement

1 Pension funds need to send stronger signals down their investment supply chain that they think engagement is important

2 Pension funds need to learn how to distinguish between different approaches to, and standards of, engagement, and choose those that best fit with the outcomes they are seeking

3 Pension funds need to build their capacity for strategic leadership so they can become a more significant partner in setting the agenda for engagement and ensuring implementation

4 'Activist' fund managers need to better manage the dilemma of competing for asset owners as clients, while also meeting the real needs of end beneficiaries

5 'Activist' fund managers need to ensure better alignment between the signals sent by specialist engagement staff and 'traditional' analysts/portfolio managers within their organisations

Box 29.2 The five challenges to 'pension fund-friendly' engagement

committee meetings at which fund managers report; and the remuneration structure. In terms of signalling to managers that engagement is important, none of these control points is currently being used as effectively as it might.

To make use of the first of these control points, pension funds can incorporate an analysis of managers' capabilities on responsible investment in general and engagement in particular as one determinant in the manager selection process. With regards to the second control point, pension funds can ensure that engagement is treated as a key deliverable of the investment service by making explicit reference to it in contracts with their fund managers. The corollary, of course, is that performance evaluation and payments should be adapted to take account of these factors. Indeed, a fund that has accepted the Institutional Shareholders' Committee (ISC)[2] principles (ISC 2002), let alone made a commitment within its statement of investment principles (SIPs) to responsible investment, would seem to be putting itself at unnecessary fiduciary risk if it then chose not to translate these responsibilities into contracts with its fund managers.

The third control point relates to pension fund meetings with fund managers, as the issues raised at these meetings send signals about what the fund's real decision-makers genuinely think. If responsible investment issues are rarely raised, this is a clear signal to fund managers about the real importance given to this issue, regardless of what is in the SIP or contract. The time that trustees have with managers is valuable, but spending 5% or 10% of this time on responsible investment issues would seem an appropriate allocation, not least because it can help to illuminate the manager's real investment beliefs. It should be a relatively straightforward task for trustees to be routinely briefed about the highest-profile issues in the portfolio so they can monitor and evaluate their fund manager's performance on engagement. These briefings should, arguably, be provided by the investment advisor. Currently, many investment consultants may not have the resources and competency to play this role but other sources are available. Member-nominated trustees, for example, can get such briefings from the Trades Union Congress (TUC) trustee network (see further Chapter 25). Or the trustee body could delegate this task to their senior executive who could then contact peer organisations who do have such in-house capacity or specialist organisations.

Finally, there is an urgent need to modify remuneration schemes for managers to incentivise long-term investing, analysis of extra-financial issues and active ownership. Exactly how this is done requires further work, but will probably include both 'carrots' for desired activities and 'sticks' for activities that are not so desirable (e.g. trading activity above a certain level). Space does not permit a detailed analysis of this issue, but it is noteworthy that a recent study comparing fund managers who were consistent deliverers of alpha with those who are bottom-quartile, concluded that the former respond much more than the latter to what the authors called 'non-financial aspects of reward'.[3]

---

2   The ISC is the umbrella body of trade associations in the financial sector and represents the Association of British Insurers (ABI), the Association of Investment Trust Companies, the National Association of Pension Funds (NAPF), and the Investment Management Association. The ISC has issued a statement of principles on the responsibilities of institutional shareholders and their agents.

3   Personal communication with Mark Unger, Russell Reynolds Associates. See also Davis 2004.

Distinguishing different types and standards of engagement

Engagement is, in some ways, a new instrument in the investment management toolkit. At this early phase in its evolution, a broad spectrum of activity can be found under one umbrella. As noted by Deloitte & Touche (2002: 17) in their detailed survey of SRI fund managers: 'engagement can mean very different things, and different levels of resourcing, to different fund managers'. Worryingly, that survey found that '10% of [fund managers] offered SRI services to clients but had no specialist staff, provided no training to the staff responsible, and carried out little or no research of companies' (Deloitte & Touche 2002: 5). In the absence of pension funds playing a major strategic role in this development to date (see further below), fund managers have had to make decisions about what they think 'engagement' should and should not be about. Not all of these judgements are, however, equally 'pension fund-friendly'.

For example, many fund managers still limit engagement—in practice, if not in policy—to traditional definitions of CG that were dominant in the 1980s and early 1990s. As a corollary, they tend to exclude or assign a very low priority to engagement on any social or environmental issues. The rationale is often a mix of reasons: for example, these issues are not material to a mainstream investor or, even if they are, they should be left to management since investors cannot double-guess boards and executives (i.e. micro-manage); and if one opens the door and considers one issue, there will be an unstoppable flood. Some of these concerns are valid but they can be addressed, not least by focusing on issues that can be considered material on the basis of credible economic or other analysis. The more fundamental issue is that if a pension fund has made a commitment to being an active and responsible investor, and wants its investment supply chain to take a professional and non-ideological approach to risk and reward, then accepting engagement limited to the old and narrowly defined CG agenda is clearly insufficient. In time, it could also become an unnecessary source of fiduciary risk, not least since the ISC principles include an explicit reference to 'the company's approach to corporate social responsibility'. It is also noteworthy that many of the recent really big discontinuous shifts in share price have been linked with CR issues. A good example of this has been the pharmaceutical sector, which has experienced growing problems as a result of weak relationships with key stakeholders, including customers and regulators. The fall in Merck's share price (almost 40%) as a result of clinical trial issues with one drug, Vioxx, is indicative of this wider trend.

Another significant difference between fund managers relates to the quality and quantity of engagement activity. This is, in general, linked to the size and experience of the teams involved. In the same way that all active fund managers assert that they can outperform the benchmark, so there are strong marketing imperatives for all managers to assert highest standards and greatest commitments to engagement—as the understated Deloitte & Touche report comments (2002: 5):

> Perhaps the most significant finding was that 17% [of SRI fund managers] claimed to use shareholder activism in their SRI 'tool-box'. It would be interesting to understand the extent to which this was actual practice, rather than policy and intention.

Closely related to this is a tendency to use the word 'engagement' when 'research' would be more accurate.[4]

The solution is clear—clients and their agents need to be able to make their own informed assessment of a manager's engagement style and assess relative performance. When USS sought to do this in 2001–2002, there were no models available and USS's internal auditor and I developed a tool for evaluating our fund managers (USS 2003), with helpful input from individuals who we knew to be highly skilled engagement professionals. Perhaps the most interesting result from this project was the statement from several fund managers that they had never been questioned about engagement issues anywhere near as rigorously before. Clearly, this lack of client interest, which translated into lack of attention by investment advisors, had sent unhelpful signals to senior executives in these fund manager organisations.

Fortunately, the situation has begun to change. Some major investment consulting firms have recently started to systematically evaluate and compare fund managers on their competencies in engagement, and other consultants are actively considering doing so. This is still pilot activity and, perhaps inevitably, there are differing areas of focus (e.g. in one case only traditionally defined CG activity is covered whereas in another CR issues are also included). Nevertheless, these developments are welcome both in their own right and because they will act as a catalyst for similar action by other consultants. Since pension funds have said that the absence of appropriate evaluation tools has been a major reason for not moving faster and further on responsible investment, these mainstream developments should help build client confidence and so stimulate informed demand. In addition, several leading fund managers are working with the UK Social Investment Forum (UKSIF) and the European Social Investment Forum (Eurosif) to develop 'transparency guidelines' on engagement and reporting which will, hopefully, soon become established as good practice guidelines for the sector as a whole.[5]

Building strategic leadership capacity on engagement

Although pension funds may accept the strategic rationale for supporting engagement, it does not automatically follow that they should build internal capacity on this issue. They would do so only if they were convinced of the strategic importance of playing a share of the leadership role associated with engagement. Again, the case for this is very strong and relates to the approach to engagement in the UK which has clear strengths but also some distinct weaknesses.

The lead for engagement activities in the UK has traditionally come from commercial service providers with a specialist interest in engagement. This is in line with a strong tradition in UK pension fund management to subcontract as much as possible to specialist service providers such as legal advisors, investment consultants and fund man-

---

4   In comparison to the UK, engagement activity is generally less developed in continental Europe and the US, where one analyst estimates that 'just over 20% is in portfolios that engage in or are willing to engage in some kind of shareholder advocacy' (Hawken 2004: 8). There are, of course, exceptions, including Ethos and Trillium Asset Management to name just two.

5   www.eurosif.org/pub2/2activ/initvs/transpev/index.shtml

agers.[6] While this approach has helped pension funds reduce their costs (at least in the short term) and to access specialist expertise that is not available in-house, it has also meant that pension funds have given away much of their power to define what the agenda for, and outcomes from, engagement and related activities (e.g. proxy voting) should be.

Inevitably, the vacuum for defining what engagement happens, how it is done and who co-ordinates it has been filled by large fund managers (who may individually own several per cent of even a FTSE 100 company) and formal trade bodies such as the NAPF and the ABI. There are also informal groupings such as the Corporate Governance Forum (for UK engagement) and the Global Institutional Governance Network (for international engagement). These actors, who have been effective and valuable advocates of shareholder rights, have three things in common. First, in practice if not in policy, their definition of engagement has focused on traditional CG issues. Second, these initiatives have been led by commercial fund managers, with little oversight by clients. Since agency issues can permeate all aspects of the client–fund manager relationship, it would be unwise to assume engagement was, in some way, uniquely free from conflict-of-interest problems.[7] Third, and linking the two above, fund manager engagement has been built on a particular interpretation of 'shareholder value'. Although an extremely valuable concept at the time it was developed, the utility of the shareholder value idea has been undermined in the last two decades by an overly fundamentalist, short-term and atomised interpretation (Mintzberg *et al.* 2002; Ghoshal 2005). To caricature only slightly, if an engagement activity was not likely to add shareholder value in the short-term to that particular fund manager, it could well be rejected, either in terms of policy or as a result of priority decisions related to limited resources.[8] Similarly, it has been hard to justify engaging with a company whose share price is doing well. Those fund managers who accepted the 'idiosyncrasies' at Wm Morrison will now acknowledge, at least in private, that this was probably a mistake.[9] To assume that fundamental CG norms—for ensuring transparency, accountability and decision-making that protects long-term investors—were less important simply because stock prices were rising has, once again, been proven short-sighted (Cannon 2004). It is noteworthy that, despite these experiences and the high-profile debate on this issue not only among academics and senior consultants (DiPiazza and Eccles 2003; Davis 2005) but

---

6   Pension funds in the Netherlands and Canada, for example, do not tend to outsource so many functions as funds in the UK and US, and some commentators have argued that funds in the former countries have better governance and performance as a result. This argument has not been systematically tested or analysed, however. How this relates to responsible investment is 'work in progress' (*IPE.com* 2004).

7   For a clear, general description of agency issues between asset owners and external investment managers, see Swensen 2000: 4-6.

8   It is noteworthy that McKinsey & Co., who have been widely considered major proponents of shareholder value-added thinking, have recently published several articles on the need to better balance short and long concerns and, in particular, to pay more attention to the extra-financial drivers of risk and reward. See, in particular, Felton and Kennan Fritz 2005 and Dobbs and Koller 2005.

9   Morrisons, a very successful regional retailer which recently acquired a bigger competitor, has traditionally been dismissive of good practice in CG arguing that its governance arrangement (e.g. a combined chief executive/chair, few independent directors, etc.) was justified in light of the com-

also business leaders themselves,[10] few SRI or CG fund managers would seem to have made this a matter for new policy or even thought-leadership activity by senior decision-makers.

Another practical consequence of informed asset owners not playing a strong role in the engagement debate is that there has been painfully slow progress on key issues such as executive remuneration. There is now solid academic evidence that investor efforts to align pay with performance have not been successful (Erturk *et al.* 2004; Jensen and Murphy 2004). Moreover, a recent study by the Boston Consulting Group concluded that recent corporate fraud scandals at companies such as Enron, WorldCom and Ahold were not caused by poor governance per se but, 'rather, they were the product of excessive stock options awarded to celebrity CEOs' (Cools 2005). Investors were repeatedly warned that they were not doing enough to align director rewards with the interests of long-term shareholders (Sykes 2002; Partnoy 2003). It is only recently, however, that stock options have fallen out of favour, although it is not clear how much of this is due to investors setting an agenda or companies reacting to underwater options and the coming requirement for options to be expensed.

Another consequence of pension funds not playing their share of the leadership challenge is that fund managers often make what seem to be arbitrary decisions about priorities for, or limits to, engagement activity. For example, several UK fund managers still do not engage with US-listed companies and it is hard to understand this decision (Thelen 2003). This is the market where many unhelpful norms are set which then have a 'contagion effect' in the UK and elsewhere (remuneration being a perfect case in point). Moreover, UK pension funds are more exposed to the US market than any other single market aside from the UK and there are few substantive language and legal differences. One reason given is that UK-based fund managers have relatively small holdings in US companies so engagement with them would not be productive. This, however, is not a convincing argument given the experience of other UK fund managers who do report value from engagement activity with US companies (Thelen 2003).[11] It is also noteworthy that some of the fund managers who do not take an active ownership approach with US companies nevertheless do undertake such work with companies in the EU or other (relatively) minor markets such as Japan and Korea, these being countries where the mechanisms for co-ordinating, and thus sharing, costs are much less advanced than in the US (Tucker 2004).

10 Perhaps the most relevant example to date is Hank McKinnell who, aside from being chief executive/chair of Pfizer is also chair of the highly influential Business Roundtable. In a speech to the Council of Institutional Investors in San Diego, California, on 4 September 2003, he said: 'Perhaps we can return to an ideal expressed by the Business Roundtable 22 years ago . . . when its foundation document said, . . . "Balancing the shareholder's expectations of maximum return against other priorities is one of the fundamental problems confronting corporate management." The Roundtable continued with these words . . . "The shareholder must receive a good return . . . but the legitimate concerns of other constituencies . . . customers, employees, communities, suppliers and society at large . . . must also have appropriate attention." If we allow shareholder interest—or executive self-interest—to trump all others . . . then we risk alienating the other stakeholders upon whom we must rely for the creation of value.'

11 It is also noteworthy that co-ordinated engagement activities with two large US companies, Pfizer and Exxon, have resulted in both companies sending teams of very senior executives to the UK. Portfolio managers in more than one of the organisations involved commented afterwards that they had better access to the company through these meetings than they had ever had before.

What can be done to bring some meaningful client oversight into the engagement debate at the strategic level? One solution would be for more pension funds to have specialist in-house staff to engage as peers with these fund management professionals and, where necessary, represent client views. Such a solution would be possible for the largest funds, but not for the many smaller ones. Hence, if pension funds were to act collectively, the resource constraints would be much less of a problem for all. This approach has had considerable success outside the UK, and specialist associations now exist in several countries which are led by large pension funds who have a serious and shared commitment to being active owners and who have low levels of conflicts of interest (e.g. 'standard' corporate pension funds and commercial fund managers are either not admitted or are in the minority).[12] These organisations include the Canadian Coalition for Good Governance (CCGG), the Dutch Stichting Corporate Governance Onderzoek voor Pensioenfondsen (SCGOP) and the Australian Council of Super Investors (ACSI). The most recent development is the decision by eight mid-sized Dutch pension funds to pool their €150 billion of assets behind a collective engagement venture dubbed Governance Platform (GP). The sponsors have hired Déminor, the shareowner advocacy firm, to engage on their behalf with troubled companies.[13]

Such bodies would be ideally suited to make considered and consensus recommendations on key matters of policy and investment belief (e.g. how shareholder value should be interpreted). They could also play an important role in delivering a robust shareholder position when agency or other issues might otherwise prevent this. An interesting example in this regard is the global engagement initiative led by ACSI which sought to prevent the 'Delawarisation' of CG standards at News International as it moved its listing from Australia to the US. While corporate management, backed by considerable legal resources, won this war, this small group of senior pension fund executives, serviced by a very small dedicated unit, won some important precedent-setting battles, not least setting up an informal collaborative network which included several fund managers. This episode has clearly been noticed by other companies considering similar strategies. The contrast with the lack of effective investor response in the UK, when BSkyB reversed over a decade of CG norms by appointing a chief executive who could not be considered independent of the chair, is striking. It is noteworthy that, since BSkyB's move, there have been, according to one experienced governance professional, several more moves to have chief executives become chairpersons and to establish executive chair positions.

---

12   One example of a UK organisation that successfully co-ordinates engagement activity by pension funds is the Local Authority Pension Fund Forum (LAPFF). In common with all pension funds who adopt an engagement overlay approach, LAPFF members face the challenge of ensuring alignment between their intentions and policies and the engagement activities of their fund managers.

13   Reported in *Global Proxy Watch*, 6 May 2005.

Managing the dilemma of competing for clients while meeting the needs of beneficiaries

The ability to offer an engagement service has now become an increasingly effective marketing tool. Thus, the costs of maintaining even a significant team of professionals can be justified when put against the financial benefits that come with winning significant new mandates. This creates a pressure to develop high-profile and distinctive brands and this pressure is starting to clash with what pension funds, as universal and diversified owners, really need.

Activism tends to focus on a sub-set of companies (typically FTSE 100 companies where there are proven shareholder value concerns or which are otherwise the subject of controversy). While not denying the need for some attention here, the rest of the market is also in need of an active ownership approach (e.g. companies that are hyperperforming without obvious reasons for why and who have weak transparency and accountability mechanisms, FTSE 250/350 companies, small and mid cap companies, etc.). Given that the fund management sector as a whole lacks adequate resources for engagement, serious questions need to be asked, from the perspective of the end beneficiary, about the value of activist fund managers duplicating workloads.

While there is undoubted benefit to be had from several managers raising the same concern with the same company, whether it is cost-effective for these managers to run separate engagement projects (often necessitating separate detailed research activity and separate time-consuming engagement meetings), is far from certain. Separate engagement projects also risk sending signals that are either not aligned or that can be interpreted by management as being so, and hence used as an excuse for inactivity. There is also the issue of several managers duplicating the low-value aspects of engagement (e.g. voting[14]) and then not having adequate resources for engagement activity which is of much higher value.[15]

There is, however, no doubt that such attention can have some impact on target companies.[16] However, it is equally clear that this incremental, company-by-company approach, has little systemic impact if the market as a whole is operating at low standards. On the issue of labour or other sustainability standards in international supply chains, for example, many high-profile FTSE 100 companies continue to show weak per-

---

14   Voting is, in and of itself, low-value. What is of value is that voting gives an opportunity for engagement. Another reason why informed voting is less effective than it should be is that many fund managers still tend to vote routinely with management and so neutralise the impact of informed votes.

15   A group of clients who are particularly poorly served at present are those who use passive fund managers with no significant engagement functions, the notable exception being Hermes. Many index managers have 1–2 staff covering the whole index. Since these funds cannot, by definition, compete on the basis of financial outperformance, there would seem to be good reason for two or more of these passive fund managers to come together to form a single engagement function with much better resourcing to service its joint clients. Such a move would also remove concerns about the free-rider effect.

16   One example is Dixons Group which, according to publicly available reports, was the subject of detailed engagement activity by Insight, ISIS (now F&C), LAPFF and others. The common focus was the company's policy and practices relating to labour standards in its supply chain. The company subsequently published its first policy on this issue.

formance, which is hardly surprising given weak performance on human capital issues much nearer to home. This links with what is, perhaps, the most problematic aspect of the current focus of engagement activity—namely, the opportunity costs (i.e. what is not done which could have been done). One obvious example of this is the lack of effective action by the majority of the SRI and CG community on human capital management in 'UK plc' (Porter and Ketels 2003; DTI 2003).

It would, of course, be completely naïve to think that 'activist' fund managers could, or even should, behave in a completely non-competitive manner on engagement. These are commercial organisations who, currently at least, have business models based on assets under management and, in that very real sense, it is a win–lose world. And competition does stimulate innovation and raising of the bar. But it is equally unrealistic to think that fund managers can 'privatise' the main benefits of activism for just its own institutional clients, without clients of other fund managers also benefiting.[17] This is particularly true when one considers the issues that are most important for universal investors (see further Chapters 14 and 19).

Managing the challenge of free-riders is inherent in any collaboration, but experience indicates that pragmatic solutions can be found. It is noteworthy that some fund managers are able to join these initiatives, while many SRI and CG managers regularly do not. Personal experience indicates that the biggest challenge to successful collaboration is lack of support from senior management and marketing colleagues for a collaborative strategy, and is less related to the size of teams per se. With increasing competition among SRI and CG fund managers, there is a perceived need to differentiate investment products in a crowded marketplace. This hyper-competitiveness undermines interest in finding pragmatic solutions to the real, but not insurmountable, challenges of free-riding. It also reduces commitment to developing the competencies, relationship and trust needed to minimise the transaction costs associated with collaboration. Perhaps most important in terms of the end beneficiary, 'lone wolf' strategies can create a cycle that has negative characteristics linked with perceived underlying agendas.

This marketing dilemma, by definition, cannot be escaped. But can it be better managed? The answer has to be yes and there are at least three components to moving forward. First, all parties could acknowledge, as part of their formal investment beliefs, that the value proposition that goes with active fund management—a zero-sum game where one manager's gain is another's loss—is simply irrelevant with regards to engagement, at least from the perspective of a universal investor. This would kick-start the process of clients and managers (including marketing professionals) becoming more open to considering the case for well-planned collaborative initiatives. Second, better-informed pension fund leaders could significantly reduce the free-rider problem by creating a context where managers needed to compete on their ability to collaborate! A simple way to do this would be to ask investment consultants to report on activity in collaborative initiatives as part of their evaluation of fund manager performance. One example of work in progress is the Institutional Investors Group on Climate Change, a unique partnership between pension funds and fund managers that many fund managers with a commitment to CG and CR have found it possible to join (see further Chapter 14). Third, fund managers could be more explicit about whether their

17   I am grateful to Dean Paatsch (Governance Information Products) for this formulation.

brand of engagement is more appropriate for retail or for institutional clients. The former have a prerogative to express their personal ethical and moral values. The vast majority of the latter do not and this difference has very practical implications. Clarity by fund managers about their priority client base and their position on key debates would help align expectations. That, in turn, would help pension funds choose fund managers who had an organisational commitment, from the chief executive down, to work according to the 'pension fund-friendly' principles outlined above.

Aligning specialist engagement staff and portfolio managers

When commentators speak about engagement, the focus is generally on specialist CG and SRI staff. One could easily forget that the most potent engagement is often done by traditional portfolio managers and analysts.[18] Yet, today, the messages that many buy-side analysts and their sell-side associates communicate to management are increasingly recognised as often being unhelpful in terms of creating long-term value and finding a more responsible balance between the needs of stakeholders and shareholders.[19] This is, arguably, the biggest engagement-related challenge and goes to the heart of the debate within the SRI and CG worlds about 'mainstreaming' and 'integration'. Portfolio managers have a role that is very clearly defined by their investment mandates—their job is, generally, to add value against a benchmark and nothing more. This message is reinforced by recruitment practices, remuneration packages, career prospects and prestige with colleagues.

What can be done with regard to this challenge? The bad news is that there are no magic bullets. The way forward depends on a co-ordinated programme of stronger leadership, better training, reshaping of performance evaluation and remuneration packages, smarter risk management and asset allocation strategies (see, generally, Rajan *et al.* 2004). Greater transparency could also help align engagement activities.[20]

---

18   A high-profile recent example was the intervention of Tom Shrager of New York-based Tweedy-Brown and other institutional investors who are credited with playing an important role in Piers Morgan's departure as editor of the *Daily Mirror*. Interestingly, financial commentators showed little concern at the time about micro-management and neither has there been much debate since about whether the action was successful in terms of shareholder value (see Greenslade 2002; Kane 2004; Luckhurst 2005).

19   This issue is articulated with great clarity in a (hypothetical) letter to a chief executive in the *Harvard Business Review* from a board director who is dismayed by the amount of management energy that goes into meeting the 'number' and other short-term expectations from analysts and investors (Fuller 2002).

20   In a positive, yet low-key, move, Insight Investment Management recently added the following sentence to its regular engagement report: 'Please note that this report only covers governance and corporate responsibility issues. It is not a complete report of Insight's engagement with companies, which also includes a large number of meetings between company executives and Insight's fund managers and analysts. These additional meetings are not currently the subject of a public report.' Whether this leads to Insight or other managers who have high-quality reporting of engagement activities choosing to extend the coverage of these reports will, no doubt, become clearer with time.

Having denied the existence of magic bullets, the most significant change would be if asset owners, investment consultants and fund managers reviewed, in a serious and hard-headed manner, the mandates they, respectively, had given and had accepted. The critical question is: 'How well aligned with long-term responsible investing principles are these mandates?' The need is for this three-way conversation to be undertaken in an honest but non-blaming manner. In all likelihood, the majority of mandates will not be well aligned with and supportive of long-term responsible investing (LTRI). If they can be adapted and if the parties concerned have the competencies needed for this kind of stewardship of assets, then a happy outcome can be expected. However, if this is not the case, asset owners (e.g. pension funds) will need to take the opportunity to bring their supply chain into greater alignment with their investment beliefs and positions. Given the extra governance implications of this kind of investing, this would inevitably be a slow process rather than a one-off change.

The various gaps in competencies were well highlighted by a competition in 2002 called 'Managing Pension Funds as if the Long Term Really Did Matter', co-sponsored by USS and Hewitt Bacon & Woodrow. One lesson for pension funds from the competition was that fund managers did not believe that funds and their consultants would give such LTRI mandates, and stick with them when the going got tough and 'regret risk' became an issue. Given the conservative nature of the pension fund sector and its historical focus on short-term, relative-return mandates, this scepticism would seem reasonable.[21] In response, a group of senior decision-makers from some of the largest pension funds in the UK and abroad have come together to form the Marathon Club. This Club, which works through a series of action-learning projects, is designed to 'stimulate pension funds and their agents to be more long-term in their thinking and actions, and place more emphasis on being responsible and active owners'. While the project is designed for personal and institutional learning, there is also an active commitment to disseminate 'good practice' ideas. One of the first projects being undertaken by the Club looks at investment beliefs relating to responsible investment and engagement.

A second important lesson from the competition was that portfolio managers needed to have a better, more rounded, understanding of the companies in which they invest and to be able to manage risk better over a long-term mandate, not least to ensure risk and reward is more accurately priced. Although there are many new competencies that may need to be developed, better research underpins many of these. Careful consideration of the various options for providing the research necessary to achieve this greater risk management competency indicates that:

- Supply by traditional research sources (i.e. sell-side and independent analysts) is the optimal approach, provided they choose to adapt

- These data need to be in the public domain (i.e. bespoke research is much less useful)

---

21   For example, as noted by Swensen (2000: 5): 'fund fiduciaries hope to retain power by avoiding controversy, pursuing only conventional investment ideas. By operating in the institutional mainstream of short-horizon, uncontroversial opportunities, committee members and staff ensure unspectacular results, while missing potentially rewarding longer-term contrarian plays.'

- Perhaps most challenging, this market development will not happen without concerned fund managers working together in an appropriate manner

These conclusions challenge how most SRI and CG fund managers have engaged with this market failure to date and, not surprisingly, they have therefore been controversial in some quarters. Space does not permit a more detailed explanation of underlying rationale but the key points are:

- Recent history indicates that no specialist research or rating agency is likely, by itself, to be able to provide quality analysis on all material investment issues, integrating extra-financial and financial analysis and covering all major markets[22]

- Since brokers remain the main conduit for information for fund managers, and play a pivotal role in the investment chain, the best way to get the mainstream to change is to change the mainstream's existing information feeds

- Bespoke research related to this newer extra-financial analysis can be of limited value since the bespoke nature militates against the market responding

- Bespoke research does not deliver value to pension funds that are passively invested

These key factors were the major drivers behind the Enhanced Analytics Initiative, a collaborative project to encourage the sell side (or other research units) to produce research which is more useful to long-term responsible investors.[23] Hopefully, many SRI and CG fund managers will decide to join this initiative and show that, while it is only natural to make use of the market failure in extra-financial research, their interests extend beyond simply perpetuating this failure. In so doing, they will also demonstrate their organisational commitment to mainstreaming this work but, most importantly, their confidence that their in-house teams will be able to add value by the way they interpret the new analysis, and that these teams will therefore be able to stay ahead of the market in this regard.

Concluding comments

In this chapter, I have highlighted a number of impediments to LTRI in general and engagement in particular, and have proposed eight recommendations which, if implemented, would help to overcome some of these challenges (see Box 29.3). The result would be that pension funds, and their service providers, would come into alignment with what their end beneficiaries really need: a secure, absolute pension, where the buying power is predictable and not undermined by unnecessary degradation of the

---

22   UBS Investment Bank announced that it had formed a 'global site licence' with the specialist research agency Innovest. It is likely that other investment banks will form partnerships with other specialist research providers.

23   www.enhanced-analytics.com

1 Ensure fund managers are formally and professionally evaluated on their responsible investment competencies by investment consultants by making it one criterion in the 'beauty parade' [IC, PF]

2 Ensure that responsible investment issues are adequately covered in contracts with service providers [PF, FM, LA]

3 Ensure that responsible investment is a regular agenda item at trustee meetings with fund managers [PF, IC, FM]

4 Ensure that staff have an informed and open-minded approach when making decisions about what to engage on and with what desired outcome [FM]. Create incentives for good performance by regular comparative reviews [IC, PF]

5 Join or establish pension fund networks to foster high-quality engagement that is based on end-beneficiary interests [PF]. Engage clients in strategy setting and evaluation [FM]. Evaluate the options available and encourage clients to join those that are most appropriate to that client [IC]

6 Provide incentives for fund managers to collaborate in addressing these issues [PF, IC]. Show leadership and organisational support for collaboration [FM]

7 Review mandates and investment beliefs/positions (e.g. on shareholder value) to make them more likely to result in LTRI [PF, IC, FM]

8 Encourage the sell side and independents to analyse material extra-financial issues by supporting the Enhanced Analytics Initiative and other continuous professional development activity [FM, PF, IC]

Key: FM = fund managers; IC = investment consultants; LA = legal advisors; PF = pension funds

Box 29.3 Recommendations for moving to a 'pension fund friendly' engagement approach

social and environmental capital on which quality of retired life depends. Such an approach would also better safeguard inter-generational equity, a core fiduciary responsibility. The investment system is highly interdependent so change by one actor will affect others. Equally, resistance by several players will reduce the impact of change by one. Hence, after each recommendation in Box 29.3, the key players who can either make things happen or block progress are highlighted.

Although the UK is well ahead of many countries with regards to engagement, developments are at an early phase and further evolution is likely, especially if there is a shift towards long-term investing and also if the 'enlightened shareholder value' approach as outlined in the Company Law White Paper is implemented. The approach to engagement in the UK (i.e. fund manager-led) has distinct advantages but also some weaknesses. Fortunately, it is relatively easy to hold on to the former and mitigate the latter by adding in a new ingredient: stronger pension fund leadership.

Whether this happens depends on trustees and, as with many other trends in this sector, a decision by a majority of just the top ten pension funds would set the norm for the sector as a whole. Such a development would represent an important and welcome evolution from the perspective of end beneficiaries. An initial step would be for the leaders of these pension funds to agree, among themselves, what they considered to be the key issues for 'UK plc' and the standards they want to see encouraged through engagement activity by the fund managers they collectively employ. One way to bring objectivity to this joint prioritisation would be to focus on those issues for which there is solid economic analysis showing the likelihood that value would be added over the long term. At a later stage, and depending on whether the trade associations wanted to take part, this work could be progressed either in collaboration with these associations or as a stand-alone project, such as the Marathon Club.

This does not mean that investment advisors and fund managers do not need to be more proactive and offer engagement and related LTRI services that are more 'pension fund-friendly'. On the contrary, this development is most certainly not a zero-sum game. Good governance and leadership, from wherever it comes, will beget better governance and leadership. Ultimately, however, it is the client's duty to look after the client's interests.

References

Cannon, H. (2004) 'Get the right managers doing the right job', *The Observer*, 28 March 2004.

Cools, K. (2005) *How Greed and Egotism Destroy Companies* (Boston, MA: The Boston Consulting Group and Stichting Management Studies).

Davis, I. (2005) 'How to escape the short-term trap', *Financial Times*, 11 April 2005.

Davis, P. (2004) 'Investment stars "prize teamwork over pay" ', *Financial Times*, 15 November 2004.

Deloitte & Touche (2002) *Socially Responsible Investment Survey 2002* (London: Deloitte & Touche).

DiPiazza, S., and R. Eccles (2003) *Building Public Trust: The Future of Corporate Reporting* (London: PricewaterhouseCoopers).

Dobbs, R., and T. Koller (2005) 'Measuring Long-Term Performance', *The McKinsey Quarterly: Value and Performance* (2005 special edition).

DTI (UK Department of Trade and Industry) (2003) *Accounting for People Task Force Report* (London: DTI).

Erturk, I., J. Froud, S. Johal and K. Williams (2004) 'Pay for Corporate Performance or Pay as Social Division', *Competition and Change* 9.1

Felton, R., and P. Kennan Fritz (2005) 'The View from the Boardroom', *The McKinsey Quarterly: Value and Performance* (2005 special edition).

Fuller, J. (2002) 'A Letter to the Chief Executive', *Harvard Business Review*, October 2002.

Ghoshal, S. (2005) 'Bad management theories are destroying good management practices', *Academy of Management Learning and Education* 4.1: 75-91.

Greenslade, R. (2002) 'Mirror's Bush attack angers US shareholder', *The Guardian*, 8 July 2002.

Hawken, P. (2004) *Socially Responsible Investing: How the SRI industry has failed to respond to people who want to invest with a conscience and what can be done to change it* (Sausalito, CA: Natural Capital Institute).

ISC (Institutional Shareholders' Committee) (2002) *The Responsibilities of Institutional Shareholders and Agents: Statement of Principles* (London: ISC).

IPE.com (2004) 'Ambachtsheer Slams Pension Fund Governance', *IPE.com*, 25 May 2004.

Jensen, M., and K. Murphy (2004) *Remuneration: Where we've been, how we got to here, what are the problems, and how to fix them* (Brussels: European Corporate Governance Institute, ECGI Finance Working Paper No. 44/2004, July 2004).

Kane, F. (2004) 'Investors pressed Bailey to sack Morgan', *The Observer*, 16 May 2004.

Luckhurst, T. (2005) 'So does Sly regret sacking Piers from the Daily Mirror?', *The Independent*, 23 January 2005.

MacNaughton, J. (2004) *A Broader Perspective on Investing and Social Policy* (Toronto: Canadian Pension Plan Investment Board).

Mercer Investment Consulting (2005) *2005 Fearless Forecast* (London: Mercer Investment Consulting).

Mintzberg, H., R. Simons and K. Basu (2002) 'Beyond Selfishness', *MIT Sloan Management Review* 44.1: 67-74.

Partnoy, F. (2003) *Infectious Greed: How Deceit and Risk Corrupted the Financial Markets* (New York: Times Books).

Porter, M., and C. Ketels (2003) *Competitiveness: Moving to the Next Stage* (London: DTI).

Rajan, A., B. Martin, D. Ledster and N. Fatharly (2004) *Raising the Performance Bar: Challenges Facing Global Investment Management in the 2000s* (London: KPMG and CREATE).

Swensen, D. (2000) *Pioneering Portfolio Management* (New York: The Free Press).

Sykes, A. (2002) *Capitalism for Tomorrow: Reuniting Ownership and Control* (Oxford, UK: Capstone).

Thelen, J. (2003) *UK Institutional Investors and US Corporate Governance: Minding the Gap?* (London: Railpen Investments and USS).

Tucker, S. (2004) 'Ready to Make a World of Difference', *FTfm*, 9 May 2004.

USS (Universities Superannuation Scheme) (2003) *How to be a Responsible Pension Fund: A Manual on How to Evaluate Your Fund Managers for Pension Funds Who Have a Commitment to Corporate Governance and/or Responsible Investing* (London: USS).

30

Shaping the market
INVESTOR ENGAGEMENT
IN PUBLIC POLICY

Nick Robins

Henderson Global Investors, UK

In the absence of public policy and regulation, investment as we currently understand would be impossible. There would be no property rights to value or exchange, and no protection against market abuse. Without public policy, today's pension and mutual fund industries simply would not exist—it has been political intervention to encourage saving for retirement and other ends that underpins much of the asset management sector. Regulation is, therefore, essential to assign rights and responsibilities along the investment chain so that both private and public interests are realised. The critical issue, of course, is to establish 'good' regulation. Where policy is well designed, it can help not only to resolve pressing economic issues, such as insider trading, but also stimulate innovation and competitiveness. Where it is badly drafted, regulation can be ineffective, costly and harm productivity.

Inevitably, for as long as there has been an investment industry, institutional investors and their associations have been involved in shaping public policy. Furthermore, as with all political actions, whether by individuals or institutions, the policy positions taken by institutional investors reflect a mix of motivations. In varying degrees, two factors have historically dominated investor lobbying: the interests of clients and beneficiaries, and the interests of the investment providers themselves, whether they be pension funds, asset managers, consultants or other actors in the chain. More recently, investors also have been challenged to go beyond the boundaries of immediate self-interest to consider their role in shaping policy for sustainable development.

Achieving sustainable development is set to involve profound changes in the structure and dynamics of the global economy: a shift that is likely to be as disruptive as any the investment world has yet faced. At the microeconomic level, the transition to sustainability is already changing the balance of risks and rewards facing different assets, in the process altering the way in which many investment and governance decisions are made. However, the sustainability imperative also extends to the wider investment framework, posing a policy challenge of identifying how current patterns of incentive and regulation need to change to address the twin issues of global poverty and environmental decline. Here, the allocation of capital, and thereby the role of the investment community, is pivotal. Investment is the bridge between an unsustainable and unjust status quo and a future that delivers quality of life for all.

This is difficult territory for most investors, and it is no surprise that the investor community remains the 'missing stakeholder' in most policy discussions on sustainable development. Policy pioneers do exist, however, drawn largely from the well-established ethical investment movement and, more recently, from pension funds. Ethical investment is best seen as part of the much wider societal trend in favour of ethical consumerism and more sustainable patterns of consumption (Co-operative Bank 2003). There is a clear rationale for ethical investors not simply to apply their values to the stocks they select, but to use their voice and influence to change the policy framework in ways that reward good business practices. It is no surprise that one of the first investor initiatives on climate policy in the UK was launched by a leading provider of ethical funds. In 1997, the 'Global Care' team at NPI (one of Henderson's forerunner companies) launched the first standardised methodology for measuring corporate greenhouse gas emissions.

The case for long-term pension funds to take an active part in sustainable development policy is also becoming compelling. Analysts such as James Hawley and Andrew Williams (see further Chapter 19) have identified the emergence of 'universal owners' who hold assets across the market, who have a long-term perspective and whose returns are derived from the performance of the economy as a whole rather than the performance of individual stocks. Unlike with individual ethical investors, fiduciary duty means that these universal owners are unable to express values in the way they manage funds on behalf of final beneficiaries, such as pensioners. However, their macroeconomic position means they can capture some of the positive externalities in the wider economy generated by responsible firms. One example could be improved overall human capital resulting from enhanced training programmes. Likewise, universal owners suffer some of the negative externalities generated by their investments. For example, investment performance could be undermined where companies face rising treatment costs due to tightening industrial pollution norms. As a result, Hawley and Williams argue that these 'universal owners come to occupy a quasi-public policy position as having an economic interest in the long-term health and well-being of society as a whole' (Hawley and Williams 2002: 157). A number of leading funds have now started to apply this logic to both corporate and policy engagement on sustainability matters. In 2001, for example, the Universities Superannuation Scheme, one of the UK's largest pension funds, led the debate among institutional investors on climate risk, first producing a scoping report (Mansley and Dlugolecki 2001) on the issue and then driving the formation of a collaborative initiative to respond to the threats, the Institutional Investors Group on Climate Change (IIGCC).[1]

Beyond these clusters of ethical investors and pioneering pension funds, most institutional investors have yet to become advocates for pro-sustainability policy frameworks. The responsible investment strategies adopted by many established pension funds and fund managers have so far concentrated on company-level analysis and engagement, stopping short of involvement in policy-making. The 'silent majority' of institutional investors continues to opt out of any form of responsible investment, instead supporting traditional lobbying positions that stress the primacy of market forces and the elimination of 'red tape'. With this group of investors, the argument in favour of policy engagement to align investment frameworks with sustainable development has yet to be made, let alone accepted.

Building on experience to date, this chapter seeks to flesh out the case for institutional investor engagement in shaping pro-sustainability policy frameworks, suggesting ways in which the lessons of advocacy learned so far can be extended more broadly through the investment system. The chapter focuses on experience in the UK, but also draws on examples in other countries to compare and contrast different styles in investor engagement on public policy.

Reaching the parts that activism cannot

A core underlying proposition that drives sustainable and socially responsible investment (SSRI) is that financial markets take insufficient account of wider social, ethical and environmental (SEE) and economic factors in investment and ownership decision-making. Markets are powerful instruments for allocating economic resources and generating wealth. Unchecked, however, market forces exhibit a range of imperfections, notably a tendency to accentuate social inequality, to externalise costs (such as pollution) and to discount the interests of future generations. Financial markets have their own particular problems, notably their volatility and their propensity to develop speculative asset bubbles, whether in property or listed equities. For investors that are serious about sustainable development, this means rethinking existing market incentives and controls so that capital is allocated and held accountable in ways that sustain and enhance not just financial returns but the social and ecological 'capital' stocks that underpin all economic activity. If this were not difficult enough, the task of aligning investment policy with sustainable development comes at a time of increasing financial complexity and follows a period of 'irrational exuberance' in global stock markets that has eroded public trust in the sector.

A number of SSRI strategies have been developed to confront these market failures: positive and negative screening; the integration of sustainability into investment decision-making; and shareholder activism. Although investors have no legal responsibility for the SEE impacts of their holdings, the case for acting on the basis of enlightened self-interest is increasingly compelling. The growth in workplace, environmental and

1   www.iigcc.org

consumer law over the past three decades makes business performance on sustainability and corporate responsibility (CR) of increasing importance for both tangible and intangible asset valuation. Corporate risk registers now include a range of social and environmental factors, not least liability for environmental clean-up or the threat of litigation for product safety. In addition, the innovative capacity of business is also being affected by social and environmental pressures, with companies who anticipate environmental measures gaining competitive advantage in the process. A number of independent studies now show how an understanding of sustainability factors can enhance value creation for investors. In early 2004, for example, the Association of British Insurers (ABI) concluded that 'incorporating social responsibility can reduce portfolio volatility and increase returns' (Cowe 2004: 6).

Much has been achieved through these essentially voluntary SSRI initiatives. As a result, financial markets are different places from what they were five years ago. However, even if all investors were to adopt screening and activist strategies—a far-reaching shift from the current situation where most investors continue to sideline social and environmental questions—this would be insufficient to address some of the structural problems raised by sustainable development. Public and private interests do not always coincide. Simply put, voluntary action cannot be relied on to internalise externalities or to universalise best practice. In case after case, there is a 'brick wall' of market forces that prevents investors and companies from pursuing what would be in their (and society's) long-term interests. The risk in the current phase of globalisation is that competitive pressures result in a levelling-down of policy frameworks, resulting in a race to the bottom that depletes human and natural capital, and makes the transition to sustainable development impossible.

This is not a new problem—indeed it has been embedded within market economies since the Industrial Revolution. In a telling example of the limits of voluntary CR, in 1863 a group of 26 pottery firms from Staffordshire (including Josiah Wedgewood & Sons) petitioned the government for regulation to control child labour: 'Much as we deplore the evils before mentioned,' stated the industrialists, 'it would not be possible to prevent them by any scheme of agreement between the manufacturers . . . [and] taking all these points into consideration, we have come to the conviction that some legislative enactment is warranted' (Marx 1860). Then, as now, one of the defining characteristics of responsible corporate (and investor) practice is to recognise the limitations of voluntary action and to argue for collective legislative action to universalise good practice through law.

All of this means that policy intervention is essential to direct the dynamism and capital of investors towards economic ends that at least do no harm to society or the environment and which preferably restores and enhances human and natural capital stocks. For ethical, universal and, now, responsible investors, the first task is to construct a clear mandate for policy engagement. Ethical investors and universal owners have an advantage in this respect as they are able, through client consultation, to construct strategies based on the perspectives of the final beneficiaries. This consultative mandate for policy engagement can be further strengthened through the explicit adoption of a conceptual basis for involvement in the policy process. For large pension funds, Hawley's and Williams's notion of the universal owner provides the strongest theoretical basis. The authors argue that acting on public policy and investment is now 'part of their fiduciary duty', and is best implemented through coalitions of like-minded institutions such as the IIGCC in Europe and the Investor Network on Climate Risk (INCR) in the USA.

To be effective in policy engagement, investors need to develop a clear vision of the role that public policy plays in economic success and sustainable development. Regulation is often typecast as 'red tape' that unnecessarily restricts commercial or individual freedoms (CORE 2004). Yet not only is public policy the *only* effective way of confronting negative externalities (such as climate change) but it can also have a positive role in transmitting knowledge through the economic system, thereby accelerating the adoption of best practice. Much of the success of today's knowledge economy is based on regulation that channels resources and effort toward activities that generate superior private and public returns. Studies going back a decade and more suggest that 'smart' regulation can enhance innovation. Professor Michael Porter, for example, was writing as early as 1991 of the way in which strict environmental standards may actually foster competitiveness. This assessment has recently been endorsed by the High-Level Group convened by the European Commission to examine Europe's competitiveness. Reporting in late 2004, the group concluded that 'well-thought out environmental policies provide opportunities for innovation, create new markets and increase competitiveness through greater resource efficiency and new investment opportunities' (Kok 2004: 35).

The paradox, of course, is that, despite this evidence, the standard business posture on most policy and regulatory questions linked to sustainable development is to resist the introduction of mandatory requirements. The reasons for this are depressingly clear. Although smart regulation can bring net benefits to both society and the economy at large, individual companies may suffer in the transition process. Those that lose out from the process of upgrading that sustainability requires are often well established and economically powerful, while the beneficiaries are often diffuse or do not yet exist. In case after case, the costs of policy intervention are overestimated while the benefits are frequently left out of the equation. For example, the Confederation of British Industry (CBI) initially claimed that the cost to British business of the EU environmental liability Directive would be £1.8 billion. The UK government now puts the cost at £18–52 million (ENDS 2005). Clearly, one of the critical roles that long-term investors can play is to act as a countervailing force to this short-term, defensive lobbying, proposing in its place effective frameworks of incentives and controls that are both pro-enterprise and pro-sustainability.

Emerging examples of investor engagement on policy

To date, few institutional investors have produced clear statements on their rationale for policy engagement that match strategies for company-level activism. In the UK, Hermes is one of the few institutional investors that explicitly confronts the issue of cost externalisation in its statement of investment principles (SIP). Addressing the issue of policy via the companies they hold, principle 10 of the Hermes Principles states that 'companies should support voluntary and statutory measures which minimise the externalisation of costs to the detriment of society at large' (Hermes 2002). Hermes makes clear that this is not 'to encourage regulation *per se*', but rather for companies 'to support measures to align shareholder interests with those of society at large'.

While formal policy statements have been lacking, a number of institutional investors have sought to influence public policy in order to get at those parts of the sustainability puzzle that voluntary action cannot reach. Over the past five years, two broad styles of policy advocacy have emerged. The first generally stresses the importance of regulation being flexible, enabling rather than constraining action. The second, by contrast, highlights the importance of regulation as a tool for universalising desired practices through mandated changes in behaviour. Both of these styles of investor advocacy have been in evidence in the hotly contested policy debates on pensions legislation and corporate disclosure.

In the UK, the SSRI community was instrumental in achieving changes in pension law in 2000 that required trustees of occupational funds to declare in their SIPs the extent (if at all) to which SEE considerations are taken into account in investment decision-making. Central to the political bargain at the heart of the reform was the absence of any requirement on trustees to actually integrate SEE, thus conferring a 'duty to consider' rather than a 'duty to act'. All that trustees were required to do was to be transparent regarding the policy they considered appropriate. Similar 'enabling' legislation has been introduced in Germany and Belgium, and is forthcoming in Italy and Spain. In Sweden, however, a more 'mandated' approach has been taken in the legislation for the AP series of pension funds. These are required to 'take ethical and environmental considerations into account without relinquishing the overall goal of a high return on capital'. The five AP funds (API, AP 2, AP 3, AP 4 and AP 7) have adopted different ways of implementing this requirement, creating a climate of competition that has stimulated interest in SSRI among other institutional investors. Compare this with the situation in the UK where recent research has found that 'about half of all pension funds do not comply with the law, since their statement of investment principles does not contain particular information on SRI' (Eurosif 2004). Poor compliance with the 2000 Pension Act provisions suggests that regulatory tightening is required. A survey of pension fund trustees, published in January 2004, for example, found that a majority believed that additional regulation is needed to make funds report on the implementation of the SIP requirement (Gribben and Faruk 2004).

Investor advocacy on corporate reporting on SEE issues has also reflected the 'enabling' and 'mandated' approaches to policy design. In the UK, institutional investors have strongly supported changes to company law that require companies to include information on employee, environmental and community issues in the narrative section of their company reports where these are important for shareholder understanding of corporate performance and prospects. Again, this would only give company directors a 'duty to consider' whether to disclose information on SEE factors. The effectiveness of this approach has yet to be tested, and will depend on the assertiveness with which investors hold companies to account for inadequate disclosure. The risk, of course, is that the experience with pension fund SIPs will be repeated and the current low levels of corporate disclosure, particularly outside the top 100 companies, will continue. The challenge for responsible investors is, therefore, to make this model of 'statutory voluntarism' work by stating clearly that they would consider voting against a company's report and accounts if it had clearly inadequate disclosure of SEE issues. In the USA, by contrast, the SSRI community has taken a clear policy stance in favour of mandatory reporting on environmental issues through stock exchange disclosure requirements. For example, in April 2004, a group of leading US state pension funds with assets totalling US$800 billion, including California, Connecticut, Maine, Maryland, New Mexico, New York State and Oregon, called on the Securities and Exchange Commission to strengthen existing reporting guidelines to require disclosure on global warming and climate risk. Commenting on the demand, Denise Nappier, Treasurer of the state of Connecticut argued that 'shareholders should not have to struggle company-by-company to get the level of analysis and disclosure they need. Disclosure of climate risk should be part of routine analysis on the 10K' (CERES 2004). This points to one of the clear benefits of regulation: namely, the establishment of common frameworks that reduce transaction costs for investors and thereby enhance market efficiency.

Beyond the issue of improved disclosure, whether by corporations or pension funds, investors have been more tentative in their policy involvement. To date, governments, politicians, business, civil society and academia have been the key actors in shaping regulation on social and environmental issues. Historically, the assumption has been that the business lobbies could adequately reflect the interests of shareholders in the policy process. However, as the weight of the sustainability imperative has grown, so investors have started to engage directly—a sign, in itself, that the interests of management and shareholders are not always aligned. For example, although the insurance industry has been a long-standing supporter of international policies to combat climate change—based on its deep understanding of the issue as a provider of risk management services—asset owners and managers have been relatively late to the negotiating table. The IIGCC is one of the few investor initiatives on social or environmental matters that has taken a clear, pro-policy standpoint. Its public statements make it clear that the group regards climate change as 'a product of market failure', making public policy 'essential not only to minimise the damage caused by climate change, but also to maximise the opportunities during the transition to a low-carbon economy'.[2] The group has also stressed that it regards understanding and influencing climate policy as 'an essential element of an effective investor strategy for enhancing long-term shareholder value in an increasingly carbon-constrained world', arguing that this is part of its members' 'fiduciary duty to their clients and beneficiaries'. This is an important step in the maturing of investor approaches to public policy, directly applying the universal owner framework to a specific issue.

The climate example also highlights how the absence of investors can lead to ineffective policy design. The UK government's White Paper on energy proposed a set of ambitious targets for encouraging the transition to a low-carbon economy, culminating in a 60% reduction in greenhouse gas emissions by 2050 (DTI 2003). Despite the scale of capital required to realise these goals, little apparent attention was given to the incentive framework that would attract investors to support the shift to clean energy (such as renewables). Following representations from the renewables industry and investors, the government accepted that existing incentives were inadequate and in December 2003 extended the Renewables Obligation from 2010–11 to 2015–16 to give investors greater confidence over long-term returns.

Climate change also highlights how far the investor community still has to travel in terms of developing a strategic approach to policy design. The International Energy

2   www.iigcc.org, accessed 10 March 2005

Agency (IEA) has estimated that the projected increase in energy infrastructure to 2030 will involve investments of some US$16 trillion, 85% of which will be in fossil fuels, with the bulk in developing countries (IEA 2004). If this 'business as usual' scenario comes to pass, the consequences for climate stability will be grim, involving a 60% increase in greenhouse gas emissions. While investors have made some useful initial inputs into the climate policy process, the nettle of designing a framework of investment incentives that steers this US$16 trillion into safe, secure and profitable energy options has yet to be grasped. Interestingly, the IEA also estimates that its alternative, high-efficiency, lower-carbon scenario would require less total investment, suggesting once again that a sustainable future is also often a cheaper and more productive one.

Levelling up

A coherent investor view on the policies needed to achieve sustainable development has yet to emerge. Perhaps, as with all political processes, it is unlikely that there is ever going to be a single position on the public policies that are needed to align investment management with sustainable development. A diversity of approaches is to be expected, and just as industry projects a variety of perspectives (contrast the positions of the CBI and the Business Council for Sustainable Energy on climate change, for example) so the investment community should not be afraid of projecting a range of views on policy design. Furthermore, institutional investors are not 'neutral' actors, and it would be naïve to expect that the simple pursuit of investor self-interest will necessarily result in sustainable or responsible outcomes. Indeed, many would argue that the primacy given to investors during the 1990s, and the elevation of shareholder value to the heart of corporate management, was a significant contributory factor in the malfeasance at Enron, Parmalat, Tyco and Shell. For Paul Hawken, one of America's leading environmental thinkers and the author of a penetrating report on the state of SSRI, 'striving to attain the highest rate of financial return is a direct cause of social injustice and environmental degradation, as it consistently leads to externalisation of costs on the environment, the future, workers or other peoples' (Hawken 2004: 6).

At this relatively early stage in the life-cycle of investor action on sustainability frameworks, it is important that ethical, universal and responsible investors—in other words, the full spectrum of investors with interests in the issues around SSRI—begin to develop explicit statements on policy engagement. Such statements could flow from existing institutional or fund-level statements on CR and corporate governance and could consider the following questions concerning mandate, mechanisms and monitoring:

- **Mandate.** How does policy engagement fulfil the interests of investors and final beneficiaries? Has any consultation been conducted to elicit investor perspectives on policy engagement? How does policy engagement fit with the institution's or fund's fiduciary duty to its clients?

- **Mechanisms.** How is this mandate implemented? What is the geographical scope? Does the institution engage directly in policy (e.g. via responses to government consultations) or indirectly to influence the policy positions taken by the companies it holds? What is the balance between individual action and collaborative efforts?

- **Monitoring.** How is the effectiveness of policy engagement measured and recorded? What feedback is received from other policy actors (notably business, politicians and officials and civil-society organisations)? How transparent is this practice to beneficiaries and other stakeholders?

The introduction of clear statements on policy engagement would enable investors to communicate how far they are willing to go in advocating regulatory action for sustainable development. Some will choose to align themselves clearly with civil society and CR pioneers in the business community, aiming for a direct influence on the policy-making process, perhaps through new alliances that are pro-enterprise, pro-sustainability and also pro-policy. Others will seek a more moderate approach, limiting their role to engaging on the public policy positions of the companies they hold. Others, again, are likely to abstain from policy discussions, arguing that this is beyond the scope of their fiduciary duty. Alongside this, more work will need to be done on the effectiveness of different strategies for policy engagement. Techniques and habits of collaborative engagement on policy matters are still in their infancy and, if investors are to fulfil their policy mission, far greater attention needs to be given to what works.

Looking ahead, a powerful set of social, demographic, technological and environmental factors are reshaping markets in tune with the needs of sustainable development. While there is strong evidence that companies with better social and environmental records can be good investments, there is also no doubt that current markets are not yet aligned with the imperative of improving the quality of life of the world's population, both now and into the future. Sustainable and responsible investors will increasingly confront a 'brick wall' of market frameworks that constrain the possibility for voluntary corporate action on sustainable development. For this reason, it is critical that investors interested in SSRI extend their focus from the company level to that of the system, aiming to create market frameworks that reward companies, and their investors, for high levels of social and environmental performance. The prize for far-sighted investors is to 'level up' policy incentives and controls at both national and international levels so that investment returns are generated as if the long-term really did matter. As a result, smart engagement on policy design looks set to become a critical part of the truly responsible investors' toolkit.

References

Cowe, R. (2004) *Risks, Returns and Responsibility* (London: ABI).

CERES (2004) 'Thirteen pension leaders call on SEC chairman to require global warming risks in corporate disclosure', press release, 15 April 2004.

Co-operative Bank (2003) *Ethical Consumerism 2003 Report* (Manchester, UK: The Co-operative Bank).

CORE (2004) *Exposing the Red Tape Myth* (London: CORE).

DTI (UK Department of Trade and Industry) (2003) *Our Energy Future: Creating a Low Carbon Economy* (London: DTI, February 2003).

ENDS (2005) 'EIC hits out at deregulation lobby', *ENDS Report* 361 (February 2005).

Eurosif (European Social Investment Forum) (2004) *Pension Programme SRI Toolkit* (Brussels: Eurosif).

Gribben, C., and A. Faruk (2004) *Will UK pension funds become more responsible? A Survey of Trustees* (London: Just Pensions).

Hawken, P. (2004) *Socially Responsible Investing: How the SRI Industry has Failed to Respond to People Who Want to Invest with a Conscience and What Can be Done to Change it* (Sausalito, CA: Natural Capital Institute).

Hawley, J., and A. Williams (2002) 'Can universal owners be socially responsible investors?', in P. Camejo (ed.), *The SRI Advantage* (Vancouver: New Society Publishers): 151-71.

Hermes (2002) *The Hermes Principles* (London: Hermes).

IEA (International Energy Agency) (2004) *World Energy Outlook* (Paris: IEA).

Kok, W. (2004) *Facing the Challenge: The Lisbon Strategy for Growth and Employment* (Brussels: High-Level Group).

Mansley, M., and A. Dlugolecki (2001) *Climate Change: A Risk Management Challenge for Institutional Investors* (London: USS).

Marx, K. (1860) 'Capital: Chapter 8—The Working Day', in L. Feuer (ed.), *Marx and Engels: Basic Writings on Politics and Philosophy* (London: Fontana, 1981).

Porter, M. (1991) 'Green Competitiveness', *New York Times*, 5 April 1991.

31

Harnessing investors to support the implementation of health and safety public policy

Steve Waygood and Rory Sullivan

Insight Investment, UK

Alan Morley

Health and Safety Executive, UK

Investors are increasingly being targeted by non-governmental organisations (NGOs) and trade unions (see further Chapters 21 and 25), among others, that wish to use investors' influence with companies to promote specific social or environmental goals. Government agencies have also sought, albeit to a lesser extent, to harness investors to assist in the implementation of public policy. This chapter reviews the efforts of the UK Health and Safety Executive[1] (HSE) to use investor influence to promote improvements in occupational health and safety, focusing, in particular, on the HSE's efforts to establish a Corporate Health and Safety Performance Index (CHaSPI). It considers whether investors have an interest in either promoting enhanced corporate occupational health and safety or factoring performance in this area into investment decisions. The chapter also discusses some of the broader public policy implications of the HSE's work in this area.

1 Britain's Health and Safety Commission (HSC) and the Health and Safety Executive (HSE) are responsible for the regulation of almost all the risks to health and safety arising from work activity in Britain. HSC describes its job as being to protect everyone in Great Britain against risks to health or safety arising out of work activities, to conduct and sponsor research, to promote training, to provide an information and advisory service, and to submit proposals for new or revised regulations and approved codes of practice. HSE's role is to help the HSC ensure that risks to people's health and safety from work activities are properly controlled.

Overview of CHaSPI

In its *Revitalising Health and Safety* strategy statement, issued in 2000, the Health and Safety Commission (HSC) set out a number of actions that were aimed at promoting greater corporate responsibility and accountability for health and safety across the private, public and voluntary sectors (DETR and HSE 2000). One of the actions proposed was to encourage investors and other key financial players to have a greater regard to health and safety management performance when making investment decisions. Institutional investors were targeted because of their potential to encourage listed companies to pay closer attention to occupational health and safety.

In 2001, the HSE commissioned Claros Consulting to assess whether demand for health and safety information existed among institutional investors. The Claros review found a reasonable level of interest in health and safety, stating: 'Investors are generally supportive of the idea that good health and safety performance is an indicator of good management' (Mansley 2002: 2), and 'the rise in interest in socially responsible investment . . . supported by government and encouraged by changes to the Pensions Act . . . offers opportunities to work with investors to promote health and safety. SRI is a potentially powerful lever if health and safety can be established as an important dimension of corporate social responsibility' (Mansley 2002: 14).

In an attempt to capitalise on investor interest and influence, the HSE commissioned Greenstreet Berman to develop a health and safety performance index as a tool for investors which would both establish a best practice framework and, by disclosing comparative health and safety performance, provide a catalyst for continuous improvement by participating companies. Greenstreet Berman employed a two-stage methodology. First, a review of other measures of health and safety performance and indices of environmental performance was conducted in order to construct a pilot version of the index. Second, the initial version of the index was piloted by ten firms. Changes to the index were made as a consequence of the findings. The initial pilots indicated that the index: was valid; was of potential use to investors; was likely to provide an incentive for larger organisations to improve their performance; and would be able to provide a valid comparison of companies within and across sectors (Marsden *et al.* 2004). The draft index was also well received by the trade press (Fidderman 2004: 23):

> [CHaSPI] is already an impressive and useful achievement. It is easy, intuitive, enjoyable to complete and can provide a simple benchmarking tool for employers and safety practitioners . . . This index will offer a valuable, quick and easily comprehensible overview of organisations for investors, employees, unions, campaigners and, indeed, health and safety journalists.

The HSC and HSE launched the draft index (see Box 31.1) at two conferences in February and March 2004, with investors representing in excess of £0.5 trillion present.[2]

---

2   Including: 3i; Barclays Global; Cazenove; CIS; Henderson; Insight; ISIS; Jupiter; Morley; Railpen Investments; Société Générale; Standard Life; Storebrand; and the Universities Superannuation Scheme.

CHaSPI* is intended to be a self-assessment tool, designed for use by large public and private sector organisations employing over 250 people (see, generally, Marsden *et al.* 2004). CHaSPI is intended to measure both management systems and processes, as well as performance. It comprises eight indicators and combines quantitative and qualitative criteria. The quantitative indicators used to generate the overall index score are:

- **Health and safety management rating.** This comprises 11 sub-indicators structured to discern the status of health and safety management within the organisation
- **Injury rate.** This requires data on injuries and the numbers of employees and contractors
- **Employee sickness absence rating.** This requires the company to provide data on either the average number of sickness absence days recorded per year per employee or the total number of days of sickness absence from work in the last year among all employees
- **Occupational health rating.** This is designed to separate and give special emphasis to a key area that is often poorly measured through 'standard' health and safety performance indicators
- **Serious incident rating.** The organisation has to consider whether it has had any such incidents and, if so, must enter the appropriate data in the relevant categories

The index score is normalised (on a scale of 0–10) to allow for direct comparisons between different companies. In addition to the data used to generate the score, companies should also provide qualitative data which give a broader picture of health and safety performance and management within the organisation. These qualitative data, which appear alongside the index score, are:

- **Conduct of highly regulated activities.** Does the organisation carry out any activities that are subject to special laws (e.g. asbestos licensing)?
- **Directors' declaration.** Has the organisation's board made a declaration that it has assessed the health and safety hazards associated with its activities and implemented an appropriate set of risk management controls?
- **Verification.** Has the data input to the index been verified and, if so, by whom?

* www.chaspi.info-exchange.com

Box 31.1 Overview of CHaSPI

While investors are seen as the primary audience for the information generated by CHaSPI, the HSE also sees that companies should support the introduction of CHaSPI for two related reasons. The first is that companies require clear and consistent health and safety performance measures as a basis for communicating with investors: 'Both investors and insurers are concerned about risk, particularly risk that is not managed effectively . . . Evidence of a comprehensive and effective OSHMS [occupational safety and health management system] can aid directors in responding to questions and concerns raised by both investors and insurers' (IOSH 2003: 20). The second is for the purposes of reporting to shareholders. Where health and safety represents a risk to key drivers of the business, directors will need to consider whether the narrative text accompanying their annual report and accounts should include an assessment of the board's performance in this area. CHaSPI offers directors a useful starting point when considering what key performance indicator(s) they judge to be the most appropriate for measuring the delivery of their health and safety strategy. An electronic, web-based version of the index was subsequently created in order to facilitate broader validation of the index. The Centre for Hazard and Risk Management at Loughborough University Business School undertook the validation. Its work involved two separate studies, carried out concurrently: namely, testing the completion and use of the index by a number of large organisations (57 organisations) and investigating the value of the index to a number of key stakeholders (25 stakeholder organisations, particularly investors and other financial players who may use CHaSPI data). Insight Investment collaborated in the second part of the study, as it supported the aim of encouraging measurable long-term improvements in corporate health and safety management. Insight also wrote to 68 companies that fell within the scope of the HSE validation exercise (i.e. the banking and insurance, chemicals, utilities, and construction and house-building sectors) to encourage their participation in the validation exercise. Loughborough University's conclusion was that (Walker and Cheyne 2005: vi):

> The research presents evidence which suggests that CHaSPI may be successful, but only after a number of issues are addressed. Overall the usability and face value was considered reasonable and CHaSPI as a whole was well received by a number of organisations who completed it.

Investor interest in health and safety

Why should investors be interested in good health and safety management in general, or an index such as CHaSPI in particular? Perhaps the most obvious reason is that poor health and safety management can damage corporate financial performance. At the macroeconomic level, the International Labour Organisation (ILO) has estimated that global financial losses due to workplace injuries and ill-health exceed US$1,250 billion (ILO 2003). In the UK, HSE's statisticians have calculated that in 2001–2002 the total costs to society of health and safety failures amounted to between £20 billion and £31.8 billion.[3] At a microeconomic (or company) level, the financial costs of poor health and

---

3   www.hse.gov.uk/statistics/pdf/costs.pdf

safety management include both direct costs in the event of health and safety incidents (e.g. fines, compensation, insurance, sick pay) as well as the indirect costs associated with such incidents (e.g. lost productivity, costs of management time in dealing with incident, reduced staff morale, tarnished corporate image).

There is limited evidence regarding how these company-level costs (and the associated benefits of good health and safety management) materialise through share prices, although the Claros Consulting report highlighted research by Westpac Investment Management and Monash University Accident Research Centre which identified a positive relationship between health and safety performance and investment returns: '[a] portfolio of good "H&S" companies outperformed consistently over the nine-year test period, by around 50–60bp on average' (Mansley 2002: 22). However, there are limitations in the short-term business case for companies to invest in good health and safety management: 'There are circumstances in which the economic benefits of investing in occupational health and safety are tenuous, and where the costs to business of implementing [health and safety] protection measures will not be offset by any resulting savings from improved economic performance' (Gunningham 1999: 201). As a consequence, investors can inadvertently motivate corporate health and safety performance that may be out of line with their own long-term interests: 'It is important to stress that the single largest impediment to improved [occupational health and safety] performance is probably the emphasis of corporations on short-term profitability . . . Because corporations are judged by markets, investors and others principally on short-term financial performance, they have difficulty justifying investment in occupational health and safety improvements with primarily long-term payoffs' (Gunningham 1999: 201).

Despite these potential conflicts of interest, there is a general recognition among investors of the importance of health and safety management as an integral part of overall risk management (Mansley 2002). There is also a general recognition that companies need to comply with legal requirements in this area. Investors recognise that the benefits of good health and safety performance are not confined to individual companies but provide a broader benefit through preventing the need for, potentially costly, regulation and/or litigation to address actual or perceived failings in corporate performance in this area. This view is generally shared by companies, with many having extremely strong commitments to health and safety; examples include BP, ICI and Rio Tinto.

While the arguments for investors to be interested in health and safety in general are reasonably clear,[4] the question is: 'Why should investors be specifically interested in CHaSPI?' There are three main reasons for investor interest. First, investors have struggled to get companies to report health and safety data in a consistent and comparable manner using standardised performance indicators. CHaSPI was seen as an important initiative in this regard, both through defining performance measures and through the 'buy-in' of key stakeholders, not just the HSE but also the Trades Union Congress (TUC) and individual trade unions. The second is that CHaSPI should offer the potential to reduce, rather than increase, the amount of data that companies are required to disclose. As discussed elsewhere in this book, questionnaire fatigue is an increasing prob-

---

4 See, for example, the case studies that HSE has produced to illustrate the business benefits that attention to health and safety can bring: www.hse.gov.uk/betterbusiness/index.htm.

lem for companies, in particular given that many questionnaires request different types of information (with the consequent transaction costs that this imposes on companies). Through reaching consensus on key health and safety indicators, CHaSPI offers the potential to simplify companies' reporting requirements to investors and to other stakeholders. The third is that, in the medium term, investors may perceive CHaSPI as offering the potential to contribute to a reduced regulatory burden on companies more generally.

Lessons learned

While it is too early to comment on the effectiveness of CHaSPI as a tool for improving occupational health and safety performance, our experience to date allows some important lessons to be drawn about the role of investors in facilitating public policy implementation, how regulators can develop initiatives that align their interests with those of other actors and the potential for CHaSPI to reduce company transaction costs. Each of these is discussed below.

Investors have actively encouraged the HSE and HSC to embrace a voluntary mechanism, and have contributed to the development of CHaSPI through ensuring that it collects information that is of use to investors. Investors have also played an important role in encouraging companies to participate in CHaSPI. For example, of the 68 companies contacted by Insight, 25 participated in the validation exercise with there being some evidence that 17 did so, at least in part, because of Insight's approach. Despite investor support to date, it is not clear whether or how investors will actually use the data provided by CHaSPI. In principle, investors could use the data to benchmark companies' performance, as an input to investment decision-making and/or as a measure of the performance of individual directors charged with overseeing occupational health and safety. However, there are two important questions that need to be addressed before CHaSPI will be widely used by investors: 'Will participation in CHaSPI improve health and safety performance?' and 'Is health and safety performance (as measured by CHaSPI) correlated with share price or other financial metrics of interest to investors?'

CHaSPI is an example of how government agencies can work with investors to develop policy that aligns the interests of both. The dialogue also allowed investors to propose other related policy measures (e.g. through encouraging the regulatory body to focus attention on poorer performers or non-participants, thereby providing an incentive to good performers to maintain their performance).

Finally, CHaSPI offers the potential to reduce health and safety reporting costs. As with many other social, ethical and environmental issues, occupational health and safety is a crowded field. There are many parties with an interest in the issue, there is a multiplicity of questionnaires and there are many, frequently divergent, opinions on what good performance should look like. CHaSPI does not (nor should it) address all these issues. However, CHaSPI should help reduce companies' transaction costs through articulating the types of information that investors require and, hopefully, over the longer term, clarifying investors' expectations of companies. For companies, CHaSPI should also allow them to say 'no' to questionnaires (e.g. from research providers) that ask questions that are not related to investors' interests. That is, while there are some increased costs directly associated with CHaSPI (e.g. data acquisition, verification and reporting), the net effect should be to reduce reporting costs and to maximise the value of collected information.

Implications for public policy

From a public policy perspective, the HSE engagement with investors opens up a very interesting policy implementation mechanism for government. By encouraging investors to act as de facto regulators, through encouraging companies to participate in CHaSPI and, potentially, holding companies to account for performance, the effect is to introduce another 'regulator' into the regulatory space. In other words, there are now two parties (investors and the HSE) using their influence to encourage companies to participate in CHaSPI. Furthermore, as CHaSPI is a public information disclosure policy measure, it also provides information to other parties (e.g. trade unions) on health and safety management and performance. This broadening of the number of parties that can exert influence on companies introduces, at least in theory, a new series of sanctions and incentives (e.g. share pricing mechanism, public ranking of companies) to the regulatory space. While these can be seen as positive developments, it may not be seen as reasonable or fair that the public or NGOs (or other non-democratically elected parties) are allowed to 'regulate' the health and safety performance of companies. It is also questionable whether such parties have the ability to police the actions or activities of companies effectively. There is also the risk, based on evidence from consumer boycott campaigns, that stakeholders will focus their attention on very large or high-profile organisations, with the majority of companies tending to escape attention.

As a policy instrument, CHaSPI is likely to be much lower-cost than the alternative of a mandatory reporting requirement, which would probably require much higher negotiation costs and a longer time to implement. As CHaSPI is voluntary, it also reduces the likelihood of strong industry opposition. However, CHaSPI may not be more effective than a mandatory requirement because many companies are unlikely to participate (e.g. because of concerns about the release of sensitive information into the public domain) and it is unclear whether stakeholders (investors, trade unions, etc.) will actually use CHaSPI as a basis for discussions with companies.[5] It is therefore important that CHaSPI is not seen as a replacement for more traditional approaches to health and safety enforcement. Even if CHaSPI is effective (in terms of participation and of empowering stakeholders other than government to engage in dialogue with companies), there will continue to be a need for regulation as a 'backstop' to ensure performance. As noted by Claros Consulting: 'Working with investors should not be seen as a substitute for other action, such as enforcement' (Mansley 2002: 2).

---

5   As discussed in Sullivan 2005, one of the issues with information-based (or disclosure) regulations is that stakeholders do not necessarily use these disclosures as a basis for engagement with companies or with policy-makers.

Finally, the UK focus of CHaSPI potentially limits its usefulness to investors. Large institutional investors have significant non-UK holdings and are interested in comparing companies in different countries. Occupational health and safety (notwithstanding the effect of EU Directives) is generally regulated at national levels. Consequently, the fact that the HSE has established an initiative that applies to UK companies may be of limited value to investors investing globally. HSE has tried to address this issue through structuring CHaSPI in a manner that allows companies to complete CHaSPI on a global basis. Specifically, the HSE allows companies not to report on certain sections (e.g. where national requirements appear to vary so that reporting on those sections is impracticable), and allows companies to report on a divisional as well as a global basis.

Concluding comments

In conclusion, CHaSPI represents an interesting model of regulatory innovation, where investors and regulators (in this case, the HSE) work together to develop a voluntary disclosure framework for health and safety performance. CHaSPI seeks to align investor and policy-makers' interests and to harness the influence available to different stakeholders to encourage higher standards of health and safety performance. While some limits and potential problems have been identified here, the regulator–investor dialogue appears to offer a potential model for similar measures in other areas (e.g. environmental performance) and for use by other regulatory bodies (e.g. Environment Agency, Food Standards Agency, Financial Services Authority). However, some caution is required in advocating greater use of the CHaSPI model. There is probably limited space for multiple benchmarks or reporting frameworks in the regulatory space. Certainly, the resources available to investors to participate in the design and implementation of such indices are limited. One problem with multiple indices is that it is frequently difficult for investors to decide which index is the most important. Another issue is that investors are interested in overall performance, which means that such benchmarks, if developed, would probably need to be developed at quite high levels of abstraction (i.e. a generic 'environmental management index' rather than indices on issues such as climate change, pollution, resource consumption, etc.).

To date, CHaSPI has been successful, although many of the key questions regarding its impact on health and safety performance remain to be answered. It also remains to be seen whether or how investors will use CHaSPI. While it is reasonable to assume that non-participation in CHaSPI will be an issue that investors may raise with companies, it is less clear whether investors will engage with companies on their performance in CHaSPI. It may be that companies proactively communicate good performance to their investors (as they presently do with initiatives such as FTSE4Good or Business in the Community's Index of Environmental Engagement), but that investors only raise the issue with non-participating or particularly poorly performing companies.

References

DETR and HSC (Department of the Environment, Transport and the Regions and Health and Safety Commission) (2000) *Revitalising Health and Safety* (London: DETR/HSC, June 2000).

Fidderman, H. (2004) 'CHaSPI: The Corporate Health and Safety Performance Index', *Health and Safety Bulletin* 327: 23.

Gunningham, N. (1999) 'Integrating Management Systems and Occupational Health and Safety Regulation', *Journal of Law and Society* 26.2: 192-214.

ILO (International Labour Organisation) (2003) *Safety in Numbers: Pointers for a Global Safety Culture at Work* (Geneva: ILO).

IOSH (Institute of Occupational Safety and Health) (2003) *Systems in Focus: Guidance on Occupational Safety and Health Management Systems* (Direction 03.1; Wigston, UK: IOSH).

Mansley, M. (2002) *Health and Safety Indicators for Institutional Investors: A Report to the Health and Safety Executive* (London: Claros Consulting).

Marsden, S., M. Wright, J. Shaw and C. Beardwell (2004) *The Development of a Health and Safety Management Index for Use by Business, Investors, Employees, the Regulator and Other Stakeholders* (London: Greenstreet Berman).

Sullivan, R. (2005) *Rethinking Voluntary Approaches in Environmental Policy* (Cheltenham, UK: Edward Elgar).

Walker, D., and A. Cheyne (2005) *Further Development of a Corporate Health and Safety Performance Management Index for Use by Business, Investors, Employees, the Regulator and Other Stakeholders: Validating the Index* (London: HSE Research Report 335, prepared by Loughborough University for the HSE).

Part V
Discussion and conclusions

32
The practice of responsible investment

Rory Sullivan and Craig Mackenzie

Insight Investment, UK

This book is about how investors might play a more positive role with regard to the social and environmental impacts of investee companies. Specifically, it is about two strategies that have emerged to do this: shareholder activism, and enhanced investment analysis and decision-making. While these approaches to responsible investment have yet to be widely adopted, there is now a significant body of experience in their application. The contributions to this book present the experience of the leading practitioners as well as the views of key stakeholders and commentators. As such, they shine a light on the practice of responsible investment—on the way in which institutional investors implement investment strategies to address their responsibilities to clients and to society, the practical issues and barriers faced in implementing such strategies, and the challenges to be faced if such strategies are to become truly mainstream investment approaches.

In Chapter 1, we posed three questions about responsible investment:

- Do responsible investment strategies actually contribute to improvements in the social, ethical and environmental (SEE) performance of companies?

- To what extent is it in investors' interest to encourage higher standards of corporate responsibility (CR)?

- Do responsible investment strategies enhance financial performance for investors?

Each of these questions is discussed further below. The hypotheses presented in Chapter 2—which are briefly summarised in the next section—are used to frame the analysis.

The scope for investor action on corporate social and environmental impacts

In Chapter 2, it was suggested that harmful corporate impacts on society and the environment have three broad sources: market failure, agency problems and bounded rationality. Chapter 2 also offered some reasons for thinking that shareholder activism and enhanced analysis of SEE issues might be expected to deliver improved corporate SEE performance with regard to agency problems and bounded rationality, but had a more limited role to play with regard to market failure.

Chapter 2 suggested that a key factor in determining whether or not investors would use responsible investment strategies was their interest in doing so and that investor interest would depend on the time horizons over which they were investing and the breadth of their investment exposure. On this basis, it hypothesised that broadly based investors with long-term performance objectives would be significantly more supportive of responsible investment strategies than those with narrow, short-term, relative performance goals.

Finally, Chapter 2 suggested that shareholder activism on agency problems and bounded rationality would be expected to deliver enhanced investment performance over time, while acknowledging that activism on market failure would sometimes be in conflict with investment performance objectives, particularly over the short term. In Chapter 4—where we discussed whether or not enhanced analysis is likely to deliver enhanced investment performance—we suggested that there are reasons for thinking that SEE issues can have a material impact on the financial performance of companies. We then suggested that, in situations where information about the financial implications of these issues for companies is available and well understood, analysts will typically take them into account. However, we also suggested that markets may not be very efficient at doing this in all cases and, as a result, there may be opportunities to deliver improved investment returns through enhanced analysis.

Does responsible investment contribute to improvements in the SEE performance of companies?

Activism

There is a growing body of evidence that investor activism can play an important role in encouraging companies to improve their CR performance. The case studies in Chapters 14–18 present a series of specific examples where investors have contributed to improvements in the quality of companies' policies, management systems and disclosures on a wide range of SEE issues, including climate change, supply chain labour standards, human rights, business ethics and access to medicines. In some cases, these have contributed to noteworthy outcomes, such as the increased access to HIV/AIDS medicines in Africa, following investor and non-governmental organisation (NGO) engagement with the pharmaceutical company GlaxoSmithKline (GSK). Investors have contributed to these outcomes through:

- **Facilitating dialogue between companies and stakeholders and/or raising stakeholder concerns with companies.** For example, as noted by Peter Frankental in Chapter 21, investors have helped to raise the profile of human rights issues with companies by supporting specific NGO campaigns and acting as a conduit for the flow of information between pressure groups and companies

- **Legitimising specific debates.** As discussed in the case studies, investors have played an important role in encouraging companies to look on issues, such as equal pay, access to medicines and human rights, as proper matters for corporate attention

- **Supporting companies that wish to take proactive measures to address specific CR issues.** An example is the investor dialogue with GSK on access to medicines, where investors encouraged GSK to increase access to its HIV/AIDS medicines in Africa

- **Encouraging companies that fall below norms of good practice to improve their performance.** For example, in Chapter 17, Will Oulton highlighted the role of investors in encouraging companies to meet the standards required to allow inclusion in the FTSE4Good indices

- **Encouraging companies to ensure that corporate governance arrangements are supportive of CR.** Chapters 15 and 16 illustrate how investors act to ensure attention is given to those aspects of CR that fall within the proper role of the board: for example, tax policy or executive incentives. The case studies also highlight the fact that not all CR issues are of strategic importance to companies nor do all CR issues need to be the subject of board attention

The case studies provide strong support for the hypothesis in Chapter 2 that investor activism can improve corporate performance with regard to both agency problems (through improving governance systems and processes) and bounded rationality (through ensuring that companies have appropriate systems and processes in place to manage CR issues). Interestingly, the case studies challenge the hypothesis that investor activism will have a more limited role to play with regard to market failure. Some investor activity (e.g. on climate change and access to medicines) has sought explicitly to engage with market failure issues, and has led to some very important outcomes. However, it is our view that investor efforts to address market failures are, overall, likely to be less effective than efforts to address agency or bounded rationality problems, reflecting the relative strengths of the arguments that investors can use. In relation to agency and bounded rationality issues, investors have emphasised business-case arguments for companies to improve performance, including the need to align the interests of shareholders and managers and to minimise the risks to shareholder value of failing to manage specific SEE issues properly. As discussed in Chapters 23 and 24, these arguments are important to allow companies to understand the reasons for investor interest in specific issues. In relation to activism on market failure, it is noticeable that investors have been reluctant to explicitly state that companies may need to act contrary to their self-interests to address the market failure. Instead, investors have tended to rely on arguments around reputation risk or the longer-term benefits of not exploiting the market failure. While such arguments may have merit, it is clear from the company case studies that these longer-term arguments will require convincing supporting evidence if they are to be persuasive.

Which strategies?

In Chapter 13, we identified main strategies used by large institutional investors as: the use of voting and other formal shareholder rights; engagement; collaboration; public benchmarking; media communications; and influencing the share price. With the exception of directly attempting to influence the share price, investors have, to a greater or lesser extent, put all of these strategies to use to encourage higher standards of CR performance.

Turning first to the formal rights of shareholders, these strategies (e.g. votes against management) are quite familiar in the context of corporate governance issues, and the use of formal voting rights has been very important in encouraging sustained improvements in corporate adherence to the Combined Code on Corporate Governance. In as much as these improvements have significantly helped reduce the risk of agency problems at the top of British companies, they will have indirectly addressed those corporate issues that arise from these problems. However, in the UK, formal shareholder rights have been rarely used, at least to date, in relation to specific CR issues. This is partly because, unlike conventional corporate governance issues, there are few routine opportunities for shareholders to vote on CR issues. As a result, shareholders are faced with a choice of either seeking to use existing voting opportunities to send a signal on CR or of filing special resolutions. There are some signs that investors are increasingly willing to take the former option. For example, in Chapter 6, Ronnie Lim notes that Morley's voting policy requires companies to disclose 'sufficient' information on SEE risks, and states that Morley may abstain or vote against companies in the FTSE 350 that fail to disclose sufficient information. There is relatively little interest in the latter approach (i.e. filing resolutions). The main reason is that it is difficult to file resolutions in the UK, with the threshold required for filing being 5% of the issued share capital or 100 investors with a nominal collective investment of at least £10,000. This is in marked contrast to the US, where filing a resolution has a much lower threshold and where special resolutions on SEE issues have been far more common.[1]

Another reason why shareholders have been less willing to use their formal rights in the UK is that the largest institutional investors tend to have good relationships with, and access to, company boards and senior management and have been able to achieve significant progress through constructive dialogue (or 'engagement'). The use of shareholder resolutions would be perceived as aggressive and undermining of these relationships, and so may prove counterproductive. As illustrated in the case studies, and also as indicated in comments from company representatives (see, for example, Chapter 23), investors' views are an important influence on the manner in which companies take action on specific CR issues. This is particularly the case in situations where there is a clear business case for companies to take action. As noted above, it is less clear whether companies will respond (or continue to respond) in situations where the busi-

---

1 See the Interfaith Center on Corporate Responsibility: www.iccr.org.

ness case is less well defined. The consequence is that investors' ability to contribute to addressing market failures (i.e. where the business case for companies to take action is weak) is likely to be weak.

Reflecting the long history of collaboration on corporate governance issues, UK investors have also sought to collaborate on a range of CR issues. Examples include formal coalitions such as the Pharmaceutical Shareowners Group and the Institutional Investors' Group on Climate Change (IIGCC), as well as more informal arrangements (see, for example, Chapter 15 where Rob Lake describes how Henderson and Insight worked together to engage with Shell in relation to its operations in Nigeria). Collaboration allows investors to present a consistent and unified voice on CR issues (thereby ensuring that companies are not facing competing and contradictory priorities from different investors) while also, depending on the issue, broadening the group of investors that work on a specific issue. Many of the collaborative initiatives have led to important changes in corporate practice, but it is too early to say whether collaboration is more or less effective than the outcomes that would be achieved by investors operating individually (or with minimal co-ordination and information sharing). In addition, issues such as free-riding, the risk of lowest-common-denominator approaches and the possibility of significant transaction costs potentially limit the utility of collaboration as an activism strategy. There are two types of free-riding that affect collaborative initiatives—where some of the participants use participation to demonstrate their 'commitment to activism' (even when their contribution has been minor) and where shareholders not party to the collaborative effort are able to claim most of the benefits resulting from the resultant improvements in corporate governance or CR performance. Collaborative investor activity has also been hampered by the lack of a clear, shared view of what standards shareholders should expect of companies in relation to CR issues. While there is a general consensus on the systems and processes (e.g. corporate policies, clearly defined responsibilities, performance monitoring, reporting) that companies should have in place, there has been a marked reluctance to say what the specific performance measures (or outcomes) should be. The challenge of achieving consensus has meant that the lowest-common-denominator approach (i.e. a focus on management systems and processes) has tended to prevail. While this is an important contribution to addressing bounded rationality issues, it is not clear how far these go towards addressing market failure issues. Finally, our experience with large-scale collaborative initiatives has been that they involve significant time and effort, tend to have long lead times and, frequently, are highly bureaucratic.

Investors have also started to use benchmarking methodologies in order to support engagement. This approach involves developing a benchmarking framework for corporate SEE performance, evaluating corporate performance against the benchmark and then producing a league table of companies based on the analysis. For example, Insight has conducted benchmarking exercises on biodiversity, environmental risk management in the house-building sector and on supply chain management. These exercises have proven very effective in stimulating companies to improve their performance. Another, larger-scale use of benchmarking is presented in Chapter 17, which is a case study on FTSE4Good. This index can be considered as a very large multi-issue benchmarking framework. FTSE has accumulated impressive evidence that the existence of this framework, and the company engagement activity surrounding it, has contributed to improvements in several hundred companies around the world. It appears that companies put a premium on remaining participants in the FTSE4Good index and are willing to improve their practice in order to meet its entry requirements.

In relation to both individual engagement and collaborative engagement, there is an ongoing debate over the appropriate management level with which investors should engage on CR issues. For mainstream analysts and corporate governance activists, most engagement is with senior executive management (generally the chief executive and finance director) and the chair of the board. In contrast, it appears that most discussions on SEE issues tend to occur with lower-level managers tasked with managing CR issues. In many cases, engaging at this lower level seems to have been effective. By supporting the proposals of the CR manager, investors may have served to empower this function within the organisation. However, many CR issues raise questions of corporate strategy, appetite for risk, internal control and executive incentives. These issues can be dealt with only by the board. The failure of investors to engage at this level on SEE issues may weaken the effectiveness of investor engagement. Although in the past it has been relatively rare for investors to engage with board members on CR issues, there are signs that this is starting to change. For example, Henderson (see further Chapter 15) has engaged with boards on tax policy and non-financial aspects of executive incentives, while the Boards and Corporate Responsibility Project developed by Insight with FTSE and Business in the Community (see Chapter 16) seeks to develop consensus about the board's role in this area.

A number of fund managers now offer a stand-alone (or overlay) activism service, where they implement activism on behalf of clients, but without managing the underlying assets. In general, this involves the investment manager voting the client's holdings and engaging with companies on behalf of clients. To date, only a limited number of large institutional investors, such as the Wellcome Trust, British Coal Board and PGGM, have decided to adopt such an approach. The advantages are that it allows pension funds to hold investment managers to account for the delivery of effective activism, and it allows for consistency in voting and engagement thereby helping ensure that investee companies receive a single unambiguous message from shareholders. The overlay or unbundled approach is not, however, without its problems. Perhaps the most obvious is that it becomes an additional cost that pension funds need to meet (as noted in Chapter 28, it could be seen as inappropriate for fund managers to be paid extra for work that, arguably, they should be doing as a standard part of their investment management activities anyway). There is also a view (see, for example, the comments by Rob Lake in Chapter 15) that activism is most effective when it is accompanied by active fund management. Our view is that this problem is avoided where an active equity manager provides the activism overlay, rather than a third party who does not manage the assets. In addition, the reality is that many pension funds currently have no effective approach to activism at all; our view is that, despite the potential disadvantages, an overlay approach to activism is significantly better than nothing at all.

What is the role of public policy?

It was suggested in Chapter 2 that long-term broadly based investors have an interest in correcting market failure, but that enhanced analysis and shareholder activism are of themselves—and absent an appropriate public policy framework—likely to be of limited value in serving this interest. From the evidence presented in this book, investors have yet to actively support strong policy measures to correct market failures. To date, and as discussed in Chapter 30, most investor activity has been focused on comparatively modest ends, such as improving transparency (e.g. the Operating and Financial Review) and requiring pension funds to explicitly state in their statement of investment principles the extent, if at all, to which they take account of SEE issues in their investment processes. Nevertheless, there are some signs that investors are increasingly willing to encourage public policy-makers to take action to address market failure issues. As just one example, the IIGCC has explicitly supported the UK government's targets to reduce greenhouse gas emissions from 1990 levels by 20% by 2020 and 60% by 2050.

Investors have three key roles in helping to correct market failures. The first, as discussed above, is through encouraging public policy-makers to take action to address market failures. Despite the limited investor activity in this regard, the examples of IIGCC and Pharma Futures (see further Chapter 26) indicate that investors are increasingly willing to contemplate (if not, as yet, actively support) public policy measures to address market failures. The second is through ensuring that existing public policy is effectively implemented. Initiatives to correct certain agency and bounded rationality problems are important contributions. The third, as discussed in Chapter 31, is to strengthen the implementation of public policy by introducing new 'regulators' (in this case, encouraging investors to promote regulatory compliance with investee companies) and introducing new incentives for companies (e.g. peer pressure, publicising investor views of individual companies). However, this third set of activities seems most likely to be effective in complementing and enhancing existing regulatory initiatives (in this case, health and safety) rather than seeking to address completely new policy issues.

Enhanced analysis

Chapter 2 suggested that enhanced analysis might be effective at encouraging improved corporate performance by improving the ability of the capital markets to give due weight to SEE risks in the pricing of shares. In turn, this would send strong signals to corporate management to manage these risks more effectively. There is considerable support in Chapters 4–12 that SEE risks may be inaccurately priced and that enhanced analysis may allow investors to exploit this inefficiency. However, there is very little discussion of whether or how this will have an effect on the behaviour of corporate management. It is generally assumed by the authors of these chapters that enhanced analysis will be socially useful, although it is not clear that the various authors have a clear view on why this might be the case; the evidence presented in the various chapters for or against this view is correspondingly weak. Further research is needed to cast light on this question.

Are investors interested in pursuing responsible investment strategies?

In Chapter 2, it was suggested that investor interest in responsible investment strategies depends on the time horizons over which they are investing, the breadth of their investment exposure and the extent to which their performance goals are measured in relative or absolute terms. It was hypothesised that broadly based investors with long-term performance objectives would tend to be significantly more supportive of investor responsibility strategies than those with narrow, short-term, relative performance goals. Does the evidence provided by the subsequent chapters in this book support this hypothesis?

In theory at least, the idea that asset owners such as pension funds have a specific role to play in encouraging moves towards sustainable societies is intuitively attractive. The reasons (as discussed in Chapters 14 and 29) include the fact that pension funds are universal owners with stakes in virtually all the investable stocks in the universe; consequently, in serving their fiduciary duty to maximise the financial return of beneficiaries over the long term, they will have an interest and an obligation to address the SEE impacts of their investments. Therefore, in theory, pension funds should fall into the category of broadly based investors with long-term performance objectives. There is some evidence that pension funds accept that their long-term, broadly based interests should lead them to support efforts to address companies' SEE impacts. However, as discussed in Chapter 2, and as reflected in the comments made by some of the authors in this book (see, for example, Chapters 20 and 29), UK pension funds—with notable exceptions such as the Universities Superannuation Scheme (USS)—have been relatively slow to take a proactive role in promoting the idea of responsible investment. The structure of the institutional investment industry is (largely) that asset owners hire fund managers to manage equities: asset owners have the ultimate rights and interests while investment managers have the practical knowledge and company relationships. Given this structure, if the long-term interests of pension funds are to be reflected in investment practice, asset managers and asset owners need to work together. That is, asset owners need to give asset managers a clear mandate to act on their behalf, and to monitor and reward performance accordingly, while asset managers need to deliver on their mandate and report their results. As yet, few pension funds have created effective mandates and performance management mechanisms (e.g. detailed implementation policies for activism, requirements to comply with the pension fund's commitments to activism in contracts with fund managers, specific objectives and performance measures for activism, performance monitoring). The consequence is that, as noted by Raj Thamotheram in Chapter 29, the signals sent from pension funds to their fund managers tend to be weak. In turn, the signals from fund managers to companies are even weaker or non-existent. Not only have the signals on activism been weak, the investment mandates awarded by pension funds have tended to be relatively short-term and focused on performance relative to specific benchmarks. The consequence is that most asset owners have created incentives for asset managers to place too little emphasis on many of the important longer-term drivers of investment value (see further the discussion of enhanced analysis below).

Apart from the question of investment mandates, are there other barriers to the delivery of effective activism? The chapters in this book point to a number. The proper monitoring (as opposed to box-ticking, compliance-based approaches) of companies is expensive and may require skills not usually found in fund managers. This issue of monitoring costs is compounded by the problem of free-riders: those that spend nothing on this type of activity reap most or all of the benefits in terms of improved performance and share price than those that incur all the costs. This problem is compounded by the reluctance, to date, of the majority of pension funds to pay for activism or to hold their fund managers properly to account for its delivery.

Another barrier to effective activism is the many conflicts of interest in investment management. For example, a fund manager may be engaging with a company whose pension fund it wishes to manage, or could be undertaking an activity where the corporate finance arm is also involved. Furthermore, pension funds could face difficulties where they are raising an issue that has not been addressed by the fund's own sponsoring company; in Chapter 20, Robert Monks and Allen Sykes note that corporate pension funds, which are controlled by corporate management, have almost never been activist in either the US or the UK. They argue that there is an implicit understanding that each company's pension fund will refrain from an activist stance in return for a reciprocal stance from all the others.

A further barrier is that the results of engagement are not always measurable, either in terms of effectiveness or the financial benefits that result from engagement. If pension funds cannot measure the difference between an effective activist fund manager and an ineffective one, it is difficult for them to choose between them. There are some efforts to address this issue. For example, a number of fund managers, including Insight Investment, F&C and Henderson, now publicly disclose information on their engagement and voting activities, and some ten fund managers have worked with the UK Social Investment Forum to develop transparency guidelines for fund managers in order to encourage fund managers to disclose information on issues such as activism policies, resources, systems and processes, outcomes achieved and reporting (see further Chapter 12). Notwithstanding these initiatives, if the financial benefits of activism cannot be measured it might be difficult for pension funds to justify the modest extra costs of activism. While, in theory, long-term, broadly based investors such as pension funds ought to be better off if agency problems, bounded rationality and certain forms of market failure are addressed, this theoretical benefit is not easy to measure. As a result, pension funds have found it difficult to justify spending money on activism and enhanced analysis on the basis of a theoretical gain. This is a particular problem for pension funds given that they have a fiduciary responsibility to serve the long-term interests of their beneficiaries.

The role of investment consultants may be particularly important in addressing these problems. To date, many investment consultants have been somewhat uninterested in the question of whether responsible investment strategies enhance or detract from investment returns. The lack of consultant interest has had the effect of reinforcing the lack of appreciation of the value of SEE activism and enhanced analysis to long-term, broadly based investors such as pension funds. The good news is that this is changing. For example, the Marathon Club initiative (see Chapter 28) and the decision by the bigger consultants in the institutional market to consider activism and research as an integral part of their research processes (see Chapters 27 and 28, and the recent announcement by Watson Wyatt that it intends to formally assess investment managers on their activism capabilities) are important signals that investment consultants may be starting to take a much more proactive approach to these issues. While assessing investment managers is a start, it remains to be seen whether investment consultants will proactively encourage their clients to explicitly address SEE issues in their investment manager appointment/reappointment processes. It also remains to be seen how much weight is attached to these capabilities in the fund manager selection process.

In conclusion, it is probable that the hypotheses set out in Chapter 2 are too pessimistic. As the case studies in this book indicate, there is significant space within many fund management houses for investors to consider long-term and broadly based issues, thus serving the long-term interests of the economy as a whole rather than short-term relative performance interests. The significant resources devoted by asset managers such as Insight, Henderson, Morley, F&C and others to this area indicates that some asset managers are willing to take their responsibilities as owners seriously. The issues described above remain significant but not insurmountable barriers to ensuring that the long-term, broadly based interests of pension funds are fully reflected in the way their assets are invested in practice. Over the last five years a number of UK pension funds and charitable foundations have found ways beyond these barriers; USS, local authority pension funds in Lothian, Aberdeen, Nottingham and elsewhere, the Environment Agency pension fund and the Wellcome Trust are good examples. A few large European pension funds, such as PGGM and Algemeen Burgerlijk Pensioenfonds in the Netherlands, have also taken action. These pension schemes and foundations have helped to create a small institutional market for responsible investment strategies, providing vital commercial support for the development of many of the activism and enhanced analysis approaches described in this book. However, the maintenance of these teams and resources in the various asset managers depends largely on demand from pension funds. In the longer term, without support from asset owners, activism by managers is unlikely to happen.

Can financial performance be enhanced through responsible investment?

Enhanced analysis

The fact that SEE issues can have a material impact on the financial performance of companies does not, of itself, mean that a focus on these issues can enhance investment performance. As discussed in Section 2 of this book, some investors have sought to generate investment outperformance through two approaches. The first is an evolution of conventional approaches to the fundamental analysis of expected company earnings, with additional research being conducted into, for example, how expected environmental regulations or patterns of social change will affect earnings expectations in the future. The second is more radical, with analysis being driven primarily by data on SEE performance rather than by financial indicators. The case studies in Chapters 5–12 lend some support to the argument that, while markets are reasonably efficient at reflecting the available information about companies in share or bond prices, not all SEE issues are recognised and properly valued by the markets. The various authors offer two broad reasons for this:

- SEE issues have not yet been identified by the market (see, for example, the assessment of the EU's REACH Regulation in Chapter 5 and the discussion in Chapter 7 of the importance of timely analysis when evaluating corporate bond credit risks)

- SEE issues have not been properly valued by the market (see, for example, the discussion in Chapter 6 of the EU's emission trading scheme and the discussion in Chapter 5 of the limitations in the data provided by companies and the inadequacies in the cost–benefit assessments conducted by companies, governments and industry associations)

As discussed in Chapter 2, it appears that there are three areas—long-term impacts, intangibles or extra-financial impacts (e.g. reputation) and uncertain impacts—that are particularly likely to be poorly evaluated or assessed (and, consequently, as offering particular opportunities for investors to add value or achieve outperformance). The case studies demonstrate that it is possible to focus on one or more of these areas and to generate outperformance through doing so. One of the interesting features of the case studies is that most focus primarily on financial analysis of the effects of SEE issues. The investment managers (with the exception of Innovest and SAM who have a more radical investment approach) who have been able to benefit from analysis of SEE issues have done so through incremental improvements to their analysis of SEE impacts on core financial metrics, rather than seeking to analyse issues such as broader impacts on corporate reputation, quality of management or impacts on intangibles. Furthermore, the time horizon used in their analysis has not been significantly longer than 'typical' investment managers.

However, the fact that some investors are able to demonstrate that they have generated outperformance through enhanced fundamental analysis or through SEE-driven analysis does not mean that all investors will seek to do so, or that investment outperformance will be achieved by all investors that seek to focus on these issues. There are three factors that need to be considered: research costs, the quality of investment research and the relevance of longer-term value drivers to short-term investment performance.

With regard to the first of these, financial analysis can be costly, in particular on SEE issues where there is often little easily available information about company performance. The accepted wisdom in financial economics is that investors should invest in research to the extent that the benefits of doing so (in terms of enhanced investment performance) outweigh the costs. In many cases, the costs of enhancing analysis on SEE issues beyond a certain point will exceed the benefits. A common theme in the investment manager case studies (specifically, Chapters 5–7, 10 and 11) is that analysing SEE issues properly (i.e. in the detail necessary to properly factor these issues into investment decisions), is resource-intensive, generally requiring a team of specialists. Given that it is by no means certain that outperformance will be achieved, these research costs are a significant barrier to investment managers investing resources in this specific area. This does not mean that investment managers will not incorporate research (e.g. from the sell side) into their analysis but, rather, that they may decide not to develop their own capacity in this area beyond a certain point.

The second commonly cited barrier to responsible investment is the quality of investment research. The research produced by sell-side brokers has been criticised for being overly focused on short-term drivers of share price rather than on long-term value drivers, extra-financial factors and uncertain events. One of the specific criticisms has been that SEE issues tend to be systematically ignored in investment research. Turning first to the question of short-term investment performance, it is important to recognise that the majority of SEE issues that can affect investment performance in the short term (i.e. material issues) tend to be reasonably well understood and reasonably well integrated into investment analysis and decision-making. These issues tend, however, not to be described by financial analysts as 'social' or 'environmental' issues, but rather in terms such as 'regulatory risk', 'tax' or 'litigation risk'. For example, tobacco litigation (which originated as an ethical and public health issue) is a well-understood investment risk and is treated accordingly in investment analysis. That is, SEE issues are treated in a similar manner to other issues that may impact on investment performance (i.e. if an issue has the potential to impact materially on a company or companies, that issue will be identified and analysed). This does not mean that all SEE issues are identified or properly valued. However, these inefficiencies are not unique to CR issues. For example, the weaknesses in the market's evaluation of the REACH Regulation (see further Chapter 5) are typical of any impending legislation in that the market tends to rely on companies bringing the issue to the attention of analysts, and the analysis of the financial implications tends to be done in a 'just-in-time' manner (i.e. once there is clarity regarding the direction of policy and when the information is required by analysts). An important corollary to the question of short-term performance is that many important SEE issues are not financially important or material (at least over the short term). A good example is the cost to mining companies of providing HIV/AIDS antiretroviral therapy, as discussed by Simon Toyne in Chapter 8. While HIV/AIDS represents one of the most important public health issues facing the world today, it does not automatically follow that this creates a short-term financial risk for companies, even those operating in the AIDS-torn countries of Africa. Toyne also notes that, while it is possible to assess the short-term costs of HIV/AIDS, it is extremely difficult to tell what the longer-term financial implications will be for companies (e.g. the availability of workers).

The third question is whether research focused on longer-term performance would actually be of value to investment managers. One of the critical conclusions from the case studies in Chapters 5–12 is that the ability of investment managers to generate outperformance from a focus on SEE issues requires either a detailed fundamental analysis process or an investment philosophy that harnesses the insights generated by an analysis of these issues into investment decision-making. However, as discussed above, given that most investment managers are required to benchmark themselves constantly against an index, and given the relatively short time horizons over which investment performance is judged, it is difficult for large investment managers to propose investment philosophies that diverge from index tracking. Consequently, it is debatable whether (even if the major analytical problems such as assessing impacts on extra-financials were resolved) there would be a significant market demand for research that gives substantially more weight to longer-term rather than shorter-term value drivers. We acknowledge that this may be a 'chicken and egg' argument as the emergence of better-quality research may enhance the legitimacy of longer-term approaches to investment and investment decision-making. However, even if these technical barriers could be overcome, the consequences of future events inevitably get discounted in investment analysis. That is, it is by no means certain that effective social controls will emerge to encourage companies to internalise negative externalities and, even if these controls do emerge, these controls will be implemented or adopted at some indeterminate time in the future (and the effect of discounting future costs means that these costs will have a lower net present value). As a consequence, even if more or better research were to emerge on longer-term value drivers, it is by no means a given that this research would be used by investment managers. Finally, research is not a free 'good'; for sell-side researchers to focus more on SEE issues they would need to expect a pay-off (e.g. the Enhanced Analytics Initiative proposes that investment managers and pension funds should allocate a minimum of 5% of their brokerage commission budgets to sell-side houses who are effective at analysing material extra-financial issues and intangibles). However, given that many investment managers have less interest in longer-term issues, it is not clear that they would be interested in allocating extra resources to this area.

The financial value of activism

The examples offered by this book offer some early support for the claim that enhanced analysis may be expected to contribute to improved investment performance. Does shareholder activism do the same? There are two questions here. The first is whether improved corporate SEE performance improves earnings and the second is whether shareholder activism is effective at achieving these changes.

An implication of the arguments presented in Chapter 2 is that, where a SEE impact is caused by agency problems or bounded rationality and companies are effective at reducing these problems, then these companies would expect to see increased earnings over time. However, for market failure issues, improved SEE performance may not pay (unless there are substantial long-term social penalties for exploiting market failure). If this argument is correct, shareholder activism to encourage companies to address agency problems, bounded rationality and market failure (where there are reasonably certain and substantial long-term penalties) should contribute to financial outperformance, but activism on other forms of market failure will not. The contributions to this book, as discussed above, provide strong evidence that shareholder activism can contribute substantially to improving corporate SEE performance, in particular in relation to agency and bounded rationality problems. However, there is limited evidence to date to support the hope that activism will be able to substantially address market failure issues. One of the most striking impressions of the chapters on activism in this book is that, while the authors discuss in detail the impacts of activism on CR performance, they pay little attention to the question of the impacts of activism on investment performance. While there is some discussion of related questions, such as whether or not there is a business case for CR, or whether or not activism on CR is compatible with the fiduciary duties of investors, the specific question of whether or not shareholder activism contributes to measurable improvements in the financial performance of particular stocks or of investment portfolios is not substantially addressed. The lack of attention to the financial performance implications of activism reflects the difficulties in attributing specific changes in share price to the effects of activism and the fact that performance benefits will tend to be shared by the market as a whole (thereby reducing relative gains). While the authors appear to be unwilling to make specific claims about the financial benefits of activism, a number argue (see, for example, Chapter 15 on activism and Chapters 6 and 7 on investment decision-making) that one of the out-comes of engagement and activism is a better understanding of companies and their value drivers. Thus, the process of engagement—whether or not directed towards achieving specific improvements in corporate performance—can provide insights that allow investment performance to be improved.

The fact that shareholder activists seem to pay relatively little attention to the impli-cations of their work for investment performance highlights another important issue: the apparent disconnect between the agendas and issues raised by socially responsible investment analysts and mainstream analysts. A number of companies (see, for exam-ple, Chapters 23 and 24 on Severn Trent and BT respectively) have noted that their chief executives have not been asked about CR issues by mainstream analysts, that main-stream analysts do not appear particularly interested in these issues and that SEE ana-lysts often do not attend the same meetings as mainstream analysts. Does this mean that SEE analysts are not relevant to the work of mainstream investment processes? Sometimes this can be a reasonable conclusion. Many of the SEE issues that have been pursued by investors through activism may not be all that material to share price. As illustrated by Simon Toyne's analysis of HIV/AIDS in the southern African mining indus-try (Chapter 8), SEE issues are often too financially insignificant to warrant analysts' attention. The consequence is that shareholder activism to encourage improved per-formance on such topics, even if successful, will not create significant financial bene-fits. However, in other circumstances, specifically those where there may be long-term penalties for companies that exploit a market failure, a more accurate conclusion would be that the difference in emphasis reflects the different time horizons of each. As discussed above, mainstream analysts are frequently more interested in short-term influences on earnings, whereas shareholder SEE activists tend to more interested in longer-term issues (i.e. those issues where the sanctions are longer-term, less certain and impact on issues such as corporate reputation). For example, using the example of GSK presented in Chapter 18, while GSK's old pricing policy for its AIDS medicines may not have been material in the short term, failure to manage the issue may have had sub-stantial long-term implications both for the company's reputation and for ongoing pub-lic support, particularly in poorer countries, for the 'trade-related aspects of intellectual property rights' (TRIPS) global regime. One of the risks for responsible investment is that companies may use this apparent disconnect between financial analysts and share-holder activists to reject engagement on CR issues.

Concluding comments

The material presented in this chapter and, indeed, the book as a whole, allows us to provide some answers to the three questions that we raised in Chapter 1. First, in rela-tion to the question of whether responsible investment strategies actually contribute to improvements in the SEE performance of companies, the case studies in this book offer encouraging evidence that shareholder activism strategies can make important contri-butions to addressing agency problems, bounded rationality issues and market failure issues. There is rather limited evidence either way on whether enhanced analysis has a similar role. However, given that a specific challenge in addressing market failures is the weakness of the business-case arguments that can be used to support company action (in particular, given that addressing the market failure is likely to entail costs for companies), improved rigour in the analysis of the long-term, uncertain and extra-financial impacts of SEE issues may strengthen the force of investors' arguments to address market failures.

On the question of whether responsible investment strategies enhance financial performance for investors, there is some limited evidence to support a positive conclusion in this regard. The reality is that demonstrating consistent investment outperformance takes many years. It is too early in the evolution of responsible investment to draw any firm conclusions on this issue.

Finally, this book has allowed us to examine the extent to which it is in investors' interest to encourage higher standards of CR. The material in the book supports the view that long-term, broadly based investors do have an interest in encouraging higher standards of CR, but that the way pension funds invest in practice may not be fully consistent with this interest. This helps explain why responsible investment strategies are not yet all that widely adopted. However, the general conclusions of Chapter 2 were probably a little too pessimistic. The chapters in this book reveal that the CR performance of companies is recognised as an important issue that many different parties to the investment process—pension funds, other asset owners, investment consultants, investment managers, trade unions, NGOs and companies themselves—are trying to address. Many of the barriers to action are starting to be addressed by these parties. If they are successful, we expect and hope to see growing support for responsible investment strategies over time.

33
Looking forwards

Craig Mackenzie and Rory Sullivan
Insight Investment, UK

By allocating capital efficiently to companies through the capital markets, investors provide the lifeblood for our economic system. This activity has a vital role to play in delivering the products, services, innovation, jobs and wealth creation that are essential to sustainable development. However, our economic system is by no means perfect. Markets and companies sometimes have harmful impacts on society and the environment. This book has sought to explore, through analysis and case studies, the extent to which investors can play a role in addressing these imperfections. We have identified three important causes of harmful corporate social and environmental impacts—market failure, agency problems and bounded rationality—and we have described two strategies by which investors may be able to address these problems: shareholder activism and enhanced analysis. Shareholder activism helps by encouraging companies to deliver stronger self-regulation, more effective governance, improved incentive structures and more rational business practices. Enhanced analysis involves giving due weight to environmental and social factors in investment decision-making, and so sends more accurate and stronger signals to companies about these issues through the capital markets.

From the case studies and other contributions to this book there are many grounds for optimism that these strategies do have a positive contribution to make to sustainable development. There is fairly clear evidence that shareholder activism, in particular, has made important contributions to addressing agency problems, bounded rationality and market failure. There are also positive indications that, as the capital markets are imperfect at valuing environmental and social factors, enhanced analysis may have a role to play in contributing to more efficient capital markets while also sending more constructive signals to companies about the importance of these issues. The fact that these strategies have a positive role to play is a very important message. At present, relatively few institutional investors attempt to implement either shareholder activism or enhanced analysis. The cause of sustainable development would be advanced if more investors were to adopt these strategies.

However, there appear to be some serious limitations in investors' ability to tackle market failure. This is bad news because problems such as climate change, collapse of natural resources and loss of biodiversity arise largely because of market failures of various kinds. We need to recognise that some of these limitations to investor action are probably immovable. For example, it is hard to see why investment analysts would attempt to incorporate companies' environmental externalities in their valuations because, in the absence of regulation to internalise these externalities, they are, by definition, external to the company's value. In such cases, government or other social interventions will be needed to address these market failures.

Fortunately, however, it may be possible to reduce or remove other limitations to investor action on market failure. This book has made very clear that many of these limitations relate to the time horizons and breadth of economic interest of investors. Where investors have long-term, economically broad investment horizons, they will often have an interest in seeing market failures corrected. While many institutional investors would appear to have the appropriate length and breadth of perspective, this book has also made clear that more may need to be done to ensure this broad, long-term perspective is reflected in investment practice. Such steps will be vital to secure the viability of the innovative approaches described in this book.

It is here that debate is presently poised. While investors (asset owners and asset managers) have demonstrated that responsible investment can make a useful contribution to reducing harmful corporate impacts on society and the environment, it is clear that more needs to be done to encourage the majority of investors to take effective action in this regard. If the objective is to make the kind of responsible investment strategies described in this book the norm, rather than the exception, it is important that pension funds and other institutional asset owners ensure that their long-term, broadly based interests are fully reflected in the way their assets are invested in practice. In the last five years considerable progress has been made in developing responsible investment strategies that are both effective and consistent with fiduciary obligations. A relatively small number of pioneering pension schemes and charitable foundations have helped to create a small institutional market for such strategies, providing vital commercial support for a small group of innovative asset management houses and research agencies to develop the activism and enhanced analysis approaches described in this book. However, these strategies will achieve their full potential only if they become widely adopted in the investment community as a whole. This will require much more widespread support from the pension funds and long-term asset owners whose interests they serve. The mainstreaming of responsible investment still has a long way to go.

Appendix 1
Innovest Intangible Value Assessment: Aracruz Celulose

Innovest
STRATEGIC VALUE ADVISORS

www.innovestgroup.com
New York: (+) 212 421-2000
London: +44 (0) 20 7073 0470
Toronto: (+) 905 707-0876
Paris: +33 (0)1 44 54 04 89
Copyright© All rights reserved. 1998-2003
Innovest Strategic Value Advisors

INTANGIBLE VALUE ASSESSMENT

May –03

Aracruz Celulose S.A.

Country:	Brazil
Ticker Symbol:	AA
Industrial Sector:	Forest products
Combined IVA Rating:	AA
Rank:	6 of 29
Sub-Factors:	
Environment:	9.0
Human Capital:	9.5
Stakeholder Capital:	9.0
Strategic Governance:	8.0
Analyst:	Juan D. Silva (+) 905.707.0876 x. 310

Intangible value comprises a growing percentage of companies' market capitalization. Innovest's IVA™ ratings analyze relative corporate performance on intangible value drivers related to the strength and sustainability of companies' competitive advantage. By assessing differentials typically not identified by traditional securities analysis, IVA™ ratings uncover hidden risks and value potential for investors.

COMPANY OVERVIEW

Core Business: Aracruz produces, distributes, and exports bleached eucalyptus pulp. The Aracruz Produtos de Madeira subsidiary produces eucalyptus hardwood lumber for the flooring and furniture markets. Geographic Focus: Aracruz own a port terminal, Portocel, and exports 97% of its product to the following markets: 37% to North America; 37% to Europe; and, 23% to Asia. Revenue Breakdown: 2002 revenues totaled US$680 million. The Lorentzen, Votorantim, and Safra groups each own 28% of Aracruz's shares. The Brazilian National Economic and Social Development Bank holds 12.5%. Operations: Facilities consist of three pulp mills, one sawmill, and a port terminal in the state of Espírito Santo. The company's forest plantations cover 0.7 million acres with 51% in the state of Bahia, and 49% in Espírito Santo. Workforce: Aracruz has 4,831 employees, including 3,037 permanent outsourced workers.

INDUSTRY DRIVING FORCES

Industry Consolidation: Tightening environmental regulations, increasing energy costs, and newly imposed duties on lumber have increased cost and capacity pressures and reduced profit margins, creating conditions conducive to mergers and acquisitions. Value Addition: On average, forest products companies generate at least two-thirds of their sales in paper and wood products manufacturing. Firms are adding value to final products, transforming them into high demand office products and building materials to increase net margins and sales volumes. Product Specialization: Engineered Wood Products (EWPs) provide a market for a wider range of species and grades, harvesting costs are often reduced, and additional silvicultural operations become economic. EWPs also allows for a high rate of waste recovery.

INTANGIBLE VALUE DRIVERS

Brand Value: Increasing demand rates from environmentally sensitive markets have driven companies to invest in brand value enhancement through sustainable forestry operations. Resource Efficiency: Companies are increasingly driven by both customer demand and tightening environmental regulations to become more resource efficient, chiefly by increasing their emphasis on recycling wood and paper products. This approach has also led to reductions in manufacturing costs. Shift to Plantations in the South: Plantations have reduced pressure on natural forests and have gained a good reputation among certification bodies when developed on barren land, with due environmental considerations. By following these guidelines, firms are still able to access environmentally sensitive markets.

PERFORMANCE / ALPHA INTENSITY MATRIX

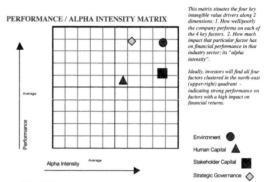

This matrix situates the four key intangible value drivers along 2 dimensions: 1. How well/poorly the company performs on each of the 4 key factors. 2. How much impact that particular factor has on financial performance in that industry sector; its "alpha intensity".

Ideally, investors will find all four factors clustered in the north-east (upper-right) quadrant - indicating strong performance on factors with a high impact on financial returns.

Environment ●
Human Capital ▲
Stakeholder Capital ■
Strategic Governance ◇

AREAS OF POTENTIAL RISK

International Reputation: Despite intense investments and partnerships to maintain good community relations, opposition to eucalyptus plantations still exists in Brazil. Several groups maintain minor campaigns against Aracruz with frequent support from international organizations, somewhat damaging the company's international reputation. This may be an impediment for earning eco-logo certification, such as the Nordic Swan.

AREAS OF COMPEITIVE ADVANTAGE

- Leader in Brazil in employee motivation programs and benefit packages, reducing turnover and enhancing local reputation.
- Strong R&D investment in improving environmental performance of plantations and sharing this knowledge through stakeholder programs.
- Sound business development policies that integrate sustainability, enhancing performance and reducing regulatory risk exposure.
- Proactive participation in the World Business Council for Sustainable Development and in local regulatory bodies has led to the implementation of proactive policies and state-of-the-art technology.

STRATEGIC PROFIT OPPORTUNITIES

- Aracruz has invested significantly in R&D programs focusing on the following in eucalyptus plantations: minimization of environmental impact, biodiversity protection, hydrological cycles, plant growth improvement, and nutrient balance. These initiatives are considered vital to ensuring the company's core business by making it sustainable. Implementation of R&D results has improved Aracruz's production and corporate reputation for sustainability.
- Aracruz's most recent innovation, Lyptus®, consists of a high-grade hardwood product line. These products are marketed as being derived from environmentally responsible forest plantations and manufacturing operations with state-of-the-art technology. FSC certification and possible eco-labeling of products could give Aracruz a premium on international markets.

RATING OUTLOOK: POSITIVE

Aracruz has been at the forefront of corporate sustainability initiatives in Brazil for some time, and continues to drive innovation in many areas. The company has been investing in reducing its exposure to regulatory and market risk, especially since its exports to North America and Europe have increased. However, the firm will need to implement an internationally recognized forest certification system in order to sustain international credibility for sound forestry practices. Aracruz is currently working on mutual recognition mechanisms for its CERFLOR forest certification system. This would help Aracruz to gain more international market share.

Innovest

STRATEGIC VALUE ADVISORS

New York: (+) 212 421-2
London: +44 (0) 20 7073 (
Toronto: (+) 905 707-(
Paris: +33 (0)1 44 54 0

INTANGIBLE VALUE ASSESSMENT

STRATEGIC GOVERNANCE: 8.0

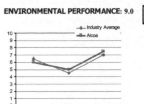

Strategy: Aracruz has evolved as a company and now includes sustainability issues in its business development strategies. Policies, programs, annual goals and indicators are in place to demonstrate its commitment. Current environmental policies cover forestry, R&D, chemical pulping activities, and energy and resource efficiency. Social issues, which are an important part of plantation development, are also integral to business at Aracruz. The company not only focuses on workers' safety but also on professional development, training, and life quality improvement. Special attention is taken to develop strategic partnerships with local communities. This policy exceeds compliance. Aracruz also works with local government and non-governmental organizations, and with international institutions such as the World Business Council for Sustainable Development to enhance and re-shape its policies and programs. Aracruz has a hard-won reputation as a progressive company with good environmental and social practices.

Adaptibility/Responsiveness: Aracruz has set up a strong governance structure not only to implement strategies that enhance its sustainability performance, but also to receive feedback from stakeholders and other external organizations. This is important in order to be able to continually monitor the accomplishment of its social and environmental goals. The company's sustainability executive positions include: Environmental Affairs, Licensing, Health & Safety, Community Relations, and R&D. The highest-ranking environmental officer is the Deputy Director of Environment.

Traditional Governance Factors: Aracruz's board of directors consists of ten independent members elected by the shareholders, at the Shareholders Meeting, for a three-year term. The board does not have an environmental committee. The Chair of the board and CEO positions are separate, reducing the chances for conflict of interest at the executive level. It is important to implement formal and inclusive mechanisms at the board level to further improve responsiveness to corporate social responsibility concerns in view of continuous regulatory changes in Brazil. It is expected that environmental regulations, and in particular regulations related to forestry, will become more stringent in the country.

HUMAN CAPITAL: 9.5

Labor Relations: Aracruz has been working to improve its recruitment strategies and its image as an employer of choice. Initiatives such as online job applications, a comprehensive benefits program, and investments in employee training and development have helped to reduce turnover and retain qualified professionals.

A total of 67% of Aracruz's employees are represented by eight labor unions in the states of Bahia, Espírito Santo, and Rio de Janeiro. Labor relations have improved through partnerships focusing on health, professional training, and employee education.

The majority of employees are male (90%). However, Aracruz promotes equality between men and women and has been the first company in the Brazilian pulp and paper sector to have women in operational jobs inside pulp plants. Women comprise 20% of the enrollment in training course conducted in partnership with government institutions. The percentage of women graduating from these courses with professional certification is even higher (26% on average).

High-Performance Workplace Practices:

Aracruz has different employee incentive programs in place. One of them is its Profit-Sharing Plan (PLR), which ensures financial recognition of the efforts of employees for six factors: pulp production, quality, workplace safety, diligence, the environment and production costs. Parameters are established annually in negotiations with labor unions. In 2001, approximately US$4 million was distributed through this program.

Aracruz's Social Security Foundation (ARUS) is a non-profit private pension institution that supplements the benefits provided under the federal pension plan. In 2001, Aracruz contributed nearly US$1 million. These funds enhance pension reserves throughout the active lifetime of participants and augment the benefits available upon retirement, disablement or death, as well as providing free life insurance. Currently, 417 individuals are covered under this plan.

The company is well known in Brazil for its comprehensive medical, hospital, and dental assistance programs available for employees. Additional benefits offered include: transportation, reimbursement of day-care center costs, group life insurance, medicine costs assistance, eye care loans, emergency loans, funeral assistance, salary supplements for disabled employees and basic food provisions.

A consulting firm, Hay do Brasil, ranks Aracruz among the top five Brazilian companies for organizational climate management. In a number of aspects surveyed, Aracruz was considered a national benchmark with the market's best practices, and a higher employee satisfaction index than the market average.

Health & Safety: Aracruz has a wide variety of health and safety programs aiming to improve employees' well-being and occupational health in operations. Despite the fact that positive esults have been achieved, the lost time accident frequency rate in 2002 was higher than the previous year, though the measured rate of severity of the accidents fell 4.6% over the same period. Company programs include: Internal Accident Prevention Commissions (CIPAs); Support Program for Smokers; Chemical Dependency Support Program; sexually transmissible diseases (STD) information sessions; and, the Professional Rehabilitation Program, which seeks new job positions for employees whose capacity to work has been reduced due to health problems.

ENVIRONMENTAL PERFORMANCE: 9.0

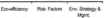

Environmental Strategy & Management: Strategy: Aracruz integrates sustainability in its core business development plan. The current policy covers forestry activities, R&D, chemical pulping, and resource efficiency. Aracruz cooperates with local and international NGOs to enhance and re-shape its environmental policy. Governance: The company does not have an environmental committee on the board. However, the CEO is sensitive to sustainability and initiated company participation in the World Business Council for Sustainable Development. Environmental Management Systems (EMS): All operations are ISO14001 certified. Aracruz is involved in Brazil's FSC standards development and has created its own forestry standards, CERFLOR, based on FSC principles. The company is looking for

Innovest

STRATEGIC VALUE ADVISORS

www.innovestgroup.com
New York: (+) 212 421-2000
London: +44 (0) 20 7073 0470
Toronto: (+) 905 707-0876
Paris: +33 (0)1 44 54 04 89
Copyright© All rights reserved. 1998-2003
Innovest Strategic Value Advisors

INTANGIBLE VALUE ASSESSMENT
Page 3

mechanisms for mutual recognition by international systems. Reporting: Aracruz publishes a comprehensive annual Environmental Report, which includes numerous indicators, research findings, and covers attendant social issues.

Risk Factors: Operational Risk: Below average exposure. The company has initiatives in place to continually reduce its environmental burden, going beyond compliance with emissions regulations. Since 1990, AOX and BOD were reduced by 93% and 91% respectively. Market Risk: The absence of a forestry-specific EMS and, therefore, lack of verifiability of forestry management practices may limit access to environmentally sensitive markets. Future FSC certification will reduce this risk. Regulatory Risk: Environmental performance improvements have reduced costs of non-compliance. ECF (Elemental Chlorine Free) and TCF (Total Chlorine Free) technologies have been implemented at different facilities.

Eco-efficiency Initiatives: Resource Use Efficiency: Aracruz has implemented a waste collection program and partners with local non-profit organizations to valorize industrial waste as raw materials and fertilizers. Aracruz continues to research and develop possible uses of industrial effluents for irrigation purposes. Energy Efficiency: Aracruz generates 92% of its electricity needs through black liquor, biomass, hydrogen, non-condensable gases, and methanol. Following Brazil's energy crisis, the company adopted a contingency plan in 2001 focusing on the reduction of internal consumption. Eco-efficiency Programs: Aracruz has increased water use efficiency at its mills by identifying opportunities to reduce consumption and reuse dregs and mud from lagoons. Water consumption was reduced 29% from 1992 to 2001. Aracruz also dedicates R&D efforts to preserving biodiversity, conserving water and optimizing the nutrient cycle.

STAKEHOLDER CAPITAL: 9.0

Local Communities: Aracruz has a wide range of initiatives and partnerships with local communities in Brazil. Programs cover education, cooperative business development, training in forestry-related activities, scholarships, and donations to schools, municipalities and local aboriginal groups. In 2002, the company earmarked expenditures totaling US$2.3 million and actually spent US$4.2 million. The budgeted 2003 expenditure is US$2 million. Aracruz's Forestry Partners Program promotes Environmental Education among farmers in the region. The company supports programs to improve employment among indigenous communities and conducts studies to restore rivers, supplying native seedlings, and technical assistance for reforestation.

Despite these efforts, some local representatives say that Aracruz's plantation work has resulted in cultural and environmental damage in the Tupinikim and Guarani communities. These ethnic groups have boycotted Aracruz operations even though they signed an agreement with the company. The demonstrations have somewhat damaged Aracruz's international reputation.

Regulators: Aracruz is helping to develop nationwide environmental legislation. Special attention is paid to the states of Espírito Santo, Bahia and Rio de Janeiro, where Aracruz operates most actively. The focus is on water resources, zoning, forests, and bio-safety. Aracruz is also seeking international endorsement of its forestry certification system, CERFLOR.

Other Stakeholders:

Customers: Customer demand has been better understood through the implementation of a Customer Service Committee. However, this committee does not deal with the improvement of corporate relations with clients or supply chain management. Supply Chain: Aracruz maintains a high level of local suppliers (40%) of materials and services through the Supplier Development Program (PRODFOR), which has a positive impact on the regional economy.

EMERGING MARKETS: Strategy: Aracruz is a company that has 100% of its manufacturing and forestry operations located in Brazil. Its strategies and management systems to address sustainability issues are discussed in the other sections of this report.

Human Rights: The company demonstrates, through the different initiatives in place for communities and employees, its commitment to maintain a zero record of human rights violations at all operations. Further, Aracruz's chairman of the board was invited in 2000 to participate in the UN's Global Compact.

Child and Forced Labor: Through partnerships with different NGOs, Aracruz helps children in need and supports the Child Labor Eradication Program. The company has specific policies against forced labor and promotes the well-being of employees and communities, as mentioned in previous sections.

Oppressive Regimes: Aracruz does not have operations or activities in countries with oppressive regimes.

SRI NEGATIVE SCREENING INFORMATION

The following information is provided for investors who for various ethical or social reasons may wish to avoid investments in companies involved in the following business areas. Innovest's IVA product uses a positive screening approach to identify superior management. Beyond assessing potential market risks, involvement in the following businesses does not impact IVA ratings.

SCREEN

Alcohol - N/A

Animal Testing - N/A

Contraception - N/A

Gambling - N/A

Genetically Modified Organisms - N/A

Nuclear Power - N/A

Pornography - N/A

Tobacco - N/A

Weapons Production – N/A

Appendix 2
Just Pensions:
Pharmaceutical Sector Note

UK
Social
Investment
Forum

www.uksif.org

Features of the pharmaceutical sector
- The pharmaceutical sector is the second largest global industry (banking is the largest).
- The US Federal Drug Administration (FDA) is the most powerful national regulatory body, driving the regulatory framework in which the sector operates globally.
- The industry is active in advancing its interests and defending its position in political arenas.

Top 10 global companies, May 2003

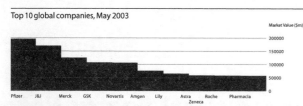

- GSK, the largest UK pharmaceutical company, ranks 3rd in the FTSE 100, comprising 8% of the index.

Indicative breakdown of revenue

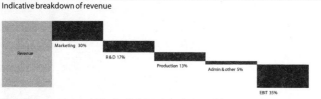

- The industry operates on a high price, high margin business model.

Lifecycle of a pharmaceutical product

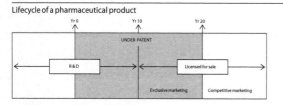

- The long time lag between patenting and licensing typically leaves an average of 5–10 yrs to maximise revenue before a patent expires.

This note forms part of a research programme to identify potentially material social, ethical and environmental risks for each industry sector. Due to the collaborative nature of the work, this analysis does not necessarily reflect the views of each of the fund managers involved.

1 Pharmaceuticals

Potentially material social, ethical & environmental risks

Please note that the short and long term risks identified in this section will apply differently to companies within the sector, according to their product range and exposure to various markets.

Short term risk		Long term risk
The FDA is increasingly seeking evidence that a new drug will deliver greater clinical efficacy than those already available, highlighting innovation as key to a company's product pipe-line. Pharmaceutical companies are dependent on their research staff for innovation. Where work-life balance, transparent business practices and external reputation are perceived to be negative, the recruitment and retention of top graduates and key staff may be influenced. A company that motivates its staff to produce innovative products in-house will avoid the costs associated with the acquisition of patents or smaller research companies.	**Product innovation**	Gene-based technologies are expected to provide the next wave of blockbuster drugs. These will target speci fic genotypes, optimizing performance and reducing side effects. However, societal concerns regarding the management of new research techniques and genetic screening are increasingly out of step with the range and scope of treatments under development. Companies risk investing in the development of techniques and treatments whose use will be delayed or restricted while public debate regarding the use of genetic information is resolved.
As bulk handlers of chemicals, the potential for the pharmaceutical industry to contribute to pollution of air, land and water from manufacturing facilities is real. Even if punitive damages for pollution incidents are not considered significant by the company, recurrent pollution incidents and fines may be viewed by regulators as an indicator of lax management and control within a company. In addition, an incident resulting in harm to human health or the environment may open the door to civil claims.	**Environmental regulation**	The continual, low level, release of pharmaceuticals, via sewage, to the water system results in a persistent presence of bioactive substances in the natural environment. Currently, there is limited understanding of the toxicity or long term consequences of this form of pollution. If linked to environmental or human health impacts, potential costs and regulatory intervention associated with rectifying any damage and preventing further impact could be significant.
The FDA approves drugs for licensing based on the evidence from clinical trials on their effectiveness and safety. Poor processes in clinical trials which breach ethical guidelines and undermine the quality of the science will adversely affect the approval process. The FDA also carries out quality audits on all facilities producing drugs for sale in the US. Its quality standards are strictly enforced, with warning letters sent to companies in cases of non-compliance, resulting in closure of a facility if corrective action is not suf ficient.	**Safety regulation**	Companies often undertake ongoing monitoring of patients for the effectiveness of drugs and the severity of side effects. Delaying the release of negative information may maintain sales in the short term, but damage the reputation of the company in the long term. Doctors may be influenced in their prescription habits if concerned that truthful information about potential side-effects is not available. Non-disclosure of known side effects which result in harm to patients may also open the door to damaging litigation. Greater scrutiny of the impacts of direct-to-consumer advertising on pricing and consumer behaviour is likely to increase the negative consequences of non or partial disclosure.
In the US, the filing of law suits against generic manufacturers to keep their cheaper products off the market has become controversial in recent years. Damages are now being awarded to generic manufacturers for loss of earnings related to such delaying tactics. New legislation will limit the use of litigation in this way. This will result in generics coming to market within the US more quickly. Branded drugs will be forced to compete on the basis of clinical effectiveness and price to retain their sales.	**Patent protection**	The response of the pharmaceutical industry to the issue of access to essential medicines in developing countries (see overleaf) has tainted its reputation and reduced public sympathy. The assumption that it is possible to contain this debate by focusing on government health provision may well prove to be mistaken, as recent challenges to pricing decisions and patent extensions in the US show. A more constructive engagement that addresses both the industry's long-term business needs as well as the health needs of citizens of developing and least developed countries is likely to be necessary in order to maintain the industry's incentive to invest in innovative research.
There is growing criticism of doctors for receiving non-financial gifts from pharmaceutical companies such as free drug samples or sponsorship to attend conferences and events, which includes generous hospitality. As guidelines to protect their independence are found to be abused, a tightening of regulation to provide a greater distance between the industry and doctors becomes more likely. Marketing strategies realigned to focus on the superior performance of a product, stemming from innovative research, would not only avoid this criticism, but also help to reduce the huge marketing expenditure of sales teams.	**Marketing strategy**	Marketing focuses on increasing brand recognition through large sales teams targeting doctors, and direct-to-consumer advertising in the US. The proliferation of 'me too' drugs (those which vary little from other treatments within the same therapeutic class) has led to an increase in the number of patients requesting, and doctors prescribing, more expensive branded drugs based on marketing information rather than clinical advice. However, the increasing use of formularies by health providers is changing the nature of information need by doctors and consumers towards the cost-effectiveness of drugs.
15% of the US market is currently unable to access medicines, as they fall between subsidised drug provision (Medicaid) and medical insurance. In addition, insurers and employers are increasingly challenging the cost of drugs they purchase. Today, 23 US states are proposing the use of formularies (lists of drugs acceptable for prescription having been evaluated for their cost effectiveness). This is expected to have a significant effect on the price of prescription drugs. Companies will increasingly need to demonstrate the clinical superiority of their products to justify premium prices.	**Pricing strategy in western economies**	As western economies become burdened by an ageing population, the associated healthcare costs present a significant threat to the high price/high margin business model on which the industry is based. With reform of the US healthcare system urgently required, the industry needs to respond appropriately to the demands for affordable drugs for the majority, or risk having discounting, shorter periods of exclusivity and/or the opening up to generic manufacturers forced upon them.

Question: How is your fund manager incorporating these risks into their company analysis?

Question: How is your fund manager engaging with companies on these risks?

Pharmaceutical Shareowners Group

Access to essential medicines in developing countries

According to the WHO, the developing world is currently facing a public health crisis of immense proportions:
- each year approximately 11 million people die from infectious diseases;
- the toll of AIDS this decade is predicted to be 46 million people, the majority of them poor;
- HIV/AIDS is a major threat to global economic development, as its victims (those in the prime of their economically active life) are the human capital upon which the activity of future markets depends.

Obstacles preventing patients receiving treatment include inadequate local health infrastructure to prevent disease, diagnose and treat patients, and the price of medicines. While governments are responsible for the provision of health infrastructure, pharmaceutical companies have been accused of not pro-actively addressing this crisis. The response of many developing country governments has been to turn to generic manufacturers to provide cheaper alternatives to branded drugs, although in some countries even these drugs are "too expensive".

Two options commonly presented to pharmaceutical companies are:
Significantly discount products in poorer countries.
However, the industry fears that these prices may be used as a benchmark for price negotiations globally and/or that the concept of pricing according to ability to pay will flow back to western markets.
Restrict intellectual property rights to allow generic manufacture of patented drugs.
However, the industry claims this undermines incentives to invest in future R&D, and will result in diversion of cheap generic drugs from developing countries into more lucrative developed world markets.

A few companies are piloting schemes offering drugs for infectious diseases on a not-for-profit basis to least developed countries. These appear to be reaping some benefits for patients, but are not widespread and as yet, do not represent a long-term solution. WTO negotiations on easing the patent restrictions on essential medicines within developing countries are now forcing companies to address the issue.

Responsible shareholders recognise that governments should take the primary role in mobilising their societies and the international community. However, they want to ensure that the companies in which they invest are responding proactively and co-operating with developing and developed country governments. They feel there are important reputational risks involved which, if mishandled, could rebound on the companies and their investors by reducing their license to operate. They also believe that emerging markets offer signi ficant growth opportunities for the sector in the medium term.

One particularly interesting development of investors 'involvement in this debate is the Pharmaceutical Shareowners Group (PSG), a group of 12 investors with £600 billion under management. The group published a statement outlining its thinking on good practice by the pharmaceutical sector. The statement includes a framework, developed in consultation with pharmaceutical companies and other informed organisations, which covers issues relating to how companies can help improve delivery of treatments in developing countries. It is the investors 'hope that this framework will become a guide for disclosure and a tool that research/rating agencies may use.

For further details see www.pharmaproject.org
or contact the PSG secretariat at info@pharmaproject.org

Abbreviations

ABI	Association of British Insurers
ABP	Algemeen Burgerlijk Pensioenfonds (Netherlands)
ACSI	Australian Council of Super Investors
AFL–CIO	American Federation of Labor–Congress of Industrial Organisations
AIDS	acquired immuno-deficiency syndrome
AIMR	Association of Investment Management and Research
AMWG	Asset Management Working Group (UNEPFI)
ART	antiretroviral therapy
ASIC	Australian Securities and Investment Commission
AWEA	American Wind Energy Association
BAT	British American Tobacco
BLA	Biologics Licence Application
BMS	Bristol-Myers Squibb
boe	barrels of oil equivalent
BRT	Business Round Table (US)
CalPERS	California Public Employee Retirement System
CalSTIRS	California State Teachers' Retirement System
CBF	Central Board of Finance (of the Church of England)
CBI	Confederation of British Industry
CCGG	Canadian Coalition for Good Governance
CEC	Commission of the European Communities
CEO	chief executive officer
CEP	Council for Economic Priorities
CES	Centre for Environmental Strategy (University of Surrey)
CFB	Central Finance Board (of the Methodist Church, UK)
CFC	chlorofluorocarbon
CG	corporate governance
CGNU	Commercial Union, General Accident and Norwich Union
CHaSPI	Corporate Health and Safety Performance Index
CHF	Swiss franc

CIS	Co-operative Insurance Society
CLEEN	Chemical Legislation European Enforcement Network
CO_2	carbon dioxide
CO_2e	carbon dioxide equivalent
CR	corporate responsibility
CRE	Corporate Responsibility Exchange (London Stock Exchange)
CREF	College Retirement Equities Fund
CROCI	cash return on cash invested
CSD	Commission on Sustainable Development (UN)
CSR	corporate social responsibility
DB	defined benefit (pension scheme)
DC	defined contribution (pension scheme)
Defra	Department for Environment, Food and Rural Affairs (UK)
DFID	Department for International Development (UK)
DJSI	Dow Jones Sustainability Index
DKK	Danish krone
DOE	Department of Energy (US)
DrKW	Dresdner Kleinwort Wasserstein
DTI	Department of Trade and Industry (UK)
E&P	earnings and profits
EAI	Enhanced Analytics Initiative
EBITDA	earnings before interest, depreciation, tax and amortisation
ECA	European Chemicals Agency
EFI	extra-financial issue
EIRIS	Ethical Investment Research Service
ENTO	European Telecommunications Network Operators Association
EOC	Equal Opportunities Commission (UK)
EPA	Environmental Protection Agency
EPS	earnings per share
ERISA	Employee Retirement Income Security Act 1974 (US)
ESG	environmental, social and governance (issues)
ETS	emissions trading scheme (EU)
EU	European Union
Eurosif	European Social Investment Forum
EV	enterprise value
EWEA	European Wind Energy Association
F&D	finding and development
FASB	Financial Accounting Standards Board (US)
FDA	Food and Drug Administration (US)
FP	Friends Provident
FRC	Financial Reporting Council (UK)
FSA	Financial Services Authority (UK)
FTSE	Financial Times Stock Exchange
FY	financial year
GCI	gross cash invested
GDP	gross domestic product
GHG	greenhouse gas

GICS	Global Industry Classification System
GP	Governance Platform (Netherlands)
GRI	Global Reporting Initiative
GSEE	governance, social, ethical and environmental (issues)
GSEES	Goldman Sachs Energy, Environmental and Social Index
GSK	GlaxoSmithKline
GTL	gas-to-liquids
H&S	health and safety
HBOS	Halifax Bank of Scotland plc
HIV	human immunodeficiency virus
HR	human resources
HSC	Health and Safety Commission (UK)
HSE	Health and Safety Executive (UK)
IASB	International Accounting Standards Board
IBES	Institutional Brokering Estimate Service
ICCR	Interfaith Center on Corporate Responsibility (US)
ICGN	International Corporate Governance Network
ICT	information and communication technology
IEA	International Energy Agency
IFA	independent financial advisor
IIGCC	Institutional Investors Group on Climate Change
ILO	International Labour Organisation
INCR	Investor Network on Climate Risk (US)
IOC	international oil company
IOSH	Institute of Occupational Safety and Health (UK)
IPR	intellectual property rights
IR	investor relations
IRR	internal rate of return
ISC	Institutional Shareholders' Committee
IT	information technology
JV	joint venture
LAPFF	Local Authority Pension Fund Forum (UK)
LSE	London Stock Exchange
LTRI	long-term responsible investment
MNT	member-nominated trustee
MSA	Master Settlement Agreement (tobacco)
MSCI	Morgan Stanley Capital International
NAPF	National Association of Pension Funds (UK)
NCE	new chemical entity
NCP	National Contact Point (for the OECD Guidelines for Multinational Enterprises)
NGO	non-governmental organisation
NOC	national oil company
NPI	National Provident
OECD	Organisation for Economic Co-operation and Development
OFR	operating and financial review (UK)
OPERS	Ohio Public Employees Retirement System (US)
PEP	personal equity plan

PIRC	Pensions and Investment Research Consultants Ltd (UK)
PSG	Pharmaceutical Shareowners Group
R&D	research and development
R&M	refining and marketing
REACH	Registration, Evaluation and Authorisation of Chemicals (EU Regulation)
REO	responsible engagement overlay
RPA	Risk and Policy Analysts Ltd
SA	Social Accountability
SAPMA	South African Pharmaceutical Manufacturers Association
SCGOP	Stichting Corporate Governance Onderzoek voor Pensioenfondsen (Netherlands)
SDS	safety data sheet
SEC	Securities and Exchange Commission (US)
SEE	social, ethical and environmental (issues)
SIF	Social Investment Forum
SIP	statement of investment principles
SME	small or medium-sized enterprise
SRI	socially responsible investment
SSE	Scottish & Southern Energy plc
SSRI	sustainable and socially responsible investment
TCG	The Climate Group
TIAA–CREF	Teachers Insurance and Annuity Association–College Retirement Equities Fund (US)
tpa	tonnes per annum
TRIPS	Trade Related Aspects of Intellectual Property Rights (WTO)
TUC	Trades Union Congress (UK)
UK	United Kingdom
UKSIF	UK Social Investment Forum
UN	United Nations
UNAIDS	Joint United Nations Programme on HIV/AIDS
UNDHR	Universal Declaration of Human Rights
UNEP	UN Environment Programme
UNEPFI	UN Environment Programme Finance Initiative
UN GC	United Nations Global Compact
US	United States
USA	United States of America
USS	Universities Superannuation Scheme (UK)
VCT	voluntary counselling and testing
VSO	Voluntary Services Overseas
WACC	weighted average cost of capital
WHO	World Health Organisation
WTO	World Trade Organisation
WWF	formerly World Wide Fund for Nature (World Wildlife Find in US)
ZAR	South African rand

About the contributors

Meg Brown managed the Just Pensions sector research programme at the UK Social Investment Forum between 2003 and 2005. Following an MSc in environment and development at the London School of Economics, Meg worked as an environmental consultant in the UK and Singapore, focusing on environmental impact and risk assessment. She is now an SRI analyst within the European Equity Research at Citigroup Investment Research.

meg.brown@citigroup.com

Dr **Peter Casson** is a Senior Lecturer in accounting in the School of Management at the University of Southampton, UK. After working as a research psychologist, including a period at the Tavistock Institute of Human Relations in London, he trained as a chartered accountant. He is now a Fellow of the Institute of Chartered Accountants in England and Wales. His research interests include issues related to senior executive and employee share participation schemes, corporate governance and accounting for complex financial instruments. He holds an undergraduate degree and a doctorate in psychology, and a master's degree in occupational psychology.

P.D.Casson@soton.ac.uk

After several years at National Westminster Bank, specialising in private trusts, pension funds and tax planning, **Ralph Edmondson** joined Eagle Star Trust Company in 1985, which was a subsidiary of B.A.T Industries at the time. At Eagle Star, he became Group Secretary and subsequently moved to B.A.T Industries to run investor relations in 1992. Following the demerger of financial services in 1998, Ralph continued in the investor relations role at British American Tobacco plc. The investor relations department is part of the Group's corporate and regulatory affairs function.

ralph_edmondson@bat.com

Steffen Erler researches chemical risk management at the Centre for Environmental Strategy, University of Surrey, as part of an Engineering and Physical Sciences Research Council doctoral programme. Steffen also conducts best-practice surveys on company preparedness and responses to EU environmental legislation. With an academic background in chemistry, psychology and engineering, he developed an interest in chemicals policy during work at Bayer AG and at the OECD Existing Chemicals Programme. In 2002, he completed a traineeship with the European Commission Enterprise DG Chemicals Unit. Recently, Steffen participated in the UK Royal Commission on Environmental Pollution's *Chemical Study*.

S.Erler@surrey.ac.uk

Andy Evans is Head of Credit Research, Fixed Income Group at Insight Investment, where he heads a team of analysts covering the corporate bond, high-yield and asset-backed security markets. Prior to joining Insight in 2002, Andy spent nine years at UBS, latterly as Head of European Credit Strategy. While at UBS, Andy was ranked No.1 in various investor surveys, ran the successful European corporate bond research and index teams, and was a founder member of the bank's portfolio risk analytics group. Andy started his career at Friends Provident where he was jointly responsible for the management of non-government bond portfolios. Andy holds a degree in economics and is an Associate of the Society of Investment Professionals.

andy.evans@insightinvestment.com

Sarah Forrest joined the Goldman Sachs energy equity research team in August 2003. She graduated from the University of Cambridge in 2004 with a PhD in chemical engineering, and received a combined bachelor degree in chemical engineering and arts in economics in 1998 from the University of Queensland, Australia.

sarah.forrest@gs.com

Peter Frankental is Economic Relations Director of Amnesty International UK. He is the co-author of *Human Rights: Is It Any of Your Business?*, a management primer on human rights jointly published in April 2000 by Amnesty International and the International Business Leaders Forum. He is also co-author of the report *Business and Human Rights: A Geography of Corporate Risk*, and has had numerous papers published on the theme of business and human rights including 'Can Branding Reinforce Human Rights?', published by Financial Times Prentice Hall in *Visions of Ethical Business*. Peter joined Amnesty in 1998 from Business in the Community, where he specialised in developing the role of the private sector in social and economic regeneration programmes. His previous career included six years as a business analyst with Johnson Matthey and four years as a systems analyst within the National Health Service. Peter holds a degree in mathematical statistics, and has subsequently undertaken postgraduate studies at the London School of Economics (MSc Econ) and at the Institute of Latin American Studies (MA).

peter.frankental@amnesty.org.uk

Dr Thilo Goodall is Head Asset Management with SAM Group where he is responsible for investment decisions and risk management, and for quantitative and macroeconomic analysis. After receiving his high school diploma, Thilo worked for a local bank in Minden (Germany) for two and a half years. He then studied economics at the Universities of Freiburg (Germany) and Madison/Wisconsin, with an emphasis on macroeconomics and econometrics. After receiving his master's degree, Thilo became an assistant to the professor at the Institute for Economic Studies, before joining SBC Brinson, the asset management division of Swiss Bank Corporation. While there, he developed long-term global risk and return scenarios and valuation and risk models, and he also set asset allocation and equity market strategies as a member of regional and global investment committees. Thilo holds a PhD in economics.

thilo.goodall@sam-group.com

Gabriela Grab Hartmann is an analyst at SAM Sustainable Asset Management, covering the household and personal products sectors. She also manages SAM's external research network and research communications. Before joining SAM, Gabriela worked as a private equity analyst specialising in eco-efficiency. Prior to that she was programme officer at the Swiss Agency for Environment, Forests and Landscape, responsible for the co-operation with international bodies such as the UN Environment Programme, the environmental programme of the OECD and the United Nations Commission on Sustainable Development. Gabriela graduated in environmental sciences at the Swiss Federal Institute of Technology Zurich, Switzerland, and holds a European master's degree in society, science and technology, with a focus on multilateral environmental policy, from the Swiss Federal Institute of Technology Lausanne, Switzerland, and the University of Oslo, Norway.

gabriela.grab@sam-group.com

Professor **James P. Hawley** is the Transamerica Professor of Business Policy and Strategy (Graduate Business Programs), School of Economics and Business Administration, and co-director of the Center for the Study of Fiduciary Capitalism at Saint Mary's College of California. In addition to authoring many articles, he is the author of two books, the first on international banks and the global monetary system, and the most recent (as a co-author with Professor Andrew T Williams) on US pension funds and the ownership of US corporations, *The Rise of Fiduciary Capitalism: How Institutional Investors Can Make Corporations More Democratic* (University of Pennsylvania Press, 2000). He is a member of the Academic Advisory Board of the Institute for Responsible Investing at Boston College, and a member of the UN Expert Commission on Responsible Investment, a project of the UN Environment Programme Finance Initiative. He received his BA from the University of Wisconsin, MA from the University of California, Berkeley and PhD from McGill University in Montreal, Canada.

jphawley@ix.netcom.com

Harish Jeswani is an engineer with many years' experience in the chemical and petrochemical sector. He is currently researching industry responses to environmental and climate change regulation at the Centre for Environmental Strategy, University of Surrey. He previously worked with BP Pakistan Exploration and Production Inc. as an environmental engineer where he was responsible for the development and implementation of ISO 14001-based environmental management systems for oil and gas exploration and production facilities. He has also worked as an environmental consultant in Pakistan involved in the implementation of environmental and energy-efficiency improvement projects for various industrial sectors. Harish has a master's degree in environmental engineering from the University of Sydney, Australia and a bachelor's degree in civil engineering from Mehran University of Engineering and Technology, Pakistan.

h.jeswani@surrey.ac.uk

Dr **Matthew Kiernan** is founder and Chief Executive of Innovest Strategic Value Advisors, Inc., a specialist investment advisory firm based in New York, Toronto, London, Paris and Melbourne. Innovest's clients include several of the leading institutional investors in North America, Europe and Asia Pacific, as well as a number of *Fortune* Global 500 industrial companies. Prior to founding Innovest, he was Director of the Geneva-based Business Council for Sustainable Development, where he led the group's initial capital markets task force. The group served as Principal Business and Industry Advisor to the UN Earth Summit in Rio de Janeiro in 1992. Prior to that, he had served as a senior partner with KPMG Peat Marwick. Matthew has lectured on environmental finance in executive programmes at the Wharton School, Columbia Business School and Oxford University. He holds advanced degrees in political science and environmental studies, and a PhD in strategic environmental management from the University of London. He is a frequent contributor to leading business and investment journals and his book, *The 11 Commandments of 21st Century Management*, is published by Simon & Schuster.

mkiernan@innovestgroup.com

Rob Lake is Head of Corporate Engagement at Henderson Global Investors. He leads Henderson's corporate governance work, as well as its engagement with companies to encourage improvements in corporate environmental and social performance. Under Henderson's corporate governance policy, key aspects of corporate responsibility standards and reporting are monitored across the whole of the company's funds under management. Rob is a member of the Association of British Insurers' Investment Committee and its SRI Guidelines Working Group; BT's Corporate Social Responsibility Leadership Panel; the UK Social Investment Forum board; the Advisory Board to the Just Pensions project on pension investment and international development; and the Global Reporting Initiative working group developing reporting guidelines for mining companies. He was also a member of the UK Department of Trade and Industry Working Group on Materiality in the Operating and Financial Review, as part of the Company Law Review. Before joining Henderson, Rob worked at the NGO Traidcraft, where as Director of Policy he worked on corporate social responsibility, corporate governance and socially responsible investment and how they relate to international development and the needs of the poor. From 1990 to

1998 Rob was at the Royal Society for the Protection of Birds, working with the EU, World Bank, United Nations, OECD and the UK government on a variety of environmental issues.

rob.lake@henderson.com

Ronnie Lim joined Morley Fund Management as Head of Research, Socially Responsible Investment, in 2003. His present responsibilities include managing four SRI research analysts, analytical sector coverage, company engagement, business development, and the development and implementation of research processes, involving the integration of SRI and corporate governance into mainstream investment. He previously worked with Credit Lyonnais Securities Asia (CLSA), most recently as Director of Equity Sales, Singapore. Prior to joining CLSA, Ronnie worked in Asian equity sales at Cazenove & Co., London. He holds the Investment Management Certificate from the UK Society of Investment Professionals, an MSc in environmental impact assessment, management and auditing (University of East Anglia) and a BSc (Hons.) in economics (Salford University).

ronnie.lim@morleyfm.com

Anthony Ling joined Goldman Sachs in 1999 as global co-ordinator for the energy equity research team. In April 2000, he was promoted to Co-Head of European Equity Research and now covers both roles. Anthony started his career in 1987 as an investment banker specialising in the oil sector. In 1990 he became an equity analyst covering exploration and production companies, graduating to the integrated European companies in 1994. Since 1995 he has consistently been ranked in the top three in all institutional surveys and in 1998, while at his previous firm, Schroders, was ranked number one in the institutional investor poll. He has been ranked in the top three in the Greenwich survey for the last three years. He received a BA in history from Oxford University in 1987.

anthony.ling@gs.com

Craig Mackenzie is Head of Investor Responsibility at Insight Investment, the asset management arm of the HBOS Group. He leads the team that is responsible for conducting research, company engagement and voting on corporate governance and corporate responsibility issues on behalf of Insight's £74 billion of assets. Previously, Craig led the creation of the highly regarded governance and SRI team at Friends Ivory & Sime (now F&C). He is a leading advocate of investor engagement and activism strategies to encourage more responsible and sustainable approaches to value creation by companies. Craig has been involved in the development of corporate responsibility initiatives at Friends Provident and HBOS. He is chair of the FTSE4Good criteria development committee, a member of the steering group for the Business in the Community Corporate Responsibility Index and the technical advisory committee for the Global Reporting Initiative. He is a former member of the advisory boards of the UK Social Investment Forum and AccountAbility. Craig is the author of *The Shareholder Action Handbook* (New Consumer, 1993) and of numerous journal articles and reports on corporate responsibility, business ethics and responsible investment. Craig previously held a research post in the Centre for Economic Psychology, University of Bath, exploring the relationships between ethics and economics. He is a Senior Visiting Fellow at the Department of Economics, University College, London and a Senior Associate at the Judge Institute, University of Cambridge. He has a combined honours degree in social science (University of Durham, UK) and a PhD in business ethics (University of Bath, UK).

craig.mackenzie@insightinvestment.com

Robert Monks is one of North America's most prominent corporate governance activists. He is also a prominent lawyer, businessman and a former US Department of Labor pensions fund regulator. In 1992, he founded Lens, the institutional activist investment fund, and is currently Chairman of Governance for Owners in the UK. He was the first to identify corporate directors, particularly non-executives, as the pivotal balance between the interests of managements and their shareholders. He is the author of four best-selling books on investment and corporate accountability. His latest book, *The New Global Investors: How Shareholders Can Unlock Sustainable Prosperity Worldwide* was published by Capstone in the UK and US in 2001.

ragmonks@ragm.com

Alan Morley is Policy Advisor to the Health and Safety Executive's business involvement team. His most recent responsibilities have included the development of the Health and Safety Performance Indicator for Small and Medium Sized Enterprises, and the ongoing development of the Corporate Health and Safety Performance Index (CHaSPI). Prior to joining this team Alan was involved in health and safety policy work for the construction, offshore and mining industries.

alan.morley@hse.gsi.gov.uk

Will Oulton is Managing Director, CRG Advisory Services Ltd, a private consultancy practice advising companies and investors on the development of corporate social responsibility practices as well as playing a leading role in the development of the global SRI market. CRG's clients include FTSE Group, where Will acts as Strategic Advisor to the chief executive, in leading the ongoing management and development of the FTSE4Good Index series. Prior to establishing his consultancy practice, Will was Deputy Chief Executive of FTSE Group, responsible for global strategy and marketing as well as the FTSE4Good Indices. While at FTSE, his roles included a three-year posting in New York to establish FTSE Americas and serving as FTSE's global sales director based in London. Earlier in his career, he worked in the London Stock Exchange indices unit, where he was Head of Commercial Management. Before this, Will spent five years in the derivatives industry, specialising in the marketing and promotion of traded options while working with the London Traded Options Market. Will holds a BSc in zoology from the University of Wales at Bangor and a Chartered Institute of Marketing (UK) Diploma from the Guildhall University in London.

will@crgadvisory.com

Adrian Payne joined the BAT Group in 1997 as Senior Scientific Advisor, following a career spanning 20 years in the pharmaceutical industry. Since 2002, Adrian has been Head of Corporate Social Responsibility at British American Tobacco. The corporate social responsibility department is part of the Group's corporate and regulatory affairs function.

adrian_payne@bat.com

Tom Powdrill is Senior Policy Officer for institutional investment at the Trades Union Congress (TUC) where he is responsible for co-ordinating union work on pension fund investment issues and maintaining the TUC Member Trustee Network. This position was created in 2002 to increase trade union involvement in the investment of workers' capital. Before joining the TUC in January 2002 Tom spent several years as a financial journalist covering pensions and fund management. Most recently he worked at *Euromoney Institutional Investor*, where he spent two years as UK Head of Content for Institutional Investor Online. Prior to that, he was editor of *Pensions Week* magazine (published by Financial Times Business).

TPowdrill@tuc.org.uk

Nick Robins is Head of SRI Funds at Henderson Global Investors in London where he is responsible for co-ordinating the fund management and research functions for Henderson's range of SRI funds for individual and institutional investors. He leads Henderson's work on climate change, producing its position paper in August 2002, and he also chairs the public policy workstream of the Institutional Investors Group on Climate Change. Nick joined Henderson as Head of SRI Research in December 2000 with over a decade's experience with the sustainable development and corporate responsibility agenda, working at the International Institute for Environment and Development, the European Commission's Environment Directorate and the Business Council for Sustainable Development. He started his professional career at the Economist Intelligence Unit, where he authored a special report in 1990, *Managing the Environment: The Greening of European Business.* He has a BA in history from Cambridge University and an MSc in international relations from the London School of Economics.

nick.robins@henderson.com

David Russell is an Advisor on Responsible Investment to the Universities Superannuation Scheme (USS). USS is the third-largest pension fund in the UK, with assets of about £25 billion and in excess of 209,000 members. To operationalise its commitment to long-term and active share ownership, USS has created a three-member responsible investment team, of which David is one. This team works with both USS's internal and external fund managers on a range of corporate governance and corporate responsibility issues. A specialist in environmental issues, David is also a steering committee member of the Institutional Investors Group on Climate Change. He was previously the environment manager for a UK DIY retail multiple, dealing with the broad spectrum of business sustainability issues. He has also been a university lecturer, specialising in environmental management systems and auditing.

drussell@uss.co.uk

Yusuf Samad is an Associate in the UK Investment Practice of Hewitt. He is a Chartered Financial Analyst and was Chair of the UK Society of Investment Professionals in 2004–2005. Prior to joining Hewitt, he had over 25 years' experience as a banker, all with Citibank. He was Managing Director for relationship banking with the fund management sector in UK and Europe. He previously managed corporate banking relationships in Pakistan and the Middle East between 1978 and 1982 and was a Programme Director at Citibank's European Training Centre. Yusuf served as a trustee of the Citibank (UK) pension scheme and as a member of its investment sub-committee. He is presently Chair of the Advisory Council of the Global Investors Workshop, a one-week seminar offered jointly by INSEAD and the CFA Institute for investment professionals in Europe. He served on the editorial board of AIMR's publication, *CFA Digest*, for three years. He holds a MBA and a BSc in electrical engineering from the University of Wisconsin-Madison.

yusuf.samad@hewitt.com

Russell Sparkes first became involved in ethical investment in the early 1980s. He is widely recognised as one of the world's leading experts on SRI, and is one of the few people to combine practice in the field with authorship of academic papers about it. His work has been published in *The Journal of Business Ethics and Business Ethics: A European Review*. *The Ethical Investor* (HarperCollins 1994) was the first UK book on SRI produced by a mainstream publisher. Russell Sparkes has travelled widely meeting SRI investors in North America, Asia and Europe. His book *Socially Responsible Investment: A Global Revolution* was published simultaneously in the UK and US by John Wiley in November 2002, and was the first authoritative examination of SRI from a global perspective. Since 1994 he has managed institutional socially responsible investment portfolios for the Central Finance Board of the Methodist Church, where he currently serves as Chief Investment Officer. He is also the Secretary of the Joint Advisory Committee on the Ethics of Investment of the British Methodist Church. For six years he was a non-executive director of the UK Social Investment Forum.

russellsparkes@btinternet.com

Dr Rory Sullivan has been Director, Investor Responsibility with Insight Investment (the asset management arm of HBOS plc) since October 2002. In this role, he is responsible for leading Insight's engagement and research activities on climate change as well as contributing to Insight's broader work on corporate governance and corporate responsibility. He has over 15 years' experience in environmental management and public policy, having worked for the private sector and government agencies in Australia, South-East Asia, Africa and Europe. His experience includes evaluating development-focused partnerships (health, education, water) on behalf of the World Bank's Business Partners for Development programme, advising Environment Australia and the OECD on the design of pollution release and transfer registers, and assisting public- and private-sector organisations with the implementation of environmental and risk management systems. He is a member of the Amnesty International (UK) Business Group and, from 1998 to 2001, was the Convenor of the Amnesty International (Australia) Business Group. In these roles, he led much of Amnesty International's work relating to trade and investment policy, and corporate accountability.

Rory is the author of *Rethinking Voluntary Approaches in Public Environmental Policy* (Edward Elgar, 2005) and (with Hugh Wyndham) *Effective Environmental Management: Principles and Case Studies* (Allen & Unwin, 2001). He was the editor of *Business and Human Rights: Dilemmas and Solution* (Greenleaf Publishing, 2003) and (with Michael Warner) *Putting Partnerships to Work* (Greenleaf Publishing, 2004). He has written over 200 articles, book chapters and papers on investment, environmental policy and development issues.

Rory holds a first-class honours degree in electrical engineering (University College Cork, Ireland), masters' degrees in environmental science (University of Manchester, UK) and environmental law (University of Sydney, Australia), and a PhD in law (Queen Mary, University of London, UK).

rory.sullivan@insightinvestment.com

Allen Sykes, a former Managing Director of Consolidated Gold Fields, has held senior positions in a number of major international companies, particularly in the capital-intensive industries of mining, energy, natural resources and transport. He has also held a number of non-executive directorships. He was co-author with A.J. Merrett of the influential best-seller, *The Finance and Analysis of Capital Projects,* which was a pioneer in the introduction of modern financial and risk analysis technique. He is the author of *Capitalism for Tomorrow: Re-uniting Ownership and Control,* published by Capstone in July 2000. He is an active adviser on international mega-projects.

maryhuggins@freeuk.com

Formerly a practising barrister, **Kerry ten Kate** was a member of the Secretariat of the UN Conference on Environment and Development (the Rio Earth Summit). She has subsequently advised governments, industry and the UN on issues ranging from conservation and sustainable development strategies to trade and environment policies. Her focus since 1994 has been on biodiversity, particularly access to genetic resources, intellectual property rights and benefit-sharing, on which she has written extensively. She was Policy Advisor at the Royal Botanic Gardens, Kew, and a member of the UK delegation to negotiations under the UN Convention on Biological Diversity and the Food and Agriculture Organisation. She is now Director of Investor Responsibility at Insight Investment.

kerry.tenkate@insightinvestment.com

Raj Thamotheram is Senior Advisor to Universities Superannuation Scheme (USS) on responsible investment, and leads a team of three, working with both USS's internal and external fund managers on a range of corporate governance and corporate responsibility issues. He has helped initiate a range of projects including the Institutional Investors Group on Climate Change, PharmaShareowners Group, Pharma Futures, the competition Managing Pension Funds as if the Long Term Really Did Matter, the Marathon Club and the Enhanced Analytics Initiative. Prior to USS, he worked as a corporate social responsibility consultant (with clients including BT, Rio Tinto, the UK Cabinet Office and the Office of the Secretary-General of the UN) and has also worked with NGOs (including Saferworld, ActionAid and the Ethical Trading Initiative). Raj was nominated by *GlobalProxyWatch*, the newsletter of international corporate governance and shareowner value, as one of ten individuals who most influenced the shape of international corporate governance in 2004.

rthamotheram@uss.co.uk

Sophia Tickell was the Director of the Pharma Futures scenario planning project for its duration from January to December 2004. This scenario planning exercise was convened by pension funds ABP (Netherlands), OPERS (US) and USS (UK) to generate discussion about the long-term future of the pharmaceutical industry and pension funds' investments in the industry. Through much of her career, Sophia has worked on international development, both as a practitioner (while living in Bolivia from 1988 to 1992) and in policy, as Oxfam GB's Senior Policy Advisor on the private sector from 1996 to 2003, where she focused on the pharmaceutical, oil and coffee industries. Sophia is the Chair of the sustainable development consultancy, SustainAbility. She is a member of Morley's SRI Advisory Committee and an adviser on the Access to Medicines Indexing project. She is the author of a number of publications, including the Pharma Futures report, *The Pharmaceutical Sector: A Long Term Value Outlook*, and *The Antibiotic Innovation Study*, published in December 2005.

tickell@sustainability.com

Stephen Timms MP was appointed UK Minister of State for Pensions Reform in 2005. He first served as MP for Newham from 1994 to 1997, and has represented East Ham as MP since 1997. Having served as Parliamentary Private Secretary (PPS) to Andrew Smith and then as PPS to Mo Mowlam, he went on to work in the Department of Social Security as both Parliamentary Under Secretary of State and Minister of State between 1998 and 1999. He then moved on to become Financial Secretary to the Treasury (when he was also Departmental Green Minister) in 1999–2000. In 2001 he became Minister of State in the Department for Education and Skills and in 2002 he became Minister of State in the Department for Trade and Industry. He then returned to the Treasury as Financial Secretary. Stephen was elected on to Newham Council in 1984, attaining the position of Council Leader between 1990 and 1994. He worked in the computing and telecommunications industry for 15 years, first for Logica and then for Ovum, before entering Parliament in 1994. He was educated at Farnborough Grammar School and studied mathematics at Emmanuel College, Cambridge University. Stephen advised Labour's Information Society Policy Forum in Opposition, and has been honorary president of the Telecommunications Users Association and a member of the Council of the Parliamentary Information Technology Committee.

Simon Toyne has worked with DrKW since 2001. He started his investment career as a capital goods analyst before moving to specialise in Pan European Mining stocks. Simon is a Chartered Financial Analyst and holds a BA in mathematics from Cambridge University.

simon.toyne@drkw.com

Dr **Chris Tuppen** is Head of Sustainable Development and Corporate Accountability at BT, co-ordinating the development of BT's global strategy across the social, environmental and economic dimensions of sustainable development. He is also responsible for producing the company's corporate accountability reports and for communicating BT's business case for corporate social responsibility. He previously led BT's environmental issues unit. Chris is chair of the Global *e*-Sustainability Initiative, in association with the UN Environment Programme, sits on the Council of the Institute of Social and Ethical Accountability, the boards of CSR Europe and the US-based Business for Social Responsibility, and the social and environmental committee of the Association of Chartered Certified Accountants (UK). He previously co-chaired the Global Reporting Initiative measurement working group and chaired the European Telecommunication Network Operators Association environmental working group.

chris.tuppen@bt.com

Jonathan Waghorn joined the Goldman Sachs energy equity research team in June 2000. Prior to joining Goldman Sachs, Jonathan worked as a drilling engineer in the Netherlands for Shell International and as an oil research analyst for Deutsche Bank/Wood Mackenzie in Edinburgh. He graduated from the University of Bristol in 1995 with a BSc and MSc in physics.

jonathan.waghorn@gs.com

Andy Wales is Group Head of Corporate Responsibility for Severn Trent Plc, a leading environmental services company. Previously he was Sustainability Director, Europe and Asia Pacific for Interface Inc. His main areas of work and interest include climate change and renewable energy, international development, SRI and human rights. He is also involved in faith-based social justice and environmental campaigns. Andy is a graduate of the Forum for the Future masters-level scholarship in sustainable development leadership and he has a degree in English literature and international development from the University of Sussex. He is currently studying on the Executive MBA programme at Warwick Business School.

andy.wales@stplc.com

Dr **Steve Waygood** is Director, Investor Responsibility at Insight Investment, the fund manager for HBOS plc. His focus is shareholder activism on corporate governance and corporate responsibility issues. He also leads the development of the three ethically screened funds managed by Insight. Steve is currently writing a book on capital market campaigns by non-governmental organisations, and co-authored *A Capital Solution: Faith, Finance and Concern for a Living Planet*. He is an elected Vice Chair of the UK Social Investment Forum and a member of both the steering group and expert group of the UN Responsible Investment Initiative. Steve holds a PhD in Socially Responsible Investment, a Post-graduate Certificate in environmental management and health, and a degree in economics.

steve.waygood@insightinvestment.com

Dr **Walter Wehrmeyer** is a Senior Lecturer in environmental business management at the Centre for Environmental Strategy at the University of Surrey. His research focuses on corporate responses towards sustainability, as well as corporate social responsibility in all its strategic and practical mani-festations. In particular, Walter examines the use of environmental performance evaluation systems and the role of culture in defining and forming environmental strategies. He is the managing editor of *Greener Management International*, and is on the editorial boards of *The Journal of Industrial Ecology* and *Environment, Development and Sustainability*.

wwehrmeyer@ surrey.ac.uk

Emma Whitaker is a Senior Consultant with Mercer's manager research team, a unit within Mercer's investment consulting practice. Based in London, she specialises in UK equity and balanced investment products. She is lead researcher on SRI and is a member of both the defined contribution and the pri-vate equity research teams. Emma is Secretary of the UK and European manager ratings review com-mittees. Emma has over 15 years' experience within the pensions and investment industry. Prior to join-ing Mercer in 1996, she worked at BZW Investment Management (now Barclays Global Investors) as part of the team responsible for the marketing of active investment management products to UK pension funds, consultants and charities. Before this, she worked within the institutional marketing team at Bar-ing Asset Management.

emma.whitaker@mercer.com

Professor **Andrew T. Williams** is a Professor of economics in the graduate business programmes at the School of Economic and Business Administration at Saint Mary's College of California. He has also been the Transamerica Professor of business policy and strategy and is the co-director of the Centre for the Study of Fiduciary Capitalism at Saint Mary's College. Along with Professor James Hawley he has con-sulted on corporate governance topics for the OECD, co-authored a number of papers and written a book titled *The Rise of Fiduciary Capitalism: How Institutional Investors Can Make Corporations More Democ-ratic* (University of Pennsylvania Press, 2000). He holds BA, MA and PhD degrees in economics from Stanford University and has published extensively in the area of corporate governance with an empha-sis on institutional investor activism.

awilliam@stmarys-ca.edu

Index